The Enterprise Engineering Series

Enterprise Engineering is an emerging discipline for coping with the challenges (agility, adaptability, etc.) and the opportunities (new markets, new technologies, etc.) faced by contemporary enterprises, including commercial, nonprofit and governmental institutions. It is based on the paradigm that such enterprises are purposefully designed systems, and thus they can be redesigned in a systematic and controlled way. Such enterprise engineering projects typically involve architecture, design, and implementation aspects.

The Enterprise Engineering series thus explores a design-oriented approach that combines the information systems sciences and organization sciences into a new field characterized by rigorous theories and effective practices. Books in this series should critically engage the enterprise engineering paradigm, by providing sound evidence that either underpins it or that challenges its current version. To this end, two branches are distinguished: Foundations, containing theoretical elaborations and their practical applications, and Explorations, covering various approaches and experiences in the field of enterprise engineering. With this unique combination of theory and practice, the books in this series are aimed at both academic students and advanced professionals.

Jan L. G. Dietz • Hans B. F. Mulder

Enterprise Design Fundamentals

Settling an Enterprise Business and Devising the Enterprise Organisation

Springer

Jan L. G. Dietz
Delft University of Technology
Delft, The Netherlands

Hans B. F. Mulder
Antwerp Management School
University of Antwerp, Antwerp, Belgium

ISSN 1867-8920 ISSN 1867-8939 (electronic)
The Enterprise Engineering Series
ISBN 978-3-031-83261-1 ISBN 978-3-031-83262-8 (eBook)
https://doi.org/10.1007/978-3-031-83262-8

This Springer imprint is published by the registered company Springer Nature Switzerland AG
The registered company address is: Gewerbestrasse 11, 6330 Cham, Switzerland

General Preface

Through the publication of this book, the 'trilogy' Enterprise Ontology-Enterprise Design-Enterprise Governance is completed. *Enterprise Ontology* [1], authored by Jan Dietz and Hans Mulder, addresses the ontological and the philosophical theories concerning enterprises[1] in the framework that is presented in Chap. 4. *Foundations of Enterprise Governance* [2], authored by Jan Hoogervorst, addresses the ideological theories, and this book addresses the technological theories. Together, the 'trilogy' covers the whole area of Enterprise Engineering, as envisioned in [3].

In the first decade of the twenty-first century, the notion of Enterprise Ontology has been developed, the idea of understanding the essence of an enterprise's organisation, abstracted from its realisation and implementation (with any technology, in particular ICT[2]). The first book [4], authored by Jan Dietz, set the scene but was yet immature. At the same time, an international group of researchers and practitioners around Enterprise Engineering was established, called the CIAO! Network,[3] and the Enterprise Engineering Institute was founded.

While studying the book, you will internalise the crucial distinction between services and products. Services are subjective; they are the affordances that products offer to customers (with needs). Products are objective; they are what the actors in the enterprise organisation bring about. The (re)design of enterprises starts with identifying the services that the customers want. It ends with identifying the products that are going to satisfy the customers and the business processes produce them.

Next to a solid theoretical presentation of Enterprise Design, this book contains also many pages that are devoted to its practical application. It makes the book

[1] In Enterprise Engineering, any cooperation of human beings to achieve some common goal is called an enterprise.

[2] ICT stands for the modern digital information and communication technology.

[3] http://ciaonetwork.org/

perfectly suited for being used as a textbook in courses on Enterprise Design and Enterprise Engineering and on the principal methodology in Enterprise Engineering: DEMO (Design and Engineering Methodology for Organisations).

Voorburg, The Netherlands — Jan L. G. Dietz
The Hague, The Netherlands — Hans B. F. Mulder
31 December 2024

Mens agitat molem

Preface by the First Author

When I started studying Electrical Engineering at Eindhoven University of Technology (The Netherlands) in 1963, "I could read the quote above", because I had got my diploma gymnasium-β a couple of months before, but I couldn't make sense of it yet. The sentence was the title of a piece of artwork, consisting of a huge rock on a pole, in front of the main building of the university. Later I understood that this is what every technical study is about: to get grip on matter, to let it do what you want.

In 1968, Edsger W. Dijkstra was appointed professor at my university in programming digital computers. He taught me that programming is not producing code but devising algorithms and that these algorithms should be proven correct. You should always keep what you do intellectually manageable, first of all by the separation of concerns between correctness and efficiency. Thus, 'moles' can also be intangible.

My graduation internship consisted of re-designing IBM's GPSS (General Purpose Simulation System) and re-implementing it in Algol60, in such a way that the users could trace back their discrete-event simulations.

This book teaches you that the most important thing in (re)designing enterprises is to keep your work intellectually manageable. It can be achieved by two separations of concerns.

The first one is the separation between function and construction, thus between the enterprise business and the enterprise organisation.

The second one is the separation between the essential model of the organisation (the ontology of the enterprise) and the implementation model.

Without these two intellectual tools, it is impossible to conceive and bring about any change in a manageable and responsible way.

Voorburg, The Netherlands
31 December 2024

Jan L. G. Dietz

Summary of the Book

The book is divided into three parts: Introduction, Theories and Applications.

The Introduction consists of three chapters. Chapter 1 is an introduction to Enterprise Engineering (EE), headed by this quote of Henry Petroski: *Science is about knowing; engineering is about doing*. Because of their increasing complexities, modern societies have an urgent need for EE. Yet the ideas of Frederic Taylor still determine the mindset of managers; a machine-like understanding of organisations still dominates practice. EE comprises three general goals: intellectual manageability, organisational concinnity and social devotion. They are achieved by the thoughtful application of Enterprise Ontology, Enterprise Design and Enterprise Governance, respectively.

Enterprise Design is often confused with Enterprise Architecture. The distinction as well as the relationship between the two notions is discussed in Chap. 2, headed by the crucial quote: *Architecture is not what you see but what shaped what you see*. Only by applying the prescriptive notion of Enterprise Architecture as adopted in this book can one achieve organisational concinnity, which is one of the general goals of EE. The current descriptive notion of architecture in the practice of organisational design and ICT-applications development is imprecise and ambiguous. Several dominant definitions of architecture are reviewed and put aside as unsatisfying.

Chapter 3 introduces the reader to the main subject of the book, namely, Enterprise Design. We take the definition of design by Herbert A. Simon as the starting point: *devising courses of action aimed at changing existing situations into preferred ones*. Undoubtedly, this definition also holds for the design of enterprises: one wants to replace the current situation (AS-IS) of an enterprise by a preferred one (TO-BE). In discussing the design process, previous research in two different fields is investigated: the work by Wolfgang Hesse in software engineering and the work of Christopher Alexander in building engineering. Viewing a design process as alternate steps of analysis and synthesis, including its iterative nature, seems to be a powerful idea.

The Theories part comprises seven chapters and is headed by two quotes, one by Kurt Lewin (*There is nothing as practical as a good theory*) and one by Sumantra Ghoshal (*There is nothing as dangerous as a bad theory*).

Chapter 4 provides an overview of all EE theories. It is headed by this quote of Albert Einstein: *Whether you can observe a thing or not depends on the theory that you use. It is the theory that decides what can be observed.* The foundations of the discipline of EE, as envisioned by the CIAO! Network,[1] consist of the CIAO! Paradigm and a number of theories. After the discussion of the paradigm, which has its origins in the communication-centric view on information systems engineering that emerged around 2000, the role of the EE theories and their relationships with the EE methods and the practice of EE is explained. A suitable classification scheme is provided, consisting of four classes: philosophical, ontological, technological and ideological. Each of the theories is briefly discussed: the EE information theory (philosophical), the EE model theory (philosophical), the EE function-construction theory (philosophical), the EE organisational operation theory (ontological), the EE system theory (ontological), the EE organisational construction theory (ontological), the EE organisational essence theory (ontological), the EE design theory (technological), the EE implementation theory (technological), the EE automation theory (technological) and the EE governance and management theory (ideological). One philosophical theory, three ontological theories and two technological theories are elaborated in this book. The other philosophical and ontological theories are discussed in the book *Enterprise Ontology* [1]. The ideological theory is extensively discussed in the book *Foundations of Enterprise Governance and Enterprise Engineering* [2].

Chapter 5 introduces the reader into the important distinction between function and construction. This EE function-construction theory, or TAO theory, is a theory about the way subjects (people) perceive the things that surround them. TAO stands for Teleology, Affordance and Ontology. The Foundations part starts with an excerpt from Gibson's theory of affordances. This theory clarifies the subjectivity of affordances. Next, the intended affordances, commonly called functions, of designed things (artefacts) are discussed. Although people are mostly and primarily interested in the functions (affordances) that things may offer them, engineers are also interested in the construction of things. Contrary to function, construction is an objective notion. Related to function is the notion of experience, defined as the sensation that an affordance evokes in the mind. The notion of value is discussed as the intensity of experience, measurable on an ordinal scale. The Elaborations part starts with a discussion of constructional models and functional models, their incommensurability and the fundamental difference between constructional decompositions and functional ones. Next, these findings are illustrated to an example of an enterprise. The Discussions part addresses three topics. The first one is the subjective nature of functional models, and the second one is the mapping from functional to constructional models. It concludes with the importance of ontological modelling and a comparison of TAO theory and TAO philosophy.

[1] For more information, visit www.ciaonetwork.org

The first and crucial ontological theory is presented in Chap. 6, headed by this quote of Henry Mintzberg: *Every organised human activity—from the making of pots to the placing of a man on the moon—gives rise to two fundamental and opposing requirements: the division of labor into various tasks to be performed and the coordination of these tasks to accomplish the activity*. The EE Organisational Operation Theory or PSI theory is a theory about the operation of organisations. PSI stands for Performing in Social Interaction. Based on the CIAO! Paradigm (cf. Chap. 4), a communication-centric view is taken on the cooperation of people in enterprises, as manifested in business processes. The fundamental notion in understanding the operation of organisations is the coordination act. It consists of a performer, an addressee, an intention and a product. The performer and the addressee are actors: subjects filling an actor role. Actor roles are the units of authority and responsibility. Coordination acts can be performed verbally, non-verbally and tacitly. They are the key elements in (business) conversations, which are the constituting parts of (business) transactions. A transaction is carried out by actors in two roles: the initiator and the executor. The executor brings about the product of the transaction. The process of a transaction is a path, possibly including iterations, through a universal transaction pattern, which consists of one main pattern and six revocation patterns. The latter serves to revert the state in the main pattern to a previous state. Because of the inherent connection between an actor role and the transaction kind of which fillers are the executor, the combination of the two is called the transactor role. Transactor roles are the universal building blocks of business processes. Performing a coordination act results in creating the corresponding coordination fact. A fundamental principle in the PSI theory is that actors act autonomously, also if they are guided by business rules. Based on this principle, definitions are developed for the notions of authority, responsibility, accountability and competence.

Chapter 7 presents the EE Organisational Construction Theory, also called OMEGA theory. It is a theory about the modular structures that can be distinguished in organisations. Based on the organisational building block (the transactor role) from the PSI theory, three kinds of coordination structures are identified and discussed: interaction structure, interstriction structure and interimpediment structure. The interaction structure of an organisation consists of tree structures, which are constituted by the initiator links between transactor roles. An interaction tree determines a business process kind. The interstriction structure of an organisation consists of the access links between transactor roles. Through access links, actors have reading access to the facts in transaction banks. The interimpediment structure of an organisation is constituted by the wait links between transactor roles. Three topics are elaborated in depth. The first one is the notion of responsibility range of a transactor role, as an extension of the responsibility area from the PSI theory. The second subject is a comprehensive way of modelling business processes, which allows for all the details that are needed, but that is still very concise. Next, several general patterns in process structures, called reference models, are discussed. To conclude, the presented structural way of thinking about business processes is compared with the currently dominant flow way of thinking.

In Chap. 8, another theory that builds on the PSI theory is discussed. The EE organisational essence theory, or ALPHA theory, is a theory about the distinction of layers of transactor roles in an organisation, based on the sort of production that transactors bring about: original, informational, documental or material. Original production comprises all production acts that result in original new facts. Examples are devising things, deciding and judging as well as manufacturing, transporting and observing things. Informational production acts comprise remembering, computing and deriving facts and sharing (remembered or derived) facts. Documental production acts comprise saving, providing and transforming documents or datasets (containing facts). Material production comprises storing, retrieving, copying, transmitting and destroying files. Accordingly, the organisation of an enterprise can be partitioned into four partial organisations: the O-organisation (O from original), the I-organisation (I from informational), the D-organisation (D from documental) and the M-organisation (M from material). The I-organisation supports the O-organisation by means of informational services (remembering and sharing facts), the D-organisation supports the I-organisation by means of documental services (saving and providing data sets or documents) and the M-organisation supports the D-organisation by means of material service (storing and retrieving files). Because original acts are the only acts that change the state of the business world of an enterprise, they must be performed by human actors. For I-, D- and M-acts, it holds that they can be taken over by artefacts, notably ICT systems, including AI artefacts (like logistic control systems and robots). However, as pointed out in the PSI theory, human actors are ultimately responsible and accountable for the acts of these artefacts. The ontological model of an enterprise's O-organisation is called its *essential model*. Like every ontological model, it is abstracted from implementation, but it is also abstracted from realisation, that is, from the supporting I-, D- and M-organisation. At the same time, it contains everything that is needed to understand the essence of an enterprise's operation. The ALPHA theory contributes to the generic EE goal of intellectual manageability by an unprecedented reduction of complexity. It also clarifies that every enterprise information system is nothing more or less than a part of the I-, D- and M-organisation that support the O-organisation, only implemented by using ICT.

Chapter 9 contains a discussion of the core theory of this book: the organisational design theory, also called BETA theory (Building from Essence with Technology and Architecture). It is a theory about the development of a system, called the object system (OS), which is going to support another system, called the using system (US). The US uses the services that are (going to be) offered by the OS. The development process is conceived as the sequence of function design, construction design and implementation design, where the notion of design corresponds fully with its definition in Chap. 3. Although the BETA theory is generally applicable, we apply it specifically to the development of O-organisations and enterprise information systems (EISs). Both Enterprise Ontology and Enterprise Architecture are crucial notions in the General System Development Process (GSDP), which is the general development model. Function design starts from the ontological model of the US, and construction design ends up in the ontological model of the OS. Implementation design consists of producing a series of implementation models that are increasingly dependent on the chosen implementation technology. In EE, the notion of architecture is exclusively used in its meaning of guidelines (principles, standards) that are applied in the system development process. Consequently, the applied architecture in a development process is a source of both functional and constructional requirements, in addition to the functional and constructional requirements that are provided by the (future) users of the OS. In order to manage the user and architectural requirements, the GRAF is presented (General Requirements and Architecture Framework).

After the ontological design of an organisation, this design must be made operational. The way from the ontological model to the implementation model of the OS is discussed in Chap. 10. Four phases are distinguished in the ETA theory (Engineering with Technological Alternatives). The first one is the implementation design. It comprises the assignment of proper technological means to the elements of the ontological model. The second phase is the actual implementation, which is the assignment of concrete technological means to the elements of the ontological model. After this phase come installation and operation. Installation concerns the allocation of specific means for specific time periods. Operation starts when 'the switch' is turned on.

The part Applications is headed by a quote of Confucius: *I hear and I forget, I see and I remember, I do and I understand.* The aim of this part of the book is to show the reader how the theories can be put into practice.

Chapter 11 presents the DEMO methodology (Design and Engineering Methodology for Organisations). It helps one to produce the essential model of an enterprise or, in general, of a Scope of Interest (which may cover a part of one enterprise or of a network of enterprises). DEMO comprises a Way of Thinking (WoT), a Way of Modelling (WoM) and a Way of Working (WoW). The WoT consists of the theories in part II of the book. The WoM consists of an integrated whole of four sub-models: the Cooperation model (CM), the Action Model (AM), the Process Model (PM) and the Fact Model (FM). The CM of a Scope of Interest (SoI) is the ontological model of its construction, thus of the identified transactor roles and the coordination structures among them. Three structures are distinguished: the interaction structure, the interimpediment structure and the interstriction structure. The AM of an SoI is the ontological model of its operation. For every internal actor role, it provides the rules that guide the role fillers in doing their work. The guidelines for responding to coordination events are called action rules (similar to business rules); the ones for performing production acts are called work instructions. The PM of an SoI is the ontological model of the state space and the transition space of its coordination world. The FM of an SoI is the ontological model of the state space and the transition space of its production world. All four sub-models are expressed in the DEMO Specification Language (DEMO-SL),[2] which comprises diagrams, tables

[2] The latest version of DEMO-SL can be downloaded freely from www.ee-instituite.org

and formal textual descriptions. For producing essential models of enterprises, the WoW of DEMO offers the OER method (Organisational Essence Revealing). It consists of a number of steps in which the four DEMO models are produced. For (re)developing organisations and enterprise information systems, DEMO offers the DAO method (Designing under Architecture from Ontology). The so-called Ford case is used for illustrating the DAO method.

Chapters 12–14 present exercises in applying DEMO, notably the DAO method, to practical organisational changes: the Pizzeria, the Library and Redesigning a National Police Force. All three of them are exercises in organisational redesign and digital transformation.

The Pizzeria is an exercise in understanding and applying the full potential of abstracting from realisation and implementation, thus focusing on the O-organisation of an enterprise. In the course of its existence, the pizzeria passes through three phases. The transition from the first to the second phase means a change in the essential model. The change appears to have interesting consequences for the allocation of authority. Despite the huge differences between the second and the third phase in terms of implementation, their ontological models do not differ.

The Library is an exercise in producing the essential model of an enterprise that offers the obtaining of usufruct of tangible things (borrowing books) and the creating of intangible things (starting and ending memberships). By applying the OER method to the narrative case description, the information is achieved on the basis of which the essential model is produced. The essential model is a stable beacon when discussing the application of the DAO method, in particular the impacts of alternative ways of implementing it. Far-reaching changes in the operational activities appear to have no or little impact on the essential model because they mainly regard implementation matters.

In Chap. 14, the redesign of a regional police force is presented. It took place in 1993 to realise the national decision of The Netherlands that the police force should be divided into 25 autonomous regions. The one discussed is the region Rotterdam-Rijnmond, comprising 5000 police officers, working for 1.2 million people. Thanks to the adoption of DEMO as the main methodology, the original idea of redoing information planning was turned into a reorganisation of the entire region. Soon the police officers understood that once you have the essential model of your organisation, you are prepared for every change, because the essential model is not dependent on region or district or any organisational structure.

Chapter 15 contains various contributions from practice. The selected applications are (1) Direct Childcare Financing, (2) Redesigning an Organisation, (3) Redesigning Asset Management, (4) Business Information Security, (5) BPMN patterns for Process Design, (6) DEMO in Airline Alliances, (7) Designing the My Number System, (8) Developing Process Ownership and (9) The Sangikyo Case. All applications are reported in the STARR framework.

The book is concluded by a glossary of the most important terms and a list of often-used abbreviations.

References

1. Dietz, J. L. G., & Mulder, J. B. F. (2024). *Enterprise ontology—A human-centric approach to understanding the essence of organisation* (Enterprise engineering) (2nd ed.). Springer Nature.
2. Hoogervorst, J. A. P. (2017). *Foundations of enterprise governance and enterprise engineering* (p. 574). Springer International Publishing.
3. Dietz, J. L. G., Hoogervorst, J. A. P., et al. (2013). The discipline of enterprise engineering. *International Journal of Organisational Design and Engineering, 3*, 28.
4. Dietz, J. L. G. (2006). *Enterprise ontology: Theory and methodology*. Springer, xiii, 243 p.

Acknowledgements

From 2006 on, our understanding of Enterprise Design has been influenced through interaction with many people. Numerous students have been a valuable whetstone, notably those at Delft University of Technology and Antwerp Management School. A similar role was also played by our colleagues in the CIAO! Network and the Enterprise Engineering Institute. We would like to mention some of them explicitly (in reverse alphabetical order): Marné de Vries, José Tribolet, Robert Pergl, Martin Op't Land, Marien Krouwel, Steven van Kervel, Joop de Jong, Jan Hoogervorst, Edward van Dipten, Joseph Barjis, Eduard Babkin and David Aveiro.

Contents

Abbreviations[1]

ADT Authorisation Delegation Table [cross-model representation form of the *Ontological Model* and the *Implementation Model* of an SoI] (Chap. 11).

AM Action Model [*aspect model* of the *ontological model* of an *organisational layer*] (Chap. 11).

APT Actor role Position Table [cross-model representation form of the *Ontological Model* and the *Implementation Model* of an SoI] (Chap. 11).

ARS Action Rule Specifications [representation form of the *Action Model*] (Chap. 11).

BAT Bank Access Table [representation form of the *Cooperation Model*] (Chap. 11).

BCT Bank Contents Table [cross-model representation form of the *Cooperation Model* and the *Fact Model*] (Chap. 11).

CM Cooperation Model [*aspect model* of the *ontological model* of an *organisational layer*] (Chap. 11).

CSD Coordination Structure Diagram [representation form of the *Cooperation Model*] (Chap. 11).

CUT Create Use Table [cross-model representation form of the *Process Model* and the *Fact Model*] (Chap. 11).

DFS Derived Fact Specifications [representation form of *Fact Model*] (Chap. 11).

et Event time (Chaps. 8 and 11).

FM Fact Model [*aspect model* of the *ontological model* of an *organisational layer*] (Chap. 11).

GRAF General Requirements and Architecture Framework (Chap. 9).

GSDP General System Development Process (Chap. 9).

[1] Hereafter, the most common abbreviations of terms in Enterprise Design, as used in this book, are explained, in alphabetical order. The chapter(s) where the term is defined is indicated between '(' and ')'.

ICT Information and Communication Technology. It combines Information Technology (IT) for information processing and information storage and Communication Technology (CT) for transmitting information.

OFD Object Fact Diagram [representation form of *Fact Model*] (Chap. 11).

PM Process Model [*aspect model* of the *ontological model* of an *organisational layer*] (Chap. 11).

PSD Process Structure Diagram [representation form of the *Process Model*] (Chap. 11).

TPD Transaction Process Diagram [representation form of the *Process Model*] (Chap. 11).

TPT Transactor Product Table [cross-model representation form of the *Cooperation Model* and the *Fact Model*] (Chap. 11).

WIS Work Instruction Specifications [cross-model representation form of the *Ontological Model* and the *Implementation Model* of an SoI] (Chap. 11).

Part I
Introduction

Part I contains the three introductory chapters to the main contents in Parts II (theories) and III (applications). In Chap. 1, the reader is introduced to the emerging discipline of Enterprise Engineering, in which a design-oriented view is taken towards organisations. One of the conceptual pillars of Enterprise Engineering is Enterprise Design, the core subject of this book. Related to Enterprise Design is the notion of Enterprise Architecture. It is presented and discussed in Chap. 2. Enterprise Architecture has a special connotation in Enterprise Engineering. Chapter 3 provides an introduction to the key notion of this book: Enterprise Design.

Chapter 1
Introduction to Enterprise Engineering

Abstract Enterprise Engineering is an emerging discipline that takes an engineering perspective on enterprises. It aims to address the problems in organisations that cannot be solved by the traditional organisational sciences. Organisational changes are conceived as situations of (re)design and (re)implementation. The conceptual pillars of Enterprise Engineering are the notions of Enterprise Ontology, Enterprise Architecture and Enterprise Governance. By applying them, three goals are, respectively, attained: intellectual manageability, organisational concinnity and social devotion.

Science is about knowing; engineering is about doing
(Henry Petroski)

In perfect agreement with Petroski's quote above, the discipline of Enterprise Engineering (EE) is about doing. The general goal of EE is to make better enterprises or to make enterprises better, in every meaning of the word. By 'enterprise', we refer to all kinds of organised human activities (like companies, agencies, institutions, supply chains, etc. but also the organisation of a birthday party). Indeed, science alone doesn't solve the problems humanity faces, engineering is needed to develop and implement effective solutions [1]. At the same time, doing without a proper understanding of what one is doing may be worse than doing nothing. That is why every serious engineering discipline is rooted in a solid theoretical foundation.

The societal need of a discipline of EE is urgent because modern societies are increasingly complex networks of an increasingly number of enterprises, with increasingly complex interrelationships. Moreover, the traditional organisational and management sciences fail to provide effective help [2]. Deming [3] provides a convincing account, which can be paraphrased as follows: almost all (94%) manifestations of inadequate enterprise performance are the inevitable result of how enterprises are organised. The purport of this finding is that only in 6% of all instances of operational failure, one can correctly blame workers. In all other cases, the cause is a fault in the design or implementation of the organisation.

Over the years, insights have been developed about how to (1) enhance the effectiveness and efficiency of enterprises; (2) effectively ensure quality, service and

J. L. G. Dietz, H. B. F. Mulder, *Enterprise Design Fundamentals*, The Enterprise Engineering Series, https://doi.org/10.1007/978-3-031-83262-8_1

customer orientation; and (3) avoid core reasons for strategic failure. One would expect that a century after Taylor published his principles of scientific management, his influence would have diminished. However, as Doz and Thanheiser observed at the end of the previous century: 'Despite the "modernisation" of corporate structures and systems, the mindset of managers appears to be remarkably similar to the Taylorist model developed at the beginning of the century' [4]. Thus, principles that follow from 'a machine-like concept of the organisation still dominate managerial practice' [ibid.]. Others argue that 'Corporations continue to operate according to a logic invented at the time of their origin, a century ago' [5].

The continuation of the Taylorist model can additionally be demonstrated by observing the increase in the number of management functions. For example, in the country where Taylor expressed his views, managers accounted for less than 1% of the labour force in 1900. Thirty years later, this figure was already 7.5%, increasing to 10.5% by 1970. By 1990, the figure was approaching 14% [6]. These increases must be understood against the background of increasing population and workforce.

The increased population of managers largely consists of people who believe that management is a profession like other professions. As the renowned quality and productivity leader Deming observed: 'Students in schools of business in America are taught that there is a profession of management; that they are ready to step into top jobs. That is a cruel hoax' [3]. This 'hoax' resulted in the widely observable management crises. An article in Standardization News (1983) stated that 'Practical all our major corporations were started by technical men—inventors, mechanics, engineers, and chemists, who had a sincere interest in the quality of products. Now, these companies are largely run by men interested in profit, not product. Their pride is the P&L[1] statement or stock report' [3].

The needed paradigm shift is provided by the emerging discipline of Enterprise Engineering. It amounts to a theory-based methodology for addressing enterprise (re-)development in an all-encompassing way. A sound and rigid theoretical foundation is crucial. As Deming states: 'Experience alone, without theory, teaches management nothing about what to do to improve quality and competitive position, nor how to do it' [3]. In view of our previous discussion, and the tenacity of Taylor's principles, little learning seems to have taken place. We posit that an explanatory theory is required to give experience meaning and, in doing so, to provide the basis for appropriately understanding enterprises.

In 2013, the paper 'The discipline of Enterprise Engineering' was published [7]. The authors are Jan Dietz and Jan Hoogervorst, but there are many co-authors. They are the key members of the Ciao! Network.[2] We list them in alphabetical order, including their main academic affiliation at that time:

Antonia Albani (University of St. Gallen, Switzerland)
David Aveiro (University of Madeira, Portugal)
Eduard Babkin (Higher School of Economics at Nizhny Novgorod, Russia)

[1] P&L stands for profit and loss.

[2] http://ciaonetwork.org/

Joseph Barjis (Delft University of Technology, The Netherlands)
Artur Caetano (University of Lisbon, IST,[3] Portugal)
Philip Huysmans (University of Antwerp, Belgium)
Junichi Iijima (Tokyo Tech, Japan)
Steven van Kervel (Delft University of Technology)
Hans Mulder (University of Antwerp, AMS[4])
Martin Op 't Land (University of Antwerp, AMS)
Henderik Proper (Radboud University Nijmegen, The Netherlands)
Jorge Sanz (IBM Research, San José, California, USA)
Linda Terlouw (Delft University of Technology)
José Tribolet (University of Lisbon, IST)
Jan Verelst (University of Antwerp)
Robert Winter (University of St. Gallen)

The academic affiliations of the main authors are, respectively, Delft University of Technology and University of Antwerp, AMS. In this founding article, three general goals are identified for EE: intellectual manageability, organisational concinnity and social devotion.

Intellectual manageability is about getting and keeping insight into and overview over complexity. People who have to govern or run enterprises, or to devise and implement substantial changes, need first of all a proper understanding of what they are doing. Current practice shows that this basic premise is often not met. Obviously, enterprise phenomena that are not properly understood cannot be addressed adequately. Consequently, the necessary changes cannot be determined, and if they can, they cannot be brought about effectively. In addition, current development approaches, for enterprises as a whole and for IT applications in particular, are cursed with combinatorial impacts of changes. So, in addition, appropriate ideas of enterprise evolvability are needed for making changes expeditious and manageable. Intellectual manageability is an indispensable quality: if you don't understand fully and deeply what you are doing, you better not do it. The goal of intellectual manageability is particularly achieved by applying the notion of Enterprise Ontology, as discussed and applied in [8].

Organisational concinnity is about designing, engineering and implementing an enterprise in such a way that the resulting operational organisation is always a coherent and consistent whole. In order to perform optimally and to implement changes successfully, enterprises must operate as a unified and integrated whole, taking into account all aspects that are deemed relevant. Many approaches to enterprise development, for example, TOGAF, are ill-suited and suffer from theoretical and methodological weakness and incompleteness [9]. It is evidently not sufficient to consider enterprise design domains like processes, the information needs of the processes, the software applications providing the information and their underlying infrastructure. A viable theory and methodology for Enterprise Engineering must be

[3] IST stands for Instituto Superior Técnico.
[4] AMS stands for Antwerp Management School.

able to address all relevant aspects, even those that cannot be foreseen presently, in a properly integrated way. It is quite obvious that organisational concinnity must be designed; it does not emerge in a natural way [10, 11]. The goal of organisational concinnity is particularly achieved by applying the notion of Enterprise Architecture, as presented and discussed in Chap. 2 and as applied in several other chapters of this book.

Social devotion is about recognising that the operation of an enterprise's organisation is brought about not by its managers but by its operational employees. In [2, 7], the importance of employee involvement and participation has been argued in order to achieve enterprise productivity, product and service quality, customer orientation, learning and innovation (and subsequent enterprise change), as well as to cope with enterprise dynamics, complexity and uncertainty leading to emerging enterprise developments. Contrary to Taylor's mechanistic view on organisations [12], EE takes a human-centric view. It considers human beings to be the 'pearls' of every enterprise. Therefore, all employees should be fully empowered and competent for the tasks they have to perform. They must be endorsed with transparent authority and have access to all information needed to perform their tasks in a responsible way. Next, managers must not only be skilled in managerial work of the kind that Deming refers to [3], they must first of all be thoroughly knowledgeable in the subject field of the enterprise they are managing. The goal of social devotion is particularly achieved by applying the notion of Enterprise Governance, as presented extensively in [2, 13].

In the founding article of Enterprise Engineering, the crucial role of the PSI theory (cf. [8], Chap. 8), there labeled ψ-theory, is discussed. In Chap. 4 of this book, the basis of its cruciality is disclosed: its being communication-centric, as opposed to information-centric (like most existing approaches to organisational engineering and IT systems engineering are). *Communication-centric* means that communication is the primary notion, defined as the sharing of thoughts between human beings [14]. The secondary notion of information is defined as the means of communicating. *Information-centric* means that information is the primary (but mostly ill-defined) notion. Communication then is defined as the exchanging of information. The supremacy of communication-centricity is elaborated in Chap. 9: the nasty problem of information requirements elicitation has vanished, and enterprise information systems are just parts of organisations, only implemented in IT. But as in the history of engineering, many better alternatives have come off worst [15], the communication-centric view has not succeeded in surpassing the information-centric view on a broad scale.

References

1. Petroski, H. (2010). *The essential engineer: Why science alone will not solve our global problems* (1st ed.). Alfred A. Knopf. x, 274 p.

2. Hoogervorst, J. A. P. (2017). *Foundations of enterprise governance and enterprise engineering* (p. 574). Springer International Publishing.
3. Deming, W. E. (1986). *Out of the crisis: Quality, productivity and competitive position*. Cambridge University Press. xiii, 507 p.
4. Doz, Y., & Thanheiser, H. (1993). Regaining competitiveness: A process of organizational renewal. In J. Hendry, G. Johnson, & J. Newton (Eds.), *Strategic thinking: Leadership and the management of change*. Wiley.
5. Zuboff, S., & Maxmin, J. (2004). *The support economy: Why corporations are failing individuals and the next episode of capitalism*. Penguin Books. xvii, 458 p.
6. Osterman, P. (1996). *Broken ladders: Managerial careers in the new economy*. Oxford University Press. 259 p.
7. Dietz, J. L. G., Hoogervorst, J. A. P., et al. (2013). The discipline of enterprise engineering. *International Journal of Organisational Design and Engineering, 3*, 28.
8. Dietz, J. L. G., & Mulder, J. B. F. (2024). *Enterprise ontology—A human-centric approach to understanding the essence of organisation* (Enterprise engineering) (2nd ed.). Springer Nature.
9. Dietz, J. L. G., & Hoogervorst, J. A. P. (2012). A critical investigation of TOGAF. In *Advances in enterprise engineering V* (LNBIP series). Spinger.
10. Keller, S., & Price, C. (2011). *Beyond performance: How great organizations build ultimate competitive advantage*. Wiley. xx, 280 p.
11. Leinwand, P., & Mainardi, C. (2011). *The essential advantage: How to win with a capabilities-driven strategy*. Harvard Business Review Press. xii, 227 p.
12. Taylor, F. W. (1911). *The principles of scientific management* (Vol. 2, pp. 1, 7–1,77). Harper & Brothers.
13. Hoogervorst, J. A. P. (2009). *Enterprise governance and enterprise engineering* (The enterprise engineering series) (Vol. 1). Springer.
14. van Reijswoud, V. E., Mulder, H. B. F., & Dietz, J. L. G. (1999). Communicative action-based business process and information systems modelling with DEMO. *Information Systems Journal, 9*, 117–138.
15. Hamer, M. (2017, 6 September). How crooks stalled the rise of electric cars for 100 years. *New Scientist*.

Chapter 2
Introduction to Enterprise Architecture

Abstract Only by applying the exclusively prescriptive notion of Enterprise Architecture as adopted in this book can one achieve organisational concinnity, which is one of the general goals of Enterprise Engineering. The current descriptive understanding of the notion in the practice of organisational design and ICT-applications development is imprecise and ambiguous. Several dominant definitions of architecture are reviewed and put aside as unsatisfying. The resulting prescriptive notion of Enterprise Architecture is the main vehicle to achieve organisational concinnity.

2.1 The Notion of Architecture

Architecture is not what you see but what shaped what you see.

The second intellectual tool for mastering the complexity of enterprises, next to Enterprise Ontology (cf. [1]), is Enterprise Architecture (cf. [2]). It is abundantly discussed in the literature about organisational change. However, Enterprise Architecture is probably also the most troublesome term in organisational design nowadays, because it is surrounded by vagueness and ambiguity. So, let us start with shedding some clarifying light on the notion of architecture.

For all engineering disciplines, it holds that the designer of an artefact, of any kind, starts from a virtually unlimited design freedom and is left with some amount, after all requirements are satisfied. The design freedom one is left with may be substantial, even in disciplines where the implementation technology is constrained by physical laws, like in building engineering, where the notion of architecture originates from. Consequently, designers are faced with the question how to use this design freedom.

Throughout history, man has answered the question in much the same way, namely, by using it for expressing a personal or collective vision on the artefact. As an example, designers of wooden walking sticks in general use their design freedom

J. L. G. Dietz, H. B. F. Mulder, *Enterprise Design Fundamentals*, The Enterprise Engineering Series, https://doi.org/10.1007/978-3-031-83262-8_2

to let the stick evoke the experience of nature, for example, by gouging pictures of nature (trees, flowers, mountains, trails, etc.) on the stick. Most craftsmen use their design freedom in a similar way. More generally, designers use their design freedom to appeal to aesthetic experiences or to impose their personal view. The way they use the design freedom is often referred to as their 'style'. By applying this notion of architecture, building architects also seek to make clear from the appearance of a building whether it is a bank office or a kindergarten or whatever the building serves to. As an additional example, designers of churches mostly use their design freedom to appeal to religion-related concepts, like devotion, hospitality and sense of safety.

Before presenting a thorough and appropriate definition of architecture for the discipline of EE, let us look at some examples from the building industry, namely, the three opera houses of which pictures are shown in Fig. 2.1: the Sydney Opera House, the Scala in Milan and the Metropolitan Opera in New York. Let us assume that their functional requirements were roughly the same and that neither of them had serious constructional constraints. The interesting question then is: Why do they look so differently? Clearly, the difference between the three opera houses is in the way in which their designers (architects) have used the design freedom that was left after all user requirements were satisfied. We leave it to the reader's knowledge or imagination what the architects wanted to express by the way they used their design freedom. It is also perfectly clear that this is what building architects call architecture: *architecture is not what you see but what shaped what you see*, as we have put above this chapter. It is the outcome of applying rules, ideas or whatever one likes to call them, to address the remaining design freedom. Therefore, instead of attempting to invent something new, let us try to adopt this 'classic' notion of architecture for the field of EE.

Fig. 2.1 Examples of architecture in the building industry

Before doing this, let us briefly review some apparently influential definitions of the term that go around and try to identify differences and commonalities between them. A rather influential definition of (Enterprise) Architecture is the one provided by Zachman.[1] It reads:

> *Architecture is that set of design artefacts, or descriptive representations, that are relevant for describing an object, such that it can be produced to requirements as well as maintained over the period of its useful life.*

There are two interesting observations to be made regarding this definition. First, architecture is not conceived as a property of an object but rather as a document or a set of documents describing the object. This is quite remarkable since its more general and colloquial meaning, which emerged from the field of building engineering, definitely includes that it is a property of an object. For example, you can say that a church is a Roman church or a Gothic one (you would not say that the drawing of the church is Roman or Gothic). Second, the architecture of an object apparently contains the information that is needed to produce the object and to maintain it. The question that comes to mind then is in what sense or to what degree this notion of architecture differs from the notion of design. The referred paper does not provide an answer to this question, unfortunately, which leads us to the opinion that Zachman's notion of architecture is at best, and with a lot of imagination, akin to the first part of another influential definition, namely, IEEE Standard 1471.[2] It reads:

> *Architecture is the fundamental organisation of a system embodied in its components, their relationships to each other and to the environment, and the principles guiding its design and evolution.*

To our view, this definition is ambiguous; it tries to accommodate two different points of view. One is architecture as the global composition and structure of a system, abstracted from details. The other one is architecture as a way to use design freedom. Let us call the first use of the term descriptive and the second one prescriptive. So, the definition of architecture by Zachman is purely descriptive, while the definition by IEEE is both descriptive and prescriptive. IEEE Standard 1471 is quite similar to the second part of the meaning assigned to the term 'architecture' by the Open Group,[3] whereas the first part of the Open Group's definition resembles Zachman's definition to a large extent. The definition of architecture by the Open Group is:

> 1. *A formal description of a system, or a detailed plan of the system at component level to guide its implementation.*
> 2. *The structure of components, their interrelationships, and the principles and guidelines governing their design and evolution over time.*

Our first comment is that we cogently reject Zachman's definition. It fails to distinguish between a concept and the way it is represented, whether in plain text or

---

[1] Concepts of the Framework for Enterprise Architecture, Zachman International Inc. 1997

[2] https://en.wikipedia.org/wiki/IEEE_1471

[3] http://www.opengroup.org/bookstore/catalog/g051.htm

diagrams or any other language (cf. [1], Chap. 6). Our next comment regards the second part of the definition by the Open Group as well as the definition by IEEE. Both are ambiguous: they convey two different definitions (a descriptive and a prescriptive one) in the same breath, which should always be avoided.

Obviously, we agree with the cited sources that understanding the construction and operation of a system in a fundamental way, abstracted from implementation details, is crucial. However, this is already contained (but in a much more effective and precise way) in the notion of ontology, as discussed in [1]. Not only does it let you get an understanding of a system (an organisation, an information system, a data or document system) that is fully abstracted from implementation details; this understanding is also thoroughly founded in a solid theoretical basis. Let us therefore use the term 'architecture' exclusively for guidelines governing the design. This leads us to the next definition of architecture in EE:

Theoretically, architecture is the normative use of design freedom.
Practically, it is a consistent and coherent set of requirements.

By requirements is meant those requirements that the designer (architect) applies in addition to the requirements that are provided by the customer or users. In order to distinguish them properly, we will refer to the last group of requirements by 'user requirements' and to the first group by 'architectural requirements'. The application of both kinds of requirements will be elaborated in Chap. 7.

The prescriptive notion of architecture is currently emerging in practice. The companies that have adopted it are, however, pioneers. Yet, the potentials of this understanding of architecture are enormous. In fact, it seems to be the only feasible way of 'translating' high-level statements, as can be found in mission and strategy documents, into operationally useful principles for developing systems (organisations, information systems, data or document systems) [3].

2.2 Achieving Organisational Concinnity

The word 'concinnity' is not common. It was chosen in [2], in order to emphasise that both meanings of the word are relevant: harmonious and skilful.[4] Organisations must be designed in such a way that they operate as a *harmonious* whole. Obviously, one may be inclined to say, but as Deming has pointed out already long ago [4], it is not a property that emerges naturally; instead it has to be designed deliberately.

In the previous section, Enterprise Architecture is presented as the main vehicle by which harmony in organisational design is achieved. Not the unclear and

[4] The original Latin meaning of concinnity is 'skilfully put together'. It emphasises that Enterprise Architecture needs *skilful* people to apply it. This skilfulness can only be acquired by training that is based on a sound theoretical basis. This is precisely what Enterprise Engineering strives for, in applying Enterprise Architecture, in applying Enterprise Ontology and in applying Enterprise Governance.

ambiguous notion that prevails in current practice but the exclusive prescriptive notion that we presented. As will become clear particularly in Chap. 7, Enterprise Architecture does the lion's share of the job. Fortunately, it is not too hard to express general strategic goals into architectural requirements (principles, standards, etc.), as discussed in [3].

But the other two pillars of EE do also contribute to achieving concinnity. Enterprise Ontology does so by offering the next three ideas for better understanding the construction and operation of organisations [1].

First, the operating principle of every organisation is that people cooperate by entering into and complying with commitments. They do so in a recurrent pattern, called the transaction pattern. At least these basic steps must be taken: request, promise, declare and accept. In addition, the complete transaction pattern covers all 'exceptions', including the revocation of each of the basic steps.

Second, next to the well-known flow structure, business processes have an intrinsic tree structure. This tree structure is most helpful in (re)designing and (re)engineering them. In fact, (re)designing and (re)engineering business processes, while knowing only their flow structure, is playing a kind of Russian roulette.

Third, in every enterprise, four organisational layers can be distinguished: the O-organisation (O from original), the I-organisation (I from informational), the D-organisation (D from documental) and the M-organisation (M from material). The ontological model of each of them is fully abstracted from their implementation. One of the important consequences is the insight that an (enterprise) information system is just (a part of) an I-organisation, only implemented in ICT.[5] Likewise, a data or document (management) system is just (a part of) a D-organisation (and the corresponding part of the M-organisation), only implemented in ICT. In Chap. 6, these distinctions will be elaborated.

Lastly, Enterprise Governance contributes to achieving organisational concinnity first by conceiving it as something in which all employees participate and second by considering these employees as the pearls of the organisation [5]. Only employees that feel esteemed by management will be observant and able to fix small disturbances of the harmony.

2.3 The Current Meaning of Architecture and Architect

In Sect. 2.1, we pointed already at the poorness of the descriptions of the notion of architecture by leading professionals. Most descriptions were published in the last decade of the previous century. In this decade, a movement started in the worldwide community of enterprise and software engineers that resulted in a disastrous blurring of the notions of architecture and architect. System and software analysts

[5] ICT stands for Information and Communication Technology. The name refers to the totality of modern devices and techniques that are used to share, store and transmit information, data and documents. ICT includes a.o. computers, databases, networks (like the Internet), etc.

started to call themselves architects, and the structure of any system or artefact was gradually called its architecture.

Unfortunately, we have to deal with this situation, which has not improved since then. On the contrary, things are only getting worse. We see only one way out, which is to stick to our prescriptive notion of architecture and to avoid as much as possible using the word 'architect'. We are aware that this is actually fighting a losing battle.

References

1. Dietz, J. L. G., & Mulder, J. B. F. (2024). *Enterprise ontology—A human-centric approach to understanding the essence of organisation* (Enterprise engineering) (2nd ed.). Springer Nature.
2. Dietz, J. L. G., Hoogervorst, J. A. P., et al. (2013). The discipline of enterprise engineering. *International Journal of Organisational Design and Engineering, 3*, 28.
3. Dietz, J. L. G. (2009). *Architecture: Building strategy into design*. SDU Publishing.
4. Deming, W. E. (1986). *Out of the crisis: Quality, productivity and competitive position*. Cambridge University Press. xiii, 507 p.
5. Hoogervorst, J. A. P. (2017). *Foundations of enterprise governance and enterprise engineering* (p. 574). Springer International Publishing.

Chapter 3
Introduction to Enterprise Design

Abstract In order to investigate the notion of Enterprise Design, we take the general definition of design by Herbert A. Simon as the starting point: devising courses of action aimed at changing existing situations into preferred ones. Undoubtedly, this definition does also hold for the design of enterprises: one wants to replace the current shape (AS-IS) of an enterprise by a preferred one (TO-BE). In discussing the design process, previous research in two different fields is investigated: the work by Wolfgang Hesse in software engineering and the work of Christopher Alexander in building engineering. Viewing a design process as alternate steps of analysis and synthesis, including the recognition of its iterative nature, seems to be a powerful idea.

3.1 What Is Design?

Before discussing what Enterprise Design entails, we will first focus on the notion of design in general. A search for 'design' on the World Wide Web yields a vast number of hits; it demonstrates the broad use of the word. In the *Merriam Webster Dictionary*, one finds the following definitions: (1) To create, fashion, execute or construct according to plan; *design* a system for tracking inventory. (2a) To conceive and plan out in the mind; he *designed* the perfect crime. (2b) To have as a purpose; she *designed* to excel in her studies. (2c) To devise for a specific function or end; a book *designed* primarily as a college textbook, a suitcase *designed* to hold a laptop computer. (3) (*archaic*) To indicate with a distinctive mark, sign or name. (4a) To make a drawing, pattern or sketch of. (4b) To draw the plans for; *design* a building, *design* a new bike.

These are the definitions for the use of the word 'design' as a transitive verb; we disregard its use as an intransitive verb or as a noun. Definitions 1, 2c and 4 match what we have in mind when thinking of design; the others seem less relevant. This already narrows down what design could be. Without any doubt, design implies

J. L. G. Dietz, H. B. F. Mulder, *Enterprise Design Fundamentals*, The Enterprise Engineering Series, https://doi.org/10.1007/978-3-031-83262-8_3

creating something that wasn't there before. We will start our investigation into the notion of design from the very general definition by Herbert A. Simon: … *devising courses of action aimed at changing existing situations into preferred ones* ([1], p. 111). A bit further on the same page, Simon stresses the broad meaning of his definition: '… schools of engineering, as well as schools of architecture, business, education, law, and medicine, are all centrally concerned with the process of design'.

3.2 The Design Process

Having agreed on the definition of design as changing an existing situation into a preferred one prompts the following question: How does one go about? In other words, how does the design process look like? There are two studies that we think deserve being investigated to find answers to this question. The first one originates from the field of software engineering and the second one from building engineering. The latter field is also referred to by the name 'architecture', but we reserve this word for a specific meaning, as discussed in Chap. 2.

Software engineering is a discipline quite close to EE; one might even conjecture that it is part of it, as far as the development of software is concerned that implements Enterprise Information Systems (cf. Chap. 8). Software design is a core subfield of software engineering. It addresses the question of how to write a computer program that, when put into operation, produces output that satisfies the requirements that were set before. Designing a piece of software is envisioned by Wolfgang Hesse[1] as a path in a two-dimensional space from a point R (R from Requirements) to a point C (C from program Code). His view is shown in Fig. 3.1. The two dimensions in the plane are *abstraction* (vertical dimension) and *formalisation* (horizontal dimension). Hesse states that the points R and C are of the same kind, namely, a description of the program. The difference between them is that R is very abstract and very informal, whereas C is very concrete and very formal (necessarily, because computers are formal machines).

[1] Methods and Tools for Software Development: A Walk through the Technology Landscape, in: *Colloquium Programmeeromgevingen, MC Syllabus 30*, CWI (Centrum voor Wiskunde en Informatica), Amsterdam, 1983.

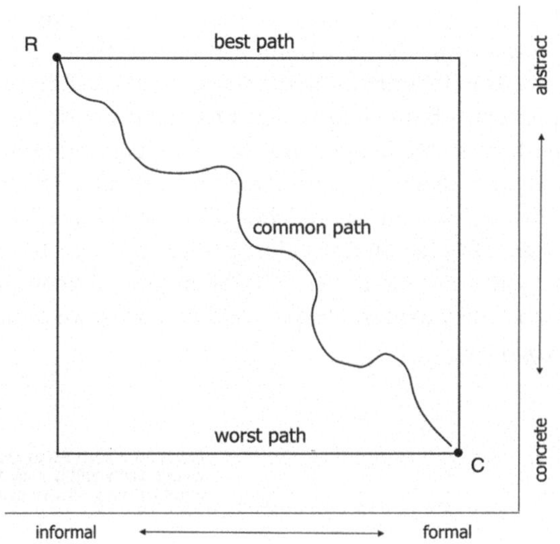

Fig. 3.1 The design process according to Hesse

According to Hesse, the way that software designers (programmers) commonly go about is quite arbitrary. It is represented in Fig. 3.1 by the line labeled 'common path'. One only knows that they start in point R and end up in point C. Figure 3.1 immediately prompts two comments. One is that ideally, point R is some undisputed fixed point. Unfortunately, in practice it often isn't. In many cases, there is quite some uncertainty about the content of R. Often, R becomes only fully clear when point C has been reached, sometimes even later: it is not uncommon in software engineering that stakeholders produce additional requirements once they understand what point C entails. The other comment is that something similar holds for point C. Software designers (or programmers) always end up with having produced code, thus in some point C. The question is whether the produced code is a proper counterpart of the requirements in point R. Both comments are at the core of the many failures of software engineering, contributing to the bad reputation of the discipline. From the very beginning, there has been a combat between people like Edsger W. Dijkstra[2] and Niklaus Wirth,[3] who wanted to address software engineering as an unprecedented intellectual challenge that requires thorough theoretical work, and people like Barry Boehm,[4] who thought that looming up problems could be solved by better project management. The evidence that this 'pragmatic' approach is doomed to fail is ubiquitous. The reader might particularly appreciate the essays that Frederick Brooks presents in [2].

[2] https://en.wikipedia.org/wiki/Edsger_W._Dijkstra

[3] https://en.wikipedia.org/wiki/Niklaus_Wirth

[4] https://en.wikipedia.org/wiki/Barry_Boehm

As pointed out in Fig. 3.1, the best path one can take is to stay on an abstract level while gradually formalising the description of the software until it is fully formalised and only needs to be transformed into program code in some programming language. This approach acknowledges that programming digital computers is an unprecedented intellectual challenge and that every (correct) computer program is an abstract mathematical machine, represented in software. This is the path that is propagated by software design approaches like 'structured programming' and 'model-driven design'. The fact that not all software engineers try to avoid the worst path is illustrated by the cartoon in Fig. 3.2. Many project managers encourage to take a 'bad' path, since they express the progress of a software project in the number of lines of code produced (!).

Fig. 3.2 Illustration of the worst path in Fig. 3.1 (https://www.pinterest.com)

In his book titled *Notes on the Synthesis of Form* [3], Christopher Alexander envisions the design process also as a path between two points. The starting point he calls P (P from problem) and the ending point S (S from solution). In line with the definition of Simon, P and S are two situations: P is a situation that is considered unsatisfying, and S is a preferred situation, to which one wants to transit. The path is envisioned as a sequence of two alternate step kinds, analysis and synthesis, as shown in Fig. 3.3, left side. In an analysis step, one develops a better understanding of the problem; in a synthesis step, one conceives a part of a preferred situation.

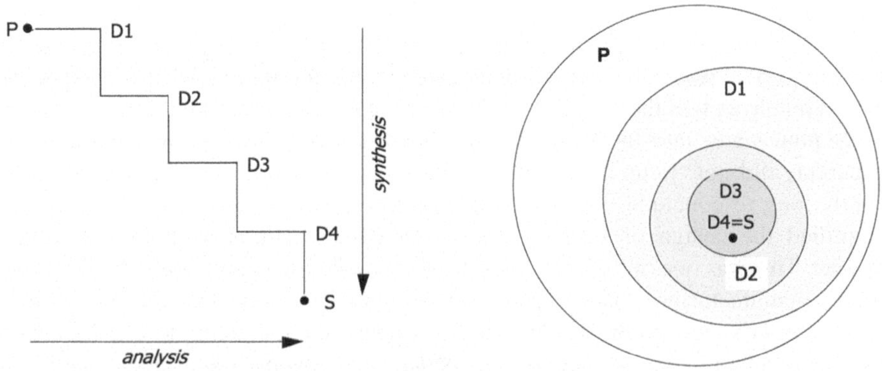

Fig. 3.3 The design process according to Alexander

We intentionally speak of 'a solution' instead of 'the solution', because there is seldom only one situation that 'solves the problem'. In every design process, there is an amount of design freedom. It means that there are a number of points S. Additional restrictions are needed to reduce the number to one (or a few). To illustrate what we mean to say, we extend the two-dimensional space to a three-dimensional one (cf. Fig. 3.3, right side). At the same time, we introduce the helicopter metaphor: we compare the design process with the process of finding a suitable landing spot for a helicopter in the dark. There is a headlamp attached to the bottom of the helicopter that produces a cone of light, thus illuminating a disk on the ground. The process starts at the height of P. There, the pilot has a view on a large area, with many seemingly suitable landing spots. However, they are hard to see because of the faint light. Therefore, she decides to descend to a lower level. The decision point is marked as D1 in Fig. 3.3. The result is that now the disk indicated by D1 on the right side is illuminated, offering a clearer sight on the ground, but the rest of the area is dark now. Note that the disregarded area (P\D1) may contain perfect landing spots.

For the design process, every switch from analysis to synthesis is the result of a design decision. Through this decision, one limits the remaining solution space, like the helicopter pilot limits the number of possible landing spots every time she decides to descend. The understanding of the design process as alternate analysis and synthesis steps clarifies that one cannot speak of *the* best solution; one can only justify that the solution one ends up with is satisfactory. In addition, one can always revoke a decision and go back to the previous analysis step. One can even keep revoking the decisions taken and end up in point P. This iterative nature of the design process is characteristic for any creative activity. In terms of the helicopter metaphor, when the pilot discovers that there is no suitable landing spot within the illuminated area, she has to revoke the previous decision, ascend and descend again elsewhere.

Alexander also warns us to resist walking upon known paths, to 'jump to conclusion'. In software engineering, these are known as design patterns; in general, people speak of best practices. As an illustration, Alexander discusses the invention of the one-hole kettle during a design contest in the 1950s [3]. Up to then, kettles had an opening to pour water into the kettle and an opening through which water could be poured out. This was the common solution to the requirement that it must be possible to pour water into the kettle and to pour water out of it. During that contest, somebody did not 'jump to conclusion' but kept analysing the requirement sufficiently long to conclude that one hole would do the job. This invention not only simplified the design of kettles, it also made the manufacturing process much cheaper. This was one of the objectives, by the way. Kettle manufacturers were interested in manufacturing processes that were substantially cheaper than the known ones.

Alexander's view on the design process supports the prevailing idea in EE that a good design is a balanced compromise between reasonable requirements and feasible specifications [4]. As an almost logical consequence, it means that one already needs a substantial amount of technical knowledge in order to fulfil adequately the role of function designer. We will elaborate this in Chap. 8.

3.3 What Is Enterprise Design?

Enterprises are more complicated than kettles. One would expect that the sciences that have enterprises (or organisations) as their primary object of interest offer help in answering the question in the title of this section. However, as pointed out in [5], they hardly do. What they offer are mainly so-called best practices. If there is nothing else, one better apply these rules of thumb of course. After all, it is the way craftsmanship originated at times past and has prospered ever since. But in EE, we want our models and methods to be based on solid theoretical grounds.

One of the ideas that are considered of paramount importance in EE is the clear and consistent distinction between the function and the construction perspective on things of whatever kind (kettles, enterprises, etc.). This distinction is clarified by the TAO theory, which is presented in Chap. 5. One of the findings of this theory is that function is a subjective notion, while construction is purely objective. Hesse doesn't seem to make this distinction; the transition from point R (function perspective) to point C (construction perspective) is presented as an unproblematic one. Yet, it is unavoidable to travel from left to right in Fig. 3.1 without 'translating' somehow functional requirements into constructional specifications.

Following Christopher Alexander (cf. Fig. 3.3), the function perspective is about analysing the problem situation and understanding the (functional) requirements regarding a preferred situation. The construction perspective is about synthesising these preferred situations, called solutions. Yet also Alexander doesn't seem to make the fundamental difference between the two perspectives and the non-trivial switch from analysis to synthesis. Still, the envisioning of the design process as alternate analysis and synthesis steps, including the iterative nature of design, is a powerful idea. We will come back to it in Chap. 8, where we present and discuss the core theory in Enterprise Design, namely, the BETA theory.

As will be elaborated and clarified in Chap. 5, we make a clear distinction between the function and the construction perspective on enterprises. Taking the function perspective, we talk about the *business* of an enterprise. Taking the construction perspective, we 'see' the *organisation* of an enterprise. Following the ALPHA theory in Chap. 7, the organisation of an enterprise can be divided into four layers, the O-organisation (O from original), the I-organisation (I from informational), the D-organisation (D from documental) and the M-organisation (M from material), according to the sort of the production in each of them: original products in the O-organisation, informational products in the I-organisation, documental products in the D-organisation and material products in the M-organisation. The O-organisation constitutes the essence of the enterprise's organisation.

Also in Chap. 7, the notion of the essential model of an enterprise is presented and discussed. It is the highest-level constructional model of the enterprise's organisation. Producing the essential model of the enterprise to be designed (often called the TO-BE situation) is considered the core of Enterprise Design. It offers everything one needs to understand the operations of the 'new' enterprise, fully abstracted though from realisation (the design of the corresponding I-organisation, D-organisation and M-organisation) and from implementation (the assignment of proper technological means to the elements in all organisational layers). Note, however, that realisation and implementation are needed to make the 'new' enterprise operational. In addition, producing the essential model of the TO-BE situation is preceded by a thorough analysis of the AS-IS situation from which one starts the design: the perceived problems and the often-conflicting interests and goals of the various stakeholders.

For the implementation of the essential model of an enterprise, the ETA theory is needed. It is presented and discussed in Chap. 9. The implementation of the supporting I-, D- and M-organisation is discussed in Chap. 8.

3.4 Current Approaches to Enterprise Design

We started the previous section by mentioning that the organisational sciences have failed up to now in offering effective help to the task of designing or re-designing an enterprise through all the phases that one has to go through according to the BETA theory, as explained in Chap. 8. Most approaches to Enterprise Design that have been developed and that are applied in practice cover only the first phase: *function design*. This phase is at the same time a complicated one. With reference to the helicopter metaphor in Sect. 3.2, there are many, and possibly conflicting, factors that determine what a satisfactory landing spot looks like.

Hereafter, we will present two current approaches to Enterprise Design that we consider useful for the function design phase: Business Model Canvas (in Sect. 3.4.1) and Solving Complex Problems (in Sect. 3.4.2). The reason for selecting these two from the plethora of available approaches is that both originate from academic research. Consequently, one has unlimited access to all published material.

For the commercial approaches, like IBM's Enterprise Design Thinking Framework,[5] this condition is not met.

3.4.1 Business Model Canvas

Because innovation and change in enterprises is speeding up (driven by, for instance, time to market, disruption, competition and compliance), professional help in addressing these challenges is needed. As an example of such help, Osterwalder and Pigneur [6] developed the Business Model Canvas (BMC) as 'a shared language for describing, visualising, assessing, and changing business models'. By business model, they understand 'the rationale of how an organisation creates, delivers, and captures value'. Applying BMC should help (1) quickly gain and share insight into the value creating potential of a business model and (2) keep the focus on this value creation while implementing the business model. Because in EE the term 'organisation' is reserved for the constructional view on enterprises (cf. Chap. 5), we use the word 'enterprise' instead of 'organisation' hereafter.

As shown in Fig. 3.4 (which is taken from [6]), a business model in BMC consists of nine parts, called areas.

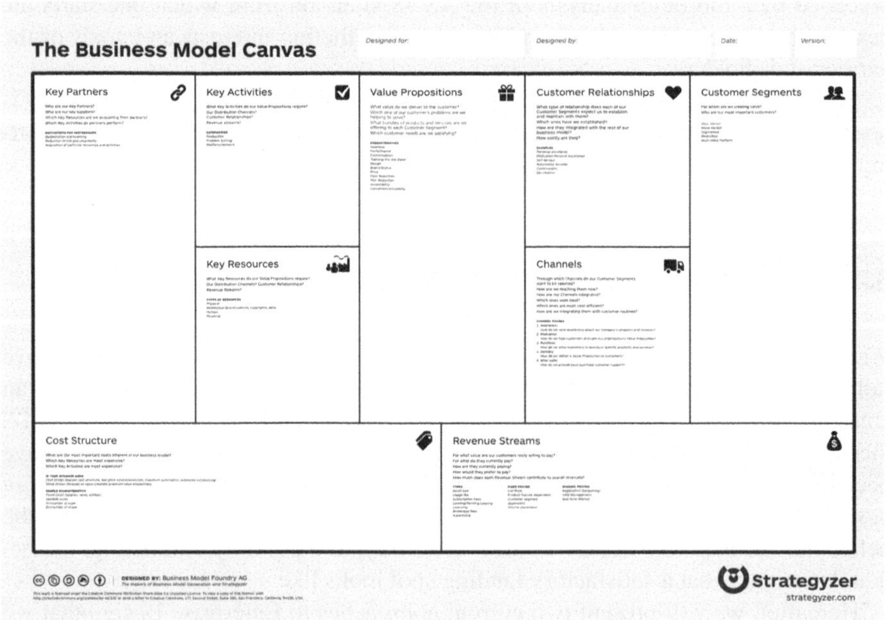

Fig. 3.4 Example of a BMC template

[5] https://www.ibm.com/design/thinking/page/framework

The notion of model in BMC is not 'the understanding of a thing within the framework of a theory, as propagated by EE' (cf. [7], Chap. 6). Actually, it is rather unclear; anything goes, it seems. Therefore, we consider the BMC as a means to 'set the scene', as a first step to structure a design process. Yet, in many cases, producing a BMC template may be sufficient, in particular when the decision-making is supported by a Group Decision Support System [8].

3.4.2 Solving Complex Problems

In order to arrive at shared goals and systematically connect them to functions, De Haan and De Heer developed the theory and method of Solving Complex Problems (SCP) [9]. SCP focuses on decision-making for solution alternatives in highly complex situations, which are characterised by multi-value and multi-stakeholder problems. In Enterprise Design, SCP can be applied as a Way of Thinking and a Way of Working to define multiple stakeholder goals and perform causality analysis to validate (expected) behaviour and benefits of alternative target situations, including their sensitivity for future change.

The Way of Thinking of SCP is as follows: *Stakeholders*[6] have interests, problems and dilemmas, expressed in a number of *goals* per stakeholder. These goals can be operationalised into *criteria*, for comparing the (expected) effect of proposed (solution) *alternatives*. Most of these criteria cannot be influenced directly; a causality analysis is needed to clarify how criteria can be sufficiently (positively or negatively) influenced by (other) *factors*. This will lead to discerning which factors can be influenced in the desired direction by the (portfolio of) *alternatives* from factors that cannot be controlled—*external factors*. Finally, the effect of the (portfolio of) alternative(s) is tested against the chosen criteria, including determining (by scenario analysis) whether its sensitivity to external factors is acceptable.

The corresponding Way of Working consists of five steps (cf. Fig. 3.5): (1) Stakeholder analysis, (2) Goal analysis, (3) Causal analysis, (4) Alternative analysis and (5) Scenario analysis.

Fig. 3.5 The way of working of SCP

[6] SCP talks about *actor analysis*; we use the term *stakeholder analysis*—because of the distinct meaning of actor in Enterprise Ontology.

3.5 Quality of Service

Next to determining the kind of service one wants to provide to the environment of an enterprise, more precisely to its customers, one has to say also something about the quality with which the service is going to be provided. For example, if the owner of a pizzeria decides to enable home delivery of pizzas, he or she has to think about how the transportation will be realised. There are many options, ranging from a pizzeria-owned van plus a pizzeria-employed driver to, for example, students with their own mopeds. In addition, the owner has to decide what the maximum transportation time should be (knowing that the pizzas will cool down during transport).

Although it seems now that Quality of Service is a subject one has to deal with when re-designing an enterprise, it is of course something one has to think about already from the beginning, when starting an enterprise. Taking the pizzeria again as the example enterprise, the owner had to determine already the quality of the pizzas that are sold. This comes down to determine the making of the dough, the amount of ingredients that are used, etc.

References

1. Simon, H. A. (1969). *The sciences of the artificial* (Karl Taylor Compton lectures). M.I.T. Press. xii, 123 p.
2. Brooks, F. P. (Ed.). (1995). *The mythical man-month: Essays on software engineering*. (Anniversary ed.). Addison-Wesley Publishing.
3. Alexander, C. (1964). *Notes on the synthesis of form*. Harvard University Press. 216 p.
4. Dietz, J. L. G. (2009). *Architecture: Building strategy into design*. SDU Publishing.
5. Dietz, J. L. G., Hoogervorst, J. A. P., et al. (2013). The discipline of enterprise engineering. *International Journal of Organisational Design and Engineering, 3*, 28.
6. Osterwalder, A., & Pigneur, Y. (2010). *Business model generation: A handbook for visionaries, game changers, and challengers* (p. 278). John Wiley.
7. Dietz, J. L. G., & Mulder, J. B. F. (2024). *Enterprise ontology—A human-centric approach to understanding the essence of organisation* (Enterprise engineering) (2nd ed.). Springer Nature.
8. Mulder, H. B. F., et al. (2005). New applications of group support systems. In *Group Decision and Negotiation Conference (GDN)*.
9. de Haan, A., & de Heer, P. (2017). *Solving complex problems—Professional group decision-making support in highly complex situations* (2nd ed.). Boom uitgevers.

Part II
Theories

There is nothing as practical as a good theory
(Kurt Lewin)

There is nothing as dangerous as a bad theory
(Sumantra Goshal)

Chapter 4 provides an overview of all Enterprise Engineering theories and their position in a clarifying framework. Chapters 5–10 contain extended summaries of the theories that underlie the notion of Enterprise Design. Every chapter is divided into three parts: foundations, elaborations, and discussions.

The *foundations* part regards the theoretical basis of the theory, its core ideas, as well as the core sources of knowledge that they rely on. It is considered to be the most stable part of a theory.

In the *elaborations* part, the link to practice is established (illustrations, methods, techniques, tools, etc.). It is presumably less stable, because new elaborations may come up in the course of time from applying the theory in practice.

The *discussions* part serves mainly to compare the EE theory, and the methods that are based on it, with comparable other approaches. Therefore, it is presumably also less stable than the foundations part, as new comparisons may become relevant in the course of time.

Chapters 4 (except Sect. 4.4.9), 5, 6, 7, and 8 are reprints of, respectively, Chaps. 4, 7, 8, 10, and 11 from the book Enterprise Ontology [1].

Reference

1. Dietz, J. L. G., & Mulder, J. B. F. (2024). *Enterprise ontology—A human-centric approach to understanding the essence of organisation* (Enterprise engineering) (2nd ed.). Springer Nature.

Chapter 4
The Enterprise Engineering Theories

Abstract The foundations of the discipline of Enterprise Engineering (EE), as envisioned by the CIAO! Network, consist of the CIAO! Paradigm and a number of theories. After the discussion of the paradigm, which has its origins in the communication-centric view on information systems engineering that emerged around 2000, the role of the EE theories and their relationships with the EE methods and the practice of EE is explained. After having been arranged in a suitable classification scheme, each of the theories is briefly discussed: the EE information theory, the EE model theory, the EE function-construction theory, the EE organisational operation theory, the EE system theory, the EE organisational construction theory, the EE organisational essence theory, the EE design theory, the EE implementation theory, the EE automation theory and the EE governance and management theory.

Whether you can observe a thing or not depends on the theory that you use.
It is the theory that decides what can be observed.
(Albert Einstein)

4.1 Introduction

In this chapter, the reader is introduced into the theoretical foundations of the discipline of Enterprise Engineering (EE), as it is developed and practised by a group of researchers and practitioners, called the CIAO! Network[1] [1]. The Italian word *Ciao*[2] is an acronym for Communication, Information, Action and Organisation.

Reprinted from J. L. G. Dietz, H. B. F. Mulder, *Enterprise Ontology*, The Enterprise Engineering Series, https://doi.org/10.1007/978-3-031-53361-7_4 (except Sect. 4.4.9).

[1] For more information, visit www.ciaonetwork.org.

[2] The Italian word *Ciao* can mean both 'hello' and 'goodbye', depending on the context. The underlying commonality is that one confirms to someone else to consider him/her as a trustworthy fellow human being.

J. L. G. Dietz, H. B. F. Mulder, *Enterprise Design Fundamentals*, The Enterprise Engineering Series, https://doi.org/10.1007/978-3-031-83262-8_4

They are the key concepts in the CIAO! Paradigm, which constitutes the basic understanding of the operation of enterprises. It also sets our engineering perspective. Even if an enterprise has not been designed consciously, changing it can be considered as redesigning and re-implementing it. At the same time, the highest appreciation is given to the 'pearls' of every enterprise: the people. Empowered with the right authority, based on competence and exerted with responsibility, they are the cornerstones of an enterprise's organisation. Without people, there is no organisation.

In order to portray the role of theories and methods in the field of EE, the CIAO! Network uses the tree metaphor, as exhibited in Fig. 4.1. The EE theories constitute the roots of the tree. They feed the trunk, which represents the EE methods, with their juices. After having been made fit for consumption by the methods, the juices ultimately reach all branches, where they cause the growth of leaves and flowers, standing for the aimed at flourishing enterprises.

As the tree grows, the need may arise to develop new methods or to graft external ones on the trunk. There is no objection against it, on the contrary, every useful contribution is welcome. The only prerequisite is that the methods are (made) compliant with the EE theories. In addition, a need may occur to develop new theories or to add external ones to the root structure. Again, the only prerequisite is that they are (made) compliant with the existing set of theories.

Fig. 4.1 The CIAO Tree

Section 4.2 contains an explanation of the CIAO! Paradigm. In Sect. 4.3, an overview of the currently existing EE theories is presented, followed by a brief summary of each of them in Sect. 4.4.

4.2 The CIAO! Paradigm

4.2.1 From Information-Centric to Communication-Centric

Up to about 1970, there were no information systems, and there was no field of information systems engineering. The application of programmed computers in enterprises, for the sake of assisting the workers and the managers, was called EDP (Electronic Data Processing). After 1970, EDP was gradually replaced by ISE (Information Systems Engineering) or like names, referring to the field that concerns the application of ICT[3] in organisations. The primal and core notion became information, generally defined as the representation of knowledge. Communication was defined as the exchange of information. The notion of action was something rather disconnected from information and communication, as was the notion of organisation, although there was the general recognition that organisation somehow implies action, communication and information. Let us call this point of view the *information-centric* view on information systems (engineering).

One of the consequences of the information-centric view is that developing (automated) information systems is considered as something that ICT professionals do 'to the side', after having elicited requirements from the people in the organisation, basically by interviewing these people. Once the system is built, it is 'implanted' in the organisation. A widely acknowledged drawback of this 'waiter' approach is that the delivered systems rarely meet the expectations of the users. In hindsight, the main reason for this failure is that requirements determination was ill-understood. Asking the members of an organisation what information they need presupposes that these people have such a comprehensive understanding of their tasks that they are able to provide complete, consistent and coherent answers. As a counter-example, embedded software engineers start with getting an appropriate understanding of the system or machine for which they are going to build supporting software. Based on this understanding, they will specify the requirements for the software system to be built.

For obscure reasons, the developers of 'embedded' software for organisations, thus the information system engineers, have never recognised the necessity to acquire an appropriate understanding of the objects of interest they want to support: organisations. As a consequence of the 'waiter' approach to requirements determination, relevant requirements are often missing, and irrelevant ones are included.

In the 1990s, an awareness emerged that the information-centric view was not sustainable anymore. The number and size of failures in information systems engineering kept increasing, and the proclaimed benefits of standard packages, notably ERP[4] systems, came along with the feeling of being armoured by the people that

[3] ICT stands for information and communication technology. It refers specially to the modern practice of applying digital electronic, optical, etc. means to process, store and transmit data.

[4] ERP stands for enterprise resource planning. It evolved in the 1990s from MRP (Materials Requirements Planning). ERP is a manufacturing and logistics approach to business processes and data management.

had to use these systems. Based on the achievements in language philosophy, notably Speech Act Theory [2, 3] and in (social) action theory, notably the Theory of Communicative Action [4], a community of researchers in information systems engineering, called LAP (Language/Action Perspective), proposed to make a paradigm shift [5]. By taking communication as the primal notion, the path was paved to a more appropriate and more integrated understanding of the other three key notions: information, action and organisation. Later, the name CIAO! Paradigm (CIAO stands for Communication, Information, Action and Organisation) has been coined for this *communication-centric* view on information systems (engineering). *Communication*[5] is now defined as the sharing of thoughts between subjects (human beings) and *information* as the means for communication. People, in organisations and in society at large, have a need to communicate, generally for the sake of making known what they are doing. Because it is impossible to do this directly, e.g. by connecting brains, they have to use the vehicle of information.

4.2.2 Communicative Action

In addition to the sharing of thoughts, communication became (also) understood as a form of *action*, by virtue of the intention in every communicative act, as explained by Habermas' Theory of Communicative Action [4]. Figure 4.2 exhibits the four constituting parts of a communicative act: the performer, the intention, the addressee and the proposition.

The *performer* and the *addressee* are subjects, i.e. human beings, particularly in their quality of social individual, which means being capable to engage in mutual commitments. The *proposition* is a state of affairs that is or that can be the case. An example of a proposition in the café situation is that a client has got a cup of coffee.

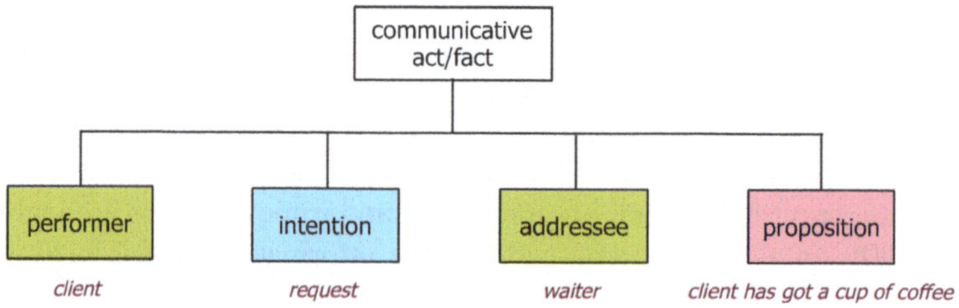

Fig. 4.2 The structure of a communicative act/fact

[5] The English word 'communicate' comes from the Latin word *communicare*, which means 'making something common' or 'sharing something with somebody'. In a more specific sense, it means 'sharing thoughts'.

The *intention* is the intent of the performer (the client) towards the addressee (a waiter), with respect to the proposition. If the intention is 'request', the performer wants the addressee to make the proposition become true. In this case, the client wants the waiter to bring her a cup of coffee. Habermas [4] tells us that in performing a communicative act, the performer raises three validity claims towards the addressee: the claim to rightness, the claim to sincerity and the claim to truth. These claims have to be assessed by the addressee, and the result of this assessment will guide her/him in the way he/she will respond. By accepting the *claim to rightness* in the above example, the waiter recognises the authority of the client to make the request. By accepting the *claim to sincerity*, the waiter expresses that he considers the client sincere in making the request. By accepting the *claim to truth*, the waiter expresses that the proposition can be made true. If all three claims are accepted, the communicative act is said to be successful. In the café example, the waiter will then respond by a promise. In case of failure, he will decline the client's request. In every communicative act, one of the validity claims is dominant. Based on this dominance, Habermas [4] distinguishes three categories of communicative acts, as well as three worlds in which these acts have effect. Figure 4.3 exhibits the distinctions. The dominance of a claim, as well as the related world, is indicated by the grey-coloured rectangles.

In the category of *constativa*, the dominant claim is the claim to truth, and the world with which they are primarily concerned is called the *objective world.* Examples of intentions in this category are question and assertion. If a railway passenger asks a railway officer for the departure time of the next train to Amsterdam, the dominant claim is the claim to truth, i.e. that the fact exists (in their shared objective world). This holds also for the answer by the officer (which would be the assertion of a fact). Facts like the departure time of trains are considered to exist in our common objective world, like the fact that the sun is shining and the current price of a glass of beer in your favourite pub. But the other two (non-dominant) validity claims must also be satisfied. In the train example, this means that the railway passenger respectively trusts the railway officer that he/she is authorised to provide the answer and that this officer will provide the correct answer.

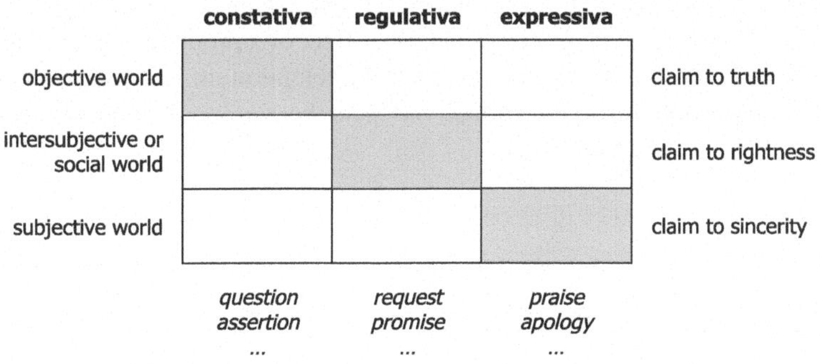

Fig. 4.3 Categories of communicative acts

In the category of *expressiva*, the dominant claim is the claim to sincerity, and the world with which they are primarily concerned is everyone's private *subjective world*. Examples of intentions in this category are praise and apologise. If the railway passenger starts his/her conversation with the railway officer by saying, 'I'm sorry to disturb you, madam, but …', then the dominant claim of this phrase is the claim to sincerity. If the officer feels that the passenger is insincere, she will most likely utter a sincerity checking sentence, and she may even ignore the passenger. Facts like feeling sorry are considered to exist in everyone's subjective world. The claim to sincerity represents the most fundamental condition for human cooperation in the broadest sense of the word, which is mutual *trust*. At the same time, it is the hardest one to verify. Moreover, trust emerges from shared values and norms among people, which do change over time. In language philosophy [6] and social action theory [4], it is assumed that people constantly check and adjust their values and norms when they are communicating. In [7], we have called this second-order communication, and we have suggested that this is the lubricating oil of organisations and of society at large.

In the category of *regulativa*, the dominant claim is the claim to rightness, and the world with which they are primarily concerned is the intersubjective or *social world*. Examples of intentions in this category are the request and the promise. If the client in the café asks the waiter for a cup of coffee, the dominant claim is the claim to rightness, i.e. the client claims that she has the authority to make the request and that she considers the waiter to be authorised to fulfil it. This holds also for the response by the waiter. Facts like being authorised to do something are considered to exist in our common intersubjective or social world. Moreover, we have created them ourselves. Assigning each other authorities (and expecting that they will be exerted in a responsible way) is the way in which we build organisations and societies [6]. This insight has important consequences. One of them is that people are basically autonomous in deciding how to respond to (intersubjective or social) events. This is the case in every enterprise and in society at large. The fundamental autonomy implies that one may disobey rules and laws if the situation asks for it. At the same time, they must act responsibly, and they can be held accountable for their deeds. Another consequence is that all facts are basically social or intersubjective.

As will be elaborated in the PSI theory (cf. [8], Chap. 8), a fact is either a coordination fact, like having requested a cup of coffee, or a production fact, like having brought a cup of coffee or having observed the temperature in a room. Even in the upcoming era of the Internet of Things, the facts that we use in our institutionalised society are always social facts.

4.2.3 Implications for Information, Action and Organisation

Let us point out next what the consequences of the communication-centric view are for the other three concepts, information, action and organisation, starting from the basic understanding that *communication* is the sharing of thoughts by human minds. Because human beings are not able to directly connect their minds, some vehicle for transmitting thoughts is needed, and this vehicle is information, or the sign, which is the preferred term in semiotics (cf. [8], Chap. 5). A major outcome of this study is the semiotic ladder, exhibited in Fig. 4.4. It clarifies the role of signs in the communication of human beings. *Information* then is the dyad of content and form, meaning that the two parts are distinguishable but not separable. The *content* is the thought that one wants to share, and the *form* is the agreed-upon perceivable sign. The content comprises both the intention (or pragmatics) and the proposition (or semantics) of the thought, and the form comprises both the formalism (or syntax) and the coding (or empirics). Contrary to the definition in Fig. 4.4, the content of a sign is often equated with the notion of *information* and the form with *data*. Unfortunately, precise definitions and their consistent use don't seem to have a high priority in current practice.

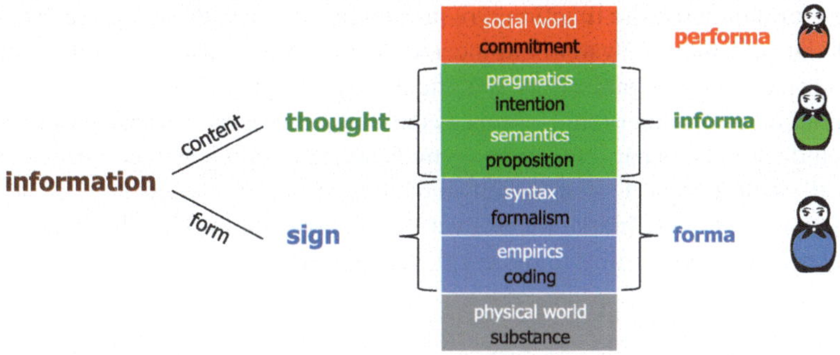

Fig. 4.4 The semiotic ladder

In the café example, the client has, at some point in time, got the thought that she wants a cup of coffee. In order to share this thought, she has to express it in a sign that is intelligible for the waiter. The proposition of the thought is 'client has got a cup of coffee', and the intention is the request. By performing the request, she enters into a commitment towards the waiter, like the waiter enters into a commitment if he performs a promise or a decline in response. The client may have expressed her thought in this English sentence, 'I'd like to have a cup of coffee, please', which constitutes the form or sign part in Fig. 4.4. The applied formalism is the English grammar, and the coding regards the representation of the words. The substance in which the sentence is inscribed consists of air vibrations that are produced by the client and then perceived by the sense of hearing of the waiter.

For the concept of *action*, the communication-centric view means that communicating is (also) acting, as discussed in Sect. 4.2.2. As Austin [2] puts it: people do things with words. In the PSI theory (cf. [8], Chap. 8), this is accentuated by distinguishing coordination acts and production acts and by combining them in the concept of the (business) transaction. The new concept of *organisation* that arises from the foregoing is a network of actors who carry out transactions in collaboration. It is a new way of looking at Mintzberg's basic idea of organisation: the need to divide labour into tasks and the need to coordinate these tasks [9]. The idea that organisation is somehow the outcome of the social interaction of cooperating human beings is not new. Since Max Weber [10], several sociologists have studied this relationship, for example, Weick [11]. However, we think that none of them has made the idea as operational as the CIAO! Paradigm does.

Having this new understanding of organisation, a new and more appropriate understanding of information systems emerges. It appears that every information system in an organisation can appropriately be conceived as some implementation of some part of the organisation. This view emphasises the being intrinsically intertwined of information systems and their supported organisations. It also clarifies why information system engineers should first of all study the construction and operation of the organisation before designing the information system. Basically, the information system is already there, because it is an intrinsic part of the organisation. Consequently, the functional requirements are also already there. The main task of the information system engineer is to find a new way of implementing a particular part of the organisation, specifically by applying ICT.

Although conceiving organisations as networks of actors who carry out transactions is indifferent to a particular management style or approach, it certainly matches very well with a high degree of self-management, as discussed in [12]. Making decisions at the lowest hierarchical level that is possible implies that one grants a high degree of responsibility to the employees on that level.

4.3 Overview of the EE Theories

Paraphrasing Einstein's quote above Sect. 4.1, EE theories are the mental glasses through which enterprise engineers observe and understand enterprises and seek to make sense of them. In addition, EE theories are the roots of the methods for improving enterprises, as illustrated in Fig. 4.1.

The presently identified EE theories are listed in Table 4.1. Next to the Greek letter that serves as the primary identifier are their names and EE references. All theories are classified in the EE Framework of Theories (Fig. 4.5), which is an adapted version of the framework that was introduced in [1]. Four categories are distinguished: philosophical, ontological, technological and ideological. The structure of Fig. 4.5 must be understood as follows. The philosophical theories underly all other theories. On top of that, the ontological theories underly both the technological theories and the ideological ones. The latter two categories do not have specific interrelationships. The classification of the theories in the framework is, to some extent, disputable, because they do not always fit in exactly one category. However, the presented classification seems to do justice to their main character.

Table 4.1 The current EE theories

Φ-theory	FI theory	EE information theory
M-theory	MU theory	EE model theory
T-theory	TAO theory	EE function-construction theory
Ψ-theory	PSI theory	EE organisational operation theory
Δ-theory	DELTA theory	EE system theory
Ω-theory	OMEGA theory	EE organisational construction theory
A-theory	ALPHA theory	EE organisational essence theory
B-theory	BETA theory	EE organisational design theory
H-theory	ETA theory	EE organisational implementation theory
N-theory	NU theory	EE automation theory
Σ-theory	SIGMA theory	EE governance and management theory

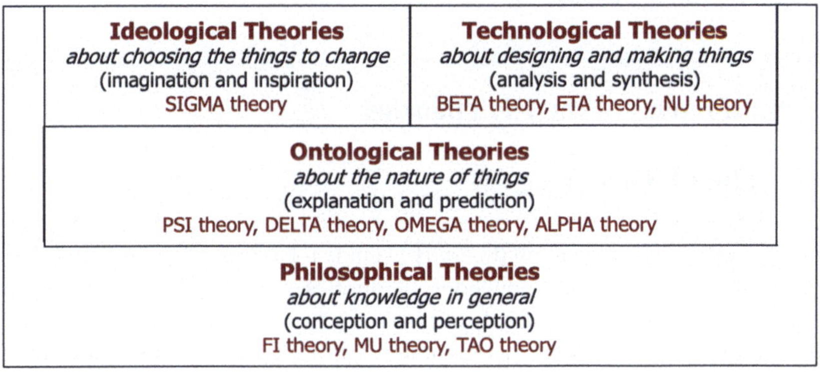

Fig. 4.5 The EE theories in the EE Framework of Theories

Philosophical theories concern the most fundamental ways in which people perceive and conceive the surrounding world, make sense of it, study it, etc. They are about knowledge in general and therefore include epistemology, phenomenology and logic. Philosophical theories are justified by their *truthfulness*. The truthfulness of a theory is established by reasoning or by judging its tenability in the face of reality.

Ontological theories are about the nature of things. They serve to explain their construction and operation and predict the consequences of changing them while completely abstracting from implementation. In EE, the things are organisations. Ontological theories are justified by their *soundness* and *appropriateness*. The soundness of an ontological theory is established by its being rooted in sound philosophical theories. The appropriateness of an ontological theory is established by the evaluation of its practical application, e.g. through expert judgments.

Technological[6] theories are about designing and building things and about putting them into operation. Generally spoken, they assist in analysing and synthesising things. Technological theories are justified by their *rigour* and *relevance*. The rigour of a technological theory is established by its being rooted in sound ontological and ideological theories. The relevance of a technological theory is established by the evaluation of its practical application, e.g. through measurements, evaluative comparisons and adoption studies.

Ideological theories are not about things themselves but about the context in which one decides on whether to make or change them. In EE, they serve to feed the imagination of people and to assist them in inspiring other people to adopt new, better ideas for running enterprises. Ideological theories cannot a priori be predicated as truthful or as sound and appropriate, nor as rigorous and relevant, even if they are rooted in rigorous and relevant other theories. One can only speak of their societal *significance*. The significance of an ideological theory boils down to the usefulness that is assigned to it by its supporters.

The summaries of the EE theories in Sect. 4.4 are presented in an order that seems to be most logical; one can read them from the first to the last without having to jump forward for explanations.

4.4 Summaries of the EE Theories

4.4.1 The FI Theory

The FI theory or EE information theory (FI stands for *Factual Information*) clarifies how people acquire factual knowledge. Semiotics provides us with the *semiotic triangle* [13], which clarifies the dyadic character of information: it is the inseparable combination of *content* (the communicated thought) and *form* (the sign that signifies the thought). In addition, Semiotics provides us with the *semiotic ladder* [14], in which a distinction is made between the semantics and the pragmatics of thoughts, thereby clarifying that a thought consists of a *proposition* and an *intention*.

The core of the FI theory is the *semiotic mill*, refined into the *ontological mill*, which is a generic framework for understanding perception and conception, exhibited in Fig. 4.6. A *fact* becomes existent in the mind when a perceived concrete thing conforms to (the prescription of form of) a *type*. Therefore, a fact is an *instantiation* of a type. In logical terms, it is a predication of a conceptual object, with the type as the predicate. The conceptual object represents a concrete object that is considered to be the *identity* of a concrete thing. The first is a member of a conceptual class, and the second is a member of a concrete class. Type and class are dyadic notions: a class is the *extension* of a type; conversely, a type is the *intension* of a class.

[6] Particularly in information and communication technology, the term 'technology' has got the meaning of means. We prefer to stick to the original meaning of the word, which stems from its Greek origin: *technè* (meaning 'making') and *logos* (meaning 'knowing'). So technology means knowing how to make.

Because the form of the thing with object 701 conforms to the type human, the conceptual fact is created in the mind that the thing is a human. In addition, factual knowledge can be acquired through communication.

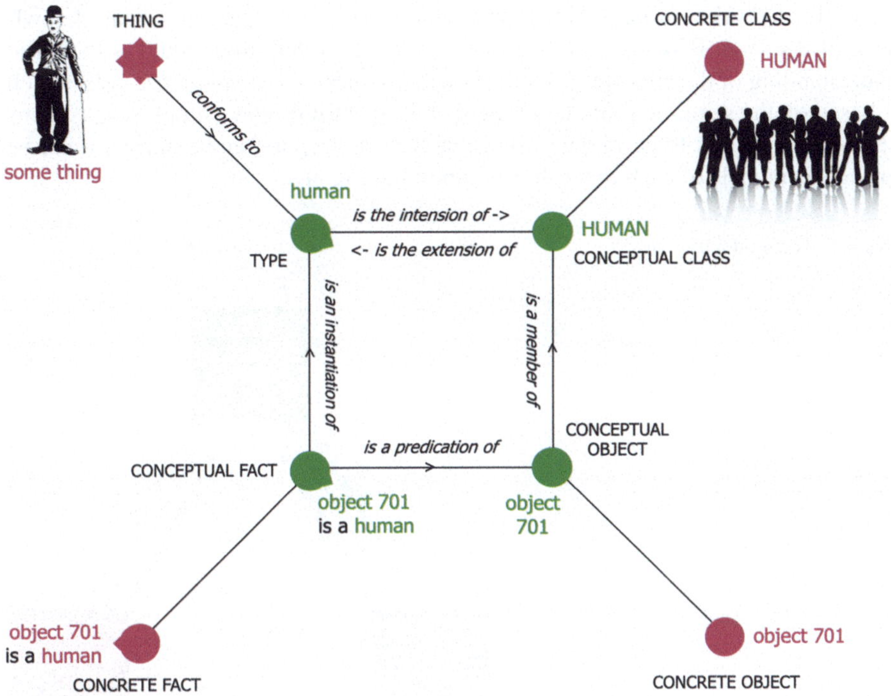

Fig. 4.6 The ontological mill

Types can be *declared*, as original new types, but they can also be *derived* from existing types. Three ways of deriving are discussed: specialisation, generalisation and aggregation. An example of *specialisation* is the definition of the type student as a specialisation of person: a student is a person for which there is an admission in which the person is the admitted person. An example of *generalisation* is the (extensional) definition of the type vehicle: the class VEHICLE is the set-theoretic union of the classes CAR, BIKE, SCOOTER, etc. An aggregation of a number of types is (extensionally) defined as the cartesian product of their classes. An example of *aggregation* is the definition of the price of an article as an attribute of the Cartesian product of article kind (e.g. apple), supplier (e.g. GreenShop) and day (e.g. today).

4.4.2 The MU Theory

The MU theory or EE model theory (MU stands for *Model Universe*) is a theory of models and modelling in general and of conceptual modelling in particular. It adopts Apostel's definition of *model* [15]: any subject using a system A to obtain knowledge of a system B is using A as a model of B. This definition conveys the basic understanding of the concept of model as a role concept. The *model triangle*, which is based on the semiotic triangle (cf. Sect. 4.4.1), clarifies how complexes (systems and aggregates) of three major sorts (concrete, conceptual and symbolic) can be viewed as models of each other. It is exhibited in Fig. 4.7.

Fig. 4.7 The model triangle

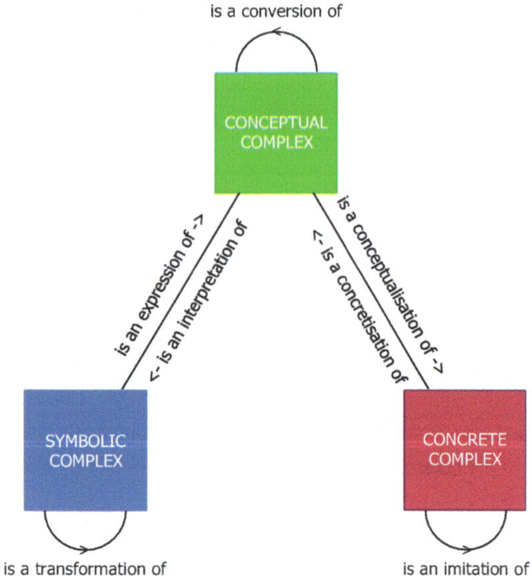

By adding two levels of abstraction (the schema level and the meta level) on top of the conceptual complex or instance level, the *General Conceptual Modelling Framework* (GCMF) emerges. It clarifies the notions of *conceptual complex*, *conceptual schema* and *meta schema*, for any Universe of Discourse or system's world. It also makes clear that these notions are logical constructs and that, consequently, any expression of them (in a suitable language) is directly transformable to first order logic. The GCMF is exhibited in Fig. 4.8.

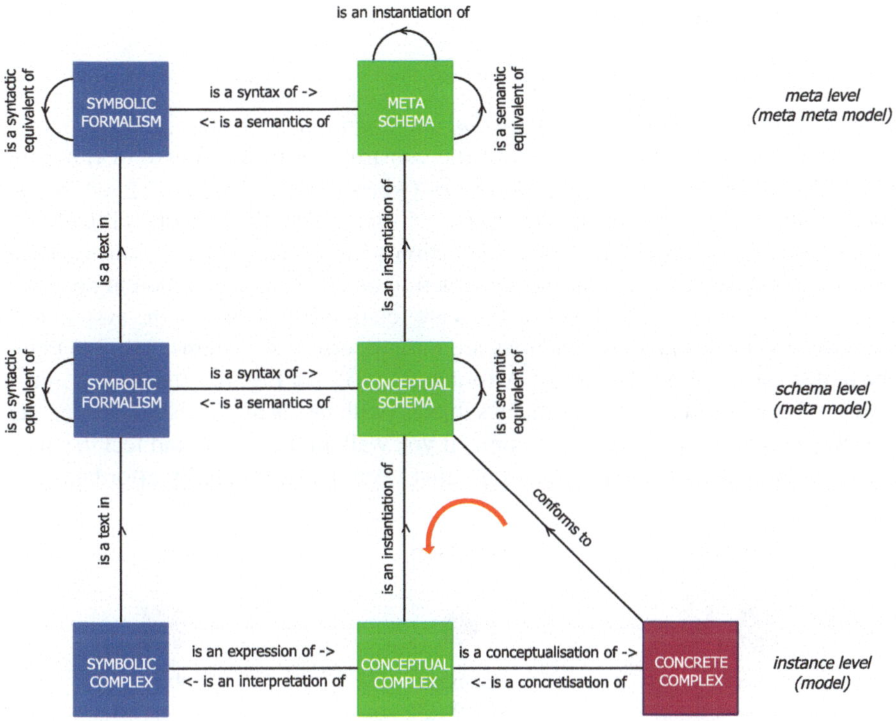

Fig. 4.8 The General Conceptual Modelling Framework

Because the form of the concrete complex conforms to the prescription of form that the conceptual schema represents, the corresponding conceptual complex is created in the mind. For communicating this 'thought', it is expressed in the symbolic formalism of the conceptual schema, yielding the symbolic complex.

In order to specify conceptual complexes, conceptual schemas and meta schemas, the *General Ontology Specification Language* (GOSL) is presented and discussed. The syntax of the language consists of graphical and textual symbols and constructs, as well as a textual part. The latter is an English-like formal language, which means that it is directly transformable to first-order logic, like the graphical part. The split between the two is a rather pragmatic one. Compared to common graphical languages for conceptual modelling, GOSL might be called minimal: it covers only the basic concepts and constructs. More complicated logical formulas can mostly better be expressed in formal textual sentences.

4.4.3 The TAO Theory

EE is an engineering approach to tackling problems in enterprises. By nature, engineers seek to understand the *construction* and *operation* of systems (where operation is defined as the manifestation of the construction in the course of time), in addition to their *functions* and *behaviours* (where a behaviour is defined as the manifestation of a function in the course of time). The TAO theory (Teleology-Affordances-Ontology) clarifies the distinction between function and construction. One of the clarifications is that the construction of a system is an inherent property of the system, whereas all of its functions are relationships between the system and stakeholders. Consequently, functions are not properties of systems. The TAO theory builds on Gibson's Theory of Affordances [16]. As Fig. 4.9 illustrates, *affordances* emerge from the perception by subjects (with needs or purposes) of concrete objects (with properties). As an example, if you walk in the woods and feel the need to sit, you may perceive that a tree trunk offers you the sit-on-ability affordance.

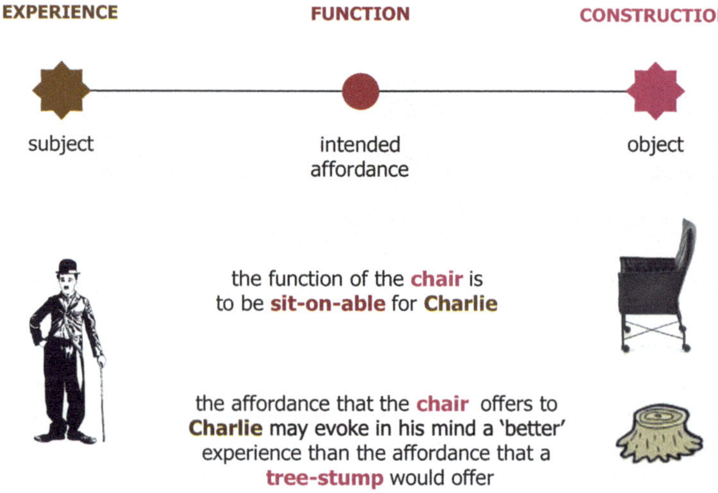

Fig. 4.9 Illustration of the TAO theory

Next to using the affordances that existing things offer, people also create things, with particular affordances in mind. These things are commonly called *artefacts*, and their intended affordances *functions*. For example, chairs have the function to be sit-on-able. In addition, one can assign (new) functions to things. For example, one can assign the function of parking lot to a square, for particular days of the week.

Consequently, a strict distinction is made between the construction and the function perspective on things. In the *construction perspective*, one studies a thing in an objective way, i.e. independent of the affordances it may offer. In the *function perspective*, one studies the affordances that a thing may offer to subjects while disregarding its construction. So, function (or affordance) is not a property of a thing but a relationship between the thing and a stakeholder. For example, to people who know to drive, cars do offer relevant functions. This does probably not (directly) hold for the members of an isolated tribe in the jungle of Brazil.

When using the affordances that things can offer them, subjects may have different *experiences*. For example, you may *value* the sit-on-ability of a chair higher than the same affordance offered by a tree trunk. Experiences are basically subjective impressions. However, they may be shared among stakeholders.

Corresponding with the function-construction distinction, two sorts of conceptual models (cf. Sect. 4.4.2) are distinguished: constructional models and functional models. A *constructional model* is a representation of the construction of concrete things, like cars. A *functional model* is a representation of the possible affordances or functions that a concrete thing may offer to someone, e.g. the driving function of a car to a (potential) driver. Next, the constructional decomposition and functional decomposition of enterprises are discussed. To distinguish between the two, it is suggested that the term 'organisation' is used when referring to the construction perspective on enterprises and the term 'business' when referring to the function perspective. A decomposition of an enterprise's organisation is a *constructional decomposition*, and a decomposition of its business is a *functional decomposition*.

4.4.4 The PSI Theory

The PSI theory or EE organisational operation theory (PSI stands for *Performing in Social Interaction*) serves to study the operation of organisations. The word 'organisation' indicates that it takes the construction perspective on enterprises. Organisations are systems in the category of social systems (cf. Sect. 4.4.3), which means that the system elements are social individuals, called actors. The operating principle is that actors enter into and comply with commitments towards each other.

An *actor* is defined as a subject (human being) in an actor role. The *actor role* determines the authority that the actor may exercise and the responsibility to do so. Commitments are raised in coordination acts, which are communicative acts in Habermas' category of regulativa (cf. Figs. 4.2 and 4.3). The result of performing a coordination act is the creation of the corresponding coordination fact. For example, performing a request act concerning some product results in the fact that the product is requested.

Coordination acts/facts are the atomic building blocks of organisational (but commonly called: business) processes. They always occur in particular patterns of interaction between subjects who play either the *initiator* role or the *executor* role in the transaction. These patterns are instances of one generic pattern, called the (business) *transaction*. The basic coordination acts in every transaction are the request (by the initiator), the promise (by the executor), the declare (by the executor) and the accept (by the initiator). The complete transaction pattern comprises in addition the decline (instead of promise), reject (instead of accept) and a revocation pattern for each of the mentioned steps. Every transaction (instance) is of a particular *transaction kind*. A transaction kind concerns one specific *product kind* and has one specific actor role as its executor role. The combination of a transaction kind and its executor role is called a *transactor role*. It is the (molecular) building block of organisations.

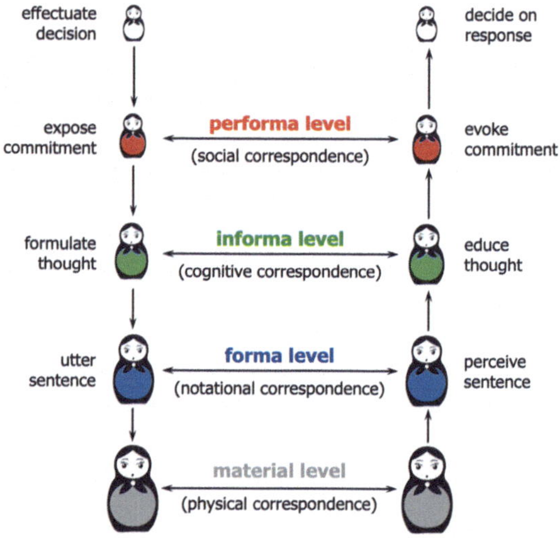

Fig. 4.10 The process of a communicative act

Based on the semiotic ladder (cf. Sect. 4.4.1), three human abilities are distinguished in performing coordination acts: *forma*, *informa* and *performa* (cf. Fig. 4.4). This distinction gives rise to three levels of correspondence in the communication between subjects: the forma level (notational correspondence), the informa level (cognitive correspondence) and the performa level (social correspondence), as shown in Fig. 4.10. To be successful, all three conditions of correspondence must be satisfied, i.e. the communication must be free of distortion. Below the forma level is the medium level, where forms are inscribed in physical substances and transported between subjects. Although evenly conditional for successful communication, the 'inner self' upper level, where a person's wisdom and love reside, the basis for his/her decisions, is considered outside the field of EE. He/she is basically autonomous in deciding how to respond to coordination events. At the same time, actors can always be held accountable, by other actors, for the acts that they decide to perform.

The structure of a coordination act/fact is exhibited in Fig. 4.2. Examples of intentions are request, promise, declare and accept. An example of a product (or independent production fact) is 'sale 1618 is completed'. As said, coordination acts occur in specific interaction patterns between two participants, called transactions. A transaction is successful if the (final) product is accepted. At that moment, the product starts to exist (comes into being). Figure 4.11 exhibits the complete transaction pattern, which is considered to be the universal pattern in all organisations. It consists of the standard pattern (middle part) and revocations patterns for all acts in the standard pattern.

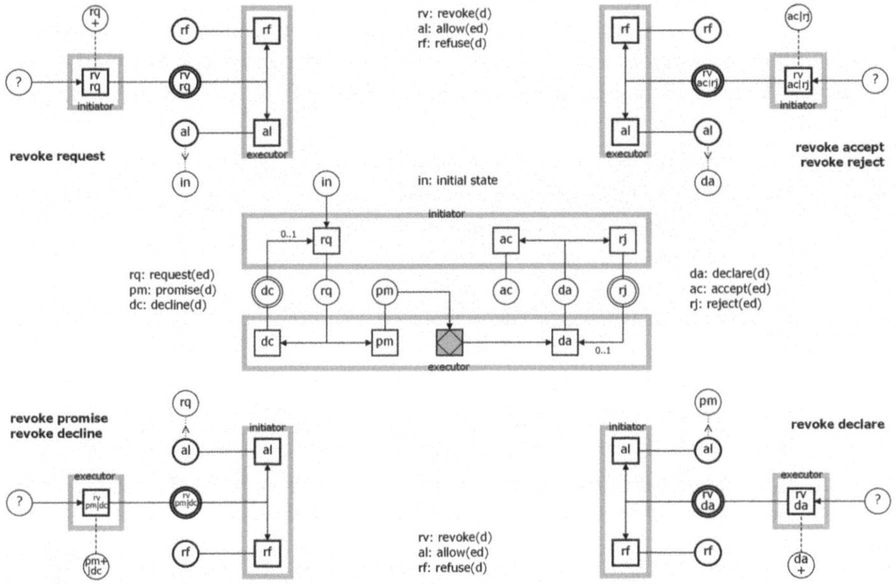

Fig. 4.11 The complete transaction pattern

4.4.5 The DELTA Theory

The DELTA theory or EE systems theory (DELTA stands for *Discrete Event in Linear Time Automaton*) is a theory of discrete event systems, both from the construction and from the function perspective (cf. Sect. 4.4.1). According to Weinberg's division of the realm of systems [17], organisations fall in the category of organised complexity: they are too organised for statistics and too complex for (mathematical) analysis. we adopt Bunge's system definition [18]: a (homogeneous) *system* is a triple (C, E, S), where C (composition) is a set of elements of some category, E (environment) is a set of elements of the same category as the elements in C and S (structure) is a set of influencing bonds among the elements in C and between them and the elements in E. Examples of categories are physical, biological and social. Organisations fall in the category of social systems.

Two sorts of conceptual systems are distinguished that may serve as models (cf. Sect. 4.4.2) of concrete systems: the *black-box* system and the *white-box* system. White-box models are suited to study the construction and operation of systems (cf. Sect. 4.4.3). Black-box models are suited to study their functionality and behaviour.

Because black-box systems don't have an internal state, the grey-box system is introduced. Well-known examples of grey-box systems are the finite automaton (or finite state machine) and the discrete event system. For a deep and formal study of grey-box and white-box models, the PRISMA model is introduced. Three ways of mutual influencing between (the elements of) systems are distinguished: *activating*, *restricting* and *impeding*.

In the PRISMA *grey-box* model, all acts by the system, and their resulting facts, are divided in *production acts/facts* and *coordination acts/facts* (cf. Sect. 4.4.4).

The PRISMA grey-box model is defined as a tuple (**P**, **R**, **I**, **S**, **M**, **A**), where:

P	is a partial function, called the *performance function*
R	is a set of C-fact types, called the *reaction base*
I	is a set of C-fact types, called the *impediment base*
S	is a set of P-fact types, called the *state base*
M	is a set of P-fact types, called the *mutation base*
A	is a set of C-fact types, called the *action base*

$$\mathbf{P} \text{ is defined as}: \wp\left(\left(\underline{\mathbf{A}} \cup \underline{\mathbf{I}}\right) * T\right) * \wp\left(\underline{\mathbf{S}} * T\right) \rightarrow \wp\left(\underline{\mathbf{M}} * D\right) * \wp\left(\underline{\mathbf{R}} * D\right)$$

where $\underline{\mathbf{Y}}$ is the union of the extensions of $\mathbf{y} \in \mathbf{Y}$ (**Y** is **A**, **I**, **M**, **R** or **S**); *T* is the discrete time scale, and *D* is the set of (positive) time delays.

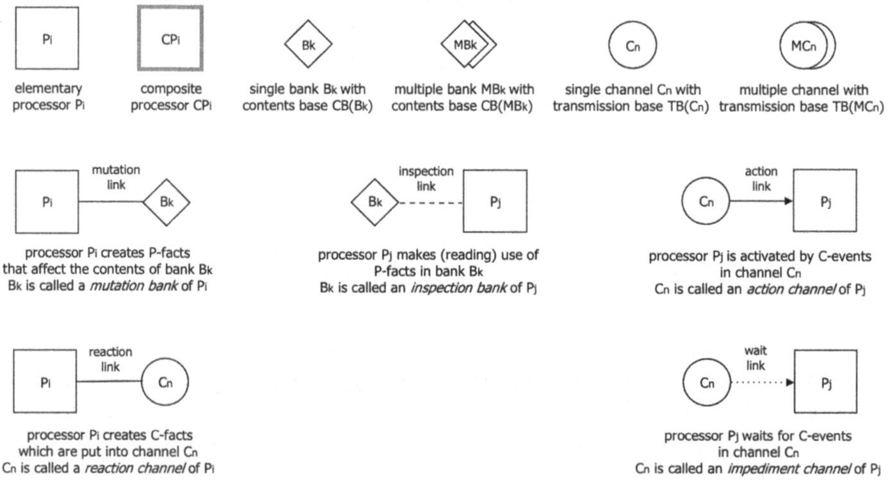

Fig. 4.12 Legend of the prismanet diagram

The PRISMA *white-box* model allows one to conceive systems as *prismanets*: networks of processors, channels and banks. The complete prismanet model of a system is divided into the construction model and the operation model. The *construction model* of a system is the part that is expressed in the prismanet diagram, whose legend is shown in Fig. 4.12. The meanings of the various links between the basic shapes (box for processors, diamond for banks and disk for channels) are expressed in an informal way. The *operation model* of a system consists of the action rules that constitute the performance function of the corresponding prisma. They reside in the processor that is the kernel of the prisma. The abstraction that is achieved through the notions of activating, restricting and impeding makes the prismanet comprehensive: no additional knowledge is needed to get a complete (ontological) understanding of the modelled system. That is why it is called the *essential model* of the system. In addition, prismanets are formalised systems; they can directly be implemented in software.

4.4.6 The OMEGA Theory

The OMEGA theory or EE organisational construction theory (OMEGA stands for *Organisational Modules Emerging from General Arrangements*) clarifies the coordination structures in which transactor roles are connected. Three basic structures are distinguished: interaction, interstriction and interimpediment.

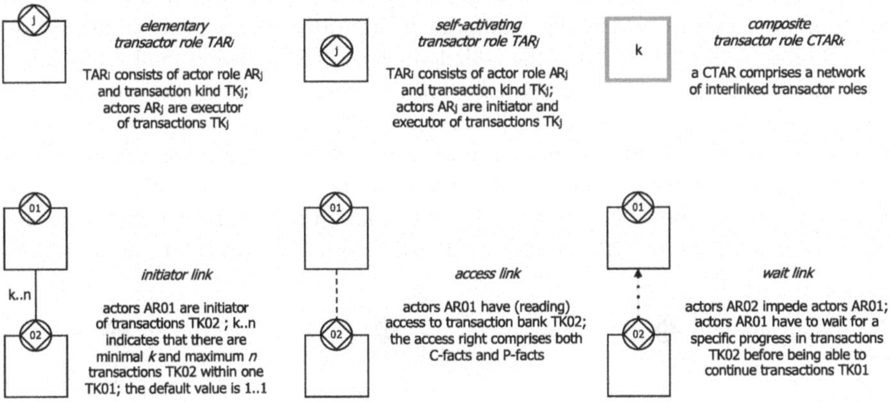

Fig. 4.13 Legend of the Coordination Structure Diagram

The *interaction structure* determines for every transactor role in the organisation which transactor roles are initiator in transactions of the corresponding transaction kind. It appears that the interaction structure of an organisation is always a set of tree structures. Consequently, the transaction kinds at any level of such a tree structure are enclosed in another transaction kind (except the 'root' of the tree) and do have enclosed transaction kinds (except the 'leaves' of the tree). The interaction structure is the inherent fundamental structure of business processes (which are commonly envisioned as flows, i.e. as sequences of events). In addition, it clarifies the responsibility ranges of actors in business processes and thus notions like process ownership and data ownership.

The *interstriction structure* determines which transactor roles may inspect the history of the transactions of other transaction kinds. These other transaction kinds may be external to the organisation (or Scope of Interest). Actors do inspect the history of transaction processes because they need to take process facts into account when deciding on acts to perform. In this way, actors restrict each other's decision freedom.

The *interimpediment structure* determines whether actors in some actor role have to put off performing specific acts until other transaction processes have reached a specific state. All three organisational structures are expressed in the *Coordination Structure Diagram* (CSD), of which Fig. 4.13 exhibits the legend. Figure 4.14 illustrates them, using the GloLog case (cf. [8], Chap. 18) as an example enterprise. The red colour of the diamonds indicates that the transactor roles belong to the O-organisation of the modelled enterprise (cf. Sect. 4.4.7). There are four interaction trees, also called *business processes* (better: process kinds). The top of the left one is a composite transactor role. The initiator link with TAR01 expresses that it contains a (unknown) transactor role that initiates transactions TK01. The top of the other three structures is a self-activating transactor role. The light-grey colour of some boxes indicates that they belong to the environment of the focus within the Scope of Interest. Each of the four processes has its own case kind: client order, supply order, ship content and container content, respectively. The evoked structural clashes [19] between them are resolved by the wait links. In addition, there are several inspection links. Figure 4.14 clearly shows the added value of product (tree) thinking in addition to flow thinking. There cannot be one 'seamless' process flow in GloLog. Instead, there are four autonomous processes, with their own process cycle, determined by their case kind. As alluded to in Sect. 4.4.5, no additional knowledge is needed to get a complete (ontological) understanding of the organisation, i.e. of the collective business processes, provided that the action rules for the transactor roles are also known. Therefore, this model is called the *essential model* of the organisation.

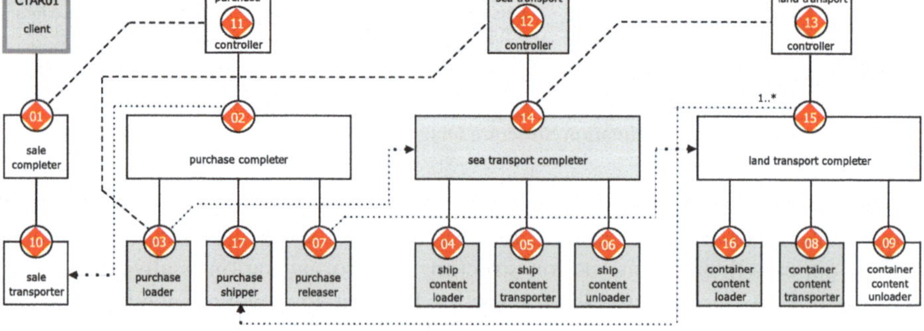

Fig. 4.14 CSD of the GloLog enterprise

There is a second kind of general arrangement that comes in addition to the ones above. It appears that every organisational structure is composed of a limited number of *reference patterns*, which often resemble legal patterns of action, like the transfer of property and the granting/obtaining of usufructuary rights.

4.4.7 The ALPHA Theory

The ALPHA theory or EE organisational essence theory (ALPHA stands for *Abstraction Layers in Production for Holistic Analysis*) is a theory about layers of transactor roles that come in addition to the compositional trees from the OMEGA theory (cf. Sect. 4.4.6). These tree structures occur in four transactor layers, which are based on the distinction of four sorts of production acts: original, informational, documental and material.

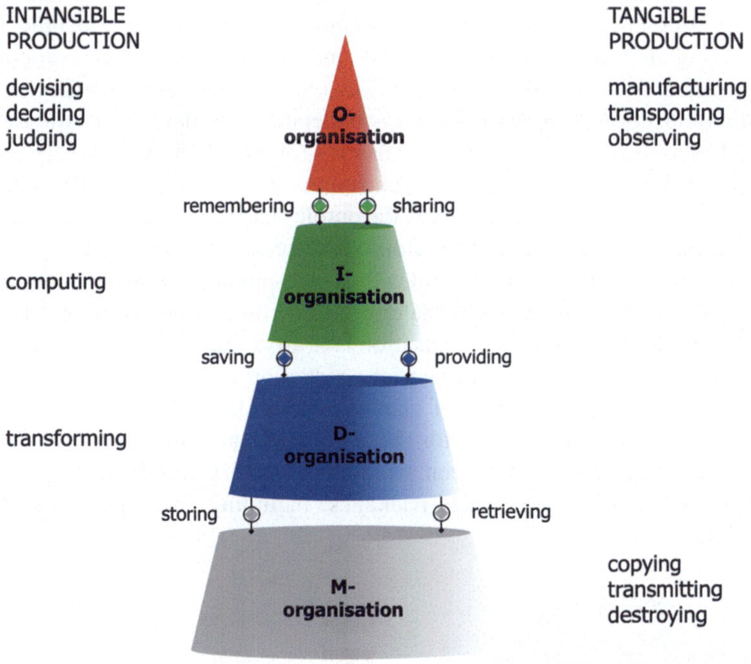

Fig. 4.15 The four aspect organisations

Original production acts bring about original production facts. Examples are devising, deciding and judging (all of them dealing with intangible things), as well as manufacturing, transporting and observing (all of them dealing with tangible things).

Informational production acts comprise remembering facts (in the state of the production or coordination world of an organisation), recalling (remembered) facts and computing or deriving facts. Computing does not change the state of a world; it only leads to presenting the state in new, possibly more intelligible, ways.

Documental production acts concern the signs (or data) that contain facts. They comprise saving, providing and transforming (documents or datasets).

Material production acts concern the physical carriers of signs, commonly called files. They comprise storing, retrieving, copying, transmitting and destroying (files).

Because original acts are the only acts that change the state of the production world of an organisation, they need to be performed by authorised and responsible actors, thus subjects in actor roles. Informational, documental and material acts may be taken over by artefacts, notably ICT systems. However, as pointed out in Sect. 4.4.4, human actors are ultimately responsible and accountable.

Corresponding with the distinct sorts of production, the actors in an organisation can be partitioned in four layers: the *O-organisation* (O from original), the *I-organisation* (I from informational), the *D-organisation* (D from documental) and the *M-organisation* (M from material). The I-organisation supports the O-organisation by means of informational services (remembering and sharing facts), the D-organisation supports the I-organisation by means of documental services (saving and providing documents) and the M-organisation supports the D-organisation by means of material services (storing and retrieving files).

By the *realisation* of an organisation is understood the devising of the I-, the D- and the M-organisation, given its O-organisation (cf. Fig. 4.15). Conversely, abstracting from realisation yields the O-organisation of an enterprise. The additional abstracting from implementation yields the ontological model of the O-organisation, also called the *essential model* of the (total) enterprise (cf. Sect. 4.4.5).

The 'pie chart' in Fig. 4.16 illustrates the correspondence between tangible production in the O-organisation and material production in the M-organisation (the production in the I- and the D-organisation is always intangible). The adjacency of tangible original production and material production expresses that the sort of an act/fact may depend on the point of view taken: sending a letter by postal mail is clearly a material documental act for the sender. Postal mail companies, however, may consider the distinction between original and material production less interesting. Their business is to transport packages, including envelops, without much regard to their contents.

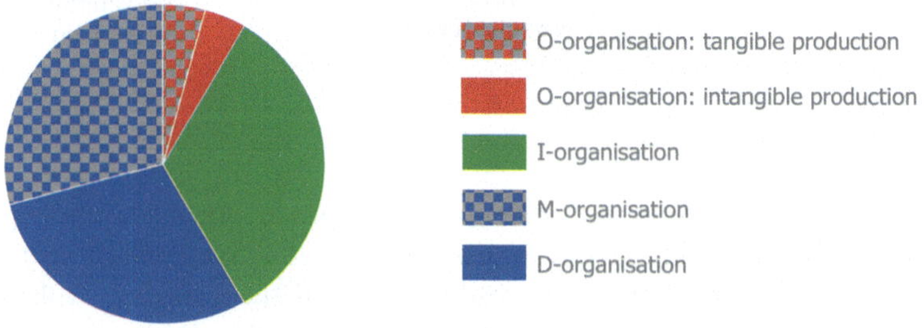

Fig. 4.16 Aspect organisations and sorts of production

4.4.8 The BETA Theory

The BETA theory or EE design theory (BETA stands for *Building from Essence with Technology and Architecture*) is a theory about designing artefacts. Where the ALPHA theory tells one how to abstract from the concrete appearance of a system (realisation and implementation), the BETA theory guides one in designing a system and in making it concrete. First, Simon's notion of *design* [20] is discussed, understood as devising a situation that is considered preferable to the current situation, as well as Alexander's notion of *design process* [21], understood as a sequence of alternate analysis (of the problem) and synthesis (of a solution) steps. In Fig. 4.17, the *General System Development Process* (GSDP) is introduced. It is a general framework for understanding the development of an *object system* for the benefit of a *using system*.

With reference to the TAO theory (cf. Sect. 4.4.3), a clear and sharp distinction is made between the function and the construction of the object system, as well as between the function and the construction of the using system, thereby clarifying that the function of the object system supports the construction of the using system. The three main phases in a design process are function design, construction design and implementation design. *Function design* starts from the ontological model of the using system, which is commonly arrived at by reverse engineering (cf. Sect. 4.4.7), and ends with the specification of the object system function. There are two inputs: *functional requirements* determined by the using system construction and *functional requirements* determined by the applicable architecture. *Construction design* starts from the object system function and ends with the ontological model of the object system. There are two inputs: *constructional requirements* determined by the using system construction and *constructional requirements* determined by the applicable architecture. *Implementation design* (also called *engineering*) starts from the ontology of the object system and ends with the fully detailed specification of a possible implementation, which can subsequently be implemented with appropriate technology. Again, the inputs are the two kinds of constructional requirements: user requirements and architectural requirements.

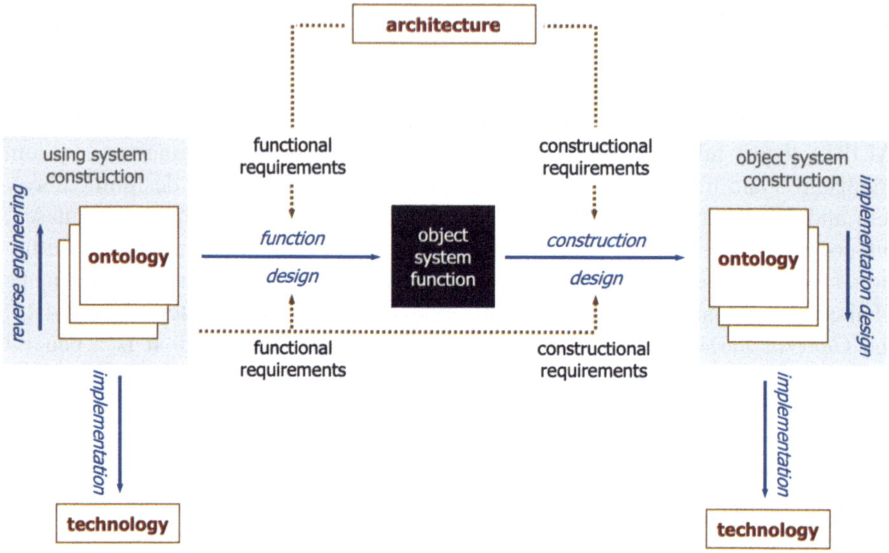

Fig. 4.17 The General System Development Process

A general problem in system development is the (too) large amount of design freedom that is left when all requirements are satisfied. Since time immemorial, the notion of *architecture* helps designers use this freedom in a purposeful and systematic way. To exemplify this, the Metropolitan Opera in New York, the Sydney Opera House and the Scala in Milan have the same basic function, namely, to offer the facilities that are needed to perform operas. Yet, their appearances are very different. One only has to look at the photos of the respective buildings to see it. Thus, whereas the functional requirements for each of the opera houses are (for the largest part) the same, the applied architectures are quite different.

The *General Requirements and Architecture Framework* (GRAF) is introduced for expressing architecture in practicable design and implementation *principles*, which are basically understood as *generic requirements* that constrain system development in addition to the specific (user) requirements.

In order to keep the BETA theory manageable, the implementation design as well as the actual implementation is taken care of by two 'sub' theories, called the IOTA and the NU theory. The NU theory regards the implementation of the object system using ICT, whereas the IOTA theory regards all other ways of implementing, including the assignment of actor roles to people.

4.4.9 The ETA Theory

The ETA theory or EE implementation theory (ETA stands for Engineering with Technological under Architecture) is a theory about the implementation of organisations. The word 'engineering' is used here in its narrow sense: it is equal to implementation design. As expressed in Fig. 4.18, the ETA theory covers both the implementation design and the implementation itself, as defined in the BETA theory: it guides the enterprise engineer in establishing the implementation model, as well as in finding, justifying and assigning technological alternatives for the actual implementation. The theory includes installation and operation, as the subsequent phases after implementation. The starting point is what has been stated already by the PSI theory: there are three technologies needed to implement an organisation: actor technology, production technology and coordination technology.

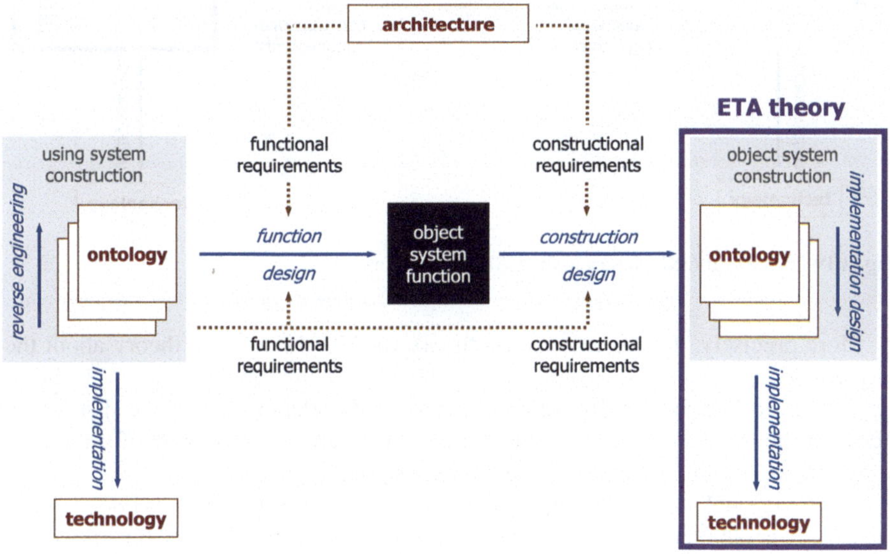

Fig. 4.18 Place of the ETA theory in the GSDP framework

4.4.10 The NU Theory

The NU theory or EE automation theory (NU stands for *Normalised Units*) is a theory concerning the construction of systems. It is complementary to the DELTA theory (cf. Sect. 4.4.5). The application of the NU theory in system development (cf. Sect. 4.4.8) results in a modular structure of the system that prevents unwanted side effects when the system undergoes changes (Fig. 4.19).

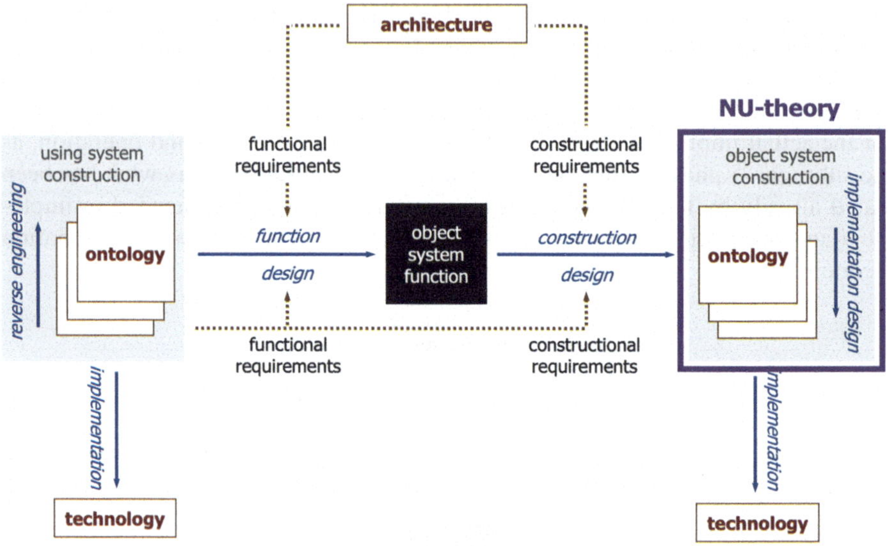

Fig. 4.19 Place of the NU theory in the GSDP framework

More precisely, the EE automation theory (or NU theory) is a theory about the implementation design of organisations where ICT is the implementation technology. Its contribution to software engineering is the elaboration of the distinction between the information-centric and the communication-centric way of producing software, as clarified by the CIAO! Paradigm in Sect. 4.2.

The traditional way of developing enterprise information systems is *information-centric*. It is characterised by having no accurate understanding of the supported organisation and by eliciting system requirements through interviewing future users and other stakeholders. In addition, developed software systems are prone to deterioration in the long run, as brought to the floor by Lehman [22]. An approach to remedy this drawback is Normalised Systems (NS) [23]. NS is information-centric though.

When taking the *communication-centric* point of view, the drawbacks of the traditional way of software engineering vanish. That is why this point of view is embraced by Enterprise Engineering. Three kinds of 'normalised units' are distinguished: transaction process steps (the organisational *atoms*), transactor roles (the organisational *molecules*) and business process kinds (the organisational *fibres*) [24]. Both the changing of each of these kinds of units and their automation are discussed. The conclusion is that organisational models that are based on the communication-centric point of view can rather straightforwardly be automated and changed, without the drawbacks of the traditional way of software engineering. There are no combinatorial effects or other unwanted side effects.

4.4.11 The SIGMA Theory

The SIGMA theory or EE governance and management theory (SIGMA stands for *Socially Inspired Governance and Management Approach*) is an ideological theory about how enterprises should be managed and governed in such a way that the people in the enterprise are maximally empowered. Traditional thinking about enterprises considers (executive) management the primary and exclusive custodians of enterprise performance. Employees, under management control, must behave instrumentally as parts of the enterprise machine. There is no employee variability: standard, predefined instrumental behaviour is required and expected. The SIGMA theory submits a fundamentally different perspective by arguing that variability in employee behaviour is crucial for operational and strategic performance. In our view, the instrumental approach to employee behaviour conflicts with moral and ethical considerations concerning employees and society at large. Current economic thinking, in which enterprises are merely seen as money-generating machines, reinforces the instrumental view on employees. It is argued that employee variability is an absolute prerequisite for aligning employee interests with enterprise performance interests. This unitarist perspective rejects any supposedly 'natural' opposition between them. The SIGMA theory is made operational through the notion of meaningful work, which is seen as an affordance (cf. Sect. 4.4.3): a relationship between employees with certain subjective needs and enterprises with certain objective properties of the work environment. The nature of these needs and properties is elucidated, clarifying at the same time that the theory is firmly grounded in the organisational sciences. The employee-centric nature of this theory aims to counteract the narrow economic theories advanced by many business schools. The discussion of these current ways of thinking reveals the fundamentally different perspective on enterprises that the SIGMA theory radiates. The SIGMA theory is extensively discussed in [25].

References

1. Dietz, J. L. G., & Hoogervorst, J. A. P. (2013). The discipline of enterprise engineering. *International Journal of Organisational Design and Engineering, 3*, 28.
2. Austin, J. L. (1962). *How to do things with words*. Harvard University Press.
3. Searle, J. R. (1969). *Speech acts: An essay in the philosophy of language*. Cambridge University Press. vii, 203 p.
4. Habermas, J. (1986). *The theory of communicative action*. Polity Press.
5. Weigand, H. (2006). Two decades of the language-action perspective. *Communications of the ACM, 49*(4), 45–46.
6. Searle, J. R. (1995). *The construction of social reality*. Free Press. xiii, 241 p.
7. Dietz, J. L. G. (2012). *Red garden gnomes don't exist*. Sapio Enterprise Engineering.
8. Dietz, J. L. G., & Mulder, J. B. F. (2024). *Enterprise ontology—A human-centric approach to understanding the essence of organisation* (Enterprise engineering) (2nd ed.). Springer Nature.
9. Mintzberg, H. (1979). *The structuring of organizations: A synthesis of the research* (Theory of management policy). Prentice-Hall International. xvi, 512 p.

10. Weber, M. (1990). Legitimate authority and bureaucracy. In D. S. Pugh (Ed.), *Organization theory*. Penguin Books.
11. Weick, K. E. (2001). *Making sense of the organization*. Blackwell Publishers. xii, 483 p.
12. Laloux, F. (2014). *Reinventing organizations: A guide to creating organizations inspired by the next stage of human consciousness* (1st ed.). Lightning Source Inc. xviii, 360 p.
13. Ogden, C. K., et al. (1923). *The meaning of meaning: A study of the influence of language upon thought and of the science of symbolism* (International library of psychology, philosophy, and scientific method). K. Paul, Trench, Trübner & co, Harcourt, Brace & Company, Inc. xxxi, 1, 544 p.
14. Stamper, R. K. (1973). *Information in business and administrative systems*. Batsford. 6, 362 p.
15. Apostel, L. (1960). Towards the formal study of models in the non-formal sciences. *Synthese, 12*, 125–161.
16. Gibson, J. J. (1979). *The ecological approach to visual perception*. Houghton Mifflin. xv, 332 p.
17. Weinberg, G. M. (1975). *An introduction to general systems thinking* (Wiley series on systems engineering and analysis). Wiley. xxi, 279 p.
18. Bunge, M. (1979). Treatise on basic philosophy ontology II: A world of systems. In *Treatise on basic philosophy 4*. Reidel.
19. Jackson, M. A. (1975). *Principles of program design. A P I C studies in data processing*. Academic Press. xii, 299 p.
20. Simon, H. A. (1969). *The sciences of the artificial* (Karl Taylor Compton lectures). MIT Press. xii, 123 p.
21. Alexander, C. (1964). *Notes on the synthesis of form*. Harvard University Press. 216 p.
22. Lehman, M. M., & Belady, L. A. (1985). *Program evolution: Processes of software change. A P I C studies in data processing*. Academic Press. xiii, 538 p.
23. Mannaert, H., Verelst, J., & de Bruyn, P. (2016). *Normalized systems—From foundations for evolvable software toward a general theory for evolvabler design*. Koppa.
24. Dietz, J. L. G. (2003). The atoms, molecules and fibres of organizations. *Data and Knowledge Engineering, 47*, 24.
25. Hoogervorst, J. A. P. (2017). *Foundations of enterprise governance and enterprise engineering* (p. 574). Springer International Publishing.

Chapter 5
The EE Function-Construction Theory

Abstract The EE function-construction theory, or TAO theory, is a theory about the way subjects (people) perceive the things that surround them. TAO stands for Teleology, Affordance and Ontology. The foundations part starts with an excerpt from Gibson's theory of affordances. This theory clarifies the subjectivity of affordances. Next, the intended affordances, commonly called functions, of designed things (artefacts) are discussed. Although people are mostly and primarily interested in the functions (affordances) that things may offer them, engineers are also interested in the construction of things. Contrary to function, construction is an objective notion. Related to function is the notion of experience, defined as the sensation that an affordance evokes in the mind. The notion of value is discussed as the intensity of experience, measurable on an ordinal scale. The elaborations part starts with a discussion of constructional models and functional models, their incommensurability and the fundamental difference between constructional and functional decomposition. Next, these findings are illustrated to an example enterprise. The discussions part addresses three topics. The first one is the subjective nature of functional models, and the second one is the mapping from functional to constructional models. The third topic is the importance of ontological modelling. The chapter concludes with a comparison of the TAO theory and the TAO philosophy.

5.1 Introduction

The theory in this chapter is labeled T-theory. The Greek capital letter is pronounced as TAO, which is an acronym for Teleology, Affordances and Ontology. It is a study of the notion of affordance and subsequently of the notions of function and construction. Therefore, the TAO theory is also called the EE function-construction

Reprinted from J. L. G. Dietz, H. B. F. Mulder, *Enterprise Ontology*, The Enterprise Engineering Series, https://doi.org/10.1007/978-3-031-53361-7_7

J. L. G. Dietz, H. B. F. Mulder, *Enterprise Design Fundamentals*, The Enterprise Engineering Series, https://doi.org/10.1007/978-3-031-83262-8_5

theory. It is classified as a *philosophical* theory in the framework of theories (cf. Chap. 4), thus a theory that is about knowledge in general.

Teleology (from the Greek words *telos*, meaning purpose, and *logos*, meaning thinking, reasoning), is the branch of philosophy in which one seeks to explain the behaviour of (animate and inanimate) things by ascribing them intrinsic purposes. Although it is broadly considered controversial, teleology has notorious defenders, like Kant in [1] and recently Nagel in [2]. The basic assumption is that animals behave in certain ways in order to achieve survival. The notion of teleology has also been introduced in cybernetics, by considering it as feedback-controlled purpose and by calling feedback-controlled systems teleological mechanisms [3].

Ontology (from the Greek words *ontos*, meaning being, and *logos*, meaning thinking, reasoning) studies questions concerning the nature of things, irrespective of the intrinsic purposes they would have or the purposes for which subjects would use them. Three phenomena are investigated in ontology. The first one is what things essentially are, so what their 'true' nature is. This subfield is called core ontology. Contemporary researchers in this field are Guarino [4] and Guizzardi [5]. The second one is how things are composed of other things. The subfield studying this phenomenon is called mereology (the Greek word *meros* means part). An authoritative work is written by Simons [6]. The third phenomenon is what the causes are of observable changes. They are studied in the subfield called aetiology (the Greek word *aitios* means cause). The PSI theory (discussed in Chap. 6) can rightly be classified as an aetiological theory.

To exemplify the foregoing, a typical *teleological* statement regarding the human heart is that it pumps blood through the arteries, for the sake of providing all organs with oxygen and nutrition (and other useful things). Note that this statement is also an anthropomorphic metaphor, drawn from our experience in using artificial, i.e. man-made, pumps. A typical *ontological* statement regarding the human heart is that its muscles alternately contract and relax and by doing so cause the blood in the arteries to flow, without investigating the why question. So, causation is definitely an interesting issue in ontology, but purpose is definitely a non-issue.

The remainder of the chapter is organised as follows: Sect. 5.2 (Foundations) introduces the notion of affordance and the related notion of function. It also discusses the distinction between function and construction. Section 5.3 (Elaborations) comprises the discussion of functional and constructional decomposition and the roles of function and construction in system design. In Sect. 5.4 (Discussions), several comparisons are made between the contributions of the TAO theory and current theoretical and practical approaches, both inside and outside the field of enterprise engineering. It concludes with a brief comparison of the TAO theory and the TAO philosophy.

5.2 Foundations

5.2.1 The Notion of Affordance

In order to connect the philosophical branches of teleology and ontology, we use the theory of affordances, developed by Gibson [7] and elaborated by Chemero [8]. In this theory, an *affordance* is defined as an action possibility which is latent in the natural environment. For example, an affordance of terrestrial surfaces is that they offer support to human beings and animals: they can stand on them, walk over them, etc. Affordances can be recognised by an intelligent subject,[1] but whether they will be recognised or not depends on the current needs or desires of the subject. So, if one doesn't have the need to sit, one may not recognise the corresponding affordance that surrounding things offer. The notion of affordance is the key notion in the TAO theory. For a thorough study of affordances, however, a few additional notions must be introduced.

The core notions on which the TAO theory is based are summarised in Fig. 5.1. There is a *subject* (shown on the left side), and there is an *object* (shown on the right side). In order to depict that the need of the subject matches the affordance that the object offers, the shapes at the top of Fig. 5.1 have protrusions. The *affordances* that the object may offer to the subject correspond with the matches of the protrusions. For example, if Charlie Chaplin (the subject) feels the need to sit, he may perceive that he can sit on a tree-stump (the object), because its height and size (the properties) offer the affordance that matches the need to sit. In other words, he perceives the sit-on-ability of the tree stump. It is crucial to keep in mind that an affordance is a *subject-object* relationship, whereas the needs of subjects are purely *subjective*, and the properties of objects are purely *objective*. Because of the unlimited (actual or imaginary) needs of human beings, the number of affordances that an object may offer is virtually unlimited.

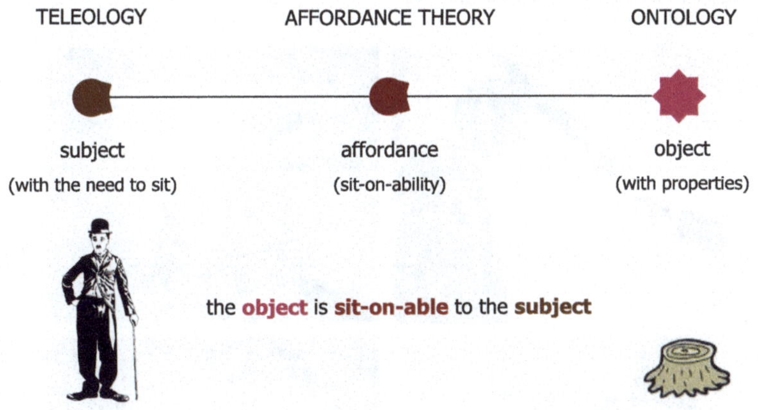

Fig. 5.1 The notion of affordance

The sit-on-ability of tree-stumps does not only hold for Charlie Chaplin but for all subjects with the need to sit, provided they have roughly the same sizes as Charlie Chaplin. That is why people are inclined to say that tree-stumps are sit-on-able

[1] Contrary to the PSI theory, subjects in the TAO theory may also be (intelligent) animals and even intelligent artefacts, next to human beings.

things. Note, however, that this tree-stump may not be sit-on-able for a 2-year-old child.

Understanding affordances as relationships between objects and subjects is crucial. Consequently, it is fallacious to say that the sit-on-ability of tree-stumps is a property of tree-stumps. If there wouldn't exist subjects with a need to sit, the notion of sit-on-ability would also not exist. But the properties of the objects that could offer this affordance would still be there.

5.2.2 Artefacts

So, it is the match between the needs of a subject and the properties of an object where affordances emerge from. But why then do people use nouns, like chair, table, hammer, screwdriver and windshield, which suggest that affordances are properties of things? The answer is that people, in addition to using 'natural' things, like tree-stumps, create and make things,[2] commonly called *artefacts*. Artefacts are designed and made with some affordance(s) in mind. For example, people make things that offer the affordance sit-on-ability; these things are called chairs. They also make things that offer the affordance sit-at-ability; these things are called tables. With respect to artefacts, we commonly do not speak of affordances but of *functions*. We say e.g. that is the function of a chair to sit on it, instead of saying that chairs offer the affordance sit-on-ability.

Fig. 5.2 Function and other affordances of an umbrella

[2] In the TAO theory, we will not make the strict distinction between the notions of object and thing as done in the FI theory. Here, the two words are considered largely synonymous.

Because artefacts may also offer unintended affordances to subjects, in addition to the intended ones (the functions), the totality of functions is a subset of the totality of affordances. Thus, like all other affordances, functions are relationships between subjects and objects, as discussed in Sect. 5.2.1 and as clarified by Fig. 5.1. To illustrate the point, Fig. 5.2 exhibits, in the lower-right part, the function, i.e. the intended affordance, of an umbrella, namely, shielding from rain.[3] But the picture also shows three other affordances that umbrellas may offer to people. Proceeding anti-clockwise, there is the affordance shielding from sun, hitting and hiding things (like a gun). In spite of these other affordances, people easily recognise the thing on all four pictures as an umbrella. The word 'umbrella' is a functional word, like the other words mentioned above: chair, table, hammer, screwdriver and windshield, and like many more words. There is nothing wrong with using functional names, as long as one is aware that they do not refer to a thing as such but to its intended affordance(s). Ontologically spoken, no thing *is* a chair, but it may be used as a chair (and intended to be used in this way). Most nouns in natural languages are functional because of people's primary interest in what they can use things for, instead of what they ontologically are. But tables are also used to sit on and chairs to sit at. In general, whenever the properties of an object match a need of a subject (that seeks to satisfy this need), the corresponding affordance emerges. Moreover, it doesn't matter whether the object is an artefact or a 'natural' thing.

In addition to designing and making artefacts, people may *assign* (new) functions to existing things, whether they are artefacts or not. Let us use Fig. 5.3 to clarify this. The building in the middle of the picture is a church, most people would say. Why? Because we have learned that buildings with such a shape are erected with the function of church in mind. But churches are sometimes (also) used as a place of shelter, for refugees. And when too few people make use of the original function of a church, it may be assigned, for example, the function of indoor playground. As for the paved area in front of the church, it is probably meant to be a village square. But these squares may be assigned various other functions, for example, marketplace (on Tuesday and Friday) and parking lot (on the other days, except Sunday). And twice per year, it may be a fair ground. In addition, the paved area may offer various unintended affordances to specific stakeholders (like rollerskate ground, dancing place, demonstration area, etc.).

[3] Actually, the English word 'umbrella' stems from the Italian word *ombrella*, which means 'giving shadow'.

Fig. 5.3 Assignments of functions

The important conclusion from these examples, once more, is that (designed or assigned) functions and other (unintended) affordances are relationships between objects (things) and subjects (people). A building is not a church per se, but it may have been designed with this function in mind, and a paved area is not a marketplace or parking lot per se, but it may have been assigned these functions (or have been designed with these functions in mind).

5.2.3 Function and Construction

Despite the fact that artefacts may offer various affordances to people, they are mostly designed with a specific function (for a specific target group) in mind. Figure 5.4 exhibits on the left side a clock that could be a showpiece in a living room. The intended function is obvious: it is a clock, i.e. it tells one what time it is. This intended function is realised by the construction behind the clock-face in the casing: the clockwork (Fig. 5.4, right side). The casing is also part of the (total) construction of the clock, and it may offer additional affordances, like being a nice piece of furniture. The clockwork itself may also be considered a beautiful piece of craftsmanship.

Fig. 5.4 Function versus construction

Thus, every function of a thing is realised by its construction. Taking the *construction* perspective on a thing (a natural thing or an artefact) means that one exclusively considers the thing as an object, without paying attention to the intended function(s) or other affordances it may offer to subjects. So, for example, we can perceive the clockwork in Fig. 5.4 just as a material thing with properties: spatial dimensions, mass, etc. without having in mind what affordances it may offer. Because the construction perspective is independent of the possible affordances of the thing, it is said to be *objective*. By this we mean that two knowledgeable persons will have or can acquire the same constructional understanding of it. As an example, if two clockwork engineers are asked to produce the Bill of Materials (BoM) of the clockwork in Fig. 5.4, by dissembling it, they will come up with the same BoM. In case they don't, at least one of them has made an error.

Taking the *function* perspective on a thing means that one exclusively considers the affordances that are offered by the thing given the purposes or needs one has in mind. For example, one could think of sitting on a chair or of using it as a temporary store, one could create a baby's crib by putting two armchairs together, etc. The distinctive characteristic of the function perspective is that we take the position of an observer who has purposes in mind for which the chair could be used. By way of metaphor, he/she looks at the chair through the 'lens of purposes' and in doing so 'sees' the affordances that the chair offers. Consequently, two persons, even if they are equipped with the same generic knowledge of chairs, could easily 'see' different affordances of the chair, dependent on the purposes they have in mind. That's why the function perspective is said to be *subjective*, although functions are actually subject-object relationships, as we have seen. In Sect. 5.3.1, we will elaborate what the distinction means for designing artefacts and for modelling them, both from the function and from the construction perspective.

5.2.4 Experience and Value

Although different things, like tree-stumps and chairs, may offer the same affordance to subjects, these affordances may very well be experienced differently. By *experience* is understood the subjective sensation that the recognition of an affordance evokes in the subject's mind (cf. Fig. 5.5).

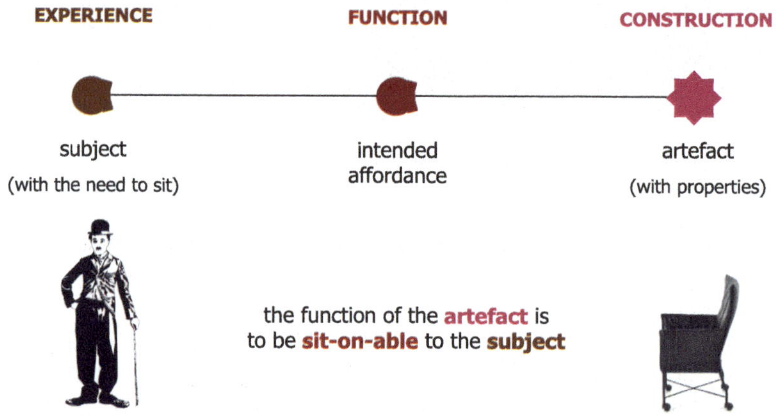

Fig. 5.5 The notion of function

For example, the sit-on-ability of the tree-stump in Fig. 5.1 may evoke a different experience in Charlie Chaplin's mind than the one offered by the chair in Fig. 5.5. On this basis, he may have a preference for one of them. Generally, subjects appear to not just look for affordances that match their needs but to also pay attention to the experiences that they evoke.

Related to the notion of experience is the notion of value. In the light of the previous discussion, it may be clear that value is not a property of a thing. Consequently, one can, in principle, not say that a thing has a particular value, like it has a particular weight. More specifically, we will define *value* as the intensity of the experience that is evoked in a subject's mind by the recognition of an affordance. The subject could express this value as an attribute of the affordance, by which value becomes measurable, although most likely only on an ordinal scale (cf. [9], Sect. 6.3.4). For example, the affordance sit-on-ability that is offered by an armchair to Charlie Chaplin could evoke in his mind a higher-ranked experience than the one that is offered by a tree-stump. He could express this by assigning to the armchair a higher value of the affordance sit-on-ability than to the tree-stump. As another example, many people nowadays rank their experience of hotel stays, restaurant visits, etc. on Web sites. In order to make this useful for other people, the subjective rankings are 'normalised' on an ordinal scale.

In contrast to value, the *price* of a thing must be considered as a property of the thing, so as something objective, regardless whether this price is the outcome of a calculation or someone's original declaration. For example, Charlie Chaplin's decision to buy a new walking pole is most likely based on balancing the price of the pole and the value that he assigns to the affordance(s) that the pole offers to him.

5.3 Elaborations

5.3.1 Constructional and Functional (De)composition

In Sect. 5.3.3, the composition and decomposition of concrete things is discussed, based on the part-of relationships between the parts of composite things, as discussed in [6]. Figure 5.11 from [9] is reproduced as Fig. 5.6. It shows the composition and decomposition of a car. Taking the foregoing into account, we need to add that the (de)composition is a constructional one, i.e. it regards purely the construction of a car, not its function(s). Therefore, the exhibited structure is called a *constructional component tree*, also known as a Bill of Materials (BoM). Obviously, the tree is not complete, it can be extended. Moreover, the exhibited decomposition does certainly not hold for all cars. Presumably, it holds for all cars with a combustion engine, but it certainly does not hold for electric cars.

A constructional component tree shows how a composite thing (the top level in Fig. 5.6) can be disassembled down to its elementary parts (the bottom level, thus the 'nuts and bolts') and how it can be (re-)assembled from these elementary parts. As every engineer knows, disassembling a car (or any other artefact) is mostly not very difficult, but re-assembling it may easily turn into a nightmare. The reason of the trouble is that there is commonly only one constructional composition of a car. This holds anyhow for the top level (the assembled car) and the lowest level (the distinct parts). Whether there is always exactly one structure of sub-assemblies in between the top and the bottom level for a particular brand and model of car is disputable, but at the same time, it is irrelevant for the argument.

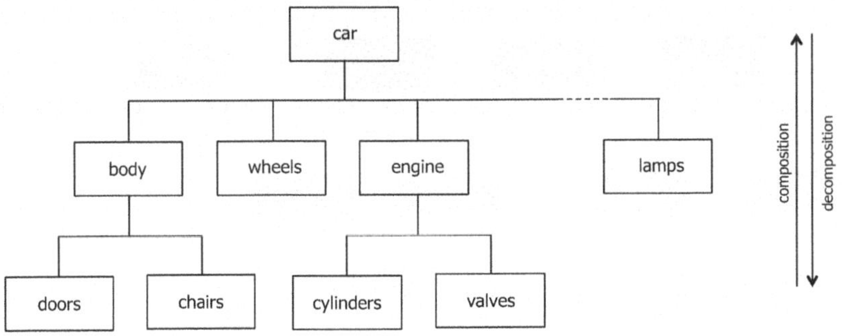

Fig. 5.6 Constructional component tree of a car

Component trees can also be applied to the functions[4] of things. Figure 5.7 exhibits (a part of) a possible functional component tree of a car. It shows a *functional decomposition* of the function driving, which most people will consider the most distinctive function of cars. Other functions could be: a cosy shelter and a status symbol. The exhibited functional model could be very useful for a driving instructor to explain to a new pupil how one drives a car. The driving function is decomposed into four subfunctions: powering, steering, lighting and seating. Both the powering and the lighting function are further decomposed, just for illustration. In addition to plain black boxes, Fig. 5.7 contains grey-lined black boxes. These boxes represent the (sub) functions that can be used through operating specific constructional parts. In general, such a constructional part is called a *user interface* to the function. In all cars, the steering function is operated by turning the steering wheel, but the constructional parts through which other functions are operated may differ between car brands and models. Fortunately, car manufacturers nowadays attempt to standardise the user interfaces. Note that these user interfaces are the only mental connections between the functions and the construction of the car and that they must be explicitly designed and implemented.

Up to now, we have intentionally avoided to use the term 'model' in discussing the constructional and functional component trees, for the simple reason that they do not comply with the definition of model as presented in [9], Chap. 6, where a (conceptual) model of a thing is the understanding of the thing within some (proper) theory. As an example, discrete event systems can be understood properly within the DELTA theory ([9], Chap. 9), more specifically within the PRISMA meta model. The part-of relation, on which the component trees are built, can hardly be called a theory. However, if component trees are integral parts of theories, there is no objection against calling structures like the ones that are exhibited in Figs. 5.6 and 5.7 models. We will go along with this habit. In addition, we will call functional component trees *black-box* models, in conformity with the DELTA theory ([9], Chap. 9), because they completely ignore the 'internals' of a system (its statics, kinematics and dynamics). Likewise, we will call constructional component trees *white-box* models.

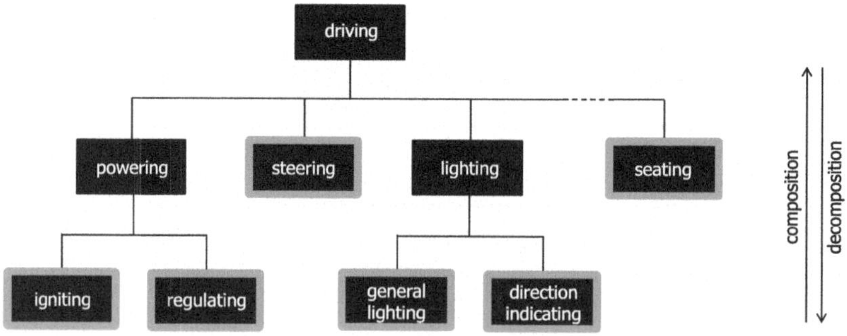

Fig. 5.7 Functional component tree of the driving function of a car

[4] From now on, we will not be strict anymore about the distinction between function and (unintended) affordance. The latter may be considered as a possible function.

Contrary to constructional decompositions (which are objective), functional decompositions are subjective. In principle, everyone can have her/his own functional model of the driving function of cars, as well as of the function(s) of other devices, like computers and vending machines. However, although these models are basically personal, they are commonly shared among groups of people. The insight that functional models are subjective sheds a clarifying light on the endless discussions about the 'correctness' of functional models. We will elaborate this topic in Sect. 5.4.

In order to show the distinction between constructional and functional component trees in a graphical way, the parts (boxes) of the first are coloured white and the parts (boxes) of the latter black. Contrary to constructional decompositions, functional decompositions may be 'endless', i.e. one can always decompose a functional component, at will, just and only because they are not (directly) related to constructions.

5.3.2 Composition and Decomposition of Enterprises

Like it holds for other composite systems, the construction and the function(s) of enterprises are generally decomposable. Let us first investigate the functional decomposition, taking the enterprise Malum, discussed in [10], as an example. The function of every enterprise is what is commonly called its *business*: the service(s) that are offered to the customers. Malum is a manufacturer and vendor of wheelbarrows.

Figure 5.8 exhibits a possible functional decomposition of the business of Malum. For the depth of the decomposition, the same criterion is applied as we did to the driving function of cars (Fig. 5.7), namely, the being able to operate the 'leaf' functions. Only three functional components are considered to be 'leaves' of the enterprise's business. The other 'black' components in Fig. 5.8 have yet to be decomposed to the 'leaf' level. The 'leaf' functions selling, paying and transporting can be operated by actors in the environment through some user interface. Examples of such actors are the clients of Malum and a transport company. The 'leaf' functions are indicated in the figure by grey-lined black boxes. These functions can be used by initiating transactions of three corresponding kinds: one that provides the service of selling, one that provides the service of paying and one that provides the service of transporting.

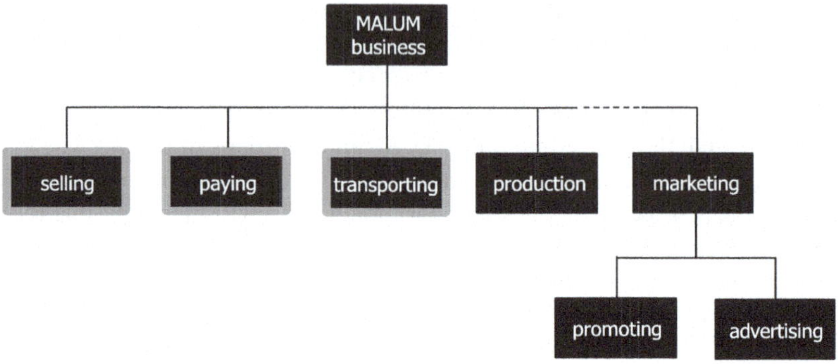

Fig. 5.8 Functional component tree of the business of Malum

We will refer to the construction of enterprises as their *organisation*. Regarding the relationship between the construction of an enterprise and its function(s), it is the organisation that realises its business, as well as all other conceivable functions, including those services that are offered to other stakeholders than the customers or clients. Figure 5.9 exhibits the constructional component tree of Malum's organisation, conceived according to the PSI theory (Chap. 6) and the OMEGA theory ([9], Chap. 10). It realises the business functions selling, paying and transporting.

Fig. 5.9 Constructional component tree of the organisation of Malum

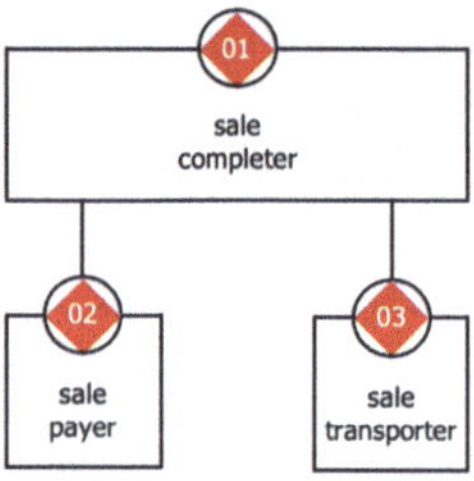

Table 5.1 Transactor product table of Malum

Transaction kind	Product kind	Executor role
01 sale completing	[sale] is completed	sale completer
02 sale paying	[sale] is paid	sale payer
03 sale transporting	[sale] is transported	sale transporter

In order to be precise as well as to illustrate the interconnectedness of the functions selling, paying and transporting, the corresponding transaction kinds in the Transactor Product Table (cf. Table 5.1) are called, respectively, sale completing, sale paying and sale transporting, where a sale is an instance of selling. The latter two turn out to be constructional components of the first one. It means that, although all three business functions are offered to the environment, paying and transporting can only be used in the context of selling. The three transactor roles are user interfaces, through which users can use the functions selling, paying and transporting. Note that the users of selling are the customers of Malum, that the users of paying are actors in the sales department, and that the users of transporting are also actors in the sales department.

As follows from the PSI theory (cf. Chap. 6), the initiators of transactions TK01 (sale completing) are the customers of Malum, and the executors are actors in the sales department. The initiators of transactions TK02 (sale paying) are actors in the sales department, and the executors are the customers of Malum. The initiators of transactions TK03 (sale transporting) are actors in the sales department, and the executors are actors in the (internal) transportation department or an (external) transportation company.

Only the building blocks in the O-organisation (cf. Chap. 7) of Malum are shown in Fig. 5.9. Those in its I-, D- and M-organisation are omitted. For a complete ontological model, the informational, documental and material component trees must be added, which would make the tree substantially bigger. However, for understanding the constructional essence of Malum, also called its essential model (cf. [9], Chap. 9), the component tree in Fig. 5.9 is the basis.

5.3.3 The Role of Function and Construction in System Design

Although this book is not about designing systems, studying the role of functional and constructional models in the design of systems appears to shed a clarifying light on them. So, let us have a look at the design process, as presented in [11]. There, system design is considered to be a part of system development, a process in which two systems play a crucial role: the object system and the using system. By the *object system* is understood the system which is going to be developed. By the *using system* is understood the system that is going to use the services (functions) of the object system.

As the explanatory example of the using system, we take the sales department of an enterprise. One of the services that the object system offers to the using system is providing the monthly turnover of the enterprise. As the explanatory example of the object system, we take a sales information system. One of the monthly products that it brings about is the result of a calculation. This result is interpreted by the using system as the monthly turnover.

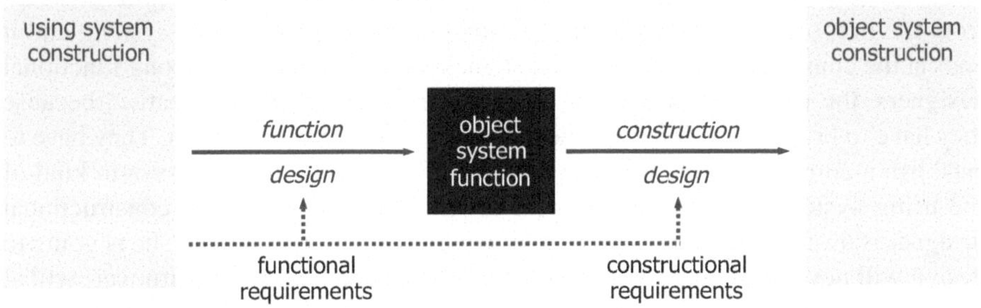

Fig. 5.10 The system design process

The complete system development process is divided into three phases: design, engineering and implementation. As said, our goal is to clarify the design process. Figure 5.10 exhibits the basic view that we consider appropriate for understanding the design process. The figure shows that the function perspective and the construction perspective on systems, as well as the corresponding black-box model and white-box model, play a crucial role in understanding the design process. Two major phases can be distinguished in the design of the object system. The first one is called 'function design' and the second one 'construction design'. Function design starts from the using system construction, which is a white-box model, and ends at the function of the object system, which is a black-box model. In line with what has been said about black-box models above, this means that the specified function of the object system does not contain any information about the construction of the object system. In other words, the function of the object system must be specified fully and only in terms of the construction of the using system.

As said, the function of the object system supports the construction of the using system. Put the other way around, the construction of the using system uses the function(s) of the object system. Why the construction of the using system, and not its function? The answer is that there must always be an alternation of function and construction in the support-use relationship of systems. A function does not support another function directly, because functions have no need for support; only constructions can have. To exemplify this, the sales department as a part of the construction of the enterprise can have a need for a sales information system. The sales department as a black box is a functional abstraction of the operational activities of selling. Conversely, the function of the object system is always and necessarily expressed in terms of the construction of the using system. So, for example, the salesmen in (the construction of) the using system may have a need to know the monthly turnover of the enterprise. The notion of turnover is a business notion that takes its meaning from the larger economic context in which the enterprise operates. The figure of the monthly turnover is something by which people in the sales department may become excited or depressed. In specifying the function of the object system, it is this rich meaning of turnover that the salesmen will express to the functional designers of the object system. Needless to say that the functional designers must possess sufficient knowledge of the enterprise in order to be well-matched sparring partners to the salesmen in the process of function design.

The nature of the second design phase, construction design, is quite different from the first one. It starts from the specified function of the object system, and it ends at the construction of the object system. Without intending to wrong functional designers, the job of constructional designers is definitely more creative, because they have to bridge the mental gap between function and construction. They have to establish a correspondence between systems of different kinds: the system kind of the using system and the system kind of the object system. The constructional designer is aware of the fact that the sales information system that he/she is going to design will never have any 'understanding' of turnover. The name 'turnover' will at best be a label, assigned to a variable in the computer program; however, this variable can equally well be named 'Mickey Mouse'. It is the task of the constructional designer to get the precise definition of turnover from the functional designer and to replace its business semantics by its formal semantics. From these formal semantics, the constructional designer devises an appropriate calculation rule. As another example for clarification, have a look at Figs. 5.6 and 5.5. Obviously, there is no simple way to arrive at the constructional model in Fig. 5.6 from the functional model in Fig. 5.5. It requires 'hard' design efforts.

The result of function design is a functional model of the object system, which by nature is a black-box model. It contains all *functional specifications* for the object system to be built. The major input for the function design phase are the *functional requirements*, which are provided by the using system (cf. Fig. 5.10). Not all functional requirements need to be contained in the functional specifications, for two reasons: first, requirements may be unfounded. Fortunately, the ontological model of the using system provides an objective yardstick for determining unfounded requirements, since the essential model of the sales department (the ontological model of its O-organisation, cf. Chap. 7) specifies the information that is needed for every actor role. All other information that the fillers of an actor role may ask for, they do not really need. Next, determining requirements includes their validation, something that can be achieved only in thorough discussions with people 'in the business'. If the ontological model of the O-organisation is taken as the starting point, one cannot forget essential requirements. Second, the functional specifications must be feasible. By this is meant that the needed object system can be implemented, given the available technology. In addition, it must be possible to finish the development process within the agreed-upon time and the agreed-upon budget.

As Fig. 5.10 indicates, the using system may also provide constructional requirements. This option is added to let people have a say in the construction of the object system. Constructional requirements regard, for example, the interface through which the services of the object system are made available to the using system.

5.4 Discussions

5.4.1 The Subjective Nature of Functional Models

As pointed at in Sect. 5.3.1, there is a persistent practical problem concerning functional modelling approaches. Examples of such models in the area of enterprise engineering are Forrester's System Dynamics Models, SADT (or IDEF0) activity models and the models expressed in Data Flow Diagrams.

The problem is that different modellers commonly produce different functional models of the same system, often to the surprise of the principal or the teacher who ordered them to produce it. It should not be surprising, for the simple reason that functional models are inherently subjective. They represent the affordances, both intended (by the designer of the system) and unintended, that the modeller perceives, steered by the needs he/she sees or feels, as discussed in Sect. 5.2. Notwithstanding, there may be a considerable amount of similarity between the different models, but that is due to the common context in which the distinct modellers work, and the preceding discussions they may have had. The bottom line is that a functional model of a system contains the affordances that the maker perceives, and the alarming point is that many modellers seem not to be aware of this subjective nature. Consequently, they conduct endless and fruitless discussions about which functional model is 'correct'. Correctness, however, is an objective notion and therefore only applicable to constructional models. As said, if two knowledgeable persons were asked to produce the constructional model of the same thing, e.g. a coffee machine, they would come up with the same model (or they made a mistake). The criterion is the resemblance of the model to the coffee machine. For functional models, there is no such criterion. Therefore, it makes little sense to talk about the correctness of functional models.

To illustrate the problem, let us have a look at the Data Flow Diagram (DFD) in Fig. 5.11. It represents a functional model, at the highest level of abstraction, of an elevator control system, as discussed in [12]. It is of the kind grey-box model, according to the DELTA theory ([9], Chap. 9), which means that it is a black-box model with an internal state. The disks (or 'bubbles') in Fig. 5.11 represent functions (also called processes), the double lines represent partial states (also called data stores), the straight arrows represent data flows and the dashed arrows represent control flows. The latter are actually also data flows but with a special role: they activate functions, whereas the 'normal' data flows consist of input to or output from functions. The names 'process' and 'data store' suggest that DFDs represent constructional models, but a simple test shows that this cannot be the case. First, in no concrete elevator control system will one find parts like elevator scheduler or elevator controller. Second, the decomposition rules of DFDs tell us that one may decompose every process into a network of (sub) processes, data stores, data flows and control flows. This may be done at will, as long as the totality of the processes, data stores, etc. is equivalent to the corresponding process at the higher level. This property is typical for functional models. Regarding constructional models, there is always a limited number of possible decompositions, and there is a definite lowest level, as discussed in Sect. 5.3.1.

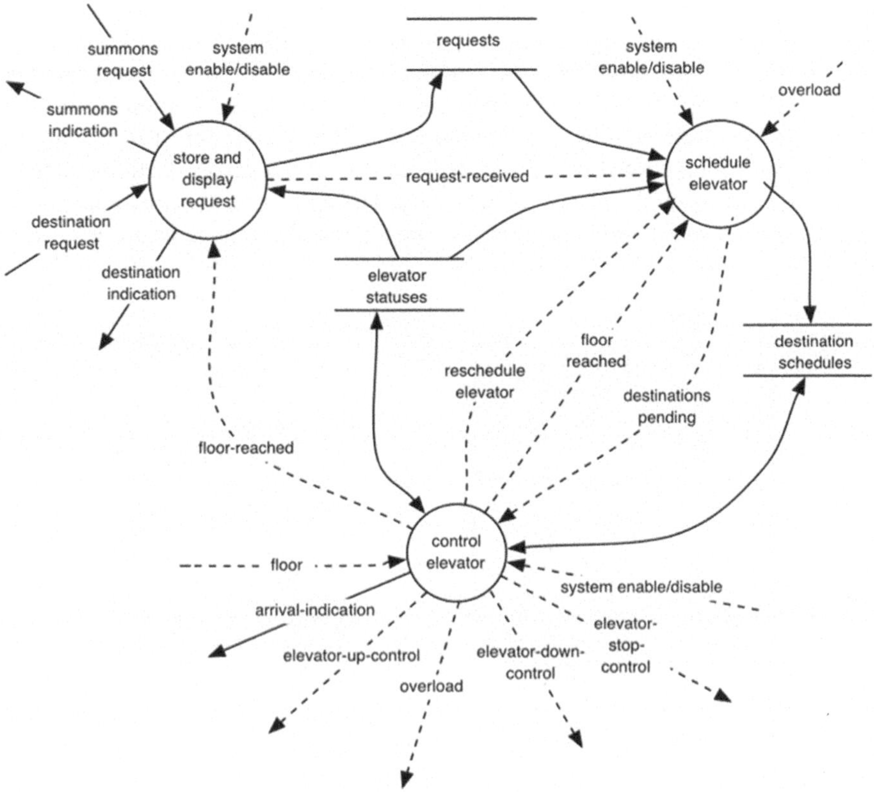

Fig. 5.11 Data flow diagram of an elevator control system

5.4.2 Can One Map Functional Models to Constructional Models?

In the current practice of enterprise engineering, notably in software engineering, but also, e.g. in business systems engineering and systems architecture, there is a widespread belief that functional models can be mapped directly to constructional models, which is fully opposite to the findings in Sect. 5.3.3. How should one understand this (mis)belief, and how could one reconcile it with the findings of Sect. 5.3.3, which are in addition compliant with the DELTA theory ([9], Chap. 9)? The answers to these questions lie in two fallacies that, for some reason, are quite common in software engineering and in computer science at large.

The first fallacy is that if one 'opens' a black-box model of a system, one gets a white-box model, where 'opening' means that one replaces the system by a structure of sub-systems. In order to illustrate the point, Fig. 1.8 in [13] is reproduced as Fig. 5.12. The figure exhibits a decomposition of the system SysA into a collection of interrelated systems SysB, SysC, etc. This decomposition can be functional or constructional (one cannot tell from the figure), but not some mix, as suggested by the figure and the clarifying text in [13]. If the boxes in Fig. 5.12 are black boxes, then the decomposition is functional and the interactions are behavioural relationships (cf. [9], Chap. 9). If they are white boxes, then the decomposition is constructional and the interactions are operational relationships (cf. [9], Chap. 9). Decomposing a functional model can only lead to structured collections of functional components (cf. Figs. 5.7 and 5.11), and decomposing a constructional model can only lead to structured collections of constructional components (cf. Fig. 5.6).

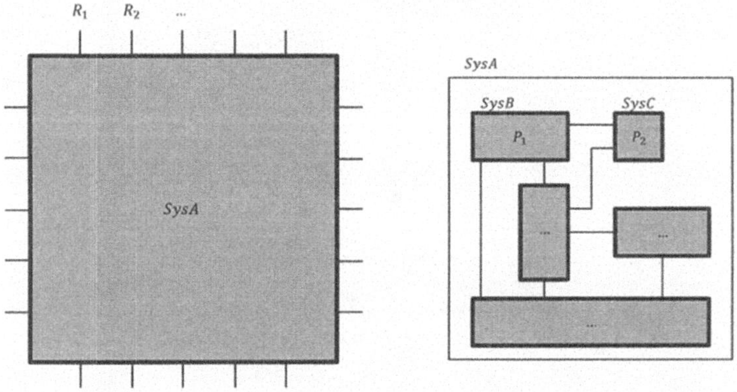

Fig. 5.12 The 'opening' of a black box

The second fallacy is that computer programming, so the production of software, can be understood as a transformation from function to construction or, more precisely, a mapping of functional requirements into software primitives ([13], Chap. 11), where the latter are considered constructional entities. The cause of this fallacy is probably that the software primitives in modern programming languages are high-level functional entities (called functions, procedures or methods, depending on the programming language). The ultimate constructional realisation of these functional entities are algorithms, thus the instructions that make the computer hardware do what one wants it to do. These algorithms must still be created, and this work is not straightforward or trivial, although there are libraries of standard algorithms where the software engineer can pick from.

Because the notion of function in current programming languages is quite blurred, and because in software engineering the dominant view on software systems is information-centric (cf. Chap. 4), a clarifying light on the second fallacy might be shed by the ALPHA theory (Chap. 7). It states that the organisation of an enterprise (so the construction perspective on the enterprise) can be divided into four partial organisations: the O-organisation, the I-organisation, the D-organisation and the M-organisation, as shown in Fig. 5.13, which is a reproduction of Fig. 6.12. The whole organisation is operating if the four partial organisations are operating and if they are connected in the way as shown in Fig. 5.13. Every *enterprise information system* is some part of the enterprise's I-organisation together with the corresponding parts of its D- and M-organisation, as indicated by the yellow trapezium.

The operation of the enterprise information system is independent of the way in which the covered parts of the I-, D- and M-organisation are implemented. As discussed in Chap. 7 and in [11], a possible implementation technology is ICT, which means that the actors are replaced by software modules or agents.

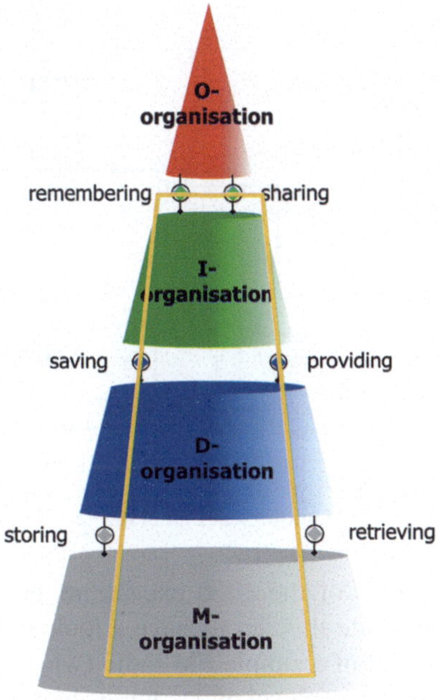

Fig. 5.13 The notion of enterprise information system

The functions that are needed by the actors in the O-organisation, and which are offered by the enterprise information system, are realised by the transactions of the general kinds remembering (of facts that are created in the O-organisation) and sharing (of original or derived facts). The issue of evolvability of information systems, which is a major issue in software engineering [14] and in systems engineering in general [13], can also be solved by redesigning the relevant parts of the I-, D- and M-organisation and subsequently re-implementing them. If ICT is the implementation technology, this implies regenerating the software, including the databases that contain representations of the facts in the O-organisation. Evolvability only concerns the implementation of a system; it is no issue at the level of the O-organisation. At this level, there is only one copy of every action, entity, fact, etc., as follows from the DELTA theory ([9], Chap. 9) and the PSI theory (Chap. 6).

5.4.3 The Importance of Ontological Modelling

As discussed in Sect. 5.3.3, devising a construction that will realise a specified function is generally the hardest task in a design process. It requires professionalism and creativity, next to thorough knowledge of the subject matter. Next, starting this process with devising the ontological model of the object system is a major help. Unfortunately, it is rarely taught in design courses, of any kind, not only in the area of enterprise engineering.

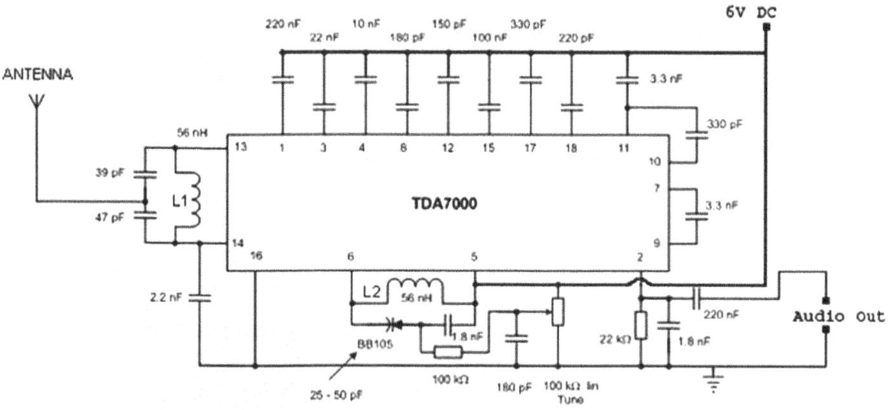

Fig. 5.14 Ontological model of the radio receiver

One of the good exceptions is electrical engineering, notably electronics. To illustrate this, let us have a look at the ontological model and the implementation model of a simple FM radio (which you may have built as a student). The detailed (i.e. lowest level of decomposition) ontological model is exhibited in Fig. 5.14.[5] The main component is an integrated circuit referred to by TDA7000. It does the lion's share of the (analog) signal processing work of the radio. It has 18 input/output ports, which take in or produce electrical signals, except ports 5 and 16, which are supplied by an electrical voltage of 6 and 0 DC, respectively. Integrated circuits, like the TDA7000, are composite components, which commonly consist of dozens of elementary components. Examples of such elementary components are transistors, diodes, capacitors, inductors and resistors. Actually, these components cannot really be found in the integrated circuit; that's why it is called integrated. Consequently, integrated circuits mostly have a quite complex functionality.

[5] Pictures and the other information of the FM radio are taken from http://pdf.datasheetcatalog.com/datasheet/philips/TDA7000_CNV_2.pdf and https://circuitswiring.com/fm-radio-with-tda7000/.

Fig. 5.15 A possible implementation of the radio receiver

In Fig. 5.14, capacitors are represented by 'double-lines', inductors by 'wired' symbols and resistors by rectangular shapes. (Note that the diagram doesn't contain transistors or diodes!) All elementary components have a specific functional behaviour, as has the integrated circuit TDA7000. Figure 5.15 exhibits a possible implementation of the ontological model. Only the right side, with the TDA7000 in the middle, is applicable. The left side contains an audio amplifier, which amplifies the audio output from the right side to a level that is needed to make it audible through a loudspeaker. The TDA7000 is implemented by the black-coloured device labeled TDA7000. It has 18 sockets, each of them implementing one of the ports in Fig. 5.14. (Note: Figures 5.14 and 5.15 do not fully correspond)

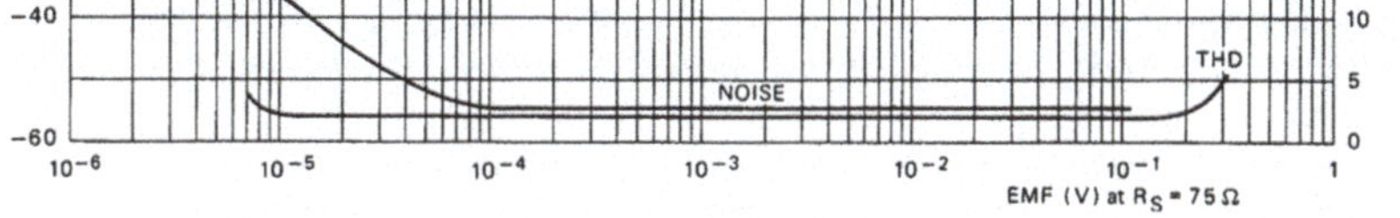

Fig. 5.16 Part of the functional specifications of the TDA7000

As said, it is the construction of a system that brings about the function(s) and additional affordances to its users and possibly to other stakeholders. The highest-level function is being a radio. This function is elaborated in more extensive and more specific functions, ending up in one or more functional component trees, like the one in Fig. 5.7, complemented by detailed behaviour specifications. As an example, Fig. 5.16 shows one of the detailed functional behaviour specifications of the integrated circuit TDA7000 that are relevant for the performance of the FM radio.

5.4.4 The TAO Theory and the TAO Philosophy

TAO, also spelled as DAO, is a metaphysical concept in ancient Chinese philosophy, among others in Confucianism. Its literal translation into English is 'the way' or 'the path' [15]. TAO is considered the source and the substance of everything that exists. Taoists seek to free themselves from the subjective influences that unavoidably stick to the human observations of the world that surrounds us and subsequently to find the human independent truth in the world. The TAO philosophy also leads to a particular way of living, the TAO ethics, which is characterised by three so-called treasures: compassion, frugality and humility.

The similarity of the TAO theory and the TAO philosophy is not only in the name.[6] The sharp distinction in the TAO theory between the function and the construction of the things that surround us, or more generally between teleology and ontology, paves the way to a crisp and clear notion of the ontological essence of systems in general (cf. [9], Chap. 9) and of organisations in particular (cf. [9], Chap. 8). But it also suggests a profound correspondence between this notion of ontological essence and the core of the TAO philosophy. We leave it to the reader to verify that this correspondence is more than mere speculation, as we leave it to the reader to discover the correspondence between the TAO ethics and the human-centric ideological foundation of Enterprise Engineering, as presented in [16].

References

1. Kant, I. (1965). *First introduction to the Critique of judgment* (The library of liberal arts). Bobbs-Merrill. xv, 55 p.
2. Nagel, T. (2012). *Mind and cosmos: Why the materialist neo-Darwinian conception of nature is almost certainly false*. Oxford University Press. x, 130 p.
3. Rosenblueth, A., Wiener, N., & Bigelow, J. (1943). Behavior, purpose and teleology. *Philosophy of Science, 10*(1), 18–24.
4. Guarino, N., Oberle, D., & Staab, S. (2009). What is an ontology? In *Handbook on ontologies* (pp. 1–17). Springer.
5. Guizzardi, G. (2005). *Ontological foundations for structural conceptual models* (CTIT). University of Twente.
6. Simons, P. (1987). *Parts—A study in ontology*. Oxford University Press.
7. Gibson, J. J. (1979). *The ecological approach to visual perception* (Vol. xv). Houghton Mifflin. 332 p.
8. Chemero, A. (2003). An outline of a theory of affordances. *Ecological Psychology, 15*(2), 181–195.
9. Dietz, J. L. G., & Mulder, J. B. F. (2024). *Enterprise ontology—A human-centric approach to understanding the essence of organisation* (Enterprise engineering) (2nd ed.). Springer Nature.
10. Dietz, J. L. G. (2012). *Red garden gnomes don't exist*. Sapio Enterprise Engineering.
11. Dietz, J. L. G. (2009). *Architecture: Building strategy into design*. SDU Publishing.
12. Yourdon, E. (1989). *Modern structured analysis*. Yourdon Press. x, 672 p.

[6] The Roman writing of the pronunciation of the Greek letter T is actually not TAO but TAU.

13. Mannaert, H., Verelst, J., & de Bruyn, P. (2016). *Normalized systems—From foundations for evolvable software toward a general theory for evolvabler design*. Koppa.
14. Lehman, M. M., Belady, L. A., & Program evolution: Processes of software change. A P I C studies in data processing. (1985). *London* (Vol. xiii). Academic Press. 538 p.
15. Puett, M. J. (2016). *The path: What Chinese philosophers can teach us about the good life* (First Simon & Schuster hardcover edition). Simon & Schuster. xvi, 204 p.
16. Hoogervorst, J. A. P. (2017). Ideological foundation. In *Foundations of enterprise governance and enterprise engineering: Presenting the employee-centric theory of organization* (pp. 355–564). Springer International Publishing.

Chapter 6
The EE Organisational Operation Theory

Abstract The EE Organisational Operation Theory or PSI theory is a theory about the operation of organisations. PSI stands for Performing in Social Interaction. Based on the CIAO Paradigm (Communication, Information, Action and Organisation), a communication-centric view is taken on the cooperation of people in enterprises, as manifested in business processes. The fundamental notion in understanding the operation of organisations is the coordination act. It consists of a performer, an addressee, an intention and a product. The performer and the addressee are actors, i.e. subjects filling an actor role. Actor roles are the units of authority and responsibility. Coordination acts can be performed verbally, non-verbally and tacitly. They are the key elements in (business) conversations, which are the constituting parts of (business) transactions. A transaction is carried out by actors in two roles: the initiator and the executor. The executor brings about the product of the transaction. The process of a transaction is a path, possibly including iterations, through a universal transaction pattern, which consists of one main pattern and six revocation patterns. The latter serve to revert the state in the main pattern to a previous state. Because of the inherent connection between an actor role and the transaction kind of which fillers are the executor, the combination of the two is called transactor role. Transactor roles are the universal building blocks of business processes. Performing a coordination act results in creating the corresponding coordination fact. A fundamental principle in the PSI theory is that actors act autonomously, also if they are guided by business rules. Based on this principle, definitions are developed for the notions of authority, responsibility, accountability and competence.

> *Every organised human activity—from the making of pots to the placing of a man on the moon—gives rise to two fundamental and opposing requirements: the division of labor into various tasks to be performed and the coordination of these tasks to accomplish the activity.*
> (Henry Mintzberg [1])

Reprinted from J. L. G. Dietz, H. B. F. Mulder, *Enterprise Ontology*, The Enterprise Engineering Series, https://doi.org/10.1007/978-3-031-53361-7_8

J. L. G. Dietz, H. B. F. Mulder, *Enterprise Design Fundamentals*, The Enterprise Engineering Series, https://doi.org/10.1007/978-3-031-83262-8_6

6.1 Introduction

The statement by Henry Mintzberg, quoted above, comprises the core problem of organising: how to divide the total amount of work, how to assign the resulting parts to workers and how to arrange the necessary coordination among them. The quote also hints to the prospect that it could be possible to understand the notion of organisation in a very general way. But how should one conceive work and workers, so that a universal notion of organisation emerges, particularly in current practice, where the pervasiveness of ICT applications[1] blurs the sight on the organisation? Achieving this goal has been the ambition of a long-lasting research that started in the early 1990s and that resulted in the present Ψ-theory. The Greek letter Ψ is pronounced as PSI, which is an acronym for Performing in Social Interaction. It is about human cooperation in enterprises, and it is classified as an ontological theory in the framework of theories (cf. Chap. 4), meaning that it is about the nature of things.

The PSI theory exclusively takes the construction perspective (cf. Chap. 5) on enterprises, thus disregarding all functional aspects. Therefore, we will try to consistently use the specific construction-oriented term 'organisation' instead of the general term 'enterprise'. The operation of an organisation is defined as the manifestation of its construction in the course of time. In concordance with the DELTA theory ([2], Chap. 9), every organisation is a discrete event system, in the category of social systems [3]. By the construction of an organisation is understood the triple of its composition, its environment and its structure (cf. [2], Chap. 9). The elements in the composition and the environment are social individuals, commonly called subjects, and the structure of an organisation consists of mutual influencing bonds between these subjects. These bonds are explained by the OMEGA theory ([2], Chap. 10).

Section 6.2 (foundations) starts with a recapitulation of the CIAO Paradigm from Chap. 4. Communication is the primal notion in understanding organisations. Communicating is (also) acting, or as Austin [4] puts it, people do things with words. In the PSI theory, this is accentuated by distinguishing coordination acts and production acts and by bringing them together in the concepts of business conversation and business transaction. In addition, the process of performing a coordination act is discussed. In Sect. 6.3 (elaborations), several time aspects of transactions are highlighted, followed by a discussion of the operating cycle of actors. Next, attention is paid to crucial factors in organisations, like authority, responsibility, accountability and competence. In Sect. 6.4 (discussions), the PSI theory is compared to several similar approaches, and the practical importance of the PSI theory is discussed.

[1] By ICT applications are understood all artefacts that are implemented using ICT (information and communication technology). They include all AI (artificial intelligence) artefacts.

6.2 Foundations

6.2.1 Recapitulation of the CIAO Paradigm

In general, the best way of addressing the potentials of a new technology is to step back and to reconsider how one actually did think about the field of application before its introduction and to find new, better ways of thinking, following Einstein's thought, 'We can't solve problems by using the same kind of thinking we used when we created them', often paraphrased as out-of-the-box thinking. Initially, the office workers in enterprises, including accountants, considered ICT[2] as a more efficient alternative for the existing paper-based data processing technology. Therefore, the original name was 'Electronic Data Processing' (EDP). It took until around 1975 before EDP was replaced by ISE (Information Systems Engineering) or by like names. The shift of attention from the form to the content of information was a paradigm shift. By this, the *information-centric* view on information systems was born.

But the wrong belief among ICT professionals that developing information systems is something that one does 'to the side', after having elicited requirements from the people in the organisation, basically by interviewing these people, persisted. Despite many improvements, this approach to requirements determination has rarely been able to achieve that the delivered systems meet the justified expectations of the users. Around 2000, a new way of thinking emerged, which took communication as the primal notion. From this *communication-centric* view on information systems, the CIAO Paradigm has evolved. The acronym CIAO stands for Communication, Information, Action and Organisation. In this paradigm, *communication*[3] is defined as the sharing of thoughts between (human) minds and *information* as the means to achieve this. As articulated by the ALPHA theory (Chap. 7), every information system can be conceived as some implementation of some part of the organisation, thereby applying ICT. The CIAO paradigm definitely solves the requirements problem: if one understands the operation of an organisation fully and properly, one also understands the (functional) requirements of a supporting information system.

In addition, communication became understood as a form of *action*. In Habermas' Theory of Communicative Action [5], the elementary instance of communication is the *communicative act*. It consists of four parts: performer, intention, addressee and proposition, as exhibited in Fig. 6.1.

---

[2] ICT stands for information and communication technology. It refers specially to the modern practice of applying digital electronic, optical, etc. means to process, store and transmit data.

[3] The English word 'communicate' comes from the Latin word *communicare*, which means 'making something common'. In a more specific sense, it means 'sharing thoughts'.

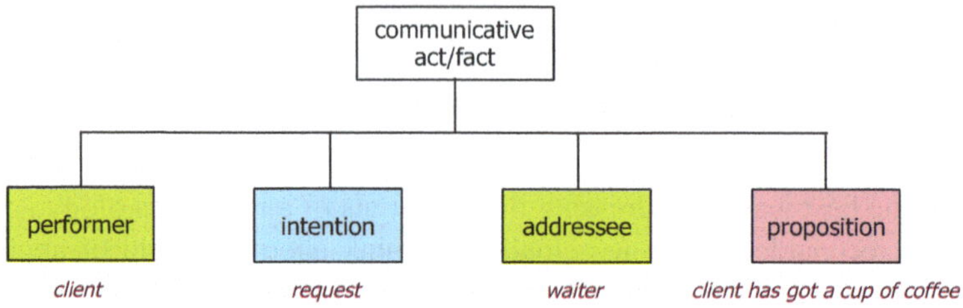

Fig. 6.1 The structure of a communicative act/fact

The *performer* and the *addressee* are human beings, in their quality of social individual, which means being capable to engage into and comply with commitments. The *proposition* is a state of affairs that is or that can be the case. The *intention* is the intent of the performer (a client in the café example) towards the addressee (a waiter in the café example), with respect to the proposition. If the intention is 'request', the performer wants the addressee to make the proposition become true. In the café case, the client wants the waiter to bring her a cup of coffee.

According to Habermas [5], the performer of a communicative act raises three validity claims towards the addressee: the claim to rightness, the claim to sincerity and the claim to truth. The claims have to be assessed by the addressee, and the result of this assessment will guide her/him in her/his response. By accepting the *claim to rightness* in the above example, the waiter recognises the authority of the client to make the request: according to the applicable societal norms or laws, she is allowed to place orders in the café. By accepting the *claim to sincerity*, the waiter expresses that he considers the client to be honest and trustworthy in making the request. It includes that she complies with the applicable terms of sale (implying, e.g. that she has to pay for the service). By accepting the *claim to truth*, the waiter expresses that he is able to make the proposition true. If all three claims are accepted, the waiter responds by a promise. Otherwise, he will decline the request, which brings the transaction process in the discussion state 'declined' (cf. Sect. 6.2.6).

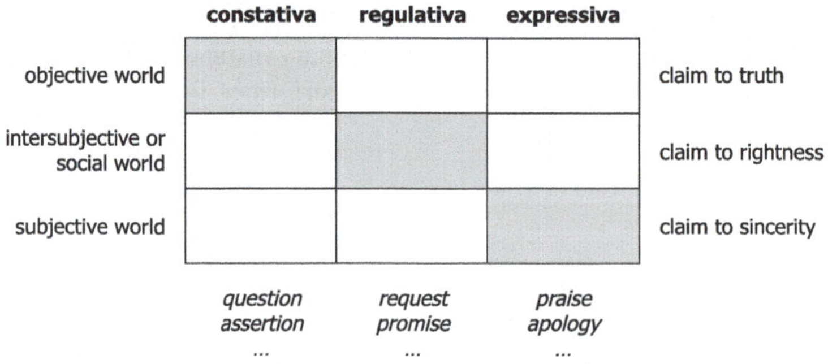

Fig. 6.2 Habermas' three categories of communicative acts

There is always one validity claim dominant. Based on this dominance, Habermas distinguishes three categories of communicative acts and three worlds in which they have effect (cf. Fig. 6.2). The dominance of a claim, as well as the related world, is indicated by the grey-coloured rectangles. In the category of *constativa*, the dominant claim is the claim to truth, and the world with which they are concerned is the *objective world*. Examples of constativa are questions and assertions. If a railway passenger asks a railway officer for the departure time of the next train to Amsterdam, the dominant claim is the claim to truth. Facts like the departure time of trains are considered to exist in the objective world. In the category of *expressiva*, the dominant claim is the claim to sincerity, and the world with which they are concerned is everyone's private *subjective world*. Examples of expressiva are praises and apologies. If the railway passenger starts by saying 'I'm sorry to disturb you, madam…', then the dominant claim in this phrase is the claim to sincerity. In the category of *regulativa*, the dominant claim is the claim to rightness, and the world with which they are concerned is the *intersubjective* or *social world*. Examples of regulativa are requests and promises. If the client in the café asks the waiter for a cup of coffee, the dominant claim is the claim to rightness, i.e. the client claims that she has the authority to make the request.

Because people are not able to directly connect their minds, some vehicle for communication is needed, and this vehicle is information or, more precisely, signs, which is the preferred term in semiotics [6]. A major outcome of this scientific field is the semiotic ladder (cf. Fig. 6.3). It clarifies the role of signs in the communication between human beings. A unit of *information* is the dyad of content and form, meaning that the parts are distinguishable but not separable. The content of an information item is the *thought* (cf. Chap. 5) that one wants to share, and the agreed-upon perceivable shapes constitute the form, thus the *sign*. The content comprises both the intention (or pragmatics) and the proposition (or semantics) of the thought, and the form comprises both the formalism (or syntax) and the coding (or empirics) of the sign.

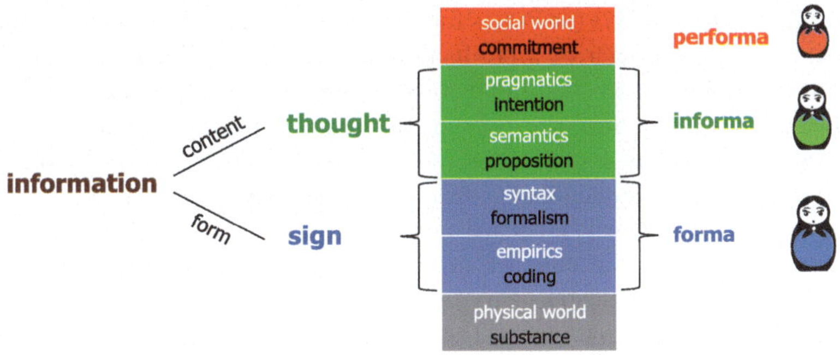

Fig. 6.3 The semiotic ladder

In the café example, the client has, at some point in time, got the thought that she wants a cup of coffee. In order to share this thought, she has to express it in a sign that is intelligible to the waiter. The proposition of the thought is 'client has got a cup of coffee', and the intention is the request. By performing the request, she enters into a commitment towards the waiter. The client may have expressed her thought in this English sentence, 'I'd like to have a cup of coffee, please', which constitutes the sign part in Fig. 6.3. The applied formalism is the English grammar, and the coding regards the construction of the words. The substance in which the sentence is inscribed consists of air vibrations, produced by the client and perceived by the waiter.

Regarding the concept of *action*, the communication-centric view means to say that communicating is acting. In the PSI theory, this is accentuated by distinguishing coordination acts and production acts (cf. Sect. 6.2.2) and by combining them in the concepts of business conversation (cf. Sect. 6.2.4) and business transaction (cf. Sect. 6.2.5). Consequently, the word 'in' in the explanation 'Performing in Social Interaction' of PSI has a twofold meaning. It means that coordination acts, like requesting a cup of coffee, are performed in communication and thus in social interaction. In addition, it means that production acts, like making and delivering a cup of coffee, are performed in patterns of social interactions (cf. Sect. 6.2.6).

The (new) concept of *organisation* is that it is a system of transactor roles, the universal building blocks of organisations (discussed in Sect. 6.2.7). There are three kinds of influencing relationships between actor roles (cf. [2], Chap. 10).

6.2.2 Work Is Production Plus Coordination

6.2.2.1 Production Acts and Facts

As postulated by the DELTA theory ([2], Chap. 9), all acts, in all systems, of all categories, can be divided into two sorts: production acts and coordination acts. By performing *production acts* (or P-acts for short), the subjects in an organisation create products. The character of a production act can be tangible (like transporting goods) or intangible (like becoming member of a library). The effect of performing a P-act is the creation of the corresponding independent P-fact, together with a number of dependent P-facts. Examples of independent P-facts are 'membership 387 is started', 'rental 1087 is concluded', 'the car of rental 1087 is issued' and 'sale 1618 is completed'. Dependent P-facts are called *dependent* because they start to exist (come into being) as a consequence of, and together with, an *independent* P-fact. Independent P-facts are mostly unary facts (concerning an entity), whereas dependent P-facts are always binary facts. They constitute the *properties* (or *attributes*) of the entity (cf. [2], Chap. 5). The combination of an independent P-fact and all of its related dependent P-facts is called a *product*.

As an example, the independent P-fact 'membership 387 is started' is an instance of the P-fact type '[membership] is started', which is a logical predication over the class MEMBERSHIP. The term '[membership]' is a placeholder, or variable, that can be instantiated; membership 387 could be one of its instances. Possible properties (or attributes) of membership 387 are that the concerned member is Shakha Mirza and that the starting day (in Julian days, cf. [2], Chap. 6) is 2458209, which equals 1 April 2018 in the Gregorian calendar.

Independent P-fact types (or product kinds) are formulated in such a way that the instances are *unique in time and space*. To illustrate this, if it is allowed that one can be a member of a tennis club several times during one's lifetime, there is only one proper way to deal with it. It is to adopt the notion of membership, whose instances are *unique in time*. By space is meant the state space of the production world (cf. Sect. 6.2.6.1). *Unique in space* means that there can only exist one membership 387 in any state of the world. In other words, membership 387 is a unique entity.

As said, the fact 'membership 387 is started' is an instance of the independent fact type '[membership] is started'. Together with its dependent facts, like 'the member of membership 387 is Shakha Mirza' and 'the starting day of membership 387 is 2458209', it is the product of a transaction of the kind TK01 'membership starting' from the tennis club Volley that is elaborated in [2], Chap. 12. Instead of these precise formulations of transaction product and independent fact type, we will hereafter often speak of P-fact or P-fact type while meaning independent P-fact or independent P-fact type or even the complete product (or product kind).

Lastly, one should be aware that a phrase like 'membership 387 is started' is just the formulation of a proposition (or independent P-fact). It is not the assertion that the proposition is true.[4] The proposition may become true at some point in time, which means that the corresponding P-fact becomes existent at that point in time.

6.2.2.2 Coordination Acts and Facts

Coordination acts (or C-acts for short) are communicative acts in Habermas' category of regulativa (cf. Fig. 6.2). Its generic structure is exhibited in Fig. 6.4, which is a refinement of Fig. 6.1. The illustrating example is taken from the case wheelbarrows, as discussed in [7]. The performer of the act is Gnome 463, in his role of buyer on behalf of the company HORTUS, and the addressee is Gnome 691, in her role of seller on behalf of the company MALUM. The proposition (now called product) is the purchase of a number of wheelbarrows. This is represented by the independent P-fact 'purchase 31416 is fulfilled' (split into the predication 'is fulfilled' and the predicated entity 'purchase 31,416') and the dependent P-facts or properties 'article

[4] In English, like in many natural languages, it is not possible to make a grammatical distinction between the formulation of a proposition and the assertion that the proposition is true. Both are expressed in the same assertive sentence.

type is Quadra 75', 'number of items is 10', 'price is 165 (in the currency of Gnomeland)' and 'delivery day is 731.513 (in the Gnomeland calendar)'. The intention of the C-act/fact is the request. By conveying this intention to Gnome 691, Gnome 463 commits himself to his request, which means that he cannot simply say at some later point in time that he was only joking. Similarly, Gnome 691 will become committed to the response that she is going to perform. C-acts are the *atoms* of business processes. They are ontologically indivisible: one performs a 'complete' request or any other C-act or none.

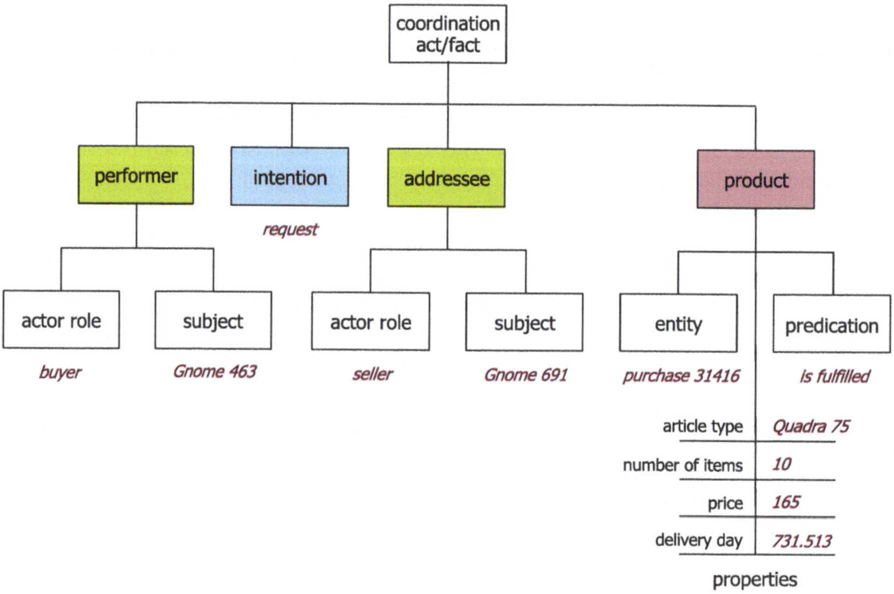

Fig. 6.4 The structure of a coordination act/fact

The coloured parts in the representation of a C-act/fact in the figure constitute the *normal form* of a C-act/fact, formally defined as follows (plus an example in which the performer and the addressee are indicated as <actor role>/<subject>):

<performer> : <intention> : <addressee> : <product>
buyer/Gnome 463 : request : seller/Gnome 691 : purchase 31416 is fulfilled

6.2.3 The Process of a Coordination Act

Corresponding with the semiotic ladder (cf. Fig. 6.3), we distinguish three abilities that communicating subjects need to dispose of: the *forma* ability (in order to deal with codings and formalisms), the *informa* ability (in order to deal with propositions and intentions) and the *performa* ability (in order to deal with commitments). These abilities are shown, on the right side of Fig. 6.3, as three shapes that human beings can take on. Note that the material world (dealing with substances) is not covered by the performa-informa-forma distinction. Sometimes, we will consider it included in the forma ability. In Fig. 6.5, the material (grey) shape is added to the elaborated explanation of the process of a coordination act, as is the blank shape, which represents the most inner self of every subject. There reside the wisdom and love that are considered to constitute the basis for deciding on how to comply with commitments. The Russian doll shapes in this figure are scaled, to illustrate that they should be understood as being enclosed in each other, from top to bottom. The first shape that one perceives is the grey one. One has to 'peel off' to reach the inner ones.

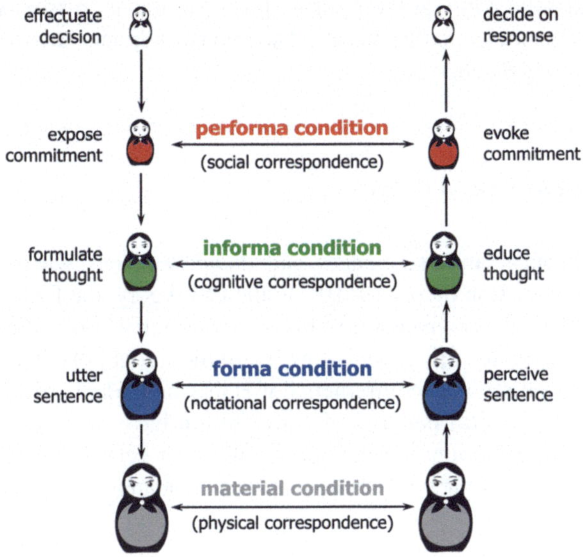

Fig. 6.5 The process of a coordination act

In order to effectuate a decision to perform a C-act, the subject on the left side of Fig. 6.5 has to expose the corresponding commitment in her/his 'red' shape, i.e. by applying its performa ability. Because it is impossible to convey the commitment directly to the addressee, he/she has to formulate, in her/his 'green' shape, a thought that contains the commitment. As we know from Sect. 6.2.1, the thought consists of a proposition and an intention. As it is impossible to share the thought directly with the addressee, the subject has to utter, in her/his 'blue' shape, a sentence that expresses the thought. In order to make the sentence perceivable to the addressee, he/she has, in her/his 'grey' shape, to inscribe the sentence in some substance and have the inscription transmitted through a proper communication channel to the addressee. This action succeeds if the message arrives undistorted. If so, the two subjects have achieved *physical correspondence*: the *material condition* is satisfied. The addressee is now able, in her/his 'blue' shape, to perceive the inscribed sentence from the transmitted substance. If he/she succeeds, the two subjects have achieved *notational correspondence*: the *forma condition* is satisfied. Next, the addressee can educe, in her/his 'green' shape, the thought from the sentence, so the contained proposition and intention. If he/she succeeds, the two subjects have achieved *cognitive correspondence*: the *informa condition* is satisfied. Then, in her/his 'red' shape, the addressee has to evoke in her/his mind the commitment that the performer of the C-act wanted to convey. If he/she succeeds, the two subjects have achieved *social correspondence*: the *performa condition* is satisfied. Lastly, the addressee has to decide on how he/she will respond in her/his blank shape, after which a similar process takes place for sharing the decision with the other subject. At every level, but specifically at the informa level, the addressee confirms or disconfirms the message. Only at the informa level can the addressee be sure that he/she understands the message thoroughly. The two participants have to communicate until this situation is reached.

6.2.4 Business Conversations

Communicative acts occur in sequences, called *conversations*, which are the objects of interest in conversation theory [8–10]. In the PSI theory, the focus is on *business conversations*, defined as conversations that take place in an institutional setting and of which the participants aim at achieving a common goal [11]. These participants are considered to satisfy the requirements of Habermas' ideal speech situation.[5] In the course of time, several patterns of conversation have been identified, like the conversation for information and the conversation for action [12]. Based on these studies, we distinguish four kinds of conversations: actagenic conversations, facta-

[5] Habermas has elucidated and elaborated the notion of 'ideal speech situation' in his book *Moral Consciousness and Communicative Action*. This a relevant quote: 'A measure of whether or not participants in communication reach agreement is the yes or no position taken by the hearer whereby he accepts or rejects the claim to validity that has been raised by the speaker. In the attitude oriented toward reaching understanding, the speaker raises with every intelligible utterance the claim that the utterance in question is true (or that the existential presuppositions of the propositional content hold true), that the speech act is right in terms of a given normative context (or that the normative context that it satisfies is itself legitimate), and that the speaker's manifest intentions are meant in the way they are expressed. When someone rejects what is offered in an intelligible speech act, he denies the validity of an utterance in at least one of three respects: truth, rightness, or truthfulness. His "no" signals that the utterance has failed to fulfil at least one of its three functions (the representation of states of affairs, the maintenance of an interpersonal relationship, or the manifestation of lived experience) because the utterance is not in accordance with either the world of existing states of affairs, our world of legitimately ordered interpersonal relations, or each participant's own world of subjective lived experience. These aspects are not clearly distinguished in normal everyday communication. Yet in cases of disagreement or persistent problematisation, competent speakers can differentiate between the aforementioned three relations to the world, thematising individual validity claims and focusing on something that confronts them, whether it be something objective, something normative or something subjective'.

genic conversations, reversiogenic conversations and cogitatiogenic conversations.[6] Henceforth, we assume that a conversation involves two participants, but we allow that a participant is the collectivity of a number of subjects (cf. Sect. 6.2.7).

An *actagenic conversation*, or *A-conversation* for short, is a conversation in which the participants strive to reach consensus about a product that one of them is going to bring about at the other's request. The key C-acts in an A-conversation are the *request* and the *promise*. Both must be present for a successful conversation, and in this order, because the promise is a response to the request. However, except for the order, they may occur at any place in the conversation. An example of an A-conversation in the café situation is given below (where C is the client and W the waiter). The request is expressed in the fourth line and the corresponding promise in the fifth line.

W:	Good morning madam. What a wonderful weather you bring with you.	
C:	Yes, indeed. It is beautiful outside. I think I will go for a walk later today.	
W:	A very good idea, I would say, madam. What can I do for you?	
C:	I think, I'd like to have a cup of coffee.	[request]
W:	I will bring it right away, madam. Anything else?	[promise]
C:	No thanks, that's all.	

A *factagenic conversation*, or *F-conversation* for short, is a conversation in which the participants strive to reach consensus about a brought-about product. The key C-acts in an F-conversation are the *declare* and the *accept*. Both must be present for a successful conversation, and in this order, because the acceptance is a response to the declaration. Except for the order, they may occur at any place in the conversation. F-conversations typically go together with A-conversations in the frame of transactions, to be discussed in Sect. 6.2.5. An example of an F-conversation in the café situation that matches the A-conversation above could be:

W:	Here you are, madam, a fresh cup of coffee, the best in town!	[declare]
C:	Ha ha, I hope so, sir. What makes you think it is the best in town?	
W:	Just gut feeling, madam. Anyway, I know no better one!	
C:	Well, let me see whether I can agree with you.	[accept]
W:	I bet you will!	

A *reversiogenic conversation*, or *R-conversation* for short, is a conversation in which the participants strive to agree on reverting (turning back) the current state in an A- or an F-conversation, in which they (also) participate. As will be shown in Sects. 6.2.6.4–6.2.6.7, one can even revert a complete transaction in this way. The key C-acts in a successful R-conversation are the *revoke*, followed by the *allow*. An

[6] The words actagenic, factagenic, reversiogenic and cogitatiogenic mean, respectively, act creating, fact creating, reversion creating and idea or plan creating.

example of an R-conversation in the café situation, right after the A-conversation above, when the waiter is already on his way to get the coffee, could be:

C:	Oh, waiter, please, on second thoughts … do you have cappuccino?	[revoke rq]
W:	Sure, madam, and it's no problem at all that you changed your mind.	[allow]
C:	Oh, thanks a lot. You are very kind. So, a cappuccino please.	[request]
W:	As you wish, madam.	[promise]

The revoke of the request is expressed in the first line, and the corresponding allows in the second one. The third and fourth line contain the new request and the corresponding promise. They are not part of the R-conversation, however. The example contains also an informational transaction (cf. Chap. 11), namely, in the last part of the first sentence and the first part of the second sentence. In this transaction, the availability of cappuccino is checked by the client and confirmed by the waiter.

As said, an A-conversation is successful if the state of being promised is reached. In case of no success, the state of the conversation can be reverted by a successful corresponding R-conversation. Likewise, an F-conversation is successful if the state of being accepted is reached. In case of no success, the state of the conversation can be reverted by a successful corresponding R-conversation. An R-conversation is said to be successful if the intended reversion is achieved, i.e. if the state of an A- or an F-conversation is reverted. In case of no success, the state in the A- or F-conversation will remain unchanged.

A *cogitatiogenic conversation*, or *C-conversation* for short, is a conversation in which the participants strive to reach consensus about a plan for future action or, more concrete, about the product of a transaction. C-conversations are typically held in preparation of a decision to perform a C-act in an A-, F- or R-conversation, in particular to settle a request or a declaration. They include notably the conversations in the discussion states that we will see in Sect. 6.2.6. Because C-conversations are mostly conducted for understanding a transaction product (more) complete or clear, the 'C' is often understood as the first letter of *completeness* or *clarity*. Contrary to the other three kinds of conversations, C-conversations are basically informational; thus, they do not contain original acts (cf. Chap. 7), like the ones we discussed up to now (cf. Fig. 6.9). We will take up informational acts in Chap. 7. Their existence and their relevance are recognised though. An example of a C-conversation in the café situation, preceding the formal part of the A-conversation above, is:

W:	Good morning madam. What a wonderful weather you bring with you.
C:	Yes, indeed, it is beautiful outside. I think I will go for a walk later today.
W:	A very good idea, I would say, madam. What can I do for you?
C:	I don't know yet. I just came in because I wanted to have something
	stimulating. I feel a bit groggy, perhaps of the wine last night.
W:	Then I can recommend a cup of coffee or, if you don't feel for it, a glass of
	fresh mint tea.
C:	Hmm, well, coffee sounds like a good idea. Let me think about it.

6.2.5 Business Transactions

A (business) *transaction*[7] is a sequence of C-acts/facts, within a specific pattern called the transaction pattern, concerning some product. It involves two actors, one in the role of *initiator* and one in the role of *executor*. An actor is a subject in filling an actor role. The notions of actor and actor role are elaborated in Sect. 6.2.7.

The best general understanding of a transaction is that it proceeds in three phases: the order phase, the execution phase and the result phase. The *order phase* is an A-conversation in which the two actors discuss and negotiate in order to come to agreement about a product (cf. Sect. 6.2.2) that the executor can promise to bring about in response to the request by the initiator. The properties (or attributes) of the product include the terms of delivery (time, price, etc.) that are common in (business) transactions. In this phase, the product is often called *proposition*. In the *execution phase*, the executor produces some product (which may differ from the promised one). The initiator is basically ignorant of what the executor does in this phase. The *result phase* is an F-conversation in which the two actors discuss and negotiate in order to come to agreement about the actually brought about product so that it can responsibly be accepted by the initiator. In this phase, the product is often called *result*. While in the order phase, basically all properties of the product are negotiable, some are still also negotiable in the result phase, notably attributes like price and delivery time. As an example in the café, the client may not be fully satisfied with the declared product if the coffee is not really warm. Instead of producing a fresh cup of coffee (something that will be discussed in Sect. 6.2.6), the two actors could agree on a lower price (Note: Paying is a separate transaction, as discussed in [2], Chap. 10).

6.2.6 Transaction Patterns

6.2.6.1 The Basic Transaction Pattern

The DELTA theory ([2], Chap. 9) postulates that the *state* of a world at some point in time is the set of facts that are created up to that point in time. The becoming existent of a fact is called an *event*. So, an event is a change of state at a particular point in time, called the *event time*. The C-acts and P-acts in an organisation cause events in, respectively, its *coordination world* (or C-world) and its *production world* (or P-world). This is illustrated in Fig. 6.6. The two subjects in the middle interact through the creation of C-facts (represented by small disks), which are the immediate results of performing C-acts (represented by small boxes). For example, the effect of performing a request is the creation of the fact of being requested. Likewise,

[7] The noun 'transaction' is related to the verb 'to transact', which originates from the Latin verb *transigere*, meaning carrying out, bringing through.

the effect of a P-act (represented by a small box) is a P-fact (represented by a small diamond). Recall that every C-act/fact concerns a specific P-fact. As will become clear, the number of C-events is always much larger than the number of P-events. The light-grey colouring of the shapes of the P-acts and P-facts will be explained later.

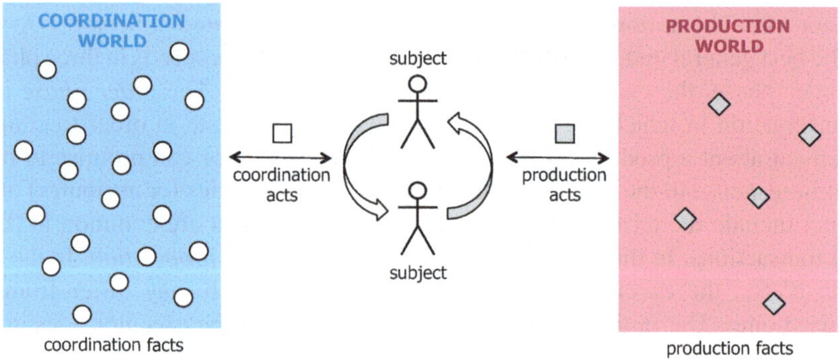

Fig. 6.6 The coordination world and the production world of an organisation

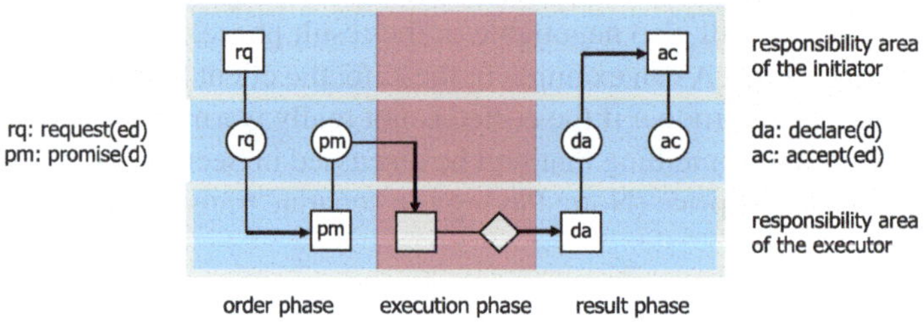

Fig. 6.7 The basic transaction pattern

In Fig. 6.7, the *basic transaction pattern* is shown. It contains the five steps that must always be performed in order to let a transaction succeed: the request and the promise in the A-conversation (the order phase), the declaration and the acceptance in the F-conversation (the result phase) and performing the P-act in between (the execution phase). The symbols used are explained in Table 6.1. In the café example, the first step is the performing of a request by the client (the initiator) for a cup of coffee, addressed to the waiter (the executor). We have entered now the order phase of the transaction. The second step is the promise by the waiter to bring the cup of coffee. With this step, the order phase ends successfully, and the execution phase starts, in which the waiter makes the cup of coffee and brings it to the client. The shapes of the P-act and the P-fact in Fig. 6.7, as well as those in Fig. 6.6, are coloured light grey to indicate that they are private to the executor. They are not directly knowable to the initiator. After this step, the waiter addresses himself to the client again and declares the result of his work, which is the fourth step. At this moment, the created P-fact is knowable to the initiator, as part of the created C-fact (cf. Fig. 6.4). We have entered now the result phase of the transaction. This phase ends successfully if the client accepts the declared result, which is the fifth transaction step.

The two light-grey lined rectangles in Fig. 6.7 indicate the *responsibility areas* of the two participants: the initiator is responsible for the request and the acceptance and the executor for the promise, the P-act and the declaration. The notion of responsibility will be elaborated in Sect. 6.3.3. In order to indicate that they are knowable to both actors, the conversation states (C-facts) are put in between these rectangles. Note that we abstract completely from the particular way in which the steps in Fig. 6.7 are performed. This abstraction is one of the key elements in calling the understanding of organisations that the PSI theory provides, *ontological*. The other key element is the being rooted of this understanding in the *atomicity* of C-acts/facts and in the *molecularity* of transaction kinds and actor roles. Note also that the pattern in Fig. 6.7 makes the communication between the initiator and the executor *asynchronous*. To illustrate this, the fact of being requested exists from the moment that the request act is performed. The addressee (thus the executor) takes notice of the fact when it suits her/him (cf. Sect. 6.3.2).

Table 6.1 Legend of the links in transaction patterns

	*causal link*: performing C-act A causes the becoming existent of C-fact F; this is identical to saying that performing A causes the occurrence of the C-event F
	*response link*: C-act A is performed in response to the occurrence of C-event F
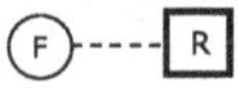	*conditional link*: in order to perform the *revocation* C-act R successfully, the C-fact F must exist (which is identical to saying that reached state F in the main process is reached)
	F+ means: the state of the main process is F or further; e.g., if F is 'declared', then F+ means that the state is 'declared' or 'accepted' or 'rejected'
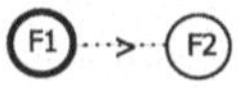	*reversion link*: reaching state F1 (in a revocation process) implies the instantaneous transition to state F2 in the main process

C-acts may be performed *verbally*, for example, by uttering sentences like 'I'd like to have a cup of coffee, please' as a way to request, but they may also be performed *non-verbally*, which means that some other act counts as the C-act (like just putting the cup of coffee in front of the client as a way of performing the declaration). In both cases, the evidence of the act is *explicit*. In addition, C-acts may be performed *tacitly*, which means that there is no evidence of acts that could count as performing them. Still they are performed, but the evidence is said to be *implicit*: they can be deduced from the presence or the absence of other acts. To illustrate this, if the waiter doesn't perform an explicit promise, the client may deduce it from the absence of an explicit decline (cf. Sect. 6.2.6). Next, when the waiter brings the cup of coffee and thereby performs the declare act, the client may deduce the promise from the presence of this act. As one may expect, tacitly performed C-acts are a major cause of business process failures: an actor may be waiting for an explicit C-event that will never occur, because the other actor thinks there is no need for it (no news is good news).

The product of a transaction, i.e. the independent P-fact together with its dependent P-facts (cf. Sect. 6.2.2), will only become existent after a successful completion of the result phase. In this way, P-acts/facts are firmly connected to C-acts/facts: the resulting product becomes existent if and when it is accepted by the initiator of the transaction. Consequently, every P-fact is the result of a successfully completed transaction (or it is derived from such original facts, cf. [2], Chap. 6).

Moreover, the initiator may accept a result that differs from the requested product. Let us take the café example again to illustrate this. Suppose that the client has asked for a double espresso and the waiter delivers a cappuccino. Most people would reject the declare act by the waiter in such a case, but it is perfectly fine if the client accepts it. The example emphasises that the most important world for human beings is Habermas' intersubjective or social world (cf. Fig. 6.2). This basic understanding of the 'nature' of P-facts reflects our basic understanding of the 'nature' of societal institutions, namely, that they are primarily intersubjective or social constructs, in accordance with the core message in [13].

The carrying out of a transaction (of whatever kind) can be taken as a generic *business process* building block, and the C- and P-acts in transactions can be taken as a generic notion of *task*, seeming to be more precise than the one that is implicitly used in Mintzberg's quote above Sect. 6.1.

6.2.6.2 The Standard Transaction Pattern

Figure 6.8 exhibits an extension of the basic pattern. Note that the diamond of the P-fact is drawn in the box of the P-act (to save space) that the phase colours are omitted and that the accept act and fact have got another place (for convenience reasons). Moreover, we have added the external state (C-fact) called 'in' (from initial). It represents the becoming existent of some state in some process. From now on, we will refer to acts and facts in the next concise way: we use the brackets '(' and ')' for a C-fact or transaction state, '<' and '>' for a P-fact and '[' and ']' for a C-act or a P-act. As an example, [rq] denotes the act of requesting, and (rq) denotes the fact of being requested.

The basic transaction process is represented by the green path. It is commonly called the success layer or happy flow. As discussed in Sect. 6.2.1, the performer of a C-act raises three *validity claims* towards the addressee: the claim to rightness, the claim to sincerity and the claim to truth. All three of them must be accepted by the addressee in order to proceed successfully. If the executor accepts the validity claims that are raised by the initiator in performing the request, he will respond by a promise. This is indicated in Fig. 6.8 by the green path from (rq) via [pm] to (pm). If one or more validity claims are not satisfied, the executor will decline the request, which brings the transaction process in the state declined. This is indicated in Fig. 6.8 by the yellow path from (rq) via [dc] to (dc).

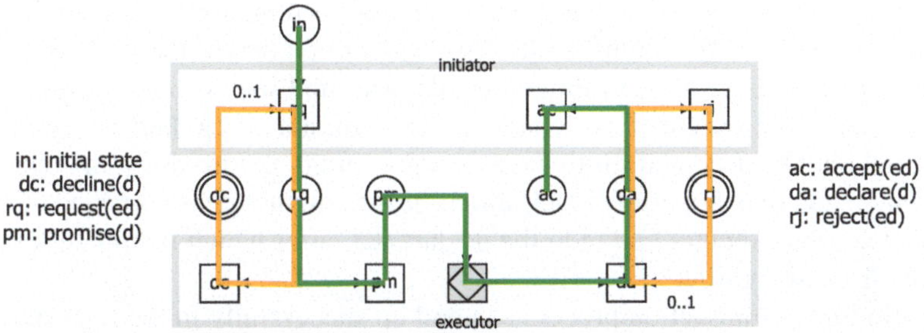

Fig. 6.8 The standard transaction pattern

The state (dc) is a *discussion* state, indicated by the double disk. Ending up there is most likely not what the initiator had in mind. If only the claim to truth was turned down (e.g. because the coffee machine is broken), the two participants can discuss other products, like a coffee later (after repair of the machine) or another drink now. If the claim to rightness or the claim to sincerity was turned down, the participants will enter a *discourse*. The social norms and social values of the participants are now at stake. Both Habermas [5] and Van Reijswoud [14] consider the discussions be carried out at a deeper conceptual layer than the success layer, which they consequently call the *discussion layer*. Likewise, they consider discourses be carried out at an even deeper layer, which they call the *discourse layer*. We adopt the distinction, as made by Habermas and Van Reijswoud between discussion and discourse, but we allow discourses to take place only 'in' discussion states.

During the discourse 'in' the state (dc), the initiator can challenge the executor to explain why a validity claim could not be accepted. Both have the opportunity to turn down the objections of the other, and they hopefully reach an agreement, so that the transaction can be proceeded. The proceeding is indicated in Fig. 6.8 by the yellow path from (dc) via [rq] to (rq). The executor can then perform the promise of the (possibly adapted) request, thus following the green path from (rq) via [pm] to (pm). Note that performing a new request is optional, as indicated by the cardinality range 0..1. The initiator can remain dissatisfied by the discussion or the discourse and do nothing, which means that the process remains in the state (dc). In Sects. 6.2.6.4–6.2.6.9, we will present ways to get out of this and other dead lock(s).

Let's assume now that the process has reached the state declared. The initiator may then accept the declared product, by which the transaction ends successfully. This is indicated in Fig. 6.8 by the green path from (da) via [ac] to (ac). But the initiator may instead reject the declare, which brings the transaction process in the state rejected, which is a *discussion* state, like the one discussed above. This is indicated in Fig. 6.8 by the yellow path from (da) via [rj] to (rj). If only the claim to truth was turned down (e.g. because the client thinks that the coffee is not fresh or not warm), the two participants may come to agree, for example, on a lower price for the client. If so, the executor performs an adapted declare, where the attribute price has got a different value. This is indicated in Fig. 6.8 by the yellow path from (rj) via [da] to (da). From there, the initiator can perform the acceptance, following the green path up to (ac). Note that a renewed declaration is optional, as indicated by the cardinality range 0..1.

The executor can also do nothing. Then the process remains in the state (rj). If the claim to rightness or the claim to sincerity was turned down, the participants will enter a *discourse*. Like we said above, social norms and social values now dominate the discourse. The executor can challenge the initiator to explain why a validity claim could not be accepted. Both have the opportunity to turn down the objections of the other, and they hopefully reach some agreement, in order to proceed the transaction. If so, the executor can redo the declare act, after which the process follows the path discussed earlier.

Concluding, a transaction process can end up successfully in the final state (ac), but it can also get stuck in one of the discussion states (dc) or (rj). The standard pattern in the middle of Fig. 6.8 offers no options to escape from these deadlock situations. There are two revocation patterns, however, that provide the escapes one may want. They come in addition to the revocations of the four basic steps (rq, pm, da and ac). By revoking a step, one wants to undo what one has performed intentionally earlier, for the reason that one has changed one's mind.

6.2.6.3 The Complete Transaction Pattern

Combining the standard transaction pattern with the revocation patterns yields the *complete transaction pattern* or CTP, exhibited in Fig. 6.9. All six R-conversations are expressed in a similar pattern. In this pattern, the boxes and disks are bold lined, in order to indicate that these conversations are at a *meta level* with regard to the main process, of which they aim to revert the current state to a previous one. The revocation of the promise and the revocation of the decline are combined, as are those of the accept and the reject, only to save space in the diagram.

An R-conversation can be initiated in response to any state in any process. Therefore, its initial state is shown in Fig. 6.9 as a C-fact named '?'. In addition, the R-conversations have a conditional link (cf. Table 6.1) from a state in the main process to the revoke act, meaning that performing the revoke is only possible if the main process has reached this state. For example, for the act [rv-rq], the condition is (rq+); thus, the state of the main process must be (rq) or further. Likewise, the condition is (pm+) for performing [rv-pm] is (pm+), (dc) for [rv-dc], (da+) for [rv-da], (ac) for [rv-ac] and (rj) for [rv-rj].

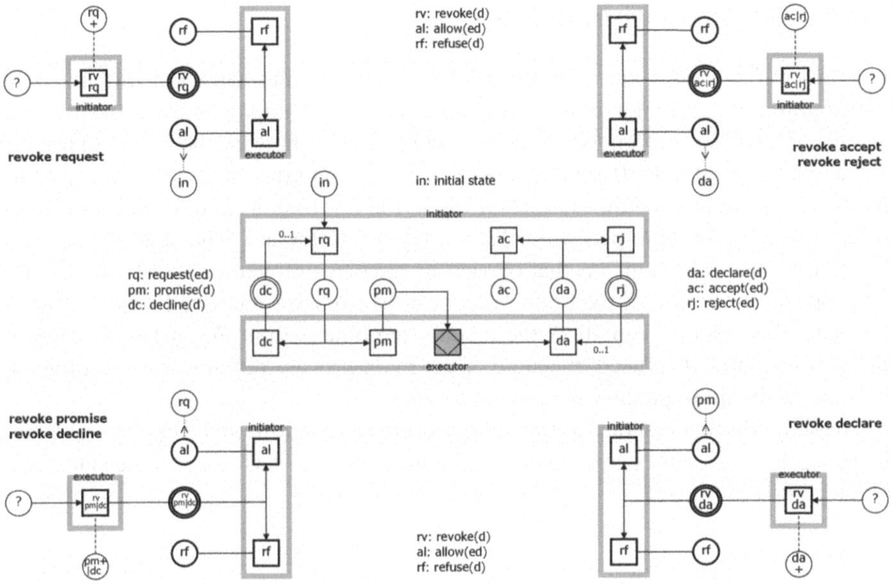

Fig. 6.9 The complete transaction pattern

If an R-conversation is successful, the state of the main process will be reverted to (in) for a revoke of the request, to (rq) for a revoke of the promise or decline, to (pm) for a revoke of the declare and to (da) for a revoke of the accept or reject, as indicated in Fig. 6.9. If an R-conversation is unsuccessful, so if it gets stuck in the corresponding discussion state, the state of the main process remains unchanged.

Concluding, every transaction process is some path (possibly including an arbitrary number of iterations) through the complete transaction pattern, starting from the state (in) and ending up either successfully in the state (ac) or unsuccessfully in one of the discussion states in the standard transaction pattern, namely, (dc) or (rj). A transaction process may also end up in the discussion state of one of the revocation patterns, so in (rv-rq), (rv-pm), (rv-dc), (rv-da), (rv-ac) or (rv-rj).

Although theoretically, every step in a transaction process should be revocable, the six R-conversations in Fig. 6.9 seem to be sufficient in practice. Revocations have a legal counterpart in the Civil Codes of many nations. In these Civil Codes, a (business) commitment cannot be made undone by one party without the explicit allowance of the other party. This legal requirement is fully accommodated by the revocation patterns as presented above. Therefore, the discussed complete transaction pattern is considered to be *universal*.

In Sects. 6.2.6.4–6.2.6.7, the revocation patterns of the basic transaction steps are presented and discussed. Those concerning the decline and the reject act are discussed in Sects. 6.2.6.8 and 6.2.6.9. If a C-act is performed by mistake, it can be *cancelled* (as long as the addressee has not responded, of course).

6.2.6.4 The Revocation of an Acceptance

After having accepted the transaction result (thus the product), the initiator of a transaction may get remorse of having done this, for example, because the product appears to be different from what one expected. He/she then has the option to revoke the accept act. Figure 6.10 exhibits the process of doing this. It starts with performing the act [rv-ac] by the initiator, resulting in the discussion state (rv-ac), indicated in the figure by the blue path from (?) via [rv-ac] to (rv-ac). The state (rv-ac) is a discussion state, which means that two actors have to sit together in order to discuss the proposed reversion of the main process or to engage even in a discourse. From this state, the executor can allow the revoke (the blue path in Fig. 6.10) or refuse it (the yellow path). If refused, the state of the main process remains (ac). If allowed, the state of the main process is reverted to (da).

The dashed line from (ac) to [rv-ac] represents the conditional link. It means that the revocation can only be performed if the main process has reached the state (ac), which is the case.

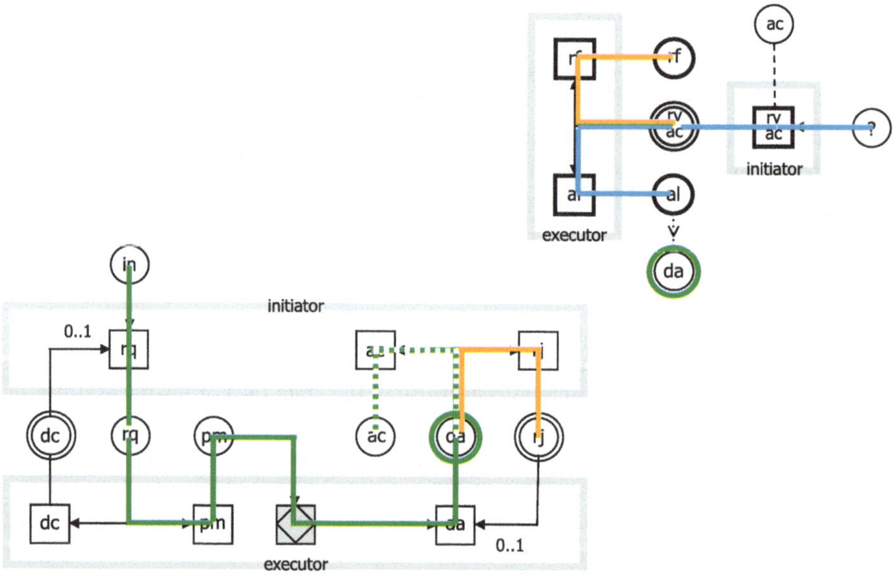

Fig. 6.10 The process of revoking an accept act

As said, the executor may allow the revoke or refuse it. If he/she allows, the main process will return to the state (da), as indicated by the green-white path in the standard pattern and by the green circle around (da). From there, the initiator is able to perform the reject, indicated by the yellow path from (da) via [rj] to (rj). Rejecting is the logical alternative to accepting. As an example in the café, the client may have accepted the delivered cup of coffee but later on discovers that the coffee is not as warm as it should be. She then may call the waiter and tell him that she doesn't want this cup of coffee. This act counts as revoking the accept act. If the waiter allows the revocation, the client can subsequently reject the declaration, by which the main process ends up in (rj). In Sect. 6.2.6.2, we have discussed how the parties can proceed from this discussion state. If the waiter refuses the revocation, the state of the main process remains unchanged, namely, (ac).

6.2.6.5 The Revocation of a Declaration

The executor of a transaction may at any point in time want to undo the declare act. Logically, this entails that he/she wants to redo the P-act and subsequently perform a new declare act. Revoking the declare act is a common response by the executor of a transaction in case the initiator has rejected the declare act, and the executor agrees, during the discussion in the state (rj), on the reason for the reject. As an example in the café, after the client has rejected the acceptance because the coffee was cold, the waiter may want to redo the P-act and the subsequent declare act. In other words, he wants to bring a new, warm, cup of coffee.

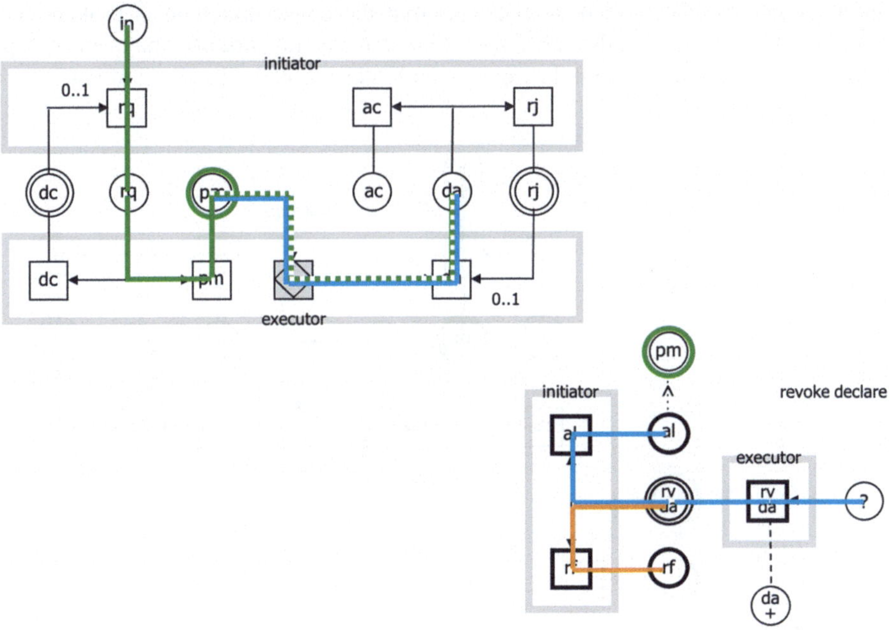

Fig. 6.11 The process of revoking a declare act

The pattern for revoking the declare act is exhibited in Fig. 6.11. It starts with performing the act [rv-da] by the executor, resulting in the state (rv-da), indicated by the blue path from (?) to (rv-da). The conditional link from (da+) to [rv-da] represents the condition that the revocation can only be performed if the state in the main process is at least (da). Thus, it can be performed from any state after, and including (da). This condition is met. The state (rv-da) is considered a discussion state, which means that the two actors have to sit together in order to discuss the proposed turning back of the main transaction process. The initiator may allow the revoke (continued blue path) or refuse it (yellow path). If he/she allows, the state of the main process will be reverted to (pm), as indicated by the green-white path in the standard pattern and by the green circle around (pm). From there, the executor is able to redo the P-act, followed by a new declare act, as indicated by the blue line. If the initiator refuses the revocation, the state of the main process remains unchanged. In Fig. 6.11, this is the state (ac).

Note that a consequence of reverting the process state to (pm) is that the P-act has to be 'undone' in some way. We will take up this topic in Sect. 6.2.6.10.

6.2.6.6 The Revocation of a Promise

The executor of a transaction may at some point in time want to undo the promise act. This will normally happen if he/she discovers that he/she cannot comply with the promise anymore. As an example in the café, the waiter may have promised the client a cup of coffee and then discovers that the coffee machine is broken. By revoking the promise, and the subsequent allowance by the initiator, they can end up in the state declined, in which they can discuss other drinks, like a cup of tea.

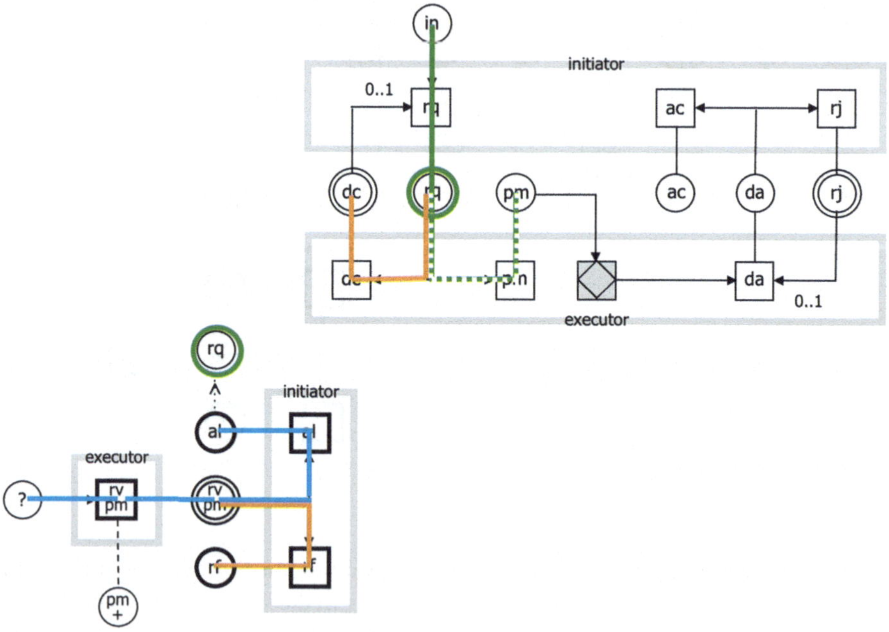

Fig. 6.12 The process of revoking a promise act

The revocation pattern of a promise is exhibited in Fig. 6.12. It starts with the revoke promise [rv-pm] by the executor, resulting in the state (rv-pm), indicated by the blue path from (?) via [rv-pm] to (rv-pm). The conditional link from (pm+) to [rv-pm] represents the condition that the revocation can only be performed if the state in the main process is (pm) or further. This condition is met. The being revoked is a discussion state, which means that the two actors have to sit together in order to discuss the proposed reverting of the main transaction process. The initiator may allow the revoke (continued blue path) or refuse it (yellow path). If he/she allows, the state of the main process will be reverted to (rq), as indicated by the green-white path in the standard pattern and by the green circle around (rq). From there, the executor can decline the request and discuss changes to the product so that he/she will be able to promise it, as indicated by the yellow path. Declining is the logical alternative to promising.

If the initiator refuses the revocation, the state of the main process remains unchanged. In Fig. 6.12, this is the state (pm). This doesn't help the initiator, however, because the executor is apparently unable to bring about what he/she wants. Therefore it seems wiser for the initiator to allow the revoke of the promise and to discuss alternatives in the state (dc). If the discussion doesn't lead to an acceptable alternative, the initiator can always revoke the request.

6.2.6.7 The Revocation of a Request

The initiator of a transaction may at some point in time want to undo the request act. As an example in the café, the client may have asked for a cup of coffee but then gets an urgent telephone call because of which she has to leave immediately. Or after she has ordered a cup of coffee, she changes her mind and wants a cup of tea instead.

The revocation pattern is exhibited in Fig. 6.13. It starts with the revoke request [rv-rq] by the initiator, resulting in the state (rv-rq), indicated by the blue path from (?) via [rv-rq] to (rv-rq). The conditional link from (rq+) to [rv-rq] represents the condition that the revocation can only be performed if the state of the main process (rq) or further. This condition is met. The state (rv-rq) is a discussion state, which means that the two actors have to sit together in order to discuss the proposed turning back of the main transaction process. The executor may allow the revoke, indicated by the continued blue path to (al) or refuse it (the yellow path). If he/she allows, the state of the main process will be reverted to (in), as indicated by the green-white path in the standard pattern and by the green circle around (in). If he/she refuses, the state of the main process remains what it is. In Fig. 6.13, this is the state (ac).

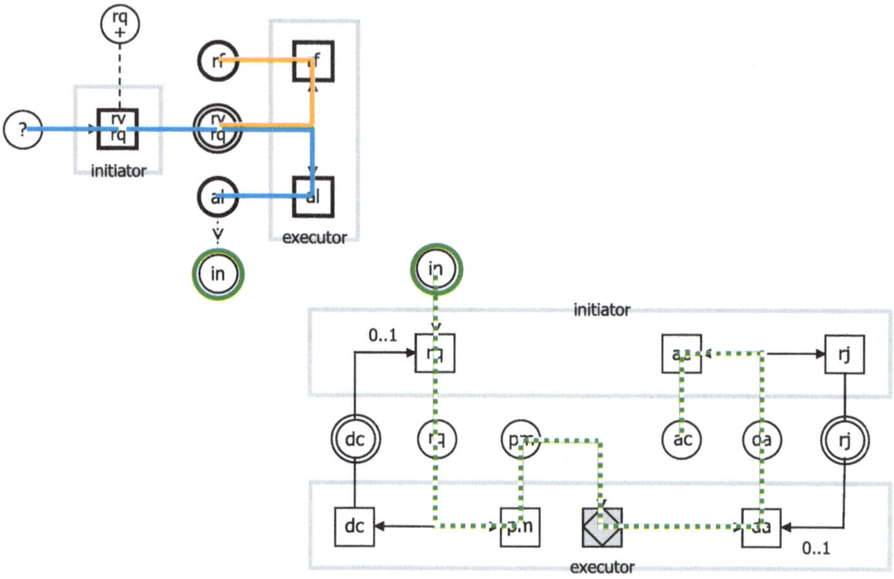

Fig. 6.13 The process of revoking a request act

So, a revoke request can even be performed from the state (ac), as shown in Fig. 6.13, when the transaction has been completed successfully. A common example is that one has bought something from a shop and returns it, e.g. because one sees no need for having it anymore. The being revoked is a discussion state, which means that the two actors have to sit together in order to discuss the proposed reversion of the main transaction process. The executor may allow the revoke (continued blue path) or refuse it (yellow path). The main process will then be reverted to the state (in), and both parties are freed of all obligations. In other words, the transaction is completely 'rolled back'. Note that in practice, there will normally also be a payment transaction. If so, the request in this transaction must also be revoked. The result is that one gets the paid amount of money back.

6.2.6.8 The Revocation of a Decline

After the executor has responded to a request with a decline, the transaction process is in the discussion state (dc), as discussed in Sect. 6.2.6.2. Next to the possibility for the initiator to perform a renewed request (with an adapted product), the executor has the option to revoke the decline. This may occur when there are new facts to take into account (which could change the response to the request) or when the executor thinks over her/his decision and concludes that it may have been made inaccurately.

In the café example, the waiter may discover right after he has declined the request for a cup of coffee because the coffee machine was broken (dissatisfaction of the claim to truth) that the machine is working again. Another possibility is that he had misjudged the client's right to ask for coffee (dissatisfaction of the claim to rightness) and now gets remorse about that decision.

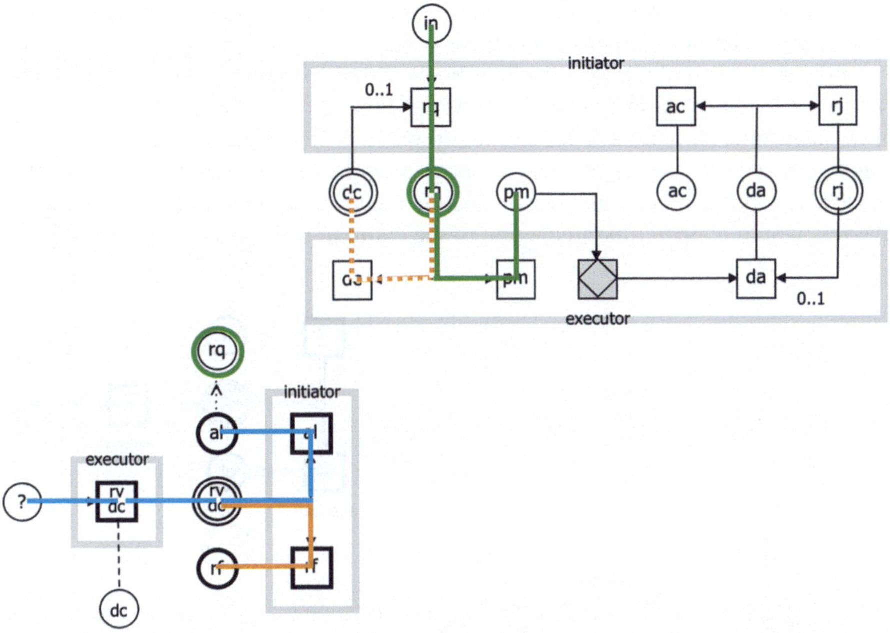

Fig. 6.14 The process of revoking a decline act

The revocation pattern of a decline is exhibited in Fig. 6.14. It starts with the revoke decline [rv-dc] by the executor, resulting in the state (rv-dc), indicated by the blue path from (?) via [rv-dc] to (rv-dc). The conditional link from (dc) to [rv-dc] represents the condition that the revocation can only be performed if the state in the main process is (dc). This condition is met. The being revoked is a discussion state, which means that the two actors have to sit together in order to discuss the proposed reverting of the main transaction process.

The initiator may allow the revoke (continued blue path) or refuse it (yellow path). If he/she allows, the state of the main process will be reverted to (rq), as indicated by the yellow-white path in the standard pattern and by the green circle around (rq). From there, the executor can perform the promise, as indicated by the green path. If the initiator refuses the revocation, the state of the main process remains unchanged. In Fig. 6.14, this is the state (dc). Note that performing the promise act is the logical alternative to the decline act.

6.2.6.9 The Revocation of a Reject

After the initiator has responded to a declare with a reject, the transaction process is in the discussion state (rj), as discussed in Sect. 6.2.6.2. Next to the possibility for the executor to perform a renewed declare (after having convinced the initiator that the product is ok), the initiator has the option to revoke the reject. This may occur when there are new facts to take into account (which could change her/his response to the declare) or when the initiator thinks over her/his decision and concludes that it may have been made somewhat inaccurately.

In the café example, after the client has rejected for good reasons, because the coffee is not really warm (dissatisfaction of the claim to truth), she may consider it in her own interest to accept the not really warm coffee because she is in a hurry. Another possibility is that she gets remorse about having refused the cup of coffee because it was brought by another person than the waiter, without prior notification that this would happen (dissatisfaction of the claim to rightness).

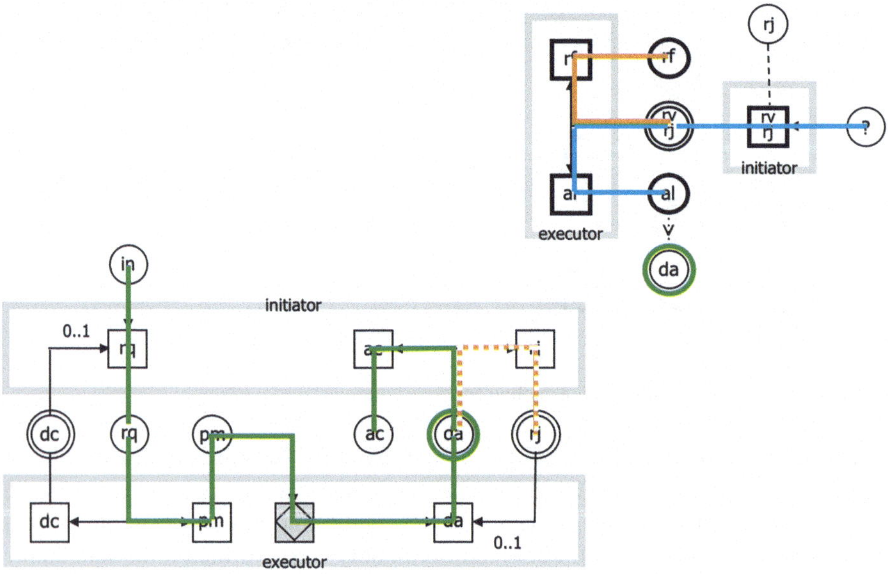

Fig. 6.15 The process of revoking a reject act

Figure 6.15 exhibits the process of revoking a reject act. It starts with performing the act [rv-rj] by the initiator, resulting in the discussion state (rv-rj), indicated in the figure by the blue path from (?) via [rv-rj] to (rv-rj). The dashed line from (rj) to [rv-rj] represents the conditional link. It means that the revocation can only be performed if the main process has reached the state (rj), which is the case. The state (rv-rj) is considered a discussion state, which means that the two actors have to sit together in order to discuss the proposed reversion of the main process.

The executor may allow the revoke, indicated by the continued blue path to (al) or refuse it (the yellow path). If he/she allows, the main process will return to the state (da), as indicated by the green-white path in the standard pattern and by the green circle around (da). From there, the initiator is able to perform the accept, indicated by the green path from (da) via [ac] to (ac). Note that performing the accept act is the logical alternative to the reject act.

6.2.6.10 Undoing a Production Act

If a revocation of a C-act leads to reverting the main process to a state before the performance of the P-act, so to (pm), (rq) or (in), the P-act must somehow be 'undone'. If the nature of this P-act is intangible, so if it was about deciding, devising or judging (cf. Fig. 11.4), the undoing may be simple. Still, costs may have incurred. Compensating for these costs is mostly done by charging them (wholly or partly) to the initiator.

In case the nature of the P-act is tangible, so if it was manufacturing, transporting or observing (cf. Fig. 11.4), the executor has almost always caused considerable costs. Whether or not he/she asks for compensation will depend on the situation. An interesting case is discussed in Chap. 13. In our café example, reverting the state of the main process to (pm), (rq) or (in) implies that costs are made in performing the production act (like producing and bringing a cup of coffee). Normally, these costs are borne by the café, but the servitude of the café, respectively, the waiter, is not endless. In normal business situations, where substantial costs may have incurred in bringing about the product, the initiator and the executor must agree on compensation. In most cases, this is sufficiently clarified in their contract.

For (business) transactions like acquiring goods, there is mostly a favour in return. Normally, this is the payment for the purchased goods or the rendered service. Note that paying is a separate transaction. It is commonly enclosed in the purchase transaction as discussed in Chap. 10, but it is a separate transaction. Rolling back the purchase transaction then implies rolling back the payment transaction. We pointed at this possibility already at the end of Sect. 6.2.6.7.

6.2.6.11 Reflections on the Complete Transaction Pattern

As becomes evident from the discussion of the complete transaction pattern above, the path of every single transaction through this pattern may comprise an arbitrary number of loops. But there are some definite landmarks. Both the order phase and the result phase (cf. Fig. 6.7) have a clear successful completion. The order phase of a transaction is completed successfully if the (latest) promised product is equal to the (latest) requested one. Likewise, the result phase of a transaction is completed successfully if the (latest) accepted product is equal to the (latest) declared one. If this is the case, the product starts to exist at the event time of the acceptance.

However, it is always possible to 'break open' a successfully completed transaction by revoking one of the basic steps. The permanent option to (try to) return to a previous state in the transaction process, long after the transaction is completed, may seem nonsensical, but it has an important practical relevance. All warranty clauses in sales contracts are actually openings to revoking one of the basic transaction steps. Understanding the settling of warranty claims and of returned goods as simple revocations in an existing transaction, instead of distinct processes, is crucial. It is an illustrative example of the reduction of complexity that EO aims to offer (cf. Chap. 3).

Next, every system has some internal mechanism that makes it 'tick' [15]. For inanimate systems, this mechanism is usually called the operating principle. Regarding animate systems, one often speaks of the vital force [16]. However, although the subjects in organisations (and other social systems) are animate systems, the organisations themselves are considered inanimate. Therefore, we speak of the operating principle of organisations, in much the same way as we speak of the operating principle of cars, aircrafts, etc. By performing coordination acts, subjects enter into and comply with commitments towards each other regarding a product to be brought about. *Commitments* are the social agencies through which people cooperate. In other words, subjects comply with commitments because they feel the social/cultural obligation to do so. We consider this 'mechanism' to be the *operating principle* of every organisation. The underlying premise, as articulated in Habermas' Theory of Communicative Action [5], is that the actors in a transaction strive to reach consensus. This is only possible if the actors *trust* each other, and this trust is verified explicitly when the claim to sincerity is assessed (cf. Fig. 6.2). Mutual trust is the fundament of every instance of human cooperation. With reference to [5], we add that the cooperation takes place in a context in which the participants are free and autonomous and in which they strive for consensus. All situations of dependence or abuse of force are excluded. In Habermas' theory, these situations are categorised as instrumental or strategic [5, 17]. Fortunately, it rarely happens in contemporary enterprises.

6.2.7 The Notion of Transactor

In all exhibited transaction patterns above, there is a clear separation between the acts that the initiator of a transaction can perform and the acts that fall within the responsibility area of the executor. In Figs. 6.8, 6.9, 6.10, 6.11, 6.12, 6.13, 6.14 and 6.15, these areas are indicated by light-grey, bold lined rectangles. We have also emphasised the importance of precisely formulating the independent P-fact of a transaction, such that it is unique in time and space (cf. Sect. 6.2.2.1). An example is '[membership] is started', where [membership] is a variable that can be instantiated, for example, to membership 387. We will take such expressions as denoting a *product kind* while being aware that it is only the expression of its independent P-fact type (cf. Sect. 6.2.2.2).

Corresponding with the notion of product kind, we will use the notion of *transaction kind*, as an attribute of every transaction (cf. Chap. 6). There is a one-to-one relationship between transaction kinds and product kinds. A proper naming of the transaction kind, in whose instances products of the kind <[membership] is started> are brought about, would be 'membership starting'. Next, we introduce the notion of *actor role*, defined as the authority to be the executor in transactions of some transaction kind. This authority can be assigned to subjects, as will be elaborated in Sect. 6.3.3. As a consequence of the definition of actor role, every transaction kind has exactly one actor role as its executor role and vice versa. An actor role may have an initiator role in several transaction kinds, however, or in none.

Figure 6.16 exhibits the graphical notation of these relationships in DEMO-SL-4.[8] The shape of a transaction kind is a diamond (the symbol of production) in a disk (the symbol of coordination), and the shape of an actor role is a box. Transaction kinds are connected to actor roles by initiator links (represented by a line between their shapes) and by executor links (represented by a line between the shapes and a small diamond at the junction of the line and the actor role shape). The cardinality range 0..1 in Fig. 6.16 indicates that transactions TK04 are optional (at least 0 times, at most 1 time).

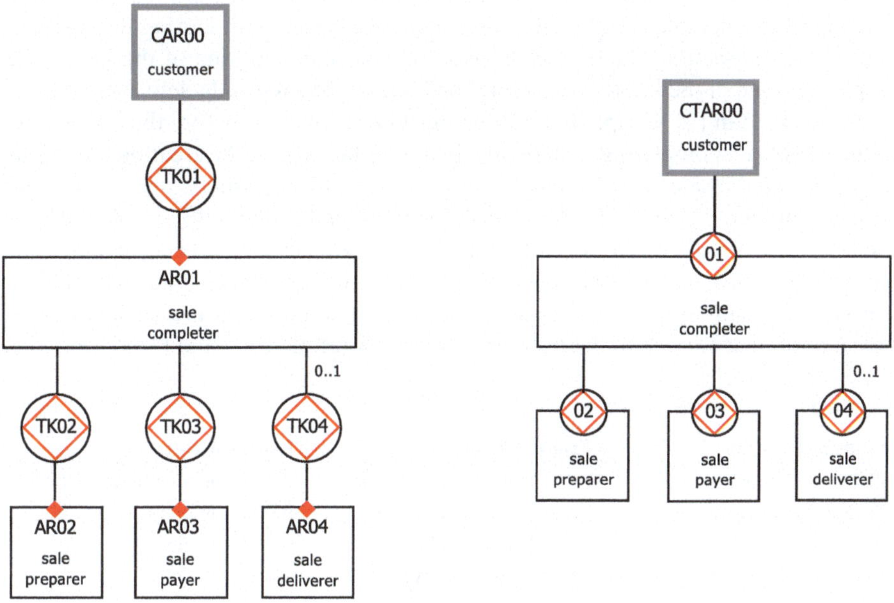

Fig. 6.16 Business process tree structure in the Pizzeria

The example organisation shown in Fig. 6.16 is the case Pizzeria (cf. Chap. 11). The red colour of the diamonds indicate that the transaction kinds and actor roles belong to the O-organisation of the Pizzeria (cf. Chap. 7). The left side of Fig. 6.16 shows that actors within the composite actor role (cf. [2], Chap. 10) CAR00 are the initiator in transactions TK01 and that actors AR01 are the executor in these transactions. At the same time, they are initiator of transactions TK02, TK03 and TK04, of which, respectively, actors AR02, AR03 and AR04 are the executors. (Note: From now on, we write ‘actors ARn’ as a shorthand for ‘actors filling actor role ARn’, ‘transactions TKn’ as a shorthand for ‘transactions of the kind TKn’ and ‘products PKn’ as a shorthand for ‘products of the kind PKn’.)

Because of the one-to-one relationship between a transaction kind and its executor role, it makes sense to combine them in one shape, as shown in Fig. 6.16 (right side). The combination of a transaction kind and its executing actor role is called

[8] DEMOSL stands for DEMO Specification Language. It is the formal definition of the ways in which DEMO models can be expressed (diagrams and formal text). The official reference document on DEMOSL can be found on www.ee-institute.org.

transactor role. The exhibited tree structure represents the same organisation as the one on the left side. When using the transactor role shape, one can just number the transactor roles, without using prefixes (like the 'TK' and the 'AR'). Transactor roles are the (molecular) *building blocks* of organisations. The links between the transactor roles in Fig. 6.16 (right side) are *initiator links*. So, like in the tree structure on the left side, actors AR01 are initiators in transactions TK02, TK03 and TK04. Table 6.2 represents the so-called Transactor Product Table of the Pizzeria. The process of completing a client order (conceived as a sale by the Pizzeria) starts with the request of a transaction of the kind 'sale completing' by a subject who fills the actor role 'customer' to someone who fills the actor role 'sale completer'. During the carrying out of this transaction, three other transactions are initiated: one of the kind 'sale preparing', one of the kind 'sale paying' and one of the kind 'sale delivering'.

As clarified in [2], Chap. 10, all three must be carried out before the transaction of the kind 'sale completing' can be finished. In other words, the creation of a product of the kind '[sale] is completed' implies three other products: one of the kind '[sale] is prepared', one of the kind '[sale] is paid' and (optionally) one of the kind '[sale] is delivered'. In the formulation of these product kinds, [sale] denotes the variable that has to be instantiated to get individual products, like 'sale 1618'. Through the bringing about of a particular product, a transactor is also said to provide a particular *service* to the initiating transactor (cf. Chap. 5 and [18]).

Table 6.2 Transactor Product Table of Pizzeria

Transaction kind	Product kind	Executor role
TK01 sale completing	PK01 [sale] is completed	AR01 sale completer
TK02 sale preparing	PK02 [sale] is prepared	AR02 sale preparer
TK03 sale paying	PK03 [sale] is paid	AR03 sale payer
TK04 sale delivering	PK04 [sale] is delivered	AR04 sale deliverer

In Fig. 6.17, it is visualised what happens if a specific transaction of the kind TK01 (sale completing) is executed. The initiating subject is Linda. By force of the operative Civil Code, she is authorised to fill the unknown transactor role within the composite transactor role CTAR00 that has an initiator link with TK01. As an actor in this role, she has the potential to initiate transactions TK01. This is expressed on the left side of the figure by the 'initiator part' of the transaction shape on the edge of the actor role shape. Mia is authorised by the Pizzeria to fill actor role AR01 (cf. Chap. 14), so she has the potential to provide the service of executing transactions TK01 (sale completing) to Linda. Her potential is expressed in Fig. 6.16 by the 'executor part' of the transaction shape on the edge of the actor role shape. As soon as Linda performs a request, a specific transaction, let's say T5189, is created. This is exhibited on the right side of the figure. In filling actor role AR01, Mia can initiate transactions TK02 (sale preparing), TK03 (sale paying) and TK04 (sale delivering). The executors in transactions of these kinds are, respectively, Mario, Linda and Edward. As soon as Mia effectuates her authorities, the transactions T5190, T5191 and T5192 are created, as shown on the right side of Fig. 6.16. As elaborated in Chap. 11, Edward is not only the executor of T5192, but he has also a delegated authority in transactions T5189, T5190 and T5191. That is the reason why he is also a filler of actor role AR01.

As soon as the transactions T5190, T5191 and T5192 are successfully completed, T5189 can be completed. Figure 6.16 does not show from which state in T5189 the other transactions are initiated by Mia and which states in transactions T5190, T5191 and T5192 Mia (or Edward) has to wait for. In order to exhibit these details, one needs to produce the Process Model of the Pizzeria (cf. Chap. 11).

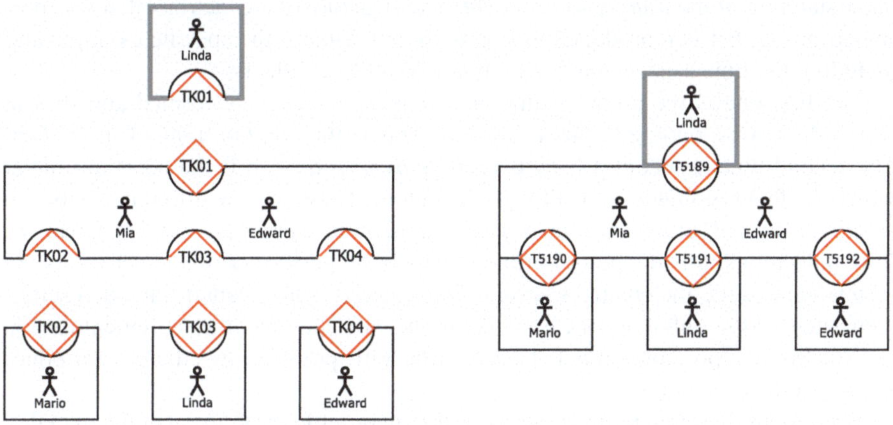

Fig. 6.17 Instantiation of the Coordination Structure Diagram of the Pizzeria

A subject may fill several actor roles, and an actor role may be assigned to several subjects, both sequentially and simultaneously. As examples in the café situation, the waiter (subject plus actor role) can at the same time be cashier (same subject, different actor role), and there may be several waiters in the café (one actor role, assigned to several subjects). Next, an actor role can be assigned to a collectivity of subjects, which means that these subjects can fill the role only together. Examples are the board of directors of a company and the general assembly of an association.

Figure 6.17 is perfectly suited to recall the crucial distinction between the subjective notion of service and the objective notion of product (cf. Chap. 5). What Linda receives according to the Pizzeria is a completed sale (which includes the home delivery of the pizza). This is the objective product. What Linda actually needs is the satisfaction of her desire for a home delivered pizza. This is the subjective service that she gets: the home-delivered pizza offers the affordance that she wants.

6.3 Elaborations

6.3.1 Time Aspects of Transactions

As we have discussed in Sect. 6.2, the process of a transaction is a sequence of C-events, starting with the request (in response to the initial state) and ending with either the acceptance (in case of success) or a reversion to the initial state (in case of failure) or being stuck in a deadlock, so in a (dc) or a (rj). Let us have a closer look now at the time aspects of C-facts and P-facts and by doing so acquire a deeper understanding of the transaction concept. The structure of a C-act/fact that was presented in Fig. 6.4 is reproduced in Fig. 6.18, but without the specific example and including the time aspects that are common to all C-acts/facts.

The first one is the point in time at which the C-act is performed and thus at which the corresponding C-fact is created. This is the *creation time* of the C-fact. The second time aspect of a C-facts is its *settlement time*. It is the point in time at which the fact is going to be dealt with. In technical systems, the difference between creation time and settlement time is used to synchronise processes (cf. [2], Chap. 9). In organisations, it is the point in time at which the performer of a C-act wants the addressee to settle the created C-event. Therefore, it is also called 'intended settlement time'. Although in most cases, like in the café example, the settlement time is asap (as soon as possible), it may be set at a specific point in time, thereby introducing a specific time delay.

Because of their inherent autonomy, actors may settle the C-event at the intended point in time, but they may also do it later or earlier. If no specific settlement time is set, the performer of the act expects the addressee to respond within a reasonable amount of time after the creation time. For example, if the client in the café asks the waiter for a cup of coffee, she assumes that the waiter responds to her request more or less instantly, not after an hour.

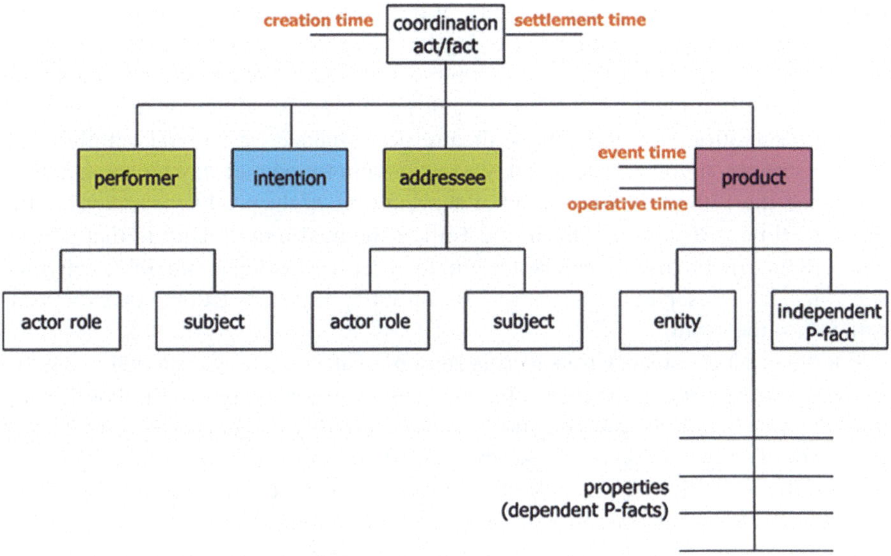

Fig. 6.18 Time aspects of coordination acts/facts

Regarding P-acts/facts, we distinguish between the event time and the operative time. (Note: because the creation time of a product is basically unknown, we disregard it.) This holds specifically for independent P-facts. The dependent facts that are related to them may be created in advance, as is illustrated by the Create Use Tables in Chap. 10. However, the event time of a dependent P-fact is always equal to the event time of the corresponding independent P-fact (and thus of the product). The *event time* of a product is by definition equal to the event time of the accept fact in the transaction in which it is brought about. If the acceptance is performed tacitly, it is considered to be equal to the event time of the declare fact.

In addition, products have an *operative time*. By this is meant the time period[9] during which the product is operative or valid. Like it holds for any other attribute, the value of the operative time may change during the transaction process, but its value at the time of performing the accept act is the definite one. Consequently, a product is operative or valid during its (accepted) operative time. In this period, the product, thus the independent P-fact and a number of dependent P-facts, is said to be effective.

Mostly, like for example in the café, the initiator wants the product to be operative asap. Therefore, the event time of a product is its default operative time. However, in a business-to-business situation, one often wants to set a specific future time. This holds for all product categories that are discussed in [2], Chap. 1: creation of things, transporting and storing, transferring ownership and granting right of

[9] As discussed in the DELTA theory (Chap. 9), every point in time is actually a time period, but possibly very small. This holds always for the attribute event time. The operative time, however, may be so large (minutes, hours, days) that one preferably speaks of a time period.

usufruct. As an example in the category of transferring ownership, you may give a money transfer order to your bank today but have the transfer effectuated on the 28th of this month. Other quite common examples are making appointments with professionals, like medical doctors for getting diagnosis, advice or treatment and making reservations for hotel stays, theatre performances, car rentals, flights, etc. So, for example, if you conclude today a reservation for a hotel stay for three nights, starting on the 13th of the next month, the event time of the product is today, but the operative time is from the 13th till the 16th of the next month. During that period, you have the right to use the booked room. In order to effectuate this right, you must check in. This is a separate transaction. By initiating this transaction, you exert your right to use the room.

For the product category transferring right of usufruct, it may even make sense to set the operative time in the *past*. This may sound strange at first sight, but it is not unusual. An example is that you subscribe to a monthly magazine, let's say during the month of May but that the subscription starts in retroaction from January on, so that you (have the right to) receive all issues of the current year. Similar advantages may hold for becoming member of an association in retroaction.

The last time aspect we like to discuss is the *life time* of an entity. To this end, we use the example in Fig. 6.19, which is taken from the case Volley (cf. [2], Chap. 12). The discussion there does not include transaction kind TK03, which we add here as the transaction kind that allows for ending memberships. The period between the event time of TK01/rq and TK01/ac can appropriately be called the prenatal phase of the membership. The event time of TK01/ac coincides with the becoming existent of PK01 '[membership] is started'. Likewise, the event time of TK03/ac coincides with the becoming existent of PK013 '[membership] is ended'. The period between the two events is properly called the existence phase of the membership. Corresponding with the name 'prenatal phase', we call the period after the occurrence of TK03/ac the postmortem phase of the membership.

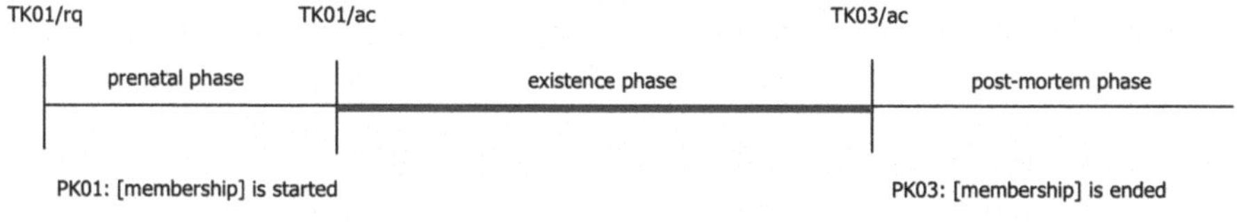

Fig. 6.19 The life time of an entity

During its existence phase, a membership is said to be valid, meaning that the associated member can exert her/his authority to play tennis and to execute other possible rights.

6.3.2 The Operating Cycle of Actors

Every actor is considered to loop constantly through its *operating cycle*, at a pace that is sufficiently frequent to deal with her/his agenda on time. The cycle begins when the actor selects an agendum (singular of agenda) to be settled (cf. Fig. 6.20). He/she may settle it at the intended settlement time (cf. Fig. 6.18) or earlier or later. Then, the actor fetches the applicable action rule and executes it. If there is no specific action rule present, he/she is led by the general guidelines (culture, policies) of the enterprise, which may have been expressed in declarative rules [19]. Because the authorisation of the actor is also based on her/his competence (cf. Sect. 6.3.3.4), he/she will also be guided by her/his professionalism. After having assessed the conditions in the action rule, the actor decides how to respond to the selected C-event. Then, the actor performs the act(s) that follow from the decision and selects the next agendum.

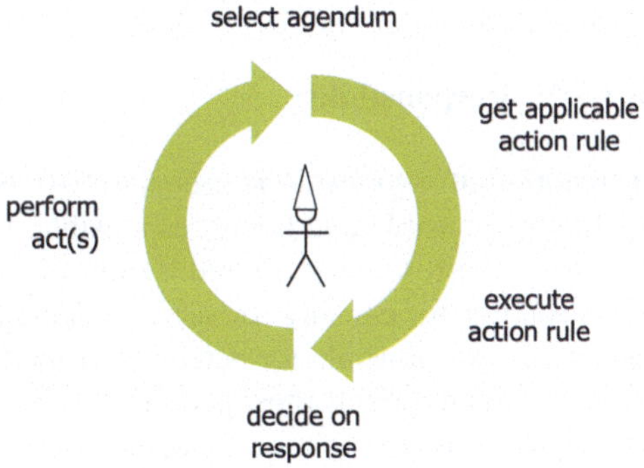

Fig. 6.20 The operating cycle of actors

6.3.3 Human Qualities in Transactions

In Sect. 6.2, the notions of responsibility and authority were briefly touched at. We have talked about the responsibility areas of the initiator and the executor in a transaction, and we have defined the notion of actor role as the authority to be executor in transactions of a specific transaction kind. Let us have a closer look at these human qualities and at two other ones, namely, accountability and competence. The definitions we will provide are not (fully) compatible with the popular RACI framework,[10] due to the fact that the RACI framework lacks a solid foundation. In contrast, the notions defined hereafter have a solid foundation in the PSI theory.

6.3.3.1 Authority

The notion of *authority* is defined as the right of a subject to perform particular acts in response to particular C-events. Taking the café situation again, the subject who

[10] See https://www.raci.com.

is referred to as waiter apparently has the authority to be executor in sale transactions, and the subject who is referred to as client apparently has the authority to be initiator in these transactions.

There are two ways in which authority can be assigned to subjects: through authorisation and through delegation. *Authorisation* is the common way in which authority is assigned to people in organisations, and it is commonly the authority of the human resource functionaries in an enterprise to authorise employees. In current practice, the unit of authorisation is mostly the functionary type: salesperson, accountant, assistant accountant, secretary, waiter, etc. In the PSI theory, the unit in which authorisation takes place is, more fundamentally and more precisely, the transactor role.

An authorisation basically includes the right to *delegate* (a part of) the authority to other subjects. Delegation may be used to deliberately relieve an actor of tasks, but sometimes it is inevitable, for physical/logistic reasons. The case Pizzeria (cf. Chap. 11) is a good example to illustrate this.

6.3.3.2 Responsibility

The notion of *responsibility* seems to have two meanings, which we will refer to as feeling responsible and being responsible. By nature, most people *feel responsible* for using the resources offered by our planet in such a way that they will not get exhausted or for causing irreversible damages to the environment. Similarly, most people feel responsible for behaving properly vis-à-vis fellow human beings. In the context of enterprises, most people feel the social obligation to exert their authority in the best way possible, so by acting professionally, by behaving properly towards other actors, etc. It corresponds with the fundamental 'social' principle in the PSI theory to base one's decisions on one's wisdom and love (cf. Sect. 6.2.3). Fortunately, most people like to be responsible for their work.

In our view, the meaning *being responsible* is the institutionalised version of feeling responsible. If someone has been assigned a particular authority (either by authorisation or by delegation), he or she is considered responsible for exerting this authority in the best possible way. As a consequence, authority and responsibility may be considered as the two sides of the same coin; none of them can exist without the other. In Sect. 6.2.6, we applied this notion already when we spoke of the responsibility areas of the initiator and the executor in carrying out transactions.

A related crucial notion in the PSI theory is *autonomy*, by which is meant that actors may deviate from the existing rules or norms. To illustrate this important point, let us take a purchaser in a manufacturing company as an example. Suppose that he/she gets the advice from the 'intelligent' purchase system to place a purchase order at a specific supplier. Normally, the purchaser would follow the advice, but suppose that he/she has heard the evening before that this supplier is going bankrupt soon. Wouldn't it be irresponsible to place the order? And doesn't he/she have a good story to justify disobeying the rule?

In order to clarify this issue, one often distinguishes in current practice between advisory and compulsory business rules. *Advisory rules* can be disobeyed but *compulsory rules* cannot. In the light of the foregoing discussion, the question is whether this distinction is tenable. Also with respect to compulsory rules, there can always be a situation that requires one to deviate from the rule. Humans are not robots.

6.3.3.3 Accountability and Liability

Responsibility seems often to be confused with *accountability*, which we define as the obligation to provide justifications of one's acts, whenever there is a need for it. Because of the basic autonomy that actors have in the PSI theory, they are accountable for all of their acts. So, if a particular subject is authorised to perform certain acts, he/she is responsible and accountable for the way he/she performs the acts, also if the authority is acquired through delegation. This becomes particularly apparent when an actor has violated the applicable business rules (for which there may be very good reasons, as we have seen). The actor will be held accountable for having deviated from the rule or the norm. In such a case, sanctions may be applied, depending on the severity of the deviation.

Related to accountability is the notion of *liability*, which means that an actor may be persecuted legally on the basis of the applicable Civil Code. With respect to liability, there is an important difference between authorisation and delegation: delegates may be held accountable for their deeds, but they are never liable. Liable is the actor who has delegated the corresponding part of her/his authority. Therefore, distinguishing between authorisation and delegation is an interesting issue in every enterprise. Ultimately, the 'big boss' is always liable.

6.3.3.4 Competence

Although one may assign any authority to any subject, one normally would do so on the basis of the subject's competence. By someone's *competence* is understood the totality of knowledge, skills and experience that a person possesses. Competence is thus a capability. Based on the PSI theory, it can be divided into production competence and coordination competence. Production competence is quite specific; it regards the being able to bring about products of one or more kinds. On the other hand, coordination competence is quite generic; it regards basically the performing of all coordination acts in the complete transaction pattern. It belongs to what are commonly called communication skills or soft skills.

To exemplify this, let us assume that someone has acquired, e.g. through education, the (production) competence of a plumber. In order to practice this competence, he/she has to get the corresponding authority from some (institutional) actor, for example, the boss of a plumbing company. Once this is done, he/she is expected to exert the authority in a responsible way, and he/she is accountable for all acts, as discussed in the previous sections. This will first of all apply to the 'real' plumbing work in the buildings of the clients of the company. But it also holds for the corresponding coordination acts. More specifically, the plumber is supposed to behave properly in the contacts with the clients.

6.4 Discussions

6.4.1 Striving for Consensus and Culture

As discussed in Sects. 6.2.4 and 6.2.6, the fundamental assumption in Habermas' theory of communicative action, and consequently of the PSI theory, is that the participants in (business) transactions strive for consensus, thus for mutual agreement. In other words, they attempt to make the transactions that they are involved in successful. This is the core of the notion of communicative action. Habermas recognises however that this precondition is not always satisfied. Therefore, he includes and discusses a fourth category of communicative acts, namely, the imperativa, where the claim to power is the dominant one. Habermas explicitly presents this category outside the region of 'proper' coordination. This is clarified in [17], which comprises a thorough comparison of Searle's speech act theory [20] and Habermas' theory of communicative action [5], yielding the next outcomes. Because Searle overlooks the orientation towards mutual agreement, he is incapable to distinguish power claims from validity claims. He considers communication primarily as an interaction between persons who try to let one another perform actions. A speech act thus succeeds if the course of action aimed at is taken. In this view, it is impossible to distinguish a situation in which the addressee acts because he/she wants to evade sanctions, from one in which he/she responds to the demand of the performer because he/she accepts the validity of her/his claims in a rational way. Otherwise said, Searle's theory is incapable to distinguish between empirical and rational coordination of action.

The central point of Habermas' critique however is that Searle fails to reveal what really makes a speech act work. This mechanism is that validity claims are criticisable, stemming from the orientation of the participants towards mutual agreement and giving rise to negotiations about the claims made. It is particularly because of this weakness in Searle's theory that his taxonomy misses several important distinctions. One of these is the distinction between speech acts that are based on power claims and speech acts that are based on validity claims (or speech acts proper).

Whether people in organisations are engaged in communicative acts that succeed because they satisfy validity claims, or in imperative coordination, i.e. exerting the power to force others to do things, is largely a matter of culture, as explained in [21]. Culture is defined as the totality of values, norms, convictions and beliefs (rational or irrational, implicit or explicit) that the members of an organisation (and of societies at large) have learned through social interaction and apply in their cooperation.

Cases about successful enterprise transformation, like the famous NUMMI case [22], show that management behaviour in the form of leadership and culture (meaning, purpose, norms and values) are the crucial determinants of enterprise success.

6.4.2 Other Approaches to Organisations as Social Systems

In the course of time, several ways of composing conversations into larger units are proposed, of which the workflow loop is probably best known [23]. It underlies the Action Workflow approach [24]. Among other things, however, it does not recognise the production act as a crucial part of a workflow loop, and it lacks the revocation patterns. The concept of workflow loop is therefore not as well founded and not as universally applicable as the (business) transaction in the PSI theory.

As discussed before, the CIAO Paradigm has evolved from the communication-centric view on information systems (cf. Sect. 6.2.1), which was developed between 1996 and 2005 by a group of researchers, who called themselves the Language-Action Perspective (LAP). In the May 2006 issue of the Communications of the ACM, the group has presented its final achievements.[11] Next to [25], which is an early sketch of the PSI theory, the issue contains presentations of comparable approaches, like e.g. the method called BAT [26].

A well-known approach to systems thinking, both in general and more specifically to organisations and information systems, is the Soft Systems Methodology (SSM) by Peter Checkland [27]. The notion that seems to come closest to the notion of organisation in the PSI theory is the notion of human activity system. It is hard to compare them, however, for many reasons, of which we present the three most important. First, SSM does not distinguish clearly between the function and the construction perspective on systems (cf. Chap. 5). Second, the human beings in SSM are not considered as the core active elements of a system. Third, SSM does not provide a theoretical explanation of the operation or behaviour of an organisation on the basis of the actions of its elements, notably the human beings in the activity system.

Sociotechnical Systems Theory (SST) is an approach to understanding the relationship between technology, individuals, organisations and society at large in the design of work places. SST includes the hardware, software, social, psychological, political, policy and legal systems that comprise the overall organisational system. SST pays particular attention to internal supervision and leadership at the level of the group and refers to it as responsible autonomy [28]. In our view, SST can very well be combined with the PSI theory and its practical bearings, through the notion of collective actor role: a team in SST can be modelled as a collective actor role.

[11] During the last meeting, in 2005, the group decided to discontinue itself. Some members continued their research activities under the name 'Pragmatic Web'.

6.4.3 The Practical Importance of the PSI Theory

The PSI theory is an intellectual instrument in clearing up the massive and seemingly unrelated details that one is faced with when trying to make sense of the observable operations of an organisation, notably of its business processes. Being based on a general understanding of human cooperation, the PSI theory is applicable to every kind of enterprise.

The most powerful innovation that the PSI theory brings to the practice of (re-) designing, (re-)engineering, (re-)implementing and running enterprises of any kind and size is the understanding that the operation of every organisation is a network of transactions and that every transaction is some path through the complete transaction pattern (CTP). In addition, every transaction is of some transaction kind, determined by the product kind of its result and by the two actor roles that the subjects who carry out the transaction fill.

A typical example of how the CTP clarifies everyday problems in doing whatever kind of business is the case Fixit (cf. [2], Chap. 13). It demonstrates that common solutions to the presented organisational problems, like help desks (to deal with customers' complaints regarding business processes) and goods-returning procedures (to deal with customers' dissatisfactions with received goods), should not be addressed as separate problem areas but instead be understood as integral parts of the notion of transaction, namely, as dealing with the 'exceptional' states declined and rejected, and with the being revoked of an acceptance, a declaration, a promise or a request.

The CTP is also a powerful help in identifying transaction steps that are apparently performed tacitly, thus for whose presence there is no evidence. Typical examples are the promise and the acceptance. In order to avoid communication costs, people rely from time immemorial on a no-news-is-good-news rule. However, this rule is also a major cause of process malfunctions, because it is doomed to fade into oblivion in the course of time. Note also that tacitly performed steps do not appear in common business process models, since these models only contain what is observable.

The notion of actor role as the unit of authority and responsibility is an effective help in unravelling the tangles of ineffective and superfluous bureaucratic measures that are a plague to consumers and citizens. Any functionary without (either assigned or delegated) authority is plainly redundant. Their only purpose is to shield the responsible persons, thus to mask their responsibility. Even in simple business processes, like in the café example discussed above, the blurring of responsibilities is annoying. When a client, in interaction with a particular waiter, has successfully carried out the order phase of a transaction to get something to drink or eat, she will not be pleased when somebody else addresses her to carry out the result phase, because it will only complicate a possible discussion in the state rejected, i.e. in case she is not satisfied with what is delivered. Unfortunately, this is the order of the day, all over the world. It is the effect of how managers are educated. They are taught that organising is about cutting costs, achieving targets and improving efficiency. What they fail to learn is a proper understanding of how organisations actually work.

References

1. Mintzberg, H. (1979). *The structuring of organizations: A synthesis of the research* (Theory of management policy). Prentice-Hall International. xvi, 512 p.
2. Dietz, J. L. G., & Mulder, J. B. F. (2024). *Enterprise ontology—A human-centric approach to understanding the essence of organisation* (Enterprise engineering) (2nd ed.). Springer Nature.
3. Bunge, M. (1979). Treatise on basic philosophy ontology II: A world of systems. In *Treatise on basic philosophy 4*. Reidel.
4. Austin, J. L. (1962). *How to do things with words*. Harvard University Press.
5. Habermas, J. (1986). *The theory of communicative action*. Polity Press.
6. Stamper, R. K. (1973). *Information in business and administrative systems* (Vol. 6). Batsford. 362 p.
7. Dietz, J. L. G. (2012). *Red garden gnomes don't exist*. Sapio Enterprise Engineering.
8. Edmondson, W. J. (1981). *Spoken discourse: A model for analysis* (Longman Linguistics Library). Longman. 217 p.
9. Grice, H. P. (1975). *Logic and conversation* (Speech acts [Syntax and semantics]) (Vol. 3). Academic Press.
10. Grice, H. P. (1978). *Further notes on logic and conversation* (Pragmatics [Syntax and semantics]) (Vol. 9). Academic Press.
11. Steuten, A. (1998). *A contribution to the linguistic analysis of business conversations within the language/action perspective*. Delft University of Technology.
12. Winograd, T., & Flores, F. (1986). *Understanding computers and cognition: A new foundation for design*. Ablex Pub. Corp. xiv, 207 p.
13. Searle, J. R. (1995). *The construction of social reality*. Free Press. xiii, 241 p.
14. van Reijswoud, V. E. (1996). *The structure of business communication: Theory, model and application*. Delft University of Technology.
15. Bunge, M. (1979). *A world of systems* (Ontology). Reidel. XVI, 314 S.
16. Bergson, H. (1913). *Creative evolution*. Macmillan. XV, 425 S.
17. Dietz, J. L. G., & Widdershoven, G. A. M. (1991). Speech acts or communicative action? In *Second European Conference on Computer Supported Cooperative Work*. Kluwer.
18. Terlouw, L. (2011). Modularization and specification of service-oriented systems. In *Computer science*. Delft University of Technology.
19. Dietz, J. L. G. (2009). On the nature of business rules. In *Advances in enterprise engineering I*. Springer.
20. Searle, J. R. (1969). *Speech acts: An essay in the philosophy of language*. Cambridge University Press. vii, 203 p.
21. Hoogervorst, J. A. P. (2017). *Foundations of enterprise governance and enterprise engineering*. Springer International Publishing. 574 p.
22. Shook, J. (2010). How to change a culture: Lessons from NUMMI. *Sloan Management Review, 50*(2), 63–68.
23. Denning, P., & Medina-Mora, R. (1995). Completing the loops. *Interfaces, 25*(3), 15.
24. Medina-Mora, R., Winograd, T., Flores, R., & Flores, F. (1992). The action workflow approach to workflow management technology. In *Conference on Computer-Supported Cooperative Work*. ACM Press.
25. Dietz, J. L. G. (2006). The deep structure of business processes. *Communications of the ACM, 49*(5), 58–64.
26. Goldkuhl, G. (2006). Action and media in interorganizational interaction. *Communications of the ACM, 49*(5), 53.
27. Checkland, P., & Checkland, P. (1999). *Systems thinking, systems practice: A 30-year retrospective* (2nd ed.). Wiley. A66, xiv, 330 p.
28. Sitter, L. U., Hertog, J. F., & Dankbaar, B. (1997). From complex organizations with simple jobs to simple organizations with complex jobs. *Human Relations, 50*(5), 497–536.

Chapter 7
The EE Organisational Construction Theory

Abstract The EE Organisational Construction Theory, also called OMEGA theory, is a theory about the modular structures that can be distinguished in organisations. Based on the organisational building block (the transactor role) from the PSI theory (cf. Chap. 6), three kinds of coordination structures are identified and discussed: interaction structure, interstriction structure and interimpediment structure. The interaction structure of an organisation consists of tree structures, which are constituted by the initiator links between transactor roles. An interaction tree determines a business process kind. The interstriction structure of an organisation consists of the access links between transactor roles. Through access links, actors have reading access to the facts in transaction banks. The interimpediment structure of an organisation is constituted by the wait links between transactor roles. Three topics are elaborated in depth. The first one is the notion of responsibility range of a transactor role, as an extension of the responsibility area from the PSI theory (cf. Chap. 6). The second subject is a comprehensive way of modelling business processes, which allows for all the details that are needed, but that is still very concise. Next, several general patterns in process structures, called reference models, are discussed. To conclude, the presented structural way of thinking about business processes is compared with the currently dominant flow way of thinking.

7.1 Introduction

The theory in this chapter is labeled Ω-theory. The Greek capital letter is pronounced as OMEGA, which is an acronym for Organisational Modules Emerging from General Arrangements. It is about the possible ways in which transactor roles (cf.

Reprinted from J. L. G. Dietz, H. B. F. Mulder, *Enterprise Ontology*, The Enterprise Engineering Series, https://doi.org/10.1007/978-3-031-53361-7_10

J. L. G. Dietz, H. B. F. Mulder, *Enterprise Design Fundamentals*, The Enterprise Engineering Series, https://doi.org/10.1007/978-3-031-83262-8_7

Chap. 6) can influence each other, as well as the modular structures that these ways of influencing give rise to. In Chap. 4, the OMEGA theory is classified as an ontological theory—meaning that it is about the nature of things.

The PSI theory (cf. Chap. 6) provides us with the most fundamental work structure in organisations, namely, the division in production and coordination, and their combined occurrence in the universal pattern of the (business) transaction. The complete transaction pattern comprises all coordination acts/facts that are necessary and sufficient for carrying out any transaction. Based on it, the PSI theory provides us also with the universal building block of organisations: the transactor (transaction processing actor) role. Every transactor role includes the complete transaction pattern. In addition, it comprises the guidelines for carrying out transactions of the corresponding transaction kind, varying from cultural norms to imperative business rules.

Section 7.2 (Foundations) starts with a summary of the PSI theory. In Sects. 7.2.2–7.2.4, the distinct coordination structures are presented that arise from the three distinct ways of influencing between transactors: the interaction structure, the interstriction structure and the interimpediment structure. All three are expressed in the Coordination Structure Diagram (CSD). The business processes in the GloLog enterprise (cf. [1], Chap. 18) are used for illustration.

Section 7.3 (Elaborations) covers three topics. In Sect. 7.3.1, the notion of responsibility range of transactors is discussed, as an extension of the notion of responsibility area from the PSI theory. In Sect. 7.3.2, the Process Structure Diagram (PSD) is introduced for understanding the three coordination structures in more detail, and the notion of business process is elucidated. Section 7.3.3 is devoted to a discussion of the reference models that emerge from the presented structures.

Section 7.4 (Discussions) is about the added value of structure thinking in business processes, next to flow thinking as well as its indispensability if it comes to changing business processes. The chapter ends with a discussion of the practical relevance of the OMEGA theory.

7.2 Foundations

7.2.1 The Organisational Building Block

In this section, the parts of the PSI theory (cf. Chap. 6) that are relevant for the OMEGA theory are resumed and elaborated. The first important notion is the notion of transaction. It is a pattern of acts, performed by actors in two roles: the initiator and the executor. The executor brings about the product of the transaction to the benefit of the initiator. In the presented complete transaction pattern, there is a clear separation between the coordination acts (C-acts) that the initiator of a transaction can perform and the C-acts that belong to the responsibility of the executor. Emphasis is put on the precise formulation of the product of a transaction, namely, in such a way that it is uniquely identified. The example of a correct formulation of a *product kind* that was used in Chap. 6 is '[membership] is started', where [membership] is a placeholder or variable in this logical predicate type. An example of an instance of the predicate type is 'membership 387 is started'. Related to the notion of product kind, the notion of *transaction kind* is introduced. It is a basic property of every transaction, and there is a one-to-one relationship between transaction kinds and product kinds. A proper naming of the transaction kind, in whose instances products of the kind '[membership] is started' are brought about, would be 'membership starting'. Next, the notion of *actor role* is introduced, defined as the authority to be the executor in transactions of a particular transaction kind. This authority can be assigned to subjects, by which these subjects become eligible to act accordingly. A proper name for the executor role of the transaction kind 'membership starting' would be 'membership starter'.

The combination of a subject and an assigned actor role is called *actor*. Only actors can act, i.e. be active in transactions. A subject may fill several actor roles, and an actor role may be assigned to several subjects, both sequentially and simultaneously. As examples from the case Rent-A-Car (cf. [1], Chap. 15), renters (subjects in an actor role) can at the same time be deposit payers (same subject, different actor role), and there are several rental completers (one actor role, assigned to several subjects). Next, an actor role can be assigned to the collectivity of a number of subjects, which means that these subjects fill the role collectively. Examples of collective actor roles are the board of directors of a company and the general assembly of an association.

Every transaction kind has exactly one actor role as its executor role and vice versa, but actor roles may have an initiator role in a number of (other) transaction kinds. The left side of Fig. 7.1 shows the graphical notation of these relationships in the DEMO Specification Language.[1] The shape of a transaction kind is a diamond (the symbol of production) in a disk (the symbol of coordination), and the shape of an actor role is a box (possibly stretched into a rectangle). A transaction kind is connected to an actor role by an initiator link, represented by a solid line between the shapes, or an executor link, represented by a solid line between the shapes plus a small black (or coloured) diamond at the junction of the line and the actor role box. Figure 7.1 shows that actors CAR00 are initiators in transactions TK01 and that actors AR01 are their executors.[2] Actors AR01 are also initiators of transactions TK02, TK03 and TK04, of which, respectively, actors AR02, AR03 and AR04 are the executors.

[1] DEMOSL stands for DEMO Specification Language. It is the formal definition of ways in which DEMO models can be expressed (diagrams and formal text). The official reference document on DEMOSL can be found on www.ee-institute.org.

[2] We will write 'actors ARn' as a shorthand for 'actors filling actor role ARn', 'transactions TKn' as a shorthand for 'transactions of the kind TKn' and 'products PKn' as a shorthand for 'products of the kind PKn'.

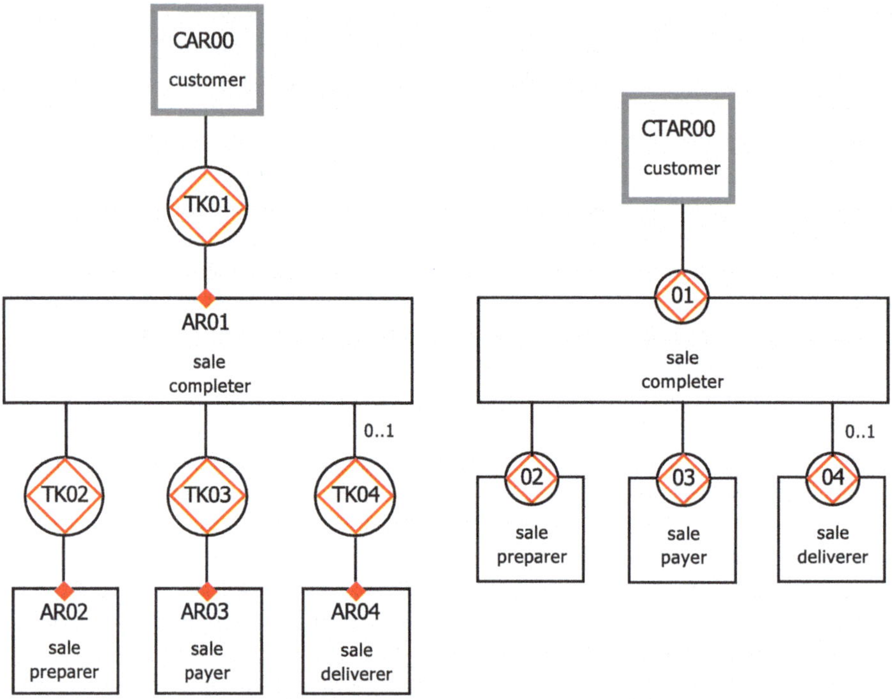

Fig. 7.1 Graphical notations of transaction kinds, actor roles and transactor roles

The transaction kind shape has two interpretations. In the *constructional interpretation*, it represents the complete transaction pattern, as discussed in Sect. 6.2.6.3. Every instance of a transaction of the transaction kind is some path, possibly including iterations, through the complete transaction pattern. In the *operational interpretation*, the transaction kind shape represents the conceptual store of all C- and P-facts in transactions of the transaction kind that are created in the course of time. Therefore, the transaction kind is now conceived as a *transaction bank*. Basically, the subjects who fill or have filled the initiator or executor role in one or more transactions of some kind have access to the contents of the corresponding transaction bank, possibly restricted to the specific transactions in which they have participated.

The *actor role shape* has also two interpretations. The *constructional interpretation* is that it represents the authority to be the executor in transactions of the transaction kind to which it is linked by an executor link. The *operational interpretation* is that it represents the guidelines, ranging from culture (norms and values) to specific action rules and work instructions, that actors filling the actor role apply when they carry out transactions. The action rules regard the role of executor of transactions of the kind to which it is linked by an executor link and the role of initiator in transactions of the kind to which it is linked by an initiator link. So, for example, actor role AR01 contains guidelines both for dealing with C-events in transactions TK01 (of which it is the executor) and in transactions TK02, TK03 and TK04 (of which it is an initiator).

Because of the one-to-one relationship between a transaction kind and its executor role, it makes sense to use one shape for the combination of the two. This shape, called *transactor role*, is shown on the right side of Fig. 7.1. Instead of using prefixes (like the 'TK' and the 'AR' that are used on the left side of the figure), we just number transactor roles. The links between the transactor roles are *initiator links*. So, for example, transactors TAR01 are initiators in transactions TK02, TK03 and TK04. Henceforth, we will talk of transactors and transactor roles, as well as of actor roles and transaction kinds. The cardinality range 0..1 in Fig. 7.1 indicates that the carrying out of a transaction TK04 within a transaction TK01 is optional.

Because transactor roles can have an initiator role in one or more transaction kinds, next to having the executor role in their 'own' transaction kind, the being connected through initiator links, constitutes tree structures, like the one shown in Fig. 7.1. To illustrate the meaning of this tree structure, we use the Pizzeria case (cf. Chap. 12). Table 7.1 represents the so-called Transactor Product Table of the Pizzeria.

Table 7.1 Transactor Product Table of the Pizzeria

Transaction kind	Product kind	Executor role
TK01 sale completing	PK01 [sale] is completed	AR01 sale completer
TK02 sale preparing	PK02 [sale] is prepared	AR02 sale preparer
TK03 sale paying	PK03 [sale] is paid	AR03 sale payer
TK04 sale delivering	PK04 [sale] is delivered	AR04 sale deliverer

The processing of a client order (which is conceived as completing a sale) starts from the request of a transaction of the kind TK01 'sale completing' by someone who fills the actor role 'customer' (an actor role within the composite actor role CAR00) to someone who fills actor role AR01 'sale completer'. During the carrying out of this transaction, three other transactions are initiated: one of the kind TK02 'sale preparing', one of the kind TK03 'sale paying' and (optionally) one of the kind TK04 'sale delivering'. All three (or two) must have been finished before the transaction of the kind TK01 'sale completing' can be finished. In other words, every product of the kind '[sale] is completed' implies three other products: one of the kind '[sale] is paid', one of the kind '[sale] is prepared' and (optionally) one of the kind '[sale] is delivered'.

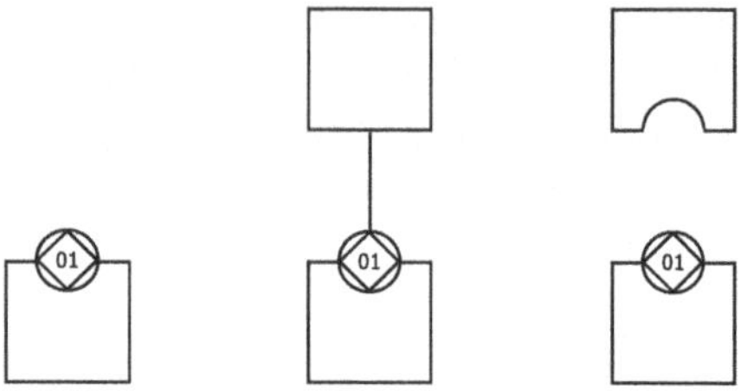

Fig. 7.2 Representations of the organisational building block

The transactor role is the construction element or *building block* of organisations, as shown in Fig. 7.2. On the left is the 'bare' building block. In the middle, this transactor role is connected to another actor role by an initiator link. By doing this, actors in this role become initiator of transactions TK01, of which actors AR01 are the executor. The construct on the right side of Fig. 7.2 represents another way of making actor roles initiator of transaction kinds. The meaning of the disk-shaped cut-away in the upper box is that actors filling the corresponding actor role become initiators in transactions TK01 by 'clicking' the transaction symbol to the cut-away. This so-called click mode will be elaborated in Sect. 7.3.2. The operational meaning of the middle and the right construct is that the initiators of transactions TK01 perform requests, to which actors AR01 respond by a promise (or a decline), and thus start the carrying out of transactions TK01, which concern products of the kind PK01. A product starts to exist as soon as the initiator has accepted it. In current business process literature, the product kinds are often also called *case kinds*.

7.2.2 The Interaction Structure

By the *interaction structure* of an organisation is understood the collective initiator links between the transactor roles, as illustrated by Fig. 7.1, right side. This is equivalent to saying that the interaction structure comprises the transaction kinds of an organisation, as well as the initiator links and the executor links that connect them to the actor roles (cf. Fig. 7.1, left side). The interaction structure is the main structure in an organisation, because it determines the business process kinds in which the products are brought about (cf. Chap. 6). Therefore, we take it as the definition: every interaction tree in an organisation is a *business process kind*. As we will see later, the top of such a tree is either an environmental or a self-activating transactor role. Both the interstriction structure (to be discussed in Sect. 7.2.3) and the interimpediment structure (to be discussed in Sect. 7.2.4) come in addition to the interaction structure.

The interaction structure of an organisation consists by definition of a number of tree structures, as will become clear hereafter. The general understanding of a tree structure is that it is a pair (P, R), where P is a set of things and R is a (binary) relation over P, commonly called a part-of relation. For every (p1, p2) ∈ R, it holds that p1 is a *part of* p2. Conversely, p2 is commonly called the *assembly* of the things x

∈ P for which it holds that (x, p2) ∈ R. The leaves of the tree, i.e. the things y in P that have no parts, so for which there is no tuple (−, y) ∈ R, are commonly called *parts*.

An interaction tree (cf. Fig. 7.1, right side) is basically always extensible by adding new transactor roles as components of the 'leaf' transactor roles. The tree structure is a direct reflection of the Bill-of-Material (BoM) structure of the corresponding product kinds.

As an example, in the Pizzeria (cf. Chap. 14), the case kind is the sale. It serves as the core entity type (cf. Chap. 6) in all four product kinds. The product structure is exhibited in Fig. 7.3 (left side), whereas Table 7.1 contains the Transactor Product Table. A product of the kind '[sale] is completed' comprises three other products as parts: '[sale] is paid', '[sale] is prepared' and '[sale] is delivered'. The last one is optional (indicated by the cardinality range 0..1) because there are also walk-in customers, for which there is no delivery transaction. Consequently, four specialisations (cf. Chap. 6) of the entity type sale are distinguished: completed sale, paid sale, prepared sale and delivered sale.

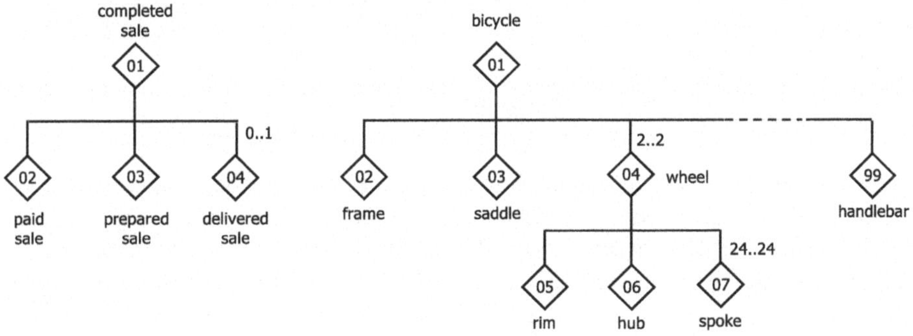

Fig. 7.3 Examples of product structures

As another example to illustrate that product structures resemble BoM like structures, a part of the BoM of a bicycle (of some bicycle kind) is exhibited on the right side of Fig. 7.3. It shows that a bicycle consists of one frame, one saddle, two wheels (indicated by the minimum and maximum cardinality), one handlebar, etc. Next, a wheel is an assembly of one rim, one hub and 24 spokes. (Note: if no cardinality range is indicated next to an initiator link, the default value 1..1 holds.) The product structure that corresponds with this BoM has the same shape. Only the names of the parts would be replaced by 'assembled bicycle', 'assembled wheel', 'acquired spoke', etc.

In order to express the coordination structures, we use the Coordination Structure Diagram (CSD) (cf. Chap. 11), whose legend is exhibited in Fig. 7.4. The upper part shows the three different sorts of transactor roles: the elementary transactor role, the self-activating transactor role and the composite transactor role.

As said, the interaction structure of an organisation consists of a number of tree structures. By definition, the top of such a tree is a self-activating transactor role. However, because many business processes in an organisation originate from the environment, the common way to represent the external 'top' transactor role of such a business process kind in a CSD is the composite transactor role (Fig. 7.4, top right).

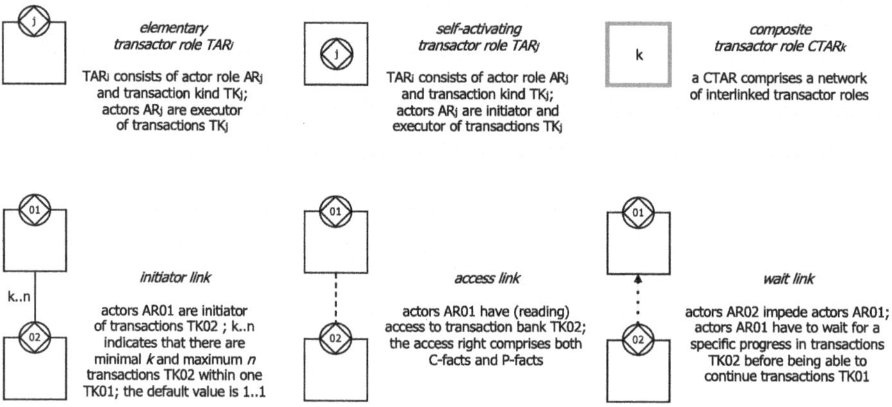

Fig. 7.4 Legend of the Coordination Structure Diagram

As shown in Fig. 7.3, a product, for example a PK01, may be composed of other products, which means that actors AR01 have to initiate other transactions in order to bring about a PK01. Figure 7.5 exhibits an interaction tree. It should be read as follows. In order to produce a PK01, actors AR01 need a PK02, a PK03 and a PK04. On their turn, actors AR02 need a PK05 and a PK06 to produce a PK02, actors AR03 need a PK08 and optionally (indicated by the cardinality range 0..1) a PK07 to produce a PK03. Likewise, actors AR04 need a PK08 and a PK09 to produce a PK04. Note that transactor role TAR08 is drawn twice, to keep the diagram orderly, but there is only one transactor role TAR08. So, transactions TK08 are initiated by either an actor AR03 or an actor AR04.

A crucial point in the OMEGA theory is that at any level in an interaction tree, the initiating actor basically does not care (and does not need to care) about what the executing actor has to do in order to produce the agreed-upon product. To illustrate this, at some point in time, the actor AR01 addresses herself/himself to the initiating actor CTAR00 and declares the creation of a product PK01. What the actor AR01 actually has done during the execution phase of the transaction TK01 is having acquired a PK02, a PK03 and a PK04 in, respectively, a transaction TK02, TK03 and TK04, as exhibited in Fig. 7.5. The transactor roles TAR02, TAR03 and TAR04 are called sub-transactor roles of TAR01. Together they constitute the subtree of TAR01. It is important to understand that every sub-transactor role may have a subtree of transactor roles itself, but this subtree does not affect the character of its products. Thus, it makes no difference for actor role AR01 whether AR02 has to initiate transactions TK05 and TK06 for producing products PK02 or not. It will always be the (same) product kind that actors AR01 and actors AR02 negotiate about and come to agreement about in transaction processes of the kind TK02. In a similar way, one may want to disregard the subtree of a transactor role.

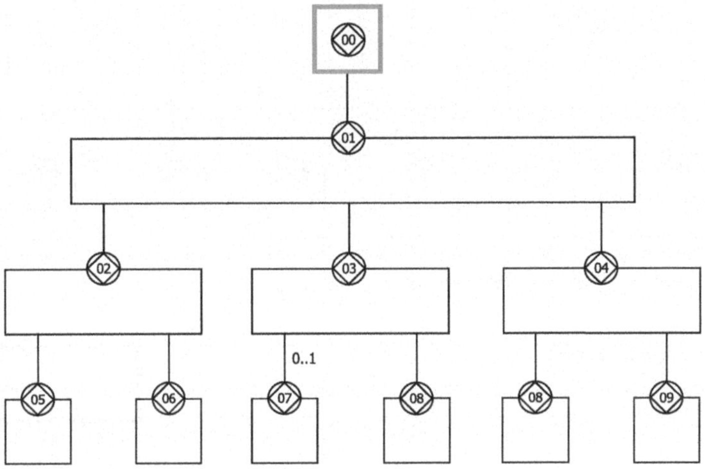

Fig. 7.5 Example of an interaction-based tree structure

The interaction tree structures in an organisation may be quite deep, i.e. have many levels, in particular if one includes the transactor roles in the I-organisation and even more if one also includes the D- and M-organisation (cf. Chap. 8). Commonly, one would only consider the transactor roles in the O-organisation, or at least start with them, as a consequence of abstracting from the I-, the D- and the M-organisation. The reason for 'hiding' a part of a tree by means of a composite transactor role, like CTAR00 in Fig. 7.5, may be that one wants to disregard it for the moment, as discussed above, or that it falls outside the chosen focus of the Scope of Interest (SoI). In the latter case, the inside of the box is coloured light grey, in order to clearly mark the focus, as is done in Fig. 7.8. In Figs. 7.6 and 7.7, the SoI as exhibited in Fig. 7.5 is narrowed down. The new focus consists of TAR02 and its components TAR05 and TAR06. For illustrative purposes, the edges of the shapes in the corresponding part of the initial SoI are blue-lined. Figure 7.7 exhibits the result. The name of the new composite transactor role (CTAR02) is arbitrarily chosen.

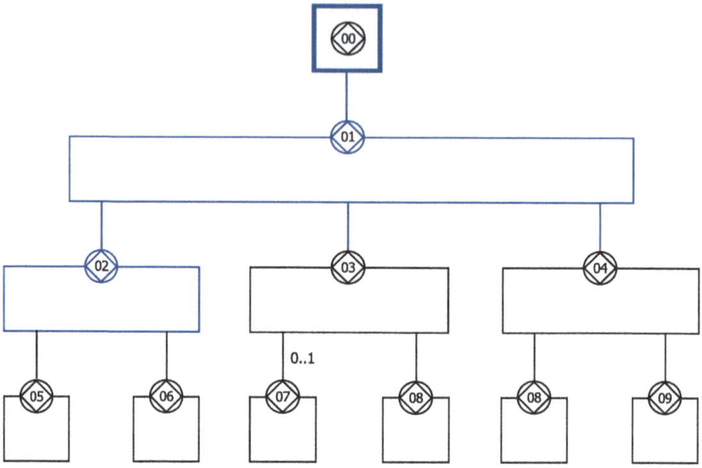

Fig. 7.6 Narrowing down a scope of interest

Fig. 7.7 The new scope of interest

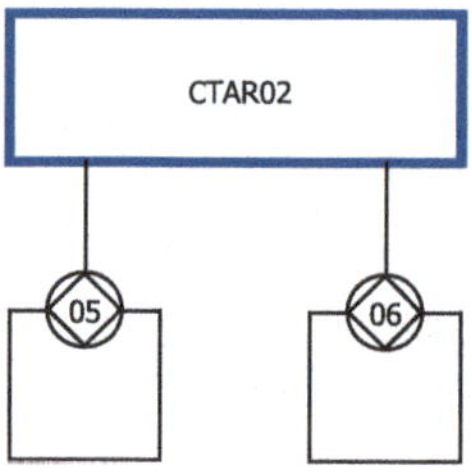

As a practical example of the interaction structure of an organisation, Fig. 7.8 exhibits this structure for the GloLog enterprise (cf. [1], Chap. 18). There are four business process kinds, represented by four distinct interaction trees: the sales process, the purchase process, the sea transport process and the land transport process. The case kind in these process kinds is, respectively, sale, purchase, ship content and container content. Only because of these different case kinds (or entity kinds) does one arrive at the four tree structures, as explained in [1], Chap. 18. The left one is initiated externally, as indicated by the composite transactor role CTAR01. The top or root of the other trees is a self-activating transactor role. The company IES within the GloLog enterprise is the focus: it comprises all white-coloured transactor role shapes. So, the grey-coloured transactor role shapes are outside the scope of IES but inside the scope of the GloLog enterprise. The red colour of the diamonds indicates that the transactor roles belong to the O-organisation of the GloLog enterprise. The structure with double-lined boxes at the top of Fig. 7.8 does not belong to the CSD; it only serves to clarify that there are four different business process kinds in the Glolog enterprise. Together, they bring about the products/services of the enterprise.

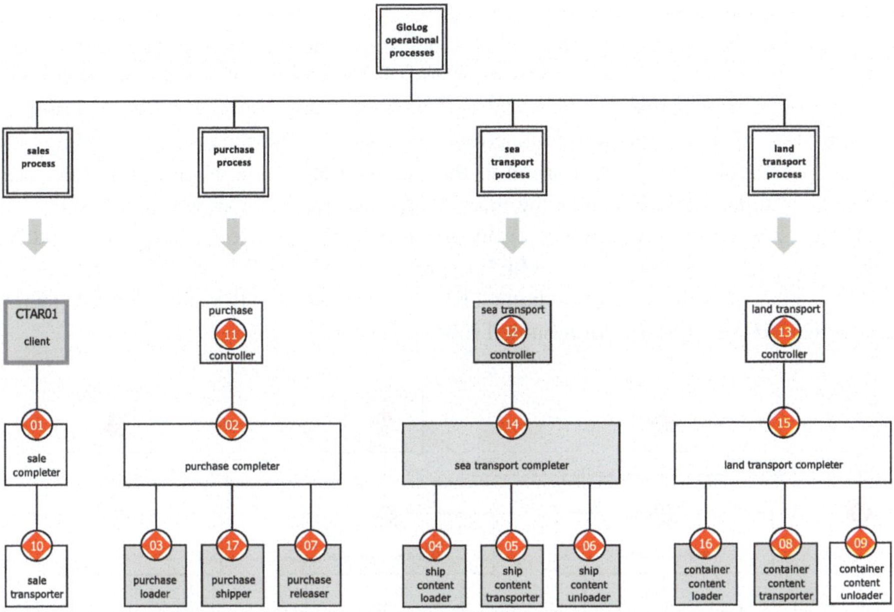

Fig. 7.8 The interaction structure in the GloLog enterprise

7.2.3 The Interstriction Structure

The second kind of link between transactor roles is the *access link*. It is presented in Fig. 7.4, in the middle of the bottom part. As discussed in Chap. 11, access links are the means to abstract from the realisation of an organisation, i.e. from the I-organisation and subsequently from the D- and M-organisation. Therefore, the right understanding of the construct in the middle of Fig. 7.4 is that actors AR01 are initiators in one or more informational transactions, through which they acquire the knowledge of facts that are contained in transaction bank TK02.

Actors AR01 need these facts in order to properly carry out transactions TK01. To this end, they have (reading) access to the contents of transaction bank TK02. The access link can also be understood as a restriction of the decision freedom of actors AR01 by actors AR02, as discussed in [1], Chap. 9. Therefore, the collective access links in an organisation are called its *interstriction structure*.[3] Interstriction is a passive way in which actors influence each other.

In carrying out a transaction, both the initiator and the executor need to keep track of the progress of the transaction, and they may also need to know the histories of earlier transactions of the same kind. Therefore, there is an access link 'under'

[3] 'Restriction' originates from the Latin verb *stringere*, meaning 'trimming' or 'curtailing'. The word 'interstriction' expresses that actors restrict each other's decision freedom or 'play area'.

every initiator link and every executor link (cf. Fig. 7.1 left side). Although they are not made visible in the CSD, they do also belong to the interstriction structure. The interstriction structure of an organisation constitutes the *state dependencies* among the contained transaction processes: the acts of the connected actors depend on the current state of the connected transaction processes, i.e. on the contents of the connected transaction banks. Commonly, the access links 'under' initiator links are considered to be excluded from the interstriction structure as shown in a CSD.

Figure 7.9 exhibits the interstriction structure in the GloLog enterprise, in addition to the interaction structure, which is presented in Fig. 7.8. It shows that actors AR11 have access to transaction bank TK01, actors AR12 to transaction bank TK03 and actors AR13 to transaction bank TK14.

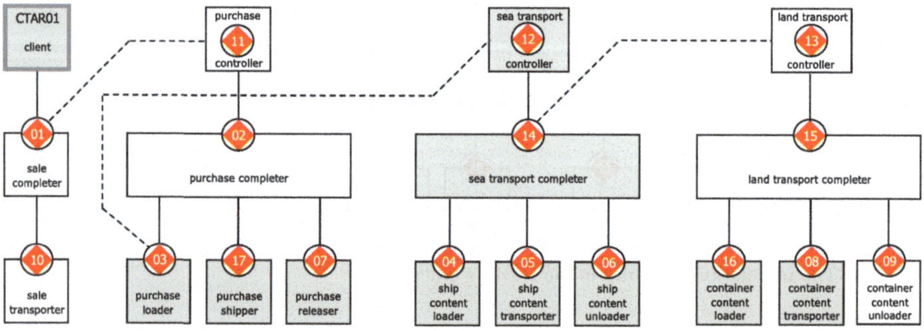

Fig. 7.9 The interstriction structure in the GloLog enterprise

7.2.4 The Interimpediment Structure

The third kind of link between transactor roles is the *wait link*. It is shown in Fig. 7.4 on the right side of the bottom part, and it should be understood as follows. The process of every transaction is a path, possibly including iterations, through the complete transaction pattern (cf. Chap. 6). Every C-act is performed in response to a C-event. The performer of the C-act may take some time before he/she responds, and this time may even exceed the intended settlement time (cf. Chap. 6), because the executor is autonomous. However, there can also be external conditions that force the performer to wait. These conditions are represented by wait links.

Collectively, the wait links represent the *interimpediment structure* of an organisation. The interimpediment structure constitutes the *process dependencies* among the transaction processes: the acts of the connected actors are held up until a specific state of the connected transaction process is reached.

The CSD in Fig. 7.10 exhibits the interimpediment structure in the GloLog enterprise, in addition to the interaction structure. The left wait link expresses that transaction processes of transactions TK10 are dependent on the progress of transactions

TK02. More specifically, the continuation of every transaction TK10 has to wait for a specific progress in some transaction TK02. In a similar way, the continuation of every transaction TK14 has to wait for a specific progress in transactions TK03 (loading goods of purchases in containers). Next, the continuation of transactions TK15 has to wait for a specific progress in transactions TK07 (release of purchases by Customs), and the continuation of transactions TK17 must wait for some progress in one or more (indicated by the cardinality range 1..*) transactions TK15 (container transports).

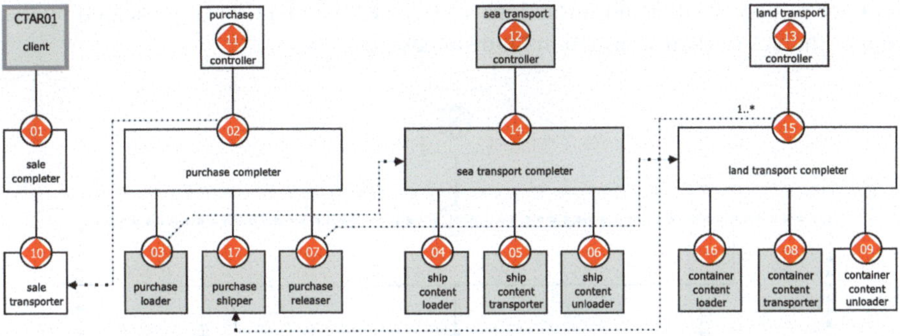

Fig. 7.10 The interimpediment structure in the GloLog enterprise

In Fig. 7.11, the three coordination structures are combined, so that one gets a comprehensive overview of the construction of the GloLog enterprise.

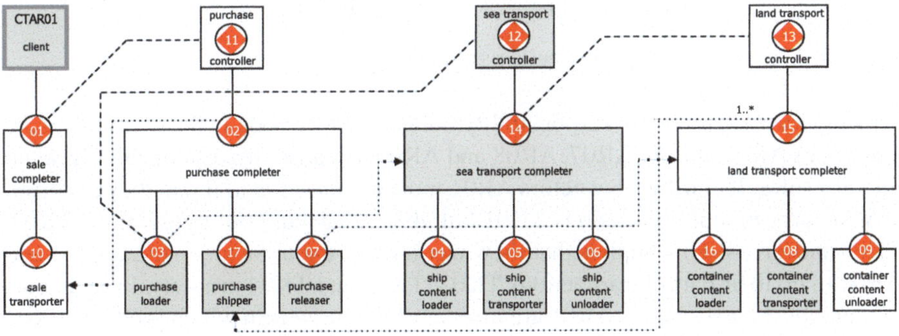

Fig. 7.11 The combined coordination structures in the GloLog enterprise

7.3 Elaborations

7.3.1 Responsibility Ranges

As discussed in Chap. 6, the two participating actors in a transaction have their own responsibility areas, which comprise the steps in the transaction process that each of them is authorised to perform. As follows from the CTP in Fig. 6.9, the responsibility area of the initiator comprises the steps rq, ac, rj, rv-rq and rv-ac (as well as allowing or refusing revocations of the promise and the declare by the executor). The responsibility area of the executor comprises the steps pm, dc, da, ex (the production act), rv-pm and rv-da (and allowing or refusing revocations of the request and the accept by the initiator). Figure 7.12 exhibits how the notion of *responsibility range* can be based on the notion of responsibility area. For example, the responsibility range of actors AR01 is indicated by the dotted-lined blue rectangle. As shown, it does not only consist of the executor responsibilities in transactions TK01 (represented by the 'lower' half of its transaction shape) but also of the initiator responsibilities in transactions TK02, TK03 and TK04 (represented by the 'upper' halves of their transaction kind shapes).

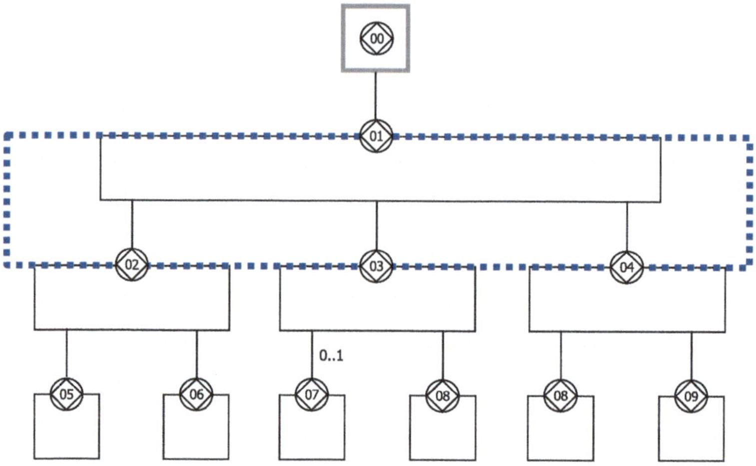

Fig. 7.12 Responsibility ranges in a business process

This extended notion of responsibility holds for every node in the tree, except the leaf nodes AR05, AR06, AR07, AR08 and AR09, because these actor roles have no initiator roles. It clarifies that actors AR01 must not only see to it that they act properly in carrying out transactions TK01 but also in carrying out transactions TK02, TK03 and TK04. This implies that they may have to exhort actors AR02, AR03 and AR04 to do their part of transactions TK02, TK03 and TK04 properly. In more current practical terms: actors AR01 are *owners* of the *process* in which products PK01 are brought about. In addition, they are *owners* of these *products* and thus of the *data* concerning them: the independent P-fact as well as the dependent P-facts that are created in transactions TK01.

7.3.2 Business Process Modelling

Although the presentation of the three kinds of coordination structures in a CSD provides a useful insight, it is often too concise for studying the business processes in detail. Notably, it is not possible to represent, in a precise way, the interimpediment structure and the intraprocess dependencies, as well as the initiations of transactions. In order to do this, the Process Structure Diagram (PSD) (cf. Chap. 11) is introduced. Below, the PSD of the sales process of the GloLog enterprise (cf. [1], Chap. 18) is presented as an example.

In Fig. 7.13, the corresponding part of interaction structure is included in the so-called click mode: the right side of Fig. 7.2 with the two parts put together. The grey-coloured thick lines correspond with the borders of the actor roles: they separate the responsibility areas in a similar way as the 'swim lanes' in BPMN [2]. The transaction kind shapes are drawn on these lines; above the line is the responsibility area of the initiator, and below the line is the responsibility area of the executor. The disk of the transaction shape is stretched horizontally, which makes it look like a 'sausage'. The diamond represents the execution phase, the part of the 'sausage' to the left represents the order phase and the part to the right represents the result phase. Consequently, one may imagine a (non-proportional) time axis from left to right.

Although the 'sausage' comprises all steps of the complete transaction pattern, only the ones that are connected to steps in other transaction kinds are shown in a PSD, and they are always put on the edge of the 'sausage'. C-acts are represented by small boxes and C-facts by small disks. The P-act is represented by a small grey box at the bottom of the (big) red diamond.

The PSD in Fig. 7.13 shows that transactions TK01 are initiated externally, thus from a different process; this is indicated by the grey colour of the small disk that is connected to [TK01/rq] by a response link. The response link corresponds with the initiator link in the CSD. Likewise, there is a response link from (TK01/pm) to [TK10/rq], expressing that transactions TK10 are initiated from the state promised of the corresponding TK01. Because of this, every transaction TK10 is said to be enclosed in a transaction TK01.

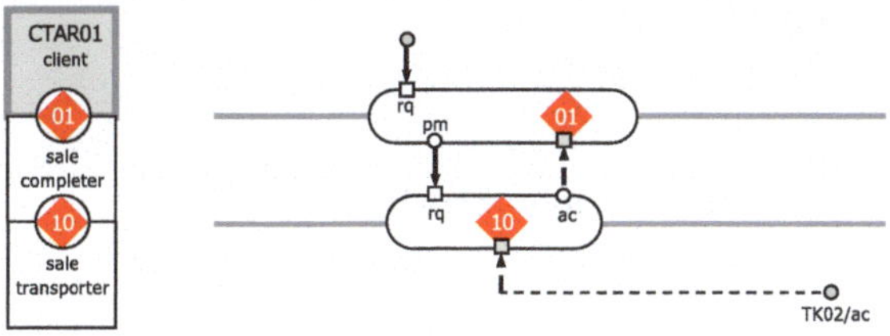

Fig. 7.13 GloLog: PSD of the sales process

The wait link from (TK10/ac) to [TK01/ex] expresses that the enclosed transaction TK10 must have reached the state (TK10/ac) before actor AR01 can proceed to perform the P-act [TK01/ex]. The interprocess wait link in Fig. 7.10 from TK02 to AR10 is made more precise in the PSD by the wait link from (TK02/ac) to [TK10/

ex]. It expresses that performing [TK10/ex] must wait until the corresponding transaction TK02 has reached the state accepted (note that a purchase instance comprises a number of sale instances). The grey colour of the small disk indicates that (TK02/ac) is a state in a process of a different business process kind.

As explained in [1], Chap. 9, the processes that are caused by a (discrete event) system are sequences of coordination events. In enterprises, these processes are commonly called *business processes*. The adjective 'business' is somewhat confusing, because it refers to the function perspective on enterprises (cf. Chap. 7). Therefore, the term 'organisational process' would be more appropriate. Nevertheless, we will adopt the term 'business process' while taking exclusively the construction perspective. As illustrated by Fig. 7.11, the four interaction (tree) structures, together with the related parts of the interstriction and the interimpediment structures, are the structures in which business processes take place. Therefore, we say that each of these tree structures corresponds with a *business process kind*. Every *business process* (instance) is some path through this structure, starting from the top transactor role (by a request for a product) and, if successful, ending in the top transactor role (by the acceptance of the product). As said, a business process kind corresponds with a BoM like product structure.

The atomic steps in every business process (instance) are coordination acts/facts (cf. Chap. 6). Because they occur always in the universal pattern of the transaction, these transactions may rightly be called the *molecules* of business processes. In Sect. 7.4.1, the structure view, as discussed above, will be compared with the currently dominant flow view in business process modelling.

The case kind of every transaction kind in a business process kind, except the self-activating transaction kind at the top, must be the same as the one at the level above it or be a part of it, like the frame in Fig. 7.3 is a part of a bicycle. If this condition is not met, the case kinds are incompatible. As an illustration, the business process structures that correspond with the product structures in Fig. 7.3 regard the same case kind or a part of it. If one is confronted with incompatible case kinds, the process structure must be split into a number of other tree structures. Because of this incompatibility, there are four distinct case kinds in the GloLog enterprise (cf. [1], Chap. 18): sale, purchase, ship content and container content. Consequently, there are four distinct business processes, only loosely coupled by access links and wait links.

7.3.3 Reference Models

The tree structures in business processes appear to contain similar patterns, which are specific for the categories of products that they bring about. These distinctions exist in addition to the product sorts that are discussed in the ALPHA theory (cf.

Chap. 8): original, informational, documental and material. In Table 7.2, the distinct categories of product kinds are listed: creating and changing, transporting and storing, transferring of ownership and obtaining usufruct. They can apply to tangible and intangible cases.

Table 7.2 Product categories

	Tangible things	Intangible things
Creating and changing	Manufacturing, changing, repairing (movable and immovable) goods	Making and adjusting decisions, advices, judgments, etc.
Transporting and storing	Transporting and storing goods or files	* Not applicable *
Transferring ownership	Buying/selling goods	Acquiring owner rights, paying, trading shares
Obtaining usufruct	Hiring/renting Space-time capacities	Using intangible things, like SaaS, movies, etc.

In the following subsections, each of the four product categories in Table 7.2 is discussed and exemplified. We do not claim that the table is exhaustive, only that it is based on many years of solid practice. The corresponding business process patterns may very well be considered *reference models* of enterprises.

7.3.3.1 Creating and Changing

By creating and changing *tangible things* is understood the making of new things (things that didn't exist before) or the extending, modifying and repairing of things. Examples of tangible things, commonly called goods, are bicycles, houses and sculptures. Things are often assemblies of other things, called their parts or components. The assembly structure of things is also called a Bill of Material (BoM). On the right side of Fig. 7.3, the BoM of a bicycle is exhibited.

In Chap. 6, the product of a transaction is defined as an independent production fact, together with its dependent facts, and a product structure is defined as a tree of independent production facts. The BoM of the bicycle in Fig. 7.3 becomes a product structure when 'bicycle' is replaced by 'assembled bicycle', 'wheel' by 'assembled wheel', 'spoke' by 'acquired spoke', etc. Note that only the real 'leaf' parts, like the rim and the hub, are acquired (or taken from the shelf); all other parts are assemblies. Figure 7.14 exhibits the CSD of the corresponding business process kind.

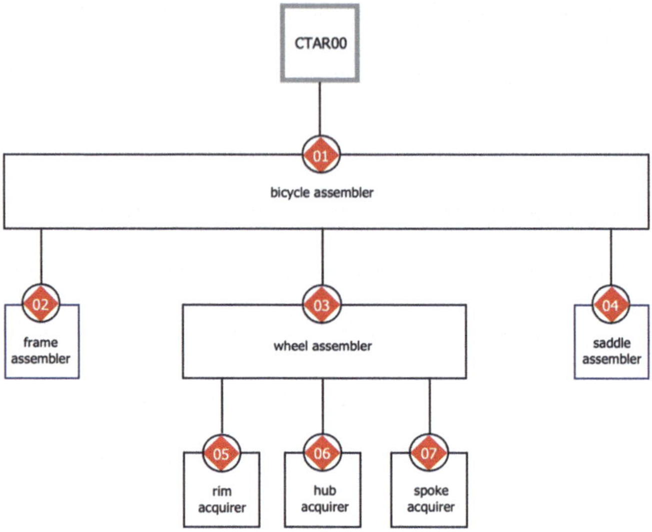

Fig. 7.14 Reference CSD for creating and changing

The creating and changing of *intangible* things, like insurance policies, building licences and judgments, is pretty much similar to what has been said about tangible things. Only the number of levels in the product structure is commonly smaller.

7.3.3.2 Transporting and Storing

Transporting and storing are exclusively associated with *tangible* things. They constitute the core of logistic operations. We have seen examples of such operations in the GloLog enterprise, as presented in Sects. 7.2.2–7.2.4 and in [1], Chap. 18. Like it is the case for creating goods, the products in transporting and storing have also BoM-like structures (cf. Fig. 7.5), and these structures can also easily be extended. As an example in the GloLog enterprise, the completion of the land transport of a container (cf. Fig. 7.8) consists of loading the container on a truck, actually transporting the container from one location to another and unloading the container. Each of these transaction kinds may have a subtree. For example, transporting the container may be decomposed into picking the container and putting it on a truck, driving the truck to the premises of IES and taking the container from the truck. It is not so hard to imagine how each of these transaction kinds, on their turn, may be further decomposed, if needed. Figure 7.15 exhibits the CSD of the resulting part of the GloLog enterprise.

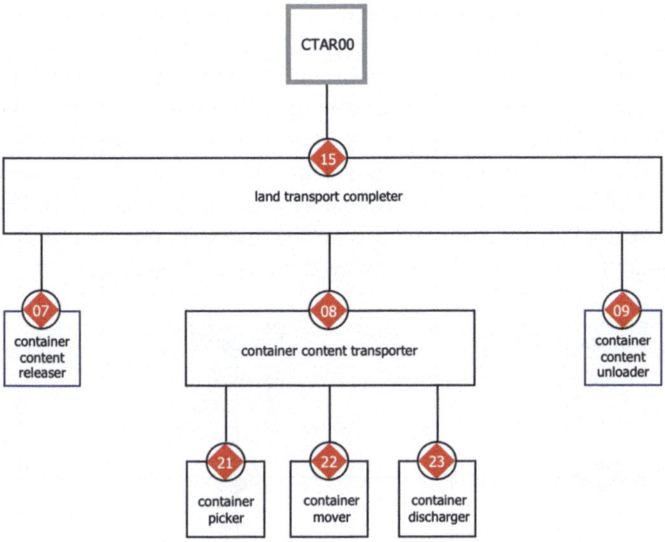

Fig. 7.15 Reference CSD of business process kinds for transporting and storing

As explained by the FI theory (cf. [1], Sect. 5.3), the form part of an information item is inscribed in some physical substance. In modern digital technologies, the physical substance is mostly electrical, magnetic or optical. In the ALPHA theory (cf. Chap. 8), the word 'file' is used to refer to the collection of physical 'inscriptions' that together carry a document (or data set). Files are transported and stored, in much the same way as goods are transported and stored. Consequently, reference models apply that are similar to the one exhibited in Fig. 7.15. For example, in order to transport a file on your computer to another computer, a number of physical actions must be performed, including the transmission of the file through a computer network.

7.3.3.3 Transferring Ownership

In most civil codes, buying and selling are the dual notions (cf. [1], Chap. 5) related to a (legal) agreement or contract between two parties about the transfer of ownership of *tangible* things from the seller to the buyer, commonly in exchange of an amount of money.

In the OMEGA theory, paying is considered a separate transaction because it results in the creation of an original product, namely, the transfer of ownership of an amount of money. Omitting the payment transaction does not affect the transfer of ownership of the goods, however. So, one can very well become owner of a thing without doing something in return, which means getting the thing for free.

As an example of the reference model that corresponds with the transfer of ownership of things, Fig. 7.16 exhibits, on the left side, the general pattern of transferring ownership. On the right side, the specific pattern for the case Pizzeria (cf. Chap. 12) is shown. The transactor roles TAR01 and TAR03 represent, respectively, the transfer of ownership of goods and the transfer of ownership of money. As said, payments are not an inherent part of an ontological model. They occur if the ownership transfer crosses the border of economic (or business) units (cf. Chap. 8). Inside such a unit, there are no payments for services. Next, transactor roles TAR02 and TAR04 in Fig. 7.16 are considered enterprise specific. If the goods can be taken from stock, there is no manufacturing (like the preparing of pizzas). Next, if the goods are taken out by the customer, there is no delivering.

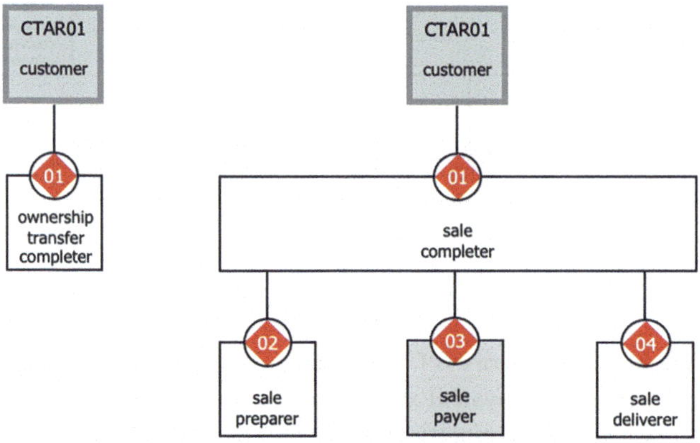

Fig. 7.16 Reference CSD in which ownership is transferred

To illustrate how buying/selling things is conceived in the OMEGA theory, transaction kind TK01 regards the fulfilment of the selling/buying contract, in this case the transfer of ownership of pizzas. The transfer of ownership of the amount to pay is represented by transaction kind TK03. Every TK03 is enclosed in a TK01. Transactions TK01 have two other components: the preparing of the pizzas (TK02) and the delivering of the pizzas to the customer's place (TK04). Note that the case kind in all product kinds is the same, namely, the sale. Sale is the conception of the product from the perspective of the supplier, as discussed in Chap. 5. From the perspective of the buyer, it is a purchase.

Next to tangible things, the ownership of intangible things can be transferred. A good example is paying. A payment is the transfer of ownership of an amount of money, and money is basically something intangible (note that banknotes and coins have a money value only by agreement of the involved social parties).

7.3.3.4 Obtaining Usufruct

Next to the transfer of ownership of goods, which basically implies a permanent right of usufruct of the owned goods, one may grant temporary usufruct of *tangible* things. These things are always space-time resources, things that one uses or occupies for some time. Figure 7.17 exhibits the most general reference model. It is a simple tree of which the top is the transaction kind TK01 (concluding of the usufruct case). There are two enclosed transaction kinds: TK02 and TK03. In a transaction TK02 (resource seizing), the user occupies the resource at the agreed beginning of the usufruct period. In a transaction TK03 (resource releasing), the user releases the occupied resource at the agreed ending of this period.

A usufruct contract concerning tangible things, like cars, houses, hotel rooms and chairs in an aircraft, a stadium or a theatre, is commonly called *renting*. As an example, if one rents a car, one gets the right to use the car for some period, and if one books a seat on a flight, one gets the right to use a chair in the aircraft with which the flight is carried out. Because payments are no inherent parts of ontological models (cf. Chap. 8), they are omitted in Fig. 7.17.

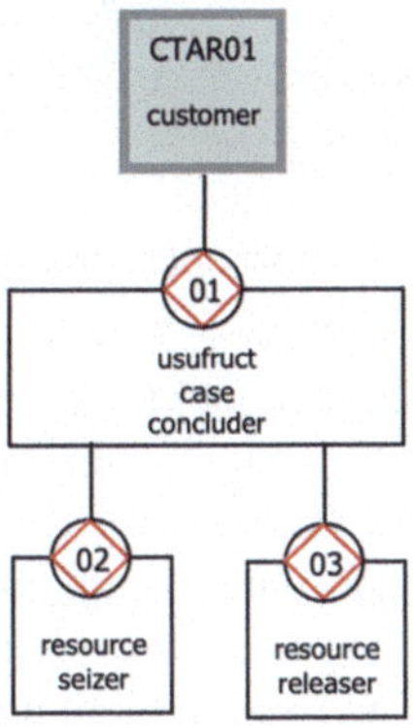

transaction kind	product kind	executor role
TK01 usufruct case concluding	PK01 [usufruct case] is concluded	AR01 usufruct case concluder
TK02 resource seizing	PK02 the resource of [usufruct case] is seized	AR02 resource seizer
TK03 resource releasing	PK03 the resource of [usufruct case] is released	AR03 resource releaser

Fig. 7.17 Reference CSD for granting usufruct

The obtaining of usufruct of intangible things (like SaaS and other 'software' on a non-proprietary basis) is also represented by Fig. 7.17, although there is no scarcity. Mostly, one gets the usufruct of a tangible thing (a file) as carrier of the intangible service one wants, but there are as many files as needed.

Seizing and releasing space-time resources are commonly called checking in and checking out, respectively. Checking in means that one shows up, at the car rental office, at the gate or at the hotel, for actually driving, flying or staying, respectively.

It corresponds with declaring that one has seized the resource, so with performing a [TK02/da]. Checking out corresponds with declaring that one has released the resource, so with performing a [TK03/da].

To the reference CSD in Fig. 7.17 belongs a typical reference PSD. It is exhibited in Fig. 7.18. What the PSD shows specifically is that the enclosed transactions TK02 (resource seizing) and TK03 (resource releasing) are initiated from the state of being requested in the enclosing TK01. In addition, performing the act [TK03/rq] has to wait for the being promised of the seizing (TK02/pm). After the releasing has also been promised (TK03/pm), the transaction TK01 can be promised. Expressed in more practical terms, concluding a usufruct case, like booking a seat on a flight or a room in a hotel, implies that one has committed oneself to check in and to check out. Not showing up for a check-in (called a no-show) means that the (in general scarce) resource cannot be occupied by somebody else.

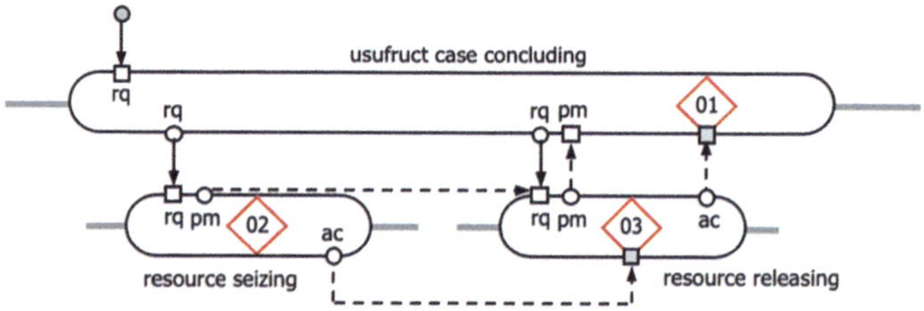

Fig. 7.18 Reference PSD for granting usufruct of tangible things

Figure 7.19 exhibits the reference model for car rental companies (cf. [1], Chap. 15). The general transaction kinds 'resource seizing' and 'resource releasing' are replaced by the more specific 'car taking' and 'car returning'. Likewise, 'usufruct case concluding' is replaced by 'car rental completing'. Because transactions of the kind TK01 (car rental completing) take place between separate economic units (namely, the renter and Rent-A-Car, two payment transactor roles are added, one for paying a deposit (TAR04) and one for paying the (final) invoice (TAR05), which may include fines).

Next to the single obtaining of usufruct, like renting a car, there are contracts that give one the right on multiple instances of usufruct. For example, by becoming member of a tennis club, one acquires the right to play on the courts of the club as often as one likes (provided there is a free court). Similarly, by subscribing to a music-streaming service, one can listen all day to one's favourite music. In these cases, there are two additional processes. The first one regards becoming a member, and the second one regards ending the membership. We will illustrate them for the case library (cf. Chap. 13). The CSD and the TPT are shown in Fig. 7.20. On the left side of the diagram are the added transaction kinds membership starting (TK01) and membership ending (TK02). When being member, one is authorised to initiate transactions TK03 (loan concluding).

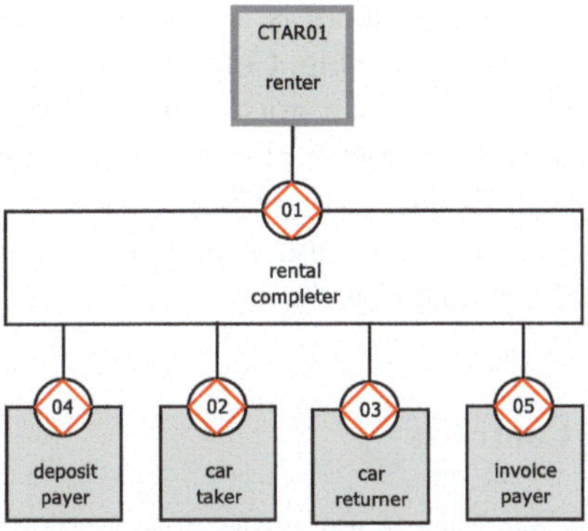

transaction kind	product kind	executor role
TK01 rental completing	PK01 [rental] **is** completer	AR01 rental completer
TK02 car taking	PK02 **the** car **of** [rental] **is** taken	AR02 car taker
TK03 car returning	PK03 **the** car **of** [rental] **is** returned	AR03 car returner
TK04 deposit paying	PK04 **the** deposit **of** [rental] **is** paid	AR04 deposit payer
TK05 invoice paying	PK05 **the** invoice **of** [rental] **is** paid	AR05 invoice payer

Fig. 7.19 Reference CSD and TPT of car rental companies

Actors AR03 will therefore check for every TK03 whether the membership under which the borrower wants to borrow a book is a valid membership, i.e. a membership that is started and not yet ended. This is represented in Fig. 7.20 by the access links from AR03 to TK01 and TK02. The general transaction kinds 'resource seizing' and 'resource releasing' (cf. Fig. 7.17) are replaced by the more specific ones 'book taking' and 'book returning'.

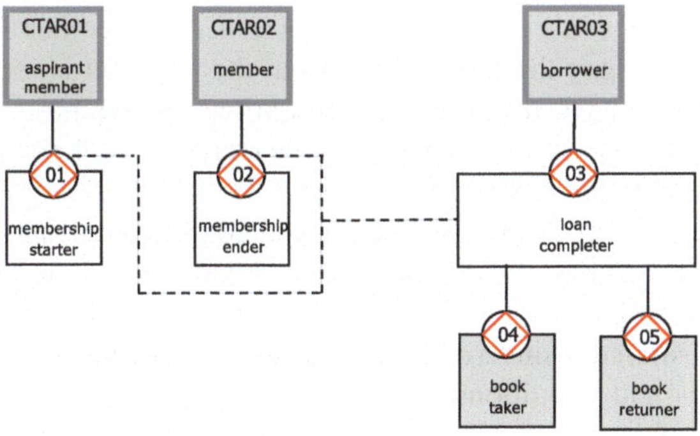

transaction kind	product kind	executor role
TK01 membership starting	PK01 [membership] **is** started	AR01 membership starter
TK02 membership ending	PK02 [membership] **is** ended	AR02 membership ender
TK03 loan completing	PK03 [loan] **is** completed	AR03 loan completer
TK04 book taking	PK04 **the** book **of** [loan] **is** taken	AR04 book taker
TK05 book returning	PK05 **the** book **of** [loan] **is** returned	AR05 book returner

Fig. 7.20 Reference CSD and TPT of libraries

In contemporary business practice, there is a tendency to offer the usufruct of things instead of transferring their ownership. Commonly, the usufruct is then often called a *service*. Renting cars is already a good example of providing and using services. In many cities, one can nowadays also rent bikes, e-bikes and scooters. Well-known examples in the ICT business are Software as a Service (SaaS) and Platform as a Service (PaaS). As discussed above, there is no scarcity of the physical carriers. They can be created if the need is there.

7.3.3.5 The Ontology of Contracts

In the preceding subsections, we have come across notions like sale (and purchase), rental and membership. They are special kinds of the general notion of contract. A contract is an agreement between parties in which the conditions regarding the mutual delivery of services is stated. The transfer of ownership of a number of pizzas in exchange of the transfer of ownership of an amount of money is a typical and well-known example of a contract. It is called a sale from the perspective of the seller and a purchase from the perspective of the buyer (cf. Sect. 5.3). Both parties may specify terms and conditions concerning such contracts. Consequently, we speak of terms and conditions of sale and of terms and conditions of purchase. Moreover, Civil Codes usually contain sections in which the rights and duties of the legal parties in legal/economic contracts are laid down.

A sale in the case Pizzeria (cf. Chap. 12) is a contract between the legal entity Pizzeria and the legal entity customer. The first is represented by Mia and the second by some person. The sale entity, thus the contract, is created at the moment that the request is performed, which means that the whole process of performing the C-act is completed (cf. Fig. 6.5). The applicable terms and conditions of sale are accessible to the customer, who is considered to comply with them when he/she performs the request in a sale completing transaction. Among other things, it implies that the customer will pay the money due when the payment is requested. Private customers commonly have no terms and conditions of purchase, but companies commonly do. If this is the case, they are considered to be known to the selling party, who is considered to comply with them.

The compliance of a customer with terms and conditions of sale may be explicitly assessed in the sincerity division of the assess part of the action rule for settling customer requests, as discussed in Chap. 11. Customers who do not comply with the rules are thus considered insincere or untrustworthy. Likewise, the compliance of a vendor with terms and conditions of purchase may be explicitly assessed in the sincerity division of the action rule for settling the promise of vendors to sell.

7.3.3.6 Enforcing Laws

Enforcing laws or rules is not a separate category in Table 7.2 but a combination of the existing ones. Still, it seems worthwhile to spend a section on this topic because it has quite some societal importance. To start with, there is no fundamental difference between the enforcement of laws by the police and, for example, the checking whether employees comply with the business rules that are in place.

There are always two processes. The first one is making laws or rules. It belongs to the category of creating and changing (intangible) things in Table 7.2. Thus, the reference model of Fig. 7.14 applies. The final product kind PK01 is a (societal) law or a (business) rule. In terms of the MU theory (cf. [1], Chap. 6), societal laws and business rules are existence laws or occurrence laws concerning some world. Collectively, these laws determine which states and/or which transitions are lawful. Because of the basic autonomy of actors, laws can be disobeyed or violated. Consequently, the P-world or C-world of an organisation can be in an unlawful state. An example of violating a societal law is driving at a speed of 120 km/h where the speed limit is 90 km/h. An example of violating a business rule is starting the membership of a tennis club for an 11-year-old kid if the minimum age is 12 years.

The second process in enforcing laws is about dealing with violations. According to the PSI theory (cf. Chap. 6), in particular Habermas' idea of discourse, the actor who violates a rule has to give account of the violation, so to explain why he/she has deviated from the rule. There may be good reasons for the violation. In the example of driving too fast, the driver could be a medical doctor who is on her way to the hospital to give medical care to a road casualty. In the example of the tennis club, the 11-year-old boy (whose name appears to be Rafael Nadal) may be considered a very promising tennis player, who would otherwise go to the rival tennis club in town. There must always be room for discussion and discourse.

But in the end, measures may be taken. There are two kinds of such measures. One aims at correcting the unlawful state. It could be an option in the tennis club case. As explained in Chap. 6, this can be achieved by revoking the promise of the tennis club official in the membership start transaction. In the subsequent discussions (and possibly discourse), the tennis club official has to convince the aspirant member that he/she is not allowed to make him member of the club.

The other kind of measure aims at trying to discourage or prohibit that the unlawful state happens again. In general, two (original) transaction kinds are needed to take measures. One is observing the violation of the law, and the other is effectuating the discouraging or prohibiting. The common way of discouraging future misbehaviour is by imposing a fine. The common way of prohibiting misbehaviour is by depriving the offender of her/his freedom, normally by imprisoning her/him. Note that these transactions belong to the category of creating and changing.

7.4 Discussions

7.4.1 Structure Thinking Versus Flow Thinking

The dominant way of thinking in business process management, as exemplified by the widespread approach BPMN [2] is *flow thinking*. By this is meant that one perceives a business process as a sequence of actions or tasks that affect an entity or case, like a purchase or sale. The word 'flow' refers to the 'flowing' of the cases through the sequence of actions. Flows are not necessarily monolithic; it may also consist of parallel (sub) flows. In the previous sections, we have introduced an alternative way of thinking about business processes, which we refer to as *structure thinking*. There are at least two situations in which flow thinking seems to be insufficient.

The first one is the situation that there are *different case kinds* in a (monolithic) process. This necessarily leads to splitting the process into parallel processes, loosely coupled by the interstriction structure and the interimpediment structure. A good example of this situation is the GloLog enterprise, whose interaction structure is exhibited in Fig. 7.8. The 'main' business process kind is the one that is initiated by the client. The other three process kinds emerge from the necessity to devise separate processes because of incompatible case kinds. Consequently, these processes are initiated internally. The four process kinds together accomplish that, at the end, the client gets the goods that he/she has ordered.

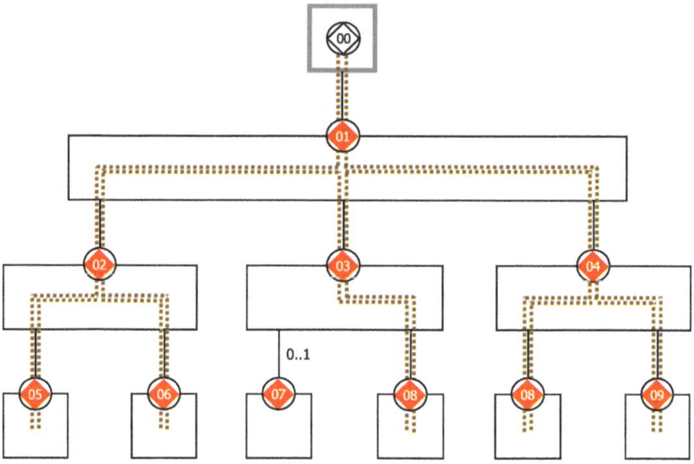

Fig. 7.21 Structure thinking versus flow thinking

The second situation is when one wants to make major changes to a business process kind. To illustrate this situation, let us have a look at Fig. 7.21, in which the interaction structure of Fig. 7.5 is copied. When applying structure thinking, one would get the next understanding of the whole process. It starts from an actor in CTAR00, who performs a request for a TK01, directed to an actor AR01. In response to it, the actor AR01 decides that he/she needs three other products in order to bring about the requested PK01, namely, a PK02, a PK03 and a PK04. So, the AR01 performs corresponding requests to, respectively, an AR02, an AR03 and an AR04. The bringing about of these products may be done in parallel, but there may also be dependencies, like the ones we have seen in Fig. 7.15. On their turn, actors AR02, AR03 and AR04 need to start transactions in which products of the kinds PK05, PK06, PK07, PK08 and PK09 are brought about. Because the PK07 is optional, as indicated by the cardinality range 0..1, Fig. 7.21 shows, for the sake of illustration, the situation in which no PK07 is needed. Note also that two products PK08 are produced: one as part of a PK03 and one as part of a PK04.

When applying flow thinking, one would primarily follow the dotted brown lines in the figure and consequently would understand the whole process basically as the next sequence of acts: [TK01/rq], [TK01/pm], [TK02/rq], [TK02/pm], [TK05/rq], [TK05/pm], [TK05/da], [TK05/ac], [TK06/rq], [TK06/pm], [TK06/da], [TK06/ac], [TK02/da], [TK02/ac], [TK03/rq], [TK03/pm], [TK08/rq], [TK08/pm], [TK08/da], [TK08/ac], [TK03/da], [TK03/ac], [TK04/rq], [TK04/pm], [TK08/rq], [TK08/pm], [TK08/da], [TK08/ac], [TK09/rq], [TK09/pm], [TK09/da], [TK09/ac], [TK04/da], [TK04/ac], [TK01/da], [TK01/ac].

Two comments are in place. The first one is that in this sequence, the possible parallel carrying out of transactions is ignored, just to keep it simple. The second comment is that the acts are indicated by their names as transaction steps, just for the sake of convenience. Other names would also be fine.

Let us point out two major drawbacks of flow thinking and illustrate them using the example above. The first drawback is that it is very hard, if not impossible, to 'see' what the consequences of changing a part of the process are for other parts. For example, if one would like to replace the process of bringing about the component PK04 in every PK01 by another process, this concerns two separated parts in the sequence, namely, the part that is represented by [TK04/rq] and [TK04/pm] and the part represented by [TK04/da] and [TK04/ac]. Moreover, one must be aware that the part in between these two, so the part that is represented by the sequence from [TK08/rq] through [TK09/ac], may also need to be changed as a consequence of changing the production of the PK04. One should also keep in mind that the transactor roles in Fig. 7.16 are original ones, i.e. they belong to the O-organisation of an enterprise (cf. Chap. 8). But every actor role will have sub-trees in the corresponding I-, D- and M-organisation. In the current practice of business process modelling, such distinctions are not made.

The second drawback of flow thinking is that it becomes easily unclear who is responsible for what. Let us take as an example the part of the process that is represented by the sequence [TK05/rq], [TK05/pm], [TK05/da], [TK05/ac], [TK06/rq], [TK06/pm], [TK06/da], [TK06/ac]. Structure thinking tells us accurately that an actor AR02 is responsible for performing the [TK05/rq], as well as the [TK06/rq]. In the usual layout of workplaces, however, actors AR05 would be located close to actors AR06, and actors AR05 would pass their work (the PK05s) to actors AR06, which could easily lead to the idea in actors AR06 that they are ordered to produce their PK06s by actors AR05. Imagine, as an example a bicycle factory where bicycles are assembled according to the BoM in Fig. 7.3 (right side). The actor who completes the frame of the bicycle passes it to her/his 'neighbour' who mounts the saddle on the frame, etc. The tree structure in Fig. 7.21 is fully clear about responsibilities: actors AR02 are initiators of transactions TK05 and TK06.

7.4.2 Transforming Flows into Trees

As said, flow thinking may be useful, in particular when one wants to explain the details of the implementation of business process kinds, but when it comes to analyse, optimise or (re)design them, flow-based knowledge is insufficient. An interesting question then is how one can transform flow structures into tree structures. The answer is provided by the combined application of the OMEGA theory, the PSI theory (cf. Chap. 6) and the ALPHA theory (cf. Chap. 8). Let us illustrate this, using the flow charts of the case Volley [3], which are reproduced in Figs. 7.22, 7.23, 7.24 and 7.25. It is about becoming member of a tennis club. Applying the ALPHA theory means distinguishing between the O-, I-, D- and M-organisation and subsequently abstracting from realisation. In Figs. 7.22, 7.23, 7.24 and 7.25, documental (thus D-organisation) as well as material (thus M-organisation) acts are indicated by 'documental' and informational (thus I-organisation) acts by 'informational', to which the letter 'P' (for production) or 'C' (for coordination) may be added. Only to original (thus O-organisation) acts, we apply in addition the PSI theory, which means that these acts are labeled as transaction steps in the complete transaction pattern. Lastly, the names of tacitly performed steps are put between '[' and ']'.

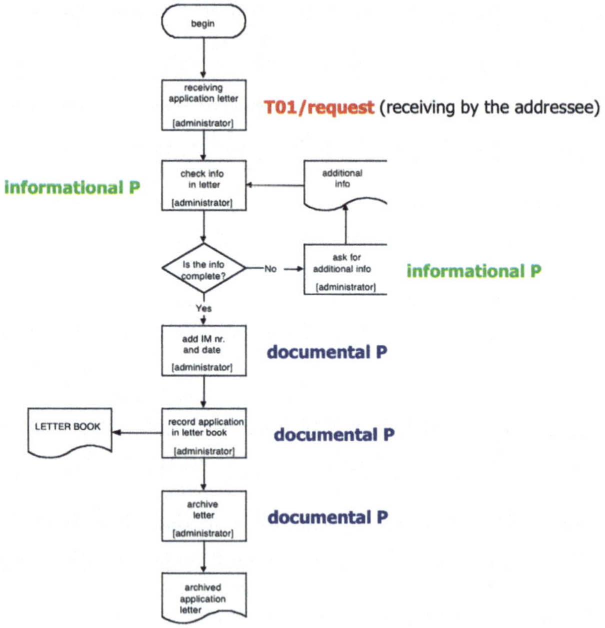

Fig. 7.22 Case Volley—Flow Chart 1

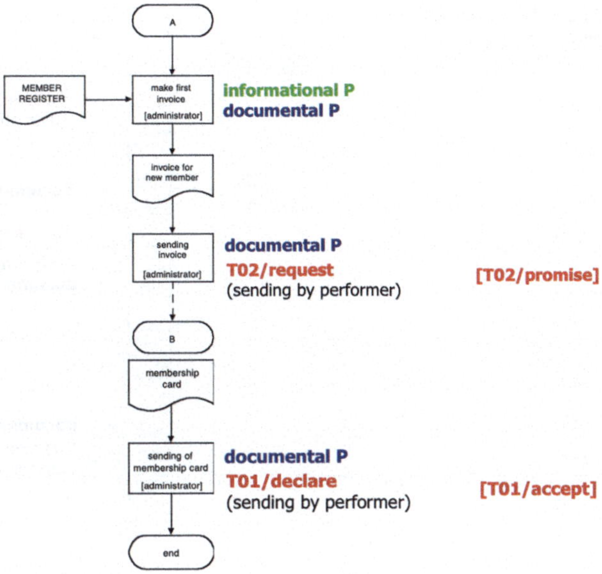

Fig. 7.23 Case Volley—Flow Chart 2

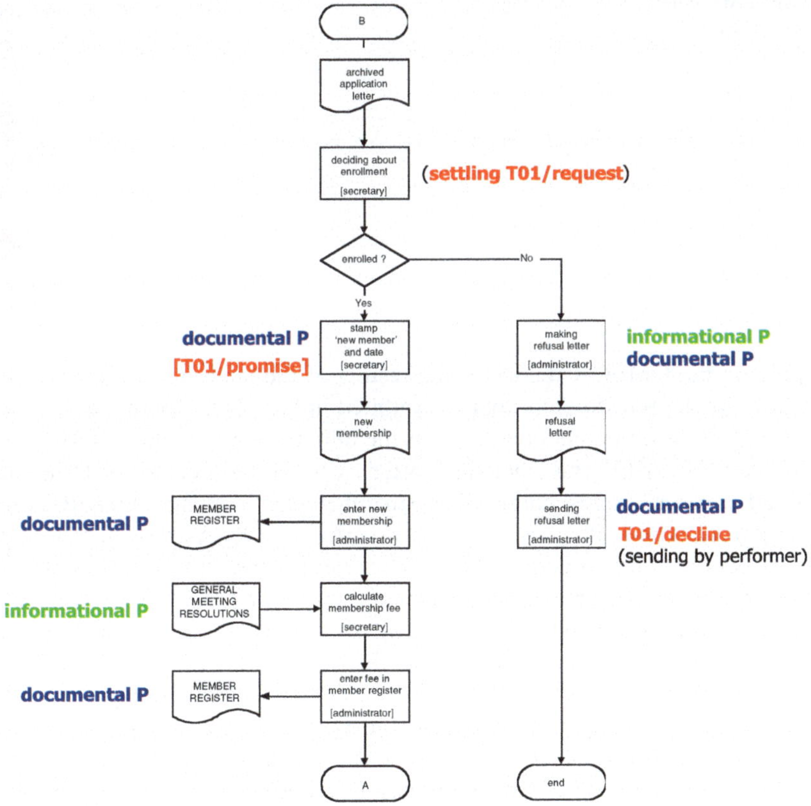

Fig. 7.24 Case Volley—Flow Chart 3

Fig. 7.25 Case Volley—Flow Chart 4

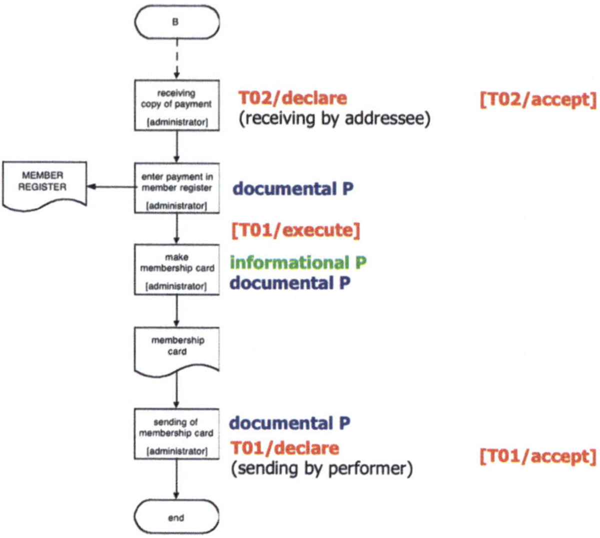

Fig. 7.26 CSD of the enterprise Volley

Applying the OMEGA theory to the results of the analysis of the flow charts yields the simple tree structure that is exhibited in Fig. 7.26. There are three actor roles: CTAR00 (aspirant member), who is the initiator of transactions TK01 (membership starting); AR01 (membership starter), who is the executor of transactions TK01 and initiator of transactions TK02 (membership payment); and AR02 (membership payer), who is the executor of transactions TK02. As shown, transactions TK02 are enclosed in transactions TK01. The tree structure in Fig. 7.26 conforms to the reference model for creating and changing (cf. Fig. 7.14).

As extensively discussed in [3], the CSD of the enterprise Volley in Fig. 7.26 shows at the same time more and less than the flow charts in Figs. 7.22, 7.23, 7.24 and 7.25. It shows more because it contains the complete transaction pattern of both transaction kinds. An important practical consequence is that one is made aware of the process 'exceptions', like the decline and the reject, and the four revocation patterns. They are easily forgotten otherwise. In addition, one is made aware that coordination acts can be performed tacitly. Tacitly performed acts are major causes of business process failures in practice. A 'no news is good news' rule could be justified in the past; it certainly is now not anymore, given the potential of modern ICT.

The CSD in Fig. 7.26 shows less because it is abstracted from the realisation and implementation of the enterprise Volley, whereas the flow charts in Figs. 7.22, 7.23, 7.24 and 7.25 show realisation and implementation details. But as one can easily check, they are not complete. Every flow chart includes what the maker (the analyst) has observed and has considered worthwhile to include. In contrast, the devising of the I-, D- and M-organisation according to the ALPHA theory (cf. Chap. 8) is systematic and therefore comprehensive, as is the implementation of all three aspect organisations.

7.4.3 The Loose Coupling of Processes

Above we have said that the distinct interaction trees in an organisation are loosely coupled through the existing interstriction and interimpediment structures. It means that the distinct business process kinds influence each other through these structures, but without the need to interact. The practical advantage is that each business process can be re-designed (and subsequently be re-engineered and re-implemented) independently of the processes with which they are connected through these structures. Only the interfaces, thus the access links and the wait links, must be properly dealt with.

The notion of loose coupling has a history in systems design that dates back to 1972 when David Parnas published his paper on the decomposing of (software) systems into modules. It is included in [4]. Without calling it loose coupling, many other researchers, like Edsger Dijkstra [5, 6] and Michael Jackson [7, 8], proceeded in the same way. A more recent approach to the modularisation of systems is normalised systems [9]. Although all of them focus on software engineering, the applied principles of modular design have a broader scope. The invariable key question is how to decompose a (too) complex system into comprehensible, manageable and maintainable parts (modules).

The OMEGA theory, as presented in this chapter, offers an approach to modularising organisations, based on the tree structures that are inherent in the products that are brought about. It is a most natural way to achieve maximum cohesion within a process tree and minimum dependencies between them, as extensively discussed in Sects. 7.2 and 7.3. As an additional illumination of the soundness of the theory, let us study the consequences of the narrowing down of the SoI in the case GloLog. To this end, Fig. 7.27 exhibits the narrowing down to the sales and the purchase processes, thus excluding or ignoring the land transport process and the sea transport process. It is indicated by the yellow lined rectangle. This rectangle cuts across several access and wait links. The question now is how these links must be represented in a CSD of the new SoI.

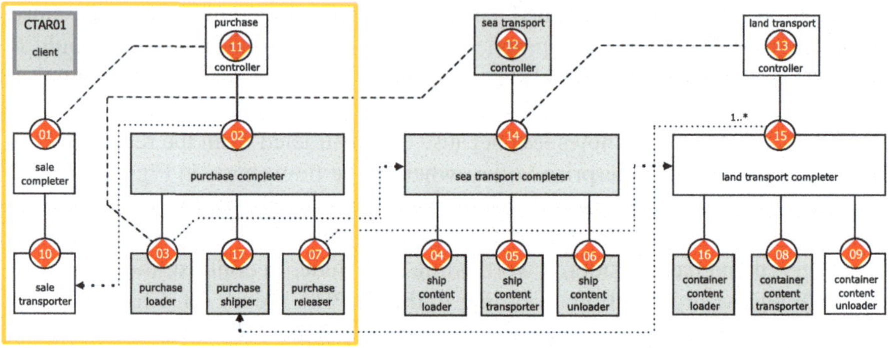

Fig. 7.27 Narrowing down the scope in the case GloLog (1)

The access link from actor role AR12 to transaction kind TK03 can just be left out because it represents an information need from outside the new scope. For similar reasons, the wait link from TK03 to AR14 and the one from TK07 to AR15 can be omitted. The only interdependency we have to take care of is the wait link from TK15 to AR17. Figure 7.28 shows how this is done, namely, by including the (now external) transaction kind TK15. In order to illustrate access links to external transaction kinds, the one to the multiple bank MTK01 is included.

Fig. 7.28 Narrowing down the scope in the case GloLog (2)

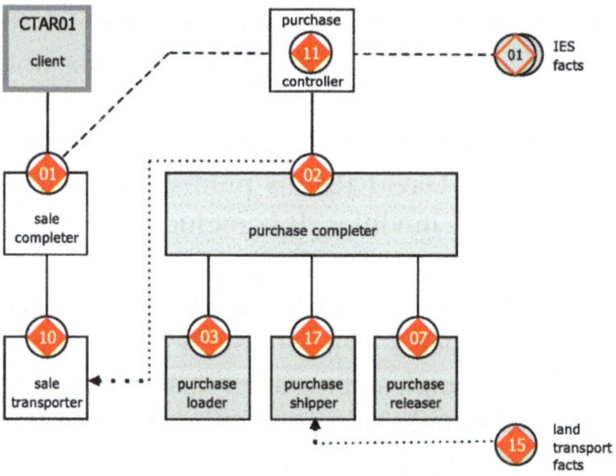

7.4.4 The Practical Importance of the OMEGA Theory

The OMEGA theory is meant to be, and has also proven to be, an intellectual instrument in discovering and profiting from the tree structures that exist in business processes, once these processes have been understood in the ontological way as provided by the PSI theory (cf. Chap. 6). The key concept on which the OMEGA theory builds is the transactor role. It is the building block of organisations and consequently of the business processes that become manifest when these organisations are operational.

The understanding of a business process as a tree of transaction processes, in the way we discussed it in Sect. 7.2.2, is probably the most important insight that the OMEGA theory offers. Therefore, it was taken as the definition of *business process*. The (interaction) tree structure resembles the product structure of the 'top' product in the tree. Consequently, the core entity or case kind in each node of a tree must be the same as the one in the higher node (the parent) or be a true part of it. Structure clashes are solved by conceiving separate trees, as demonstrated for the case GloLog. The provided insight is lacking in contemporary approaches to business process modelling, like BPMN [2, 10], UML [11, 12], Aris [13] and ArchiMate [14]. Concluding, it should not be a surprise that these approaches offer little help when major process changes are at stake.

The tree structure also allows for a clear and precise discussion of the often vaguely defined notions of process and data ownership (cf. Sect. 7.3.1). The combination of tree thinking and flow thinking for practical business process analysis was demonstrated in Sects. 7.4.1 and 7.4.2.

The second important insight is that the dependencies between (interaction) tree structures can simply be expressed in an additional *interstriction structure* and an additional *interimpediment structure*. The first one represents the *state dependencies* among business processes, so the situations in which for performing a process step, the state of another business process is taken into account. The second one represents the *process dependencies* among business processes, so the situations in which one has to wait for a specific progress in another business process in order to perform a step (in the current process). The precise nature of the impediments can be expressed in the PSD, as discussed in Sect. 7.3.2.

The third practical insight that the OMEGA theory provides is that there are only a few really different process structures. In Sect. 7.3.3, we have called them *reference models*. They may remain a subject of ongoing research, but it looks like one can do with a limited number of 'fibre' structures, on top of the 'molecules' and 'atoms' as presented in [15]. They can be used as building blocks to construct the essential model of any enterprise in a short amount of time.

References

1. Dietz, J. L. G., & Mulder, J. B. F. (2024). *Enterprise ontology—A human-centric approach to understanding the essence of organisation* (Enterprise engineering) (2nd ed.). Springer Nature.
2. Mendling, J., & Weidlich, M. (2012). *Business process model and notation. Proceedings of the 4th International Workshop, BPMN 2012, Vienna, Austria, September 12–13, 2012* (Lecture notes in business information processing). Springer. p. 1 online resource.
3. Perinforma, A. P. C. (2015). *The essence of organisation*. Sapio Enterprise Engineering.
4. Parnas, D. L., Hoffman, D. M., & Weiss, D. M. (2001). *Software fundamentals* (Collected papers by David L. Parnas). Addison-Wesley. xxiv, 664 p.
5. Dijkstra, E. W. (1970). *Notes on structures programming*. Technological University Eindhoven.
6. Dijkstra, E. W. (1976). *A discipline of programming* (Prentice-Hall series in automatic computation). Prentice-Hall. XVII, 217 p.

7. Jackson, M. A. (1975). *Principles of program design. A P I C studies in data processing*. Academic Press. xii, 299 p.
8. Jackson, M. A. (1983). *System development* (Prentice-Hall International series in computer science). Prentice/Hall International. XIV, 418 p.
9. Mannaert, H., Verelst, J., & de Bruyn, P. (2016). *Normalized systems—From foundations for evolvable software toward a general theory for evolvabler design*. Koppa.
10. Dumas, M., et al. *Fundamentals of business process management* (2nd ed.). 1 online resource.
11. ACM Digital Library. (2010). *UML: Unified Modeling Language*. ACM Digital Library.
12. Scott, K. (2001). *UML explained*. Addison-Wesley. xviii, 151 p.
13. Scheer, A.-W. (1999). *ARIS—Business process modeling*. 2., completely rev. and enl. ed (p. XIX, 218 S). Springer.
14. Group, T.O. (2010). *ArchiMate** 1.0 Specification? Technical Standard*. Van Haren Publishing. 1 online resource (161 p.).
15. Dietz, J. L. G. (2003). The atoms, molecules and fibres of organizations. *Data and Knowledge Engineering, 47*, 24.

Chapter 8
The EE Organisational Essence Theory

Abstract The EE organisational essence theory, or ALPHA theory, is a theory about the distinction of layers of transactor roles in an organisation, based on the sort of production that transactors bring about: original, informational, documental or material. Original production comprises all production acts that result in original new facts. Examples are devising things, deciding and judging as well as manufacturing, transporting and observing things. Informational production acts comprise remembering, computing and deriving facts and sharing (remembered or derived) facts. Documental production acts comprise saving, providing and transforming documents or data (containing facts). Material production comprises storing, retrieving, copying, transmitting and destroying files. Accordingly, the organisation of an enterprise can be partitioned into four partial organisations: the O-organisation (O from original), the I-organisation (I from informational), the D-organisation (D from documental) and the M-organisation (M from material). The I-organisation supports the O-organisation by means of informational services (remembering and sharing facts), the D-organisation supports the I-organisation by means of documental services (saving and providing data or documents) and the M-organisation supports the D-organisation by means of material service (storing and retrieving files). Because original acts are the only acts that change the state of the 'business' world of an enterprise (i.e. the production world of its O-organisation), they must be performed by human actors. For I-, D- and M-acts, it holds that they can be taken over by artefacts, notably ICT systems, including AI artefacts (like logistic control systems and robots). However, as pointed out in the PSI theory, human actors are ultimately responsible and accountable for the acts of these artefacts. The ontological model of an enterprise's O-organisation is called its essential model. Like every ontological model, it is abstracted from implementation, but it is also abstracted from realisation, i.e. from the supporting I-, D- and M-organisation. Yet it contains everything that is needed to understand the essence of an enterprise's operation. The ALPHA theory contributes to the generic enterprise engineering goal of intellectual manageability

Reprinted from J. L. G. Dietz, H. B. F. Mulder, *Enterprise Ontology*, The Enterprise Engineering Series, https://doi.org/10.1007/978-3-031-53361-7_11.

J. L. G. Dietz, H. B. F. Mulder, *Enterprise Design Fundamentals*, The Enterprise Engineering Series, https://doi.org/10.1007/978-3-031-83262-8_8

by an unprecedented reduction of complexity. It also clarifies that every enterprise information system (EIS) is nothing more or less than a part of the I-, the D- and the M-organisation that support the O-organisation, only implemented by using ICT.

8.1 Introduction

The EE organisational essence theory is also labeled A-theory. The Greek capital letter is pronounced as ALPHA, which is an acronym for Abstraction Layers in Production for Holistic Analysis. It is about layers of transactor roles that can be discerned in every organisation. The ALPHA theory is an *ontological* theory in the framework of theories, as presented in Chap. 4. Thus, it is a theory about the nature of things.

Four layers of transactor roles (cf. Chap. 6) are distinguished, based on the four distinct sorts of production acts: original, informational, documental and material. The distinction corresponds with the performa, informa, forma and matter level in coordination, as presented in Chap. 6. Accordingly, the organisation of an enterprise is a layered structure of four partial organisations: the *O-organisation* (O from original), the *I-organisation* (I from informational), the *D-organisation* (D from documental) and the *M-organisation* (M from material). The I-organisation supports the O-organisation by means of informational services (remembering and sharing facts), the D-organisation supports the I-organisation by means of documental services (saving and providing data or documents) and the M-organisation supports the D-organisation by means of material services (storing and retrieving files).

Original production acts result in original (new) production facts. Examples are devising things, deciding and judging (all of them concerning intangible things) and manufacturing, transporting and observing things (all of them concerning tangible things). *Informational production* acts comprise remembering facts, computing or deriving facts and sharing (remembered or derived) facts. *Documental production* acts concern the signs (documents or data) that contain facts. They comprise saving, providing and transforming documents or data. *Material production* acts concern the substances in which signs are inscribed. They comprise storing, retrieving, copying, transmitting and destroying files. Because original acts are the only acts that change the state of the 'business' world of an enterprise (i.e. the production world of its O-organisation), they must be performed by human actors. Informational, documental and material acts can be taken over by artefacts, notably ICT systems, including AI artefacts (like logistic control systems and robots).

The remainder of the chapter is organised as follows. Section 8.2 (Foundations) starts with discussing the four organisational layers, as well as the corresponding sorts of actors and products, on the basis of the semiotic ladder. Next, the notion of the essential model of an enterprise is presented. Section 8.3 (Elaborations) starts with deepening the key concepts that are discussed in Sect. 8.2. Next, the notions of realisation and implementation are elaborated. It comprises a discussion of the differences between actors and agents (artificial intelligence), and it will lead to the understanding of (enterprise) information systems as inherent parts of organisations. In Sect. 8.4 (Discussions), two topics are addressed. One is the distinction between an enterprise's organisation and the boundary of its business, thereby clarifying the notion of (in- and out-) sourcing. The other topic is the current debate on AI and the position that is taken in this discussion by the discipline of Enterprise Engineering (EE).

8.2 Foundations

8.2.1 The Organisational Layers

The FI theory (cf. [1], Chap. 5) provides us with the semiotic ladder (cf. Fig. 8.1). It clarifies the role of signs in the communication between human beings. Information is defined as the means for communication (cf. Chap. 4). A unit of *information*, commonly called an information item, is a dyad of content and form: the two parts are distinguishable but not separable, like the two sides of a coin. The content of an information item is the *thought* to be conveyed, and the form consists of perceivable patterns (letters, numerals and other symbols), collectively called the *sign*. The thought comprises both the intention (or pragmatics) and the proposition (or semantics), and the sign comprises both the formalism (or syntax) and the coding (or empirics). Signs are 'inscribed' in some material or physical substance, like clay tablets, paper sheets or electromagnetic items.

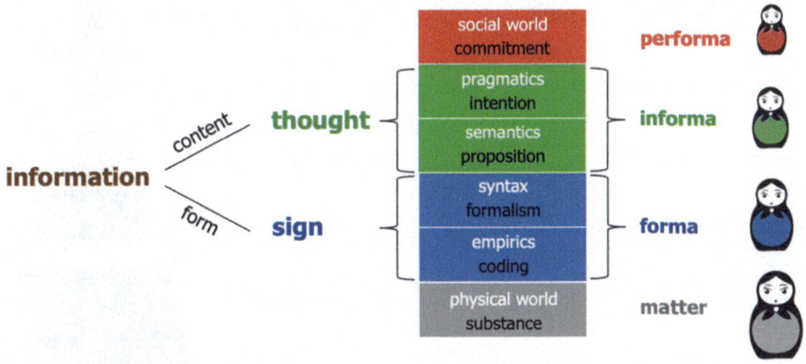

Fig. 8.1 The semiotic ladder

In accordance with the semiotic ladder, the PSI theory (cf. Chap. 6) distinguishes three abilities of communicating subjects: the *forma* ability (to deal with empirics and syntax), the *informa* ability (to deal with semantics and pragmatics) and the *performa* ability (to deal with the social impact of communication). These abilities are shown, on the right side of Fig. 8.1, as three shapes that human beings can take on. Although the material world (dealing with substances) is not covered by the performa-informa-forma distinction, we have added this shape to the figure however.

In Chap. 6, the performa, informa, forma and matter abilities or shapes are used to clarify the distinct levels in the process of performing coordination acts. Here, we will apply them to clarify the distinction that can be made in every enterprise between four organisational layers, based on the following sorts of production acts: original, informational, documental and material.

A production act (or P-act for short) is called *original* if it creates new facts in the business world of the enterprise. An example of an original P-act is the decision by a salesperson in a flower shop to sell a bouquet of flowers to a customer.

A production act is called *informational* if it concerns the remembering, sharing or deriving of business facts. Shared facts may be original, thus created in an original production act, or derived. Derivation comprises both mathematical computation and logical deduction. Note that the derivation of facts does not change the state of the world; it only presents the state in more convenient ways. Computing the daily turnover of a flower shop is an example of an informational act. It does not change the performed sales, but it presents them in a more intelligible way.

A production act is called *documental* if it concerns the saving and providing of documents or data (which contain original facts that need to be remembered). Also transforming documents or data, like changing the docx format of a document into PDF, is a documental act.

A production act is called *material* if it concerns the storing and retrieving of files that carry the documents or data. Material production also includes copying, transmitting and destroying files.

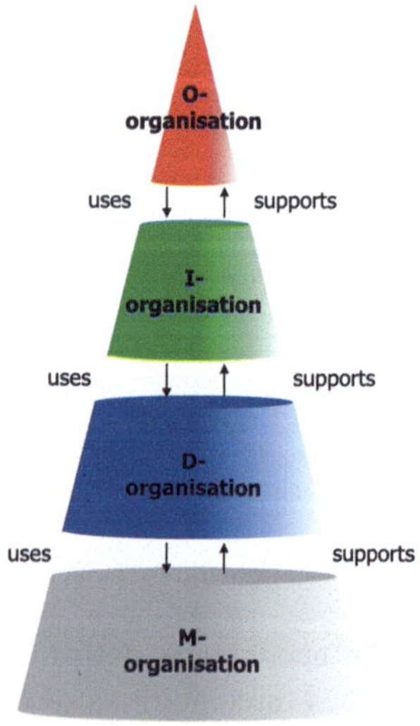

Fig. 8.2 The organisational layers

In accordance with the distinction between original, informational, documental and material production, the total organisation of an enterprise is divided into four layers of partial organisations (cf. Fig. 8.2). The four partial organisations are, respectively, called *O-organisation* (from Original), *I-organisation* (from Informational), *D-organisation* (from Documental) and *M-organisation* (from Matter).

All original production acts are performed by actors in the O-organisation (called *O-actors* for short), all informational production acts are performed by actors in the I-organisation (called *I-actors* for short), all documental production acts are performed by actors in the D-organisation (called *D-actors* for short) and all material production acts are performed by actors in the M-organisation (called *M-actors* for short). The relationship between the partial organisations is that the M-organisation *supports* the D-organisation, the D-organisation *supports* the I-organisation and the I-organisation *supports* the O-organisation. Conversely, the O-organisation *uses* (the services of) the I-organisation, the I-organisation *uses* (the services of) the D-organisation and the D-organisation *uses* (the services of) the M-organisation.

8.2.2 Organisational Layers and Sorts of Actors

As explained in Chap. 6, actors collaborate through carrying out transactions. Corresponding with the distinction between the O-, the I-, the D- and the M-organisation, we distinguish between original or *O-transactions*, informational or *I-transactions*, documental or *D-transactions* and material or *M-transactions*. In Fig. 8.3, O-actors are represented by figurines with red hats, I-actors by figurines with green hats, D-actors by figurines with blue hats and M-actors by figurines with grey hats.

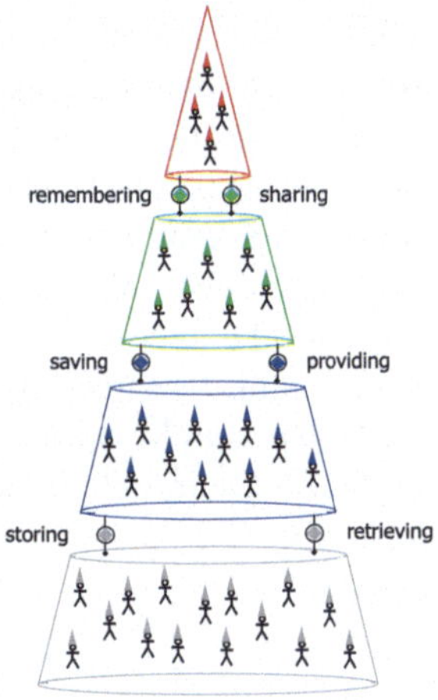

Fig. 8.3 Organisational layers with corresponding O-, I-, D- and M-actors

The figurines in Fig. 8.3 are actors, so subjects filling an actor role. Consequently, the same subject may be present in the O-organisation with a red hat, in the I-organisation with a green hat, in the D-organisation with a blue hat and in the M-organisation with a grey hat. This is quite common, in all enterprises. Sometimes, people perform original, sometimes informational, sometimes documental and sometimes material acts. But the distribution of these sorts of acts over individual persons may differ substantially. People whose organisational function is to sell or purchase will mainly perform original acts (and then be an O-actor). In contrast, accountants will mainly perform informational acts, like reasoning (and then be an I-actor), bookkeepers will mainly perform documental acts (and then be a D-actor) and postmen mainly perform material acts, like transporting letters (and then be an M-actor).

In addition to the transaction kinds that exist within the I-organisation, there are two general I-transaction kinds between the O-organisation and the I-organisation, as shown in Fig. 8.3: *remembering* facts and *sharing* facts. Transactions of these kinds are initiated by O-actors and executed by I-actors. O-actors are able to do this by taking on their informa shape (cf. Chap. 6). Similarly, there are two general D-transaction kinds between the I-organisation and the D-organisation: *saving* documents (or data) and *providing* documents (or data). I-actors are able to initiate transactions of these kinds by taking on their forma shape. Likewise, there are two general M-transaction kinds between the D-organisation and the M-organisation: *storing* files (as the material inscription or epigraph of documents and data) and *retrieving* files. D-actors are able to initiate transactions of these kinds by taking on their matter shape.

So, one of the services that the I-organisation offers to the O-organisation is that O-actors can ask I-actors to remember (original) facts. Likewise, they can ask to share (original or derived) facts. Note that O-actors create facts but do not remember them. If they want facts to be remembered, they need to initiate a remembering transaction, and if they want to know facts, they need to initiate a sharing transaction. For example, the salesperson in a flower shop fills the O-actor role seller when selling flowers, and in this actor role, he/she does not remember what has been sold. In order to have sales facts remembered, he/she must ask an actor in the I-organisation to remember them. This I-actor may be the same person as the O-actor. Continuing the flower shop example, the I-actor who has to remember the sales facts may feel the need to document these facts in order not to forget them. To this end, he or she may write down sales facts and ask a D-actor to save the notes. Likewise, an I-actor may ask a D-actor to provide saved documents or data. Both actors may be the same person, and they may also be the same person as the I-actor. Lastly, the D-actor needs to ask an M-actor to store the sheet of paper on which the sales facts are written down. Later, he/she may ask an M-actor to retrieve the sheet of paper or make a copy of it.

8.2.3 Organisational Layers and Sorts of Production

Let us have a closer look now at the distinct kinds of production acts and corresponding products, as presented in Sect. 8.2.1, in order to get a deeper understanding of the relationships between the O-organisation of an enterprise on the one hand and its I-, D- and M-organisation on the other hand.

As explained in Chap. 6, the key characteristic of all *original* production acts is that they result in new facts in the production world of its O-organisation. In Fig. 8.4, a distinction is made between intangible production (left side) and tangible production (right side). Examples of *intangible* production acts are all kinds of devising (thinking up, designing), deciding and judging. These acts create original facts, always and everywhere. They also constitute the majority of production acts in contemporary enterprises. To illustrate this, every sale or purchase implies an original decision by an authorised and responsible actor, and every advice or consultation is an original judgement, which also requires an authorised and responsible executor.

Examples of *tangible* production acts are all manufacturing acts and all logistic acts, like transporting. This is quite obvious. Less obvious may be that observing things are also tangible acts. Let us take, as an example, the measurement of water heights. Most people are able to 'measure' the water height in rivers and canals by looking at the rulers that are placed on the sides, here and there. These observations, however, have no significance for the decision by the captain of a barge on the route to take through the waters. He/she needs an authorised measurement, which is usually provided by a particular government agency. The authorised employees of this agency determine the water heights on which skippers rely. If needed, they will hold the agency responsible and possibly accountable, if things go wrong. In modern institutionalised societies, we want and need to do 'business' in this way [2].

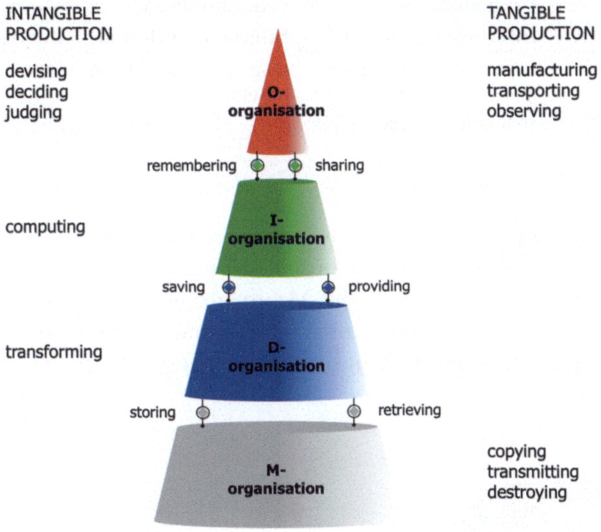

Fig. 8.4 Organisational layers and sorts of production

The characteristic of all *informational* production acts is that they are intangible, because they are acts by the human mind, and the resulting products are thoughts. Also *documental* production is, by nature, *intangible*. As illustrated in Fig. 8.1, it regards dealing with *signs*. More common words for signs are 'documents' and 'data', although one normally thinks of *documents* as reports, books or letters and one normally thinks of *data* as multiple, structured signs. Because the operations on documents and data are the same, there is no reason to make a distinction between them. From now on, we will speak of documents, thereby including *datasets*.

Like De Jong did in [3], we put a partial organisation below the D-organisation in order to deal properly with all material operations on documents. As shown in Fig. 8.4, they comprise the storing, copying, transmitting, destroying and retrieving of *files*, which are the physical carriers of documents. The distinction between documents and files is important. Every file is the carrier of a document. Conversely, every document may be inscribed in a number of files, commonly called copies of the document. A document is saved by storing the file(s) that carry it, and it is provided by retrieving (and possibly copying and transmitting) files. Only files can be destroyed; documents cannot. But if all files that carry a document are destroyed, the document has to be considered lost. This often-undesirable situation can only be avoided by proper document management (which is actually file management).

Table 8.1 summarises the various production acts in Fig. 8.4 while also distinguishing between interface acts and internal acts. The create act (O-organisation, internal) comprises the tangible and intangible acts in the upper part of Fig. 8.4.

Table 8.1 Summary of the production acts in the aspect organisations

O-organisation		I-organisation		D-organisation		M-organisation	
Interface	**Internal**	**Interface**	**Internal**	**Interface**	**Internal**	**Interface**	**Internal**
	create *fact*	remember *fact* share *fact*	compute *fact* recall *fact*	save *doc* provide *doc*	transform *doc*	store *file* retrieve *file*	copy *file* transmit *file* destroy *file*

On closer view, there is quite some resemblance between the tangible acts in the O-organisation and the material acts in the M-organisation. Actually, there is no difference between storing files in the M-organisation and storing goods in the O-organisation, between transmitting files and transporting goods, etc. Consequently, the M-organisation in one enterprise can be the O-organisation in another enterprise.

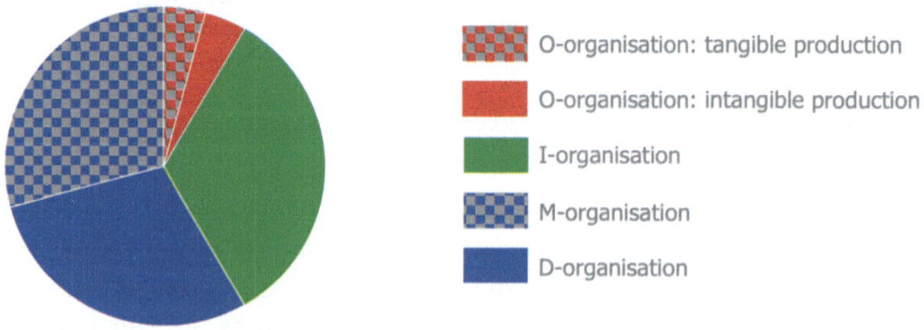

Fig. 8.5 Tangible and material production

In Fig. 8.5, we have visualised this resemblance by the two-coloured 'pie parts': the production in the O-organisation by the part with red and grey boxes and in the M-organisation by the part with blue and grey boxes. Therefore, creating a book or a technical drawing (or any other file) is at the material level similar to manufacturing a car or any other tangible thing. Tangible things need to have some material place to be. For documents and datasets, it holds that any file in which they are inscribed also needs some material (physical) place to be.

8.2.4 The Essential Model of an Enterprise

In [1], Chap. 9, the essential model of a system is defined as an ontological model, thus a model of its construction (cf. Chap. 5) that is fully abstracted from realisation and implementation. Based on this notion, we will develop in this section the notion of essential model for enterprises. Figure 8.6 illustrates what it means to abstract from *realisation*, i.e. from the supporting I-, D- and M-organisation, and thus to focus on the O-organisation.

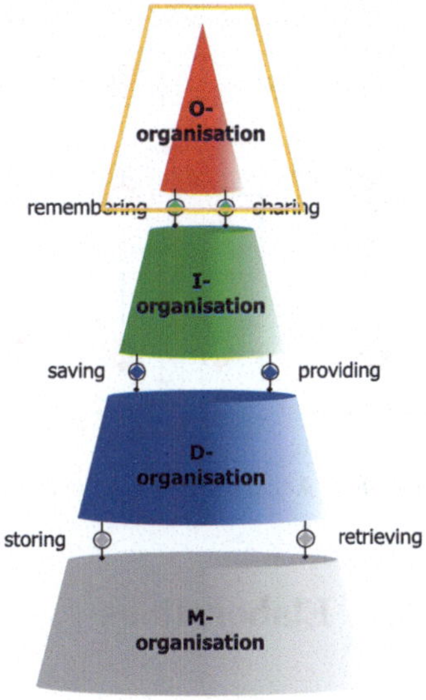

Fig. 8.6 Abstracting from realisation

By understanding the construction and operation of the O-organisation, one understands that part of an enterprise's organisation that brings about its business. The I-organisation supports the operation of the O-organisation, but it is not part of it. For a full understanding of the operation of the O-organisation, we can therefore confine ourselves to the interface between the O- and the I-organisation, thus to the remembering and sharing transaction kinds between them, of course in addition to understanding the internals of the O-organisation itself.

Ontologically spoken, all created facts, both coordination facts and production facts, exist in the corresponding world, from their event time on (cf. Chap. 6), and they will exist forever. Therefore, the remembering transaction kinds in Fig. 8.6 can be accommodated by considering created facts to be 'put' in the 'bank' of the O-transaction kind. This bank is the conceptual container of all facts that are created in the carrying out of transactions of the concerned kind (cf. Chap. 7). To accommodate the sharing transaction kinds, we introduce the notion of *access* right: actors who need to know facts from a transaction bank get reading access to the bank. In Chap. 7, this access right is expressed by means of an access link from the actor role to the transaction kind. In case one needs derived facts, the access links go to all transaction banks where the 'ingredient' original facts reside from which the derived facts are produced. To illustrate this, Fig. 7.9 is reproduced as Fig. 8.7. As an example of an access link, let us explain the link from the self-activating actor role AR11 to the transaction bank TK01. Actors AR11 periodically compose purchase orders from sales orders. To do this, they need to know the facts in the transaction bank of TK01.

We are now ready to define the *essential model* of an enterprise as the ontological model of its O-organisation, including the taking care of the remembering and sharing transactions, as explained above.

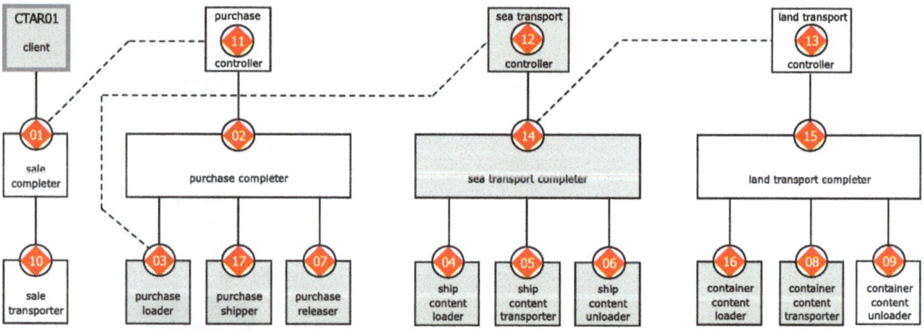

Fig. 8.7 Access links in the essential model of the GloLog enterprise

8.3 Elaborations

The discussions in Sect. 8.2 have culminated in the notion of the essential model of an enterprise, which is arrived at by abstracting from realisation, as well as from implementation (by definition ontological means abstracted from implementation). In this section, we will investigate organisations the other way around, based on [3]. First, we will take up the task to clarify how one can systematically devise the ontological models of the supporting I-, D- and M-organisation, from the ontological model of the O-organisation of the enterprise. This will be done in Sects. 8.3.1 and

8.3.2. In Sects. 8.3.3–8.3.7, we will discuss how the ontological models of the four partial organisations can be implemented, in order to arrive at a constructional model of an enterprise at such a level of detail that it can be put into operation straightforwardly. Along the same lines of reasoning, the notion of enterprise information system will be presented in Sect. 8.3.8.

8.3.1 Devising the Ontological Model of the I-Organisation

As discussed in Sect. 8.2, the interface between an enterprise's O-organisation and I-organisation consists of two general transaction kinds: remembering and sharing. In transactions of both kinds, the executor is an I-actor, and the initiator is an O-actor in her/his informa (green) shape. Remembering concerns the C-facts and P-facts that the O-actor creates and wants to be remembered. Sharing concerns the (original or derived) C-facts and P-facts that the O-actor needs to know.

An O-actor initiates transactions when he/she is settling an agendum,[1] as discussed in the PSI theory (cf. Chap. 6) and the DELTA theory (cf. [1], Chap. 9). As also discussed in these theories, actors constantly loop through their operating cycle, checking every time whether there are agenda to settle, as shown in Fig. 8.8. They have permanent access to their agenda through a sharing transaction kind. At the beginning of a cycle, an actor selects an agendum to settle. Next to knowing the agendum to be settled, O-actors must also know the action rule to be executed. The next step is therefore to fetch the corresponding action rule, through a sharing transaction. Action rules are also facts, but created by another part of the enterprise, outside the O-organisation that we are focussing at.

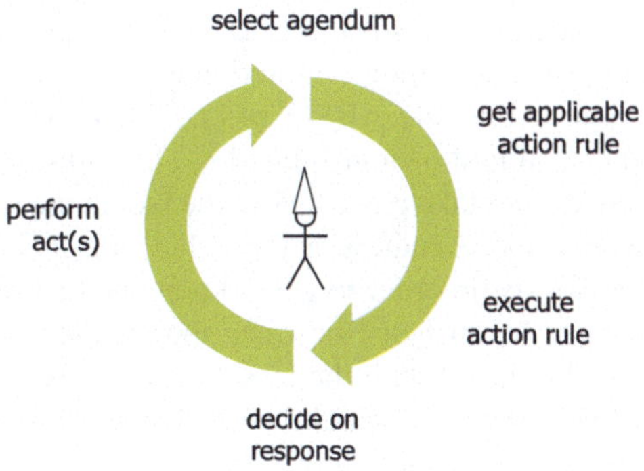

Fig. 8.8 The operating cycle of actors

In order to illustrate how the interface between an enterprise's O-organisation and I-organisation looks like, Table 8.2 exhibits one of the action rules for the case Rent-A-Car (cf. [1], Chap. 15). Note that the fetching of the agenda and the fetching

[1] The Latin word *agendum* means 'thing to do'. The plural of 'agendum' is 'agenda'.

of the action rule are taken for granted. Moreover, we assume that a new instance of the core entity type, namely, 'rental', is created, together with its dependent facts, in the response part of the action rule (outside our SoI) in which the (external) request is performed. They are also remembered at that time.

The *event part* of the action rule begins with the *when-clause*. It specifies the agendum to settle (in this case, 'rental completing **for** [rental] **is** requested'). This request is created by an actor who is filling the role of initiator in the transaction at hand, and it is settled by the actor who is filling the role of executor (cf. Chap. 6).

The *assess part* of an action rule is an expression of the business rule that is in place. It is effectively a set of facts that must exist (must be the case). The first two facts in the assess part of Table 8.2 concern the coordination world; the others concern the production world. Note that most P-facts are derived facts; they need to be computed by actors in the I-organisation. Obviously, precise specifications of these derived fact types must be available to the I-actors. As explained in Chap. 10, producing them is considered to be part of producing the Fact Model. In order to get knowledge of these facts, the executing actor initiates corresponding sharing transactions. This is indicated in the assess part in Table 8.2 by the pair of brackets '**sha**' and '**ahs**' that enclose the facts to be shared.

The *response part* starts with the sentence that expresses the human autonomy of the executing actor. He/she is allowed to violate the business rule but can be held accountable for it (cf. Chap. 6). The remainder of the response part is a formulation of the C-acts that are performed as the outcome of executing the action rule. In this case, it is either the promise in completing the rental or the decline of the request.

After an agendum is settled, it is marked as such, and this C-fact is remembered. In order to enable that the created C-events can become knowable to the actors who have to settle them, the executing actor initiates the corresponding remembering transactions. This is indicated in the response part in Table 8.2 by the pair of brackets '**rem**' and '**mer**', printed in green, that enclose the facts to be remembered.

In action rule ARS-3 in [1], Chap. 15, a *while-clause* is added to the when-clause. It is shown in Table 8.3. This while-clause specifies that the execution of the rule cannot take place before the fact in the while-clause has started to exist. In other words, the executing actor is held up in executing the rule until this fact exists. Obviously, in order to get to know the fact (deposit paying **for** [rental] **is** accepted), it must be enclosed between the brackets '**sha**' and '**ahs**'. The executing actor is now burdened with the task to constantly watch the occurrence of the event in the while-clause for which he/she has to wait. The DELTA theory (cf. [1], Chap. 9) offers an elegant solution to this operational problem, by means of the notion of trigger.

Table 8.2 Example of an action rule from the case Rent-A-Car

event part	**when** rental completing **for** [rental] **is** requested
assess part	**sha** **the** performer **of the** request **is the** renter **of** [rental]; **the** addressee **of the** request **is a** rental completer; **the** starting day **of** [rental] **is in the** rental horizon **of the** year **of** **the** starting day **of** [rental]; **the** ending day **of** [rental] **is in the** rental horizon **of the** year **of** **the** ending day **of** [rental]; **the** ending day **of** [rental] **is equal to or greater than** **the** starting day **of** [rental]; **the** duration **of** [rental] **is less than or equal to the** max rental duration **in the** year **of the** starting day **of** [rental]; **the** expiration day **of the** driving license **of the** driver **of** [rental] **is equal to or greater than the** ending day **of** [rental]; **the** number of free cars **in the** car group **of** [rental] **on** every day **in** **the** rental period **of** [rental] **is greater than zero** **ahs**
response part	**if** *performing the action after **then** is considered justifiable* **then** **rem** promise rental completing **for** [rental] **to the** renter **of** [rental] **mer** **else** **rem** decline rental completing **for** [rental] **to the** renter **of** [rental] * justification of declining * **mer**

According to the PSI theory (cf. Chap. 6), the product of a successfully carried out transaction starts to exist at the moment that the accept act is performed. Let us investigate here what this means for the design of the I-organisation. In Table 8.4, the action rule is presented in which the returning of the car of a rental in the case Rent-A-Car is completed. If the accept act is performed (in the then-clause of the response part), the product of the transaction must start to exist in the P-world at the same time. To indicate that this is the case, a corresponding sentence (coloured red) is added to Table 8.4, for clarifying the effect of an accept act (which is an act in the C-world) on the state of the P-world. Note: the red-coloured line is not part of the action rule; it is only added for clarification.

Table 8.3 Example of an action rule from the case Rent-A-Car

event part	**when** rental completing **for** [rental] **is** promised **while** **sha** deposit paying **for** [rental] **is** accepted **ahs**
assess part	**assess** *rightness*: * no specific condition * *sincerity*: * no specific condition * *truth*: * no specific condition *
response part	**if** *performing the action after* ***then*** *is considered justifiable* **then** * select car of rental * **rem** request car taking **for** [rental] **to the** driver **of** [rental] **with the** requested ot **of** car taking **for** [rental] **is** **within the** starting day **of** [rental]; **the** requested car **of** car taking **for** [rental] **is the** car **of** [rental] **mer**

Table 8.4 Example of an action rule in which a product is created

event part	**when** car returning **for** [rental] is declared
assess part	**sha** **the** performer **of the** declaration **is the** driver **of** [rental]; **the** addressee **of the** declaration **is some** rental completer; **the** declared car **of** car returning **for** [rental] **is the** promised car **of** car returning **for** [rental] **ahs**
response part	**if** *performing the action after* ***then*** *is considered justifiable* **then** **rem** accept car returning **for** [rental] **to the** performer **of the** declaration **the** car **of** [rental] **is** returned **mer** **else** **rem** reject car returning **for** [rental] **to the** performer **of the** declaration request penalty payment **for** [rental] **to the** driver **of** [rental] **with** * reason for rejecting * **mer**

We have clarified above how the general interface transaction kinds between an enterprise's O-organisation and I-organisation are put into effect in action rules, using the case Rent-A-Car for illustration. In addition to these transaction kinds, there are a number of other transaction kinds needed, which are internal to the I-organisation, of which both the initiator role and the executor role are filled by I-actors. Table 8.2 contains several examples of derived fact types for whose derivation such transaction kinds are needed. One of them is the fact type <**the** number of free cars **in the** car group **of** [rental] **on** every day **in the** rental period **of** [rental] **is greater than zero**>. Computing the truth value of this predication will encompass various additional internal transaction kinds in the I-organisation.

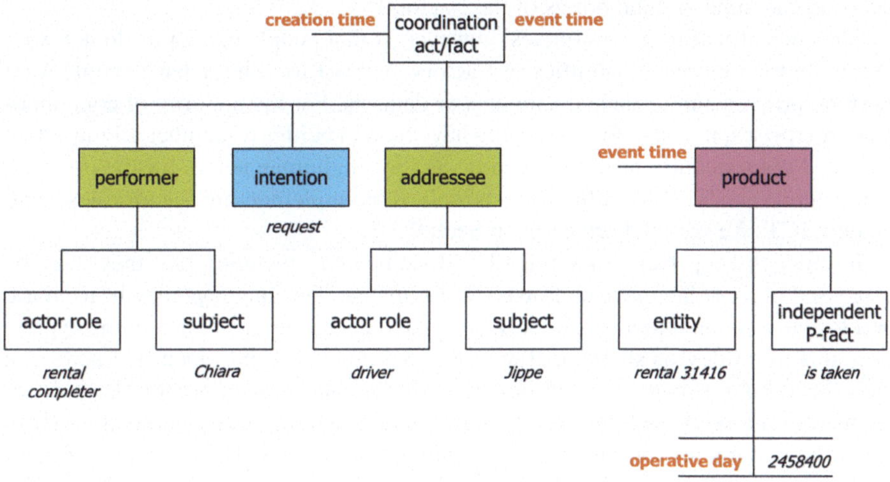

Fig. 8.9 The structure of a coordination act/fact

As can be deduced from the action rule in Table 8.2, the unit of factual knowledge to be remembered by I-actors is the C-fact. This should not be a surprise, because the C-act/fact is the atomic element of business processes, as discussed in Chap. 6. To clarify this, we reproduce in Fig. 8.9 the structure of a C-act/fact, as presented in Fig. 6.18. The example C-act/fact is taken from the first remembering act in the response part of Table 8.2. It assumes that the subject (person) Chiara fills the role of rental completer, that the subject (person) Jippe fills the role of driver, that it is about rental 31416 and that the operative (taking) day is 2458400 (on the Julian time scale).

The remembered C-fact is an agendum for Jippe in his role of driver. It will be shared with him at the proper moment, i.e. at the event time of the C-fact. In order to settle the agendum, Jippe will also be supplied with the appropriate action rule(s). The product 'rental 31416 is taken' means that the car of rental 31416 is taken. This car has been assigned to the rental in the informally specified line * select car of rental * in Table 8.3.

8.3.2 Devising the Ontological Model of the D-Organisation

Thanks to the semiotic triangle (cf. [1], Chap. 5), we have been able above to abstract completely from the sign aspect, i.e. the form of information, and to focus on the thought aspect, i.e. its content. But as said, content cannot exist without form: information is the dyad of content and form. Let us therefore now study the consequences of the acts of I-actors for the D-organisation of an enterprise.

As an intermediate step, imagine that all I-actors are human and that they all have an unlimited capability of remembering facts and of computing derived facts. In such a 'utopian' situation, there is no need for the supporting D-organisation (note that actually, the D-organisation and the supporting M-organisation are now, respectively, in the mind and the brains of the I-actors).

The current reality in enterprises, however, is that people cannot or do not want to rely on the rational capabilities of I-actors. At least for a large part, people want to store, process and retrieve documents or datasets. For the majority of contemporary enterprises, it is also impractical to have human beings remember all important facts and consequently need to ask, time and again, human actors for the information that one needs. This problem can be solved by implementing I-actor roles using modern ICT. We will elaborate this in Sect. 8.3.5.

In order to keep facts, they must be 'documented', meaning that they must be expressed in some language and saved for future use. The language may be a natural or a formal one, or something in between, like the structured English in the expression of action rules, as shown in Tables 8.2, 8.3 and 8.4. Consequently, I-actors, in their forma (blue) shape, need to initiate saving transactions in order to keep documents (or data sets) for future use and to initiate providing transactions in order to get saved documents (or data sets), as exhibited in Fig. 8.4. The executors of these transactions are D-actors. In addition, D-actors may need to transform documents (or datasets). An example in human communication is the transformation of Morse code to English. An example in the exchange of data between computers is the transformation from EBCDIC to ASCII.

8.3.3 Devising the Ontological Model of the M-Organisation

In order to save documents or datasets, they need to be inscribed in some physical matter, as discussed in Sect. 8.2.3. The results are files. Files can be stored, retrieved, copied, transmitted and destroyed. Those are the P-acts that M-actors can perform. As discussed in Sect. 8.2.3, there is no principal difference between an M-organisation and a (material or tangible) O-organisation. Therefore, there is no need to discuss the devising of the ontological model of an M-organisation separately.

8.3.4 Actors and Agents

By devising the ontological model of a suitable I-organisation and subsequently the ontological model of a suitable D- and M-organisation for the O-organisation of an enterprise, the largest part of making the essential model of the enterprise operative is done. But we are not finished yet; the four ontological models must still be implemented. Implementation means allocating proper technological means[2] to the elements of an ontological model. An important class of these elements are the actor roles.

As clarified in Chap. 6, only subjects, so human beings, can bear the responsibility of actor roles. Therefore, a perfectly safe implementation of actor roles would be to assign them exclusively to subjects. However, subjects are outperformed, in orders of magnitude, by modern ICT artefacts in doing informational and documental work. So, the question is not whether using ICT is feasible for implementing actor roles but how we should understand this application of ICT and what the limits are. As the first step in answering the question, let us call an ICT artefact filling an actor role an *agent*, like we have called a subject filling an actor role an actor (cf. Chap. 6). The question then is what it means to have agents perform P-acts and C-acts while keeping in mind that agents cannot be held accountable for their deeds.[3]

8.3.4.1 Documental and Material Transactions

We begin by answering the foregoing question with respect to D-transactions and M-transactions. The only acceptable way of addressing the problem seems to be that there is no objection to having agents carrying out D-transactions (and the supporting M-transactions) but that there must always be an actor who is ultimately responsible for the work and who can be held accountable for what the agents do. As an illustrating example, let us consider the replacement of the internal (paper-based) postal mail service in a company by an email system. Clearly, the head of the internal postal mail service is held responsible and, if the need is there, accountable for the (mal-)functioning of the system. He or she is the person that one would address in case of a problem. In our view, the same functionary should be addressed if the email system doesn't function properly, because this functionary has apparently decided to replace the current implementation of the postal mail system by a modern one. Naturally, if the cause of the problem is the ICT system, this functionary would address, on her/his turn, the people who are responsible for the technical

[2] We intentionally speak of technological means instead of technology, although this meaning inflation is quite common nowadays. We prefer to stick to the original meaning of the word technology, which stems from its Greek origin *technè* (meaning 'making') and *logos* (meaning 'knowing'). So technology is knowing how to make.

[3] I am aware that the issue of responsibility and accountability with respect to agents or to other 'intelligent' things is currently a topic of debate in the adoption of the achievements of AI. For the moment, I choose to consider 'intelligent' things as unable to bear responsibility.

performance of the ICT system. But he or she would have acted in a similar way if there would have been 'technical' problems in the internal postal mail service.

So, if one accepts the crucial idea of an actor bearing the ultimate responsibility, and if one implements this solution properly, there is nothing that would withhold the use of agents in carrying out documental and material transactions.

For executing P-acts, this is fully clear, whereas for performing C-acts, we need some additional reasoning, because C-facts are commitments between social individuals. The only acceptable solution regarding C-acts seems to be that we consider agents to *mimic* actors. This philosophical stance preserves the primacy of human beings to act as social individuals; human beings possess exclusively the ability to enter into and comply with commitments. It is also an effective measure to avoid the anthropomorphic trap. As explained by psychology, anthropomorphism is the innate tendency of people to attribute human traits to non-human things. As an example, people normally think that there is nothing wrong with calling a bicycle or a laptop stupid once in a while. As long as one is aware of producing anthropomorphic explanations concerning the behaviour of non-human things, there is no objection. But the borderline is thin, very thin. Time and again, it appears to be too tempting for people to ascribe human traits to things.

8.3.4.2 Informational Transactions

Regarding I-transactions, the answer to the question whether agents can perform P-acts and C-acts is similar to the answer given above. As an example for illustration, recall what happened on 11 May 1997 when Gary Kasparov lost to Deep Blue. Kasparov was upset, as seemed the entire chess world. There was even talk of the end of chess, because what would be the point of playing chess when machines would always win? Consider a simple counter-example. For quite some time, people use forklift trucks to lift heavy weights. Everyone would burst into laughter if a newspaper headline would read 'weightlifter beaten by forklift truck'. So, why didn't we do the same when reading the headline 'Gary Kasparov beaten by Deep Blue'? The only reason why we didn't is that we were not yet used to human chess players being beaten by artefacts. But playing chess can still be an exciting pastime for people, and chess tournaments can simply not allow chess computers to participate.

The key to dealing with artefacts properly is exactly the notion of *mimicking*. The proper way of understanding Kasparov's (alleged) defeat is that Deep Blue didn't play chess at all. It just did what is the only thing computers can do: computing. Any further attribution of human-like qualities to the computer is stepping into the anthropomorphic trap. To be very precise, computing is actually an ability of human (or other animal) intelligence. It is quite correct, and even advisable, to say that computers don't compute. The only thing they actually do, and at which they are extremely good, is very fast manipulation of symbols, following strict instructions. Why then do we call these machines computers? There are two explanations. One is our tendency to anthropomorphism, as discussed above. The other one is our evenly strong tendency to assign functional names to the things we use, in particular to the artefacts we make, as discussed in Chap. 5. That's why you can say that computers compute.

8.3.4.3 Original Transactions

If it comes to performing original P-acts, like devising, deciding and judging but also like manufacturing, transporting and observing (cf. Fig. 8.4), assigning artefacts to actor roles is no option anymore. This strict position follows from the basic philosophical position as presented in Chap. 8: our world is a socially constructed world [2]. We assign actor roles to each other, and in doing so, we bestow each other with authority and responsibility. Of course, people can and do make mistakes, but accepting failures is part of the societal game. And for substantial misdemeanour, we have our judicial system: we can and do bring people to court; we can and do condemn people; we can and do punish them. At the same time, we can and do have compassion with the condemned; we can and do help them in becoming 'normal' members of the society again. In the light of this nucleus of modern social existence, the crucial question is: could we ever treat artefacts (agents, robots) in a similar way? This is one of the most difficult philosophical questions modern man has to face and come to grips with. In our view, the only acceptable answer is no. The current tendency to conceive agents as full-fledged social individuals is treading on thin ice. An illustrating example is the decision by the government of Saudi Arabia to grant a robot the same civil rights as human citizens.[4] Declaring robots to be citizens, or holding self-driving cars responsible for causing accidents, is not only thoughtless but is also a dangerous idea. They could mark the dawn of a non-human era in human history, possibly even the end of human civilisation.

The consequence of our strict position is that artefacts, notably ICT artefacts, may be used to support O-actors to a large extent but that they can never take over the authority and responsibility. As an example for illustration, a judge may be supported by all possible 'intelligent' advisors in arriving at her or his judgement (and he or she better does so), but the judgement is made by an authorised human being. Only he or she is responsible and can be held accountable.

Having said this, and having always this strict position in mind, there is a way of co-existence with artefacts that can be acceptable in modern societies. It is the way that we alluded to already, when discussing the use of artefacts in carrying out documental and informational transactions. In the concrete example of the judicial system, it would mean that a judge would be allowed to have 'intelligent' agents produce facts that count as the judge's decisions but that the judge is ultimately responsible and accountable. Actually, most Western countries apply this idea in the case of traffic offences, for example. There is nothing wrong with automatic jurisdiction in this case, as long as the accused has the right to go against the decision. In terms of the PSI theory, to revoke her/his implicit accept act (cf. Chap. 6).

---

[4] On 28 October 2017, Saudi Arabia declared a robot to be a citizen (http://wgntv.com/2017/99/28/meet-sophia-the-first-robot-declared-a-citizen-by-saudi-arabia/).

8.3.5 Implementing the M- and D-Organisation of an Enterprise

From the discussion in Sect. 8.3.3, it is clear that carrying out D-transactions can very well be mimicked by agents, as long as there is a clear sight on the (human) actor who is responsible and accountable for their deeds. So, when taking this precaution, there is no objection to having agents do all the work in D-transactions. In other words, the D-organisation can be fully automated, if one likes. But how should one proceed in achieving it? The answer to this question is provided by the DELTA theory (cf. [1], Chap. 9), notably the PRISMA model. As discussed in [1], Sect. 9.3.2, the generic transaction prismanet is the key to implementing any organisation (O-, I- or D-organisation) by means of ICT. There are only three kinds of components that need to be implemented: processors, channels and banks. A processor is basically an algorithmic procedure that is activated by C-events in its action channel and that may be impeded by wait events in its impediment channels. In order to get the information that is needed to execute the procedure, the processor must have access to its inspection channels and its inspection banks. Channels can be implemented by a bus that connects all processors and through which the processors can send C-facts to each other. In addition, these C-facts must be stored for future inspection by the processor or by other processors. In a similar way, banks can be implemented as directly accessible storages, like computer memories.

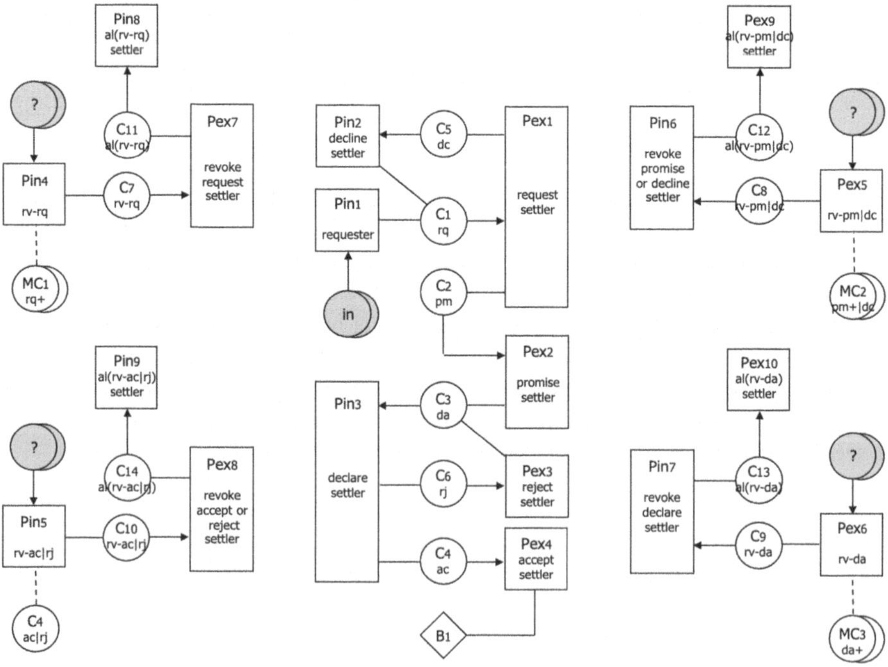

Fig. 8.10 The generic transaction prismanet

In Fig. 8.10, the generic transaction prismanet from the DELTA theory ([1], Fig. 9.14) is reproduced. Likewise, [1], Fig. 9.15 is reproduced as Fig. 8.11. Together, the pictures give the insight that we need for choosing the appropriate ICT means in implementing the D-organisation. It tells us that agents, the replacements of actors, are composed of 19 processors. They must be connected by some sort of bus through which they can exchange the various kinds of C-facts, as exhibited in Fig. 8.10. Note that actually five more processors are needed to deal with the events in the external (grey-coloured) channels in Fig. 8.10. In addition, some way of implementing banks is needed, for storing the resulting products, thus the documents (or datasets). This holds for every transaction kind in which the composite processors, the agents, are involved. Every agent is the executor of one transaction kind, but it may be initiator of a number of transaction kinds (cf. Chap.10). In this way, arbitrarily large tree structures can be constructed. In doing so, most of the external (grey-coloured) channels, mentioned earlier, become internal channels, i.e. of the kinds shown in Fig. 8.11. But there will always be some left as external channels. They are what one normally calls the input and output terminals of a system.

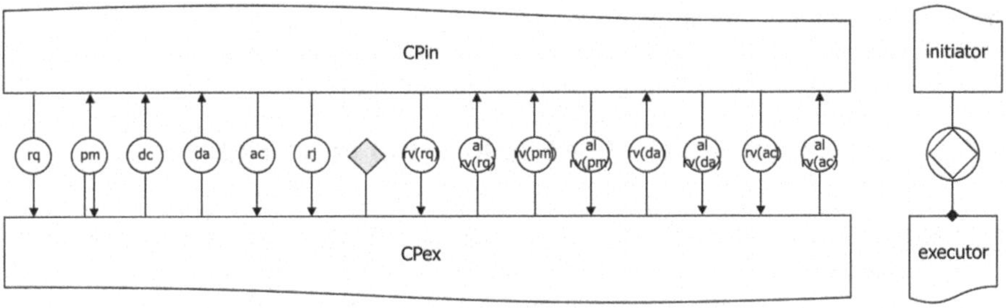

Fig. 8.11 Composite processors an organisational building blocks

As for the agents themselves, they can be implemented as computer programs. In case of a procedural programming language, an agent is a collection of procedures, one for every trigger kind that it should be able to respond to. In case of an object-oriented language, it is an object class comprising a method for every trigger kind. Of course, some work needs to be done, but the generality of the solution, as discussed above, makes that one can endlessly extend an implementation in an almost effortless way, once the general solution is there. Applying ICT in this way would be no less than a revolutionary breakthrough in computer programming, at least as far as supporting business processes is concerned.

8.3.6 Implementing the I-Organisation of an Enterprise

What has been said in Sect. 8.3.4 regarding the D-organisation is in no way specific for D-organisations; it also does hold for implementing I-organisations. So, in implementing I-organisations, one can take advantage of the knowledge and experience one has got in implementing D-organisations. But there is an even greater advantage to be gained, since we know that the products of the saving transactions and the providing transactions between the I-organisation and the D-organisation concern facts that are created or used by O-actors, for example, the C-fact (rental completing **for** rental 1993 **is** requested) or the independent P-fact (<rental 1993 **is** completed>) together with its dependent facts, like <**the** renter **of** rental 1993 **is** Adam> and <**the** driver **of** rental 1993 **is** Eve>.

In such cases, one can profit from the verity that every information item is the dyad of content and form. Concerning elementary facts, as in the examples above, it would be sufficient that I-agents are told to remember facts, as well as to compute or to share facts. Modern programming languages are already made for creating I-agents. One doesn't have to bother about how the forms of the facts are saved and possibly transformed. In other words, the design of the D-organisation, as well as the M-organisation, is taken care of by the compiler or interpreter (and the computer platform). In Sect. 8.3.3, we have referred to this ability of programming languages as the mimicking of human rational abilities. Agents do not remember, compute and share facts in the way humans do. Instead, they mimic these abilities by performing documental and material acts in well-designed and well-controlled ways, ways that preserve the semantic meaning of the data.

8.3.7 Implementing the O-Organisation of an Enterprise

As discussed in Sect. 6.3.3.3, one must be very careful in assigning actor roles in an O-organisation to artefacts, but it is certainly possible. To illustrate this 'relaxed' position, we reproduce the prismanet diagram of a part of the Rent-A-Car organisation ([1], Fig. 9.12) as Fig. 8.12. It is the PRISMA white-box model of the operations of the actor role rental completer. The six processors can be implemented as computer programs. The algorithm or logic is provided by the corresponding grey-box model. To illustrate this, Table 9.2 from [1] exhibits the grey-box model of processor P1. The performance rules are sufficiently formalised to express them in a programming language.

As said, the channels can be implemented by a bus, which connects all processors and which transmits C-facts between the processors (including the environmental ones, which are not shown in Fig. 8.12). Every processor will pick the ones that it needs to process and ignore the other ones. As also said, the banks can be implemented by the computer's memory (and external storages if necessary). This holds for bank B1 but also for the external multiple banks (MB1, MB2 and MB3) which contain various facts that the processors need when being active. Together with channels C1, C2 and C3, they constitute the terminals of the exhibited system, the connectors with the outside world.

In Fig. 8.4, a distinction is made between tangible and intangible production. Examples of tangible P-acts are manufacturing, transporting and observing. Examples of intangible production acts are devising, deciding and judging. One should be aware that this distinction does not affect the nature of P-facts. Every P-fact is an elementary state of affairs in the production world of an organisation, like every C-fact is an elementary state of affairs in its coordination world (cf. Chap. 6). Consequently, every P-fact (like every C-fact) is represented by a logical predicate and expressed in an elementary sentence. For example, the sentence 'rental 1993 **is** completed' expresses the fact that rental 1993 is completed, and the sentence '**the** car **of** rental 1993 **is** returned' expresses the fact that the car of rental 1993 is returned.

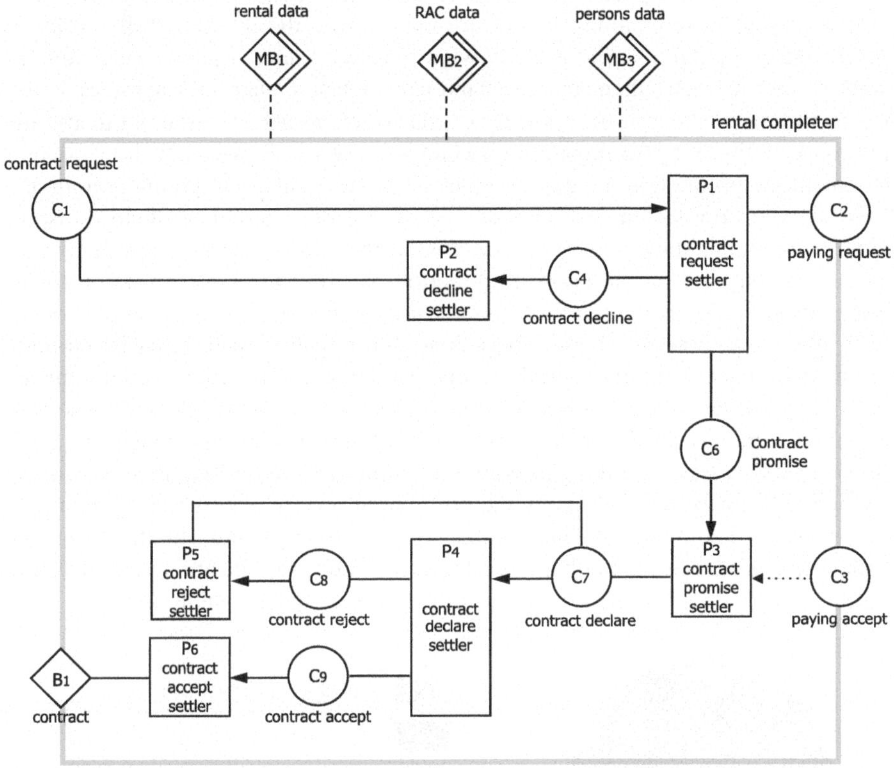

Fig. 8.12 Prismanet diagram of a part of the Rent-A-Car organisation

Let us have a closer look at these examples. The first sentence is a predication of the entity rental 1993. Although this entity is for sure a concrete thing (cf. [1], Chap. 5), it is also intangible: one cannot grasp it or observe it. In contrast, the entity in the predication <**the** car **of** rental 1993 **is** returned> is a particular car. Cars are tangible: they can be grasped and observed. And of course, cars are also concrete things. As follows from the examples, it doesn't matter for the faculty of predications to represent facts—that the predicated entities are tangible or intangible. But for creating the entities, the difference is quite relevant and important. Intangible entities are created as just the result of a mental act. For example, as soon as the C-fact (rental completing **for** rental 1993 **is** requested) is created, the entity rental 1993 is also created, just by conceiving it. There is nothing else needed. But creating a car is a different story. Like any tangible thing, it needs to be manufactured somehow. And as long as teleportation is not a reality, returning a car to a particular branch of Rent-A-Car implies the physical transport of the car to the branch's location.

So far so good, but what about tangible things that are the object of operations in the lower right side of Fig. 8.4, so of operations like storing copying, transmitting and destroying? Indeed, we have labeled these operations material, but it appears that they can quite easily turn into (original) tangible ones. As an example, the transporting of folders (containing letters, forms, etc.) by the internal mail service is clearly a documental material act. But what if such a folder contains spice nuts for Santa Claus? Clearly, then, the act cannot be labeled material anymore; it has become an original act of transporting goods. To elaborate the issue, let us use the 'pie chart' in Fig. 8.13 for illustration (which is a copy of Fig. 8.5). It shows clearly that material production in the O-organisation and material production in the D-organisation border on one another. By having the internal postman transport folders containing spice nuts, we have crossed the border. Let us cross the border once more, but now in the opposite direction, so from the O-organisation to the D-organisation. An example of such a crossing is the original creation of a document, like the writing of a book. There is no doubt that in essence, writing a book (or any document) is an immaterial original act. However, in order to communicate the contents, it has to be expressed in sentences in some language, and these sentences must be inscribed in some physical substance, like being printed on paper. This is basically the same thing as communicating facts by writing them down and having the forms be transported by the postal mail service or by entering them, via a keyboard, in a computer and having them transmitted by email. But the difference is that the contents of the book are not facts in some O-organisation, and therefore writing a book (or any other kind of document) needs special attention.

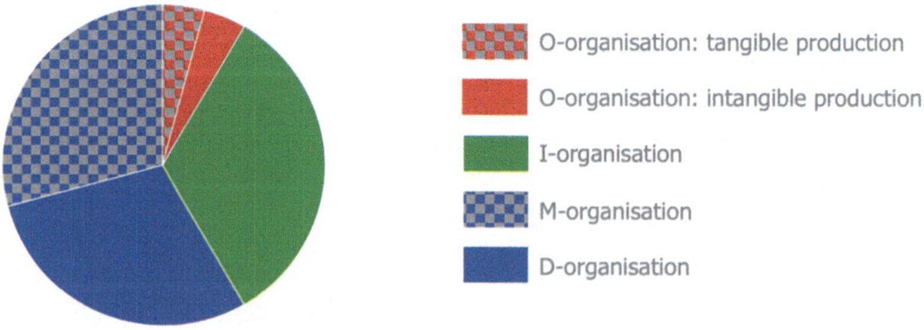

Fig. 8.13 Tangible and material production

For the sake of clarification, suppose we are studying an organisation in which this P-fact can be created: <book title 23929 **is** written>. The entity book title 23929 consists of the text of the book, and it is this text that one wants to save, provide and possibly to transform (cf. Fig. 8.4). Another but similar example of a P-fact is

<technical drawing 9829 **is** made>. The entity technical drawing 9829 consists of 'graphical text', i.e. expressions in some graphical language, and this 'text' must be saved, provided and possibly transformed. Even though the 'graphical text' could also be conceived as a dataset, the meaning of the graphical expressions is not relevant when the P-fact <technical drawing 9829 **is** made> is created, like the meaning of the contents of book title 23929 is not relevant when the P-fact <book title 23929 **is** written> is created.

Therefore, creating a book or a technical drawing or any other document is, at the documental level, similar to manufacturing a car or any other tangible thing. Tangible things need to have some place to be. For documents, it holds that any file in which they are inscribed also needs some physical place to be. Documents (or datasets) can very well be handled by the D-organisation of an enterprise. We only have to allow that O-actors, in their forma (blue) shape, initiate saving transactions as well as providing transactions with D-actors. So, this we do. It would mean some modification of Figs. 8.4 and 8.5, but we leave them as they are.

8.3.8 Enterprise Information Systems

From the time that the term 'information system' became the common reference to ICT applications that are intended to support people in organisations (around 1973), its understanding has hardly changed. The primal notion in this view is information, generally defined as the representation of knowledge, while communication is subsequently defined as the exchange of information. In Chap. 4, we have referred to it as the *information-centric* view.

One of the consequences of the information-centric view is that developing (automated) information systems is considered something that ICT professionals do 'at home', after having elicited requirements from the people in the organisation, basically by interviewing these people. Once the system is built, it is 'implanted' in the organisation. A widely acknowledged drawback of this approach is that the delivered systems rarely meet users' expectations. The main cause of this failure is that requirements determination is ill-understood. Interviewing the members of an organisation for determining information requirements is pretty much like asking the parts of a machine (like a car) what information they need in order to properly operate and cooperate. Every embedded software engineer would start to get an appropriate understanding of the machine for which he/she is going to build supporting software. Based on this understanding, he/she would specify the requirements for the software system to be built. He/she knows that the parts could never tell you, even if they were able to speak. As a consequence of the interviewing approach to requirements determination in the field of enterprise information systems, relevant requirements are often missing, and irrelevant ones are included. For obscure reasons, information system engineers have never recognised the necessity to acquire first of all an appropriate understanding of their primal objects of interest: enterprises. The extension of 'information system' to 'enterprise information system' (EIS) didn't contribute to a better understanding, only to a better delineation of the application area.

As explained in Chap. 4, the CIAO paradigm (Communication, Information, Action and Organisation) provides us with the *communication-centric* view on information systems. It entails that they are integral parts of the supported organisations and that they will always be like this, regardless of the technology that is used to implement them. The path to this new understanding was paved by the achievements in language philosophy, notably Speech Act Theory [4, 5], and in (social) action theory, notably the Theory of Communicative Action [6]. Communication[5] is defined as the sharing of thoughts between subjects (human beings) and information as the means for communication (cf. [1], Chap. 5). The bottom line is that people, in organisations and in society at large, have a need to communicate. Since it is impossible to do this directly, they use the vehicle of information. The new understanding emphasises the being intrinsically intertwined of information systems and the supported organisations. It also clarifies why information system engineers should first of all study the construction and operation of the organisation before designing information systems. Basically, the information system is already there: it is an intrinsic part of the organisation. Consequently, the functional requirements are also already there. It is the task of the 'new' information system engineer to find a better way of implementing the particular part of the organisation, most likely by applying ICT.

When we discussed the deduction of the ontological model of the I-, the D- and the M-organisation of an enterprise, we have already applied this communication-centric view. Combined I-, D- and M-organisations are the entire enterprise information system, because together they offer all information services that actors in the O-organisation need. The orange-lined shape in Fig. 8.14 shows this crucial understanding: every EIS is some part of the enterprise's I-organisation and the corresponding part of the D- and the M-organisation. But what about the 'automation' of the O-organisation? In other words, what about the replacement of O-actors by agents? Aren't these agents part of the enterprise information system? For sure they are because they cannot be elements of the O-organisation, so they must be elements of the I-organisation. The proper understanding of these agents is therefore that they are 'sham red': they are green (informa), but they have a red (performa) skin, so to speak.

---

[5] The English word 'communicate' comes from the Latin word *communicare*, which means 'making something common' or 'sharing something with somebody'. In a more specific sense, it means 'sharing thoughts'.

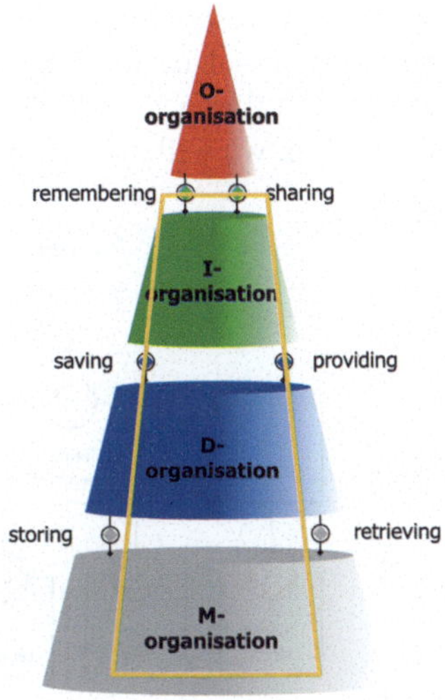

Fig. 8.14 The notion of enterprise information system

To illustrate this, suppose that we would fully automate the actor role rental completer in the Rent-A-Car company (cf. Chap. 12). Then we must first extend the I-organisation with an actor role that is a true copy of the O-actor role rental completer. Next, we transform all action rules for this actor role into algorithms, simply by replacing all occurrences of the line '**if** *performing the action after* ***then*** *is considered justifiable*' by the line '**if true**', meaning that the Boolean value of the conjunction of the predications in the assess part is true. The third step is to implement the actor role, by means of ICT. As discussed in Sect. 8.3.6, this comes down to implementing the prismanet that is shown in Fig. 8.12. The actor role rental completer comprises the operations of the processors P1 through P11. In terms of software engineering, it would be represented by a set of procedures if a procedural language is used and by an object class if an object-oriented language is used. If, in the new situation, a customer wants to rent a car, he or she addresses an agent in the role rental completer (e.g. via a Web page) to perform the request that is specified in the when-clause in Table 8.2. The resulting C-fact (e.g. rental completing **for** rental 1993 **is** requested) is remembered by some agent and shared with the rental completer agent in order to settle it. The addressee of the response act, which is either the promise or the decline of the request, is the (human) actor.

8.4 Discussions

8.4.1 The Boundary of an Enterprise

In [7], the term B-organisation (B from Business) of an enterprise is used instead of O-organisation. This has led to quite some confusion since its publication, because the delineation of the ontological model of an enterprise's O-organisation (as well as of the corresponding I- and D-organisation) does not necessarily coincide with the institutional or legal boundary of the enterprise. Hereafter, we will discuss important differences, which sometimes are quite subtle. As the leading example for illustration, we will use again the case Rent-A-Car (cf. [1], Chap. 15).

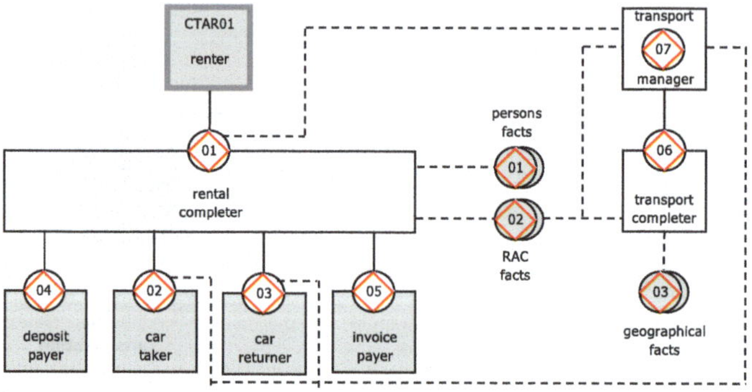

transaction kind	product kind	executor role
TK01 rental completing TK02 car taking TK03 car returning TK04 deposit paying TK05 invoice paying TK06 transport executing TK07 transport managing	PK01 [rental] **is** completed PK02 **the** car **of** [rental] **is** taken PK03 **the** car **of** [rental] **is** returned PK04 **the** deposit **of** [rental] **is** paid PK05 **the** invoice **of** [rental] **is** paid PK06 [transport] is executed PK07 transport managing **for** [day] **is** done	AR01 rental completer AR02 car taker AR03 car returner AR04 deposit payer AR05 invoice payer AR06 transport executer AR07 transport manager

Fig. 8.15 CSD and TPT of Rent-A-Car

In Fig. 8.15, the Cooperation Model (cf. Chap. 10) of the O-organisation of the case Rent-A-Car is represented, expressed in a Coordination Structure Diagram (CSD) and a Transactor Product Table (TPT). The figure also exhibits the chosen Scope of Interest (SoI). Within this scope, our focus is determined by the white (i.e. non-grey)-coloured actor role shapes and transaction kind shapes. The notion of SoI is an important one. Practically spoken, one always chooses some SoI, guided by the problems one wants to study. During this study, one may get the need to adjust the SoI, by enlarging it or by reducing it. This makes the ontological notion of an enterprise basically independent of the legal and/or economic notion. Although it is not very likely that one goes beyond the boundary of the enterprise (because the enterprise 'has' the problems to be studied and has called in your help), it is not impossible to do it.

But what then constitutes an enterprise? When does the focus in Fig. 8.15 coincide with the boundary of the enterprise Rent-A-Car and thus comprise its business? The key to answering these questions is the sourcing of the actor roles, which is a matter of implementation. According to the description of the case Rent-A-Car, the internal actor roles (thus the actor roles inside the focus) in Fig. 8.15, so actor roles AR01, AR06 and AR07, are filled by subjects who are employed by the company (i.e. who are on the payroll). In contrast, actor roles in the environment (i.e. outside the focus but inside the SoI), thus AR02, AR03, AR04 and AR05, are not filled by employees of the company. As for the external information sources, the multiple transaction kinds MTK1, MTK2 and MTK3, both the initiators and the executors are fully outside the SoI. The focus in Fig. 8.15 is said to coincide with the boundary of the legal/economic enterprise.

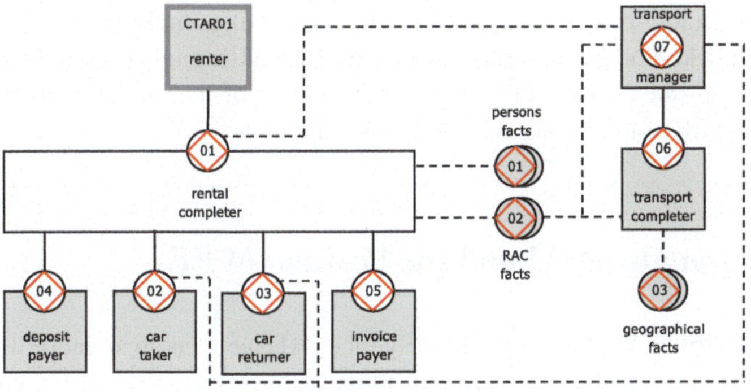

transaction kind	product kind	executor role
TK01 rental completing	PK01 [rental] **is** completed	AR01 rental completer
TK02 car taking	PK02 **the** car **of** [rental] **is** taken	AR02 car taker
TK03 car returning	PK03 **the** car **of** [rental] **is** returned	AR03 car returner
TK04 deposit paying	PK04 **the** deposit **of** [rental] **is** paid	AR04 deposit payer
TK05 invoice paying	PK05 **the** invoice **of** [rental] **is** paid	AR05 invoice payer
TK06 transport executing	PK06 [transport] **is** executed	AR06 transport executer
TK07 transport managing	PK07 transport managing **for** [day] **is** done	AR07 transport manager

Fig. 8.16 CSD and TPT of Rent-A-Car after outsourcing car transportations

Now suppose that the directors of the company decide to outsource the transportation of cars between the branches, presumably for economic reasons, to the company TransCar, which is specialised in transporting cars. This decision would mean that actor roles AR06 and AR07 are no more filled by employees of Rent-A-Car but by employees of TransCar. Then the boundary of Rent-A-Car and the SoI in Fig. 8.15 do not coincide anymore, because actor roles AR06 and AR07 have become environmental actor roles. However, the new focus may still be an interesting one, given the problems or issues at hand. Note that actor roles AR06 and AR07 in Fig. 8.15 still belong to the chosen SoI.

Figure 8.16 contains the CSD and TPT of Rent-A-Car in the new situation. Making actor roles AR06 and AR07 environmental actor roles is the first step in establishing the new situation, in which TransCar takes care of the transportation of cars between the branches of Rent-A-Car. But it is not enough. The salaries of the employees of TransCar who fill actor roles AR06 and AR07 now are debit entries for TransCar, as are various additional costs. These costs must somehow be covered by payments made by Rent-A-Car. There are several options to arrange this. One of them is that Rent-A-Car pays for every transportation. Then we would need to extend the Cooperation Model (CM) of Rent-A-Car with a payment transaction kind in which TransCar is the initiator and Rent-A-Car the executor. But the two companies could also agree on long-term cost coverages, which would lead to other changes of the CM.

In addition, new implementations must be devised and made operational of the inspection links that cross the (economic) border of the enterprise Rent-A-Car, like for example the links from AR07 to TK01, TK02 and TK03.

Outsourcing actor roles is not limited to actor roles in the O-organisation. It may also hold for actor roles in the I-organisation (like making statistics), the D-organisation (like document management) and the M-organisation (like file management). Also in these cases, the ontological models of the I-organisation and the D-organisation will not change, only their implementations.

8.4.2 The Debate on AI and the Position of EE

The advances in the field of artificial intelligence (AI) have taken an incredible pace, and the societal areas that are influenced by the achievements of AI increase at an incredible pace too. Fortunately, there is also a critical debate going on about the benefits as well as the threats of AI, on a worldwide scale. Even more importantly, not only scientists and engineers participate in the debate but also influential voices from other fields, notably philosophers. Among the recent influential contributions are the ones by Yuval Harari [8] and Daniel Dennett [9].

In Sect. 8.3.3, we have already touched on a few topics in the current debate on AI. In what follows, we only want to summarise the position that is taken by the discipline of EE. The current dominant line of reasoning of the proponents of AI is that if the 'intelligence' of artefacts, in particular robots, keeps increasing, it will arrive at a point where these artefacts could confidently be treated as fellow human beings; they will even be a lot smarter than human beings. There are two serious flaws in this line of reasoning.

The first one is the notion of intelligence itself. As pointed out in Sect. 8.3.3, the human faculty of 'intelligence' can only be ascribed to ICT artefacts by way of an anthropomorphic metaphor. Only in this perspective is it okay, e.g. to call your laptop stupid. But of course, laptops cannot be stupid nor can any other things, natural or man-made. Stupidity is the exclusive privilege of human beings. Actually, the term 'artificial intelligence' is perfect, as long as one takes it literally and thus as long as one considers AI artefacts not really but artificially intelligent. In other words, their 'intelligence' is mimicked. An example that we have discussed in Sect. 6.3.3.2 is the mimicked ability of Deep Blue to play chess. As also pointed out in this context, it is actually incorrect to say that computers compute. What these machines do, and at which they are extremely good, is manipulating symbols according to prescribed rules. This holds also for what are nowadays called self-learning machines. The fact that these machines are able to generate such rules by and for themselves doesn't make them more than symbol manipulators.

The second serious flaw in the current debate on AI is that by merely increasing the 'intelligence' of artefacts, they will at some stage of their development be able to make decisions, like human beings do. The misunderstanding here is that making decisions would be a matter of intelligence. It is not. Making decisions is a faculty of human beings in their role of social individual, being able to enter into and comply with commitments. The faculty is strongly connected to authority and responsibility (and accountability), as explained by the PSI theory (cf. Chap. 6). This is exactly why the recent granting of citizenship to a robot by the government of Saudi Arabia, which we mentioned in Sect. 6.3.3.3, is a rather thoughtless act, if not stupid.

But EE doesn't have a monopoly on wisdom, and the insights may change in the course of time. Therefore, we conclude with a quote by Stephen Hawkins: 'AI will be either best or worst thing for humanity'.

8.4.3 The Practical Importance of the ALPHA Theory

The ALPHA theory is meant to be, and has also proven to be, an intellectual instrument in discovering and profiting from the four layers of transactions and actors that exist in all organisations and business processes, once they have been understood in the ontological way as provided by the PSI theory (cf. Chap. 6). The key concept on which the ALPHA theory builds is the semiotic ladder (cf. [1], Chap. 5). It yields the distinction between these human capabilities: performa, informa, forma and material. In the PSI theory, the distinction clarifies the process of coordination acts. In the ALPHA theory, it gives rise to conceiving four aspect organisations in every enterprise: the O-organisation, the I-organisation, the D-organisation and the M-organisation.

The crucial notion of the essential model of an enterprise is primarily rooted in this distinction. It is the ontological model of the enterprise's organisation (thus a constructional model that abstracts from its implementation) that in addition abstracts from its realisation (thus from the I-, the D- and the M-organisation; cf. Fig. 8.5). The result is an ontological model of the O-organisation in which the interface with the supporting I-organisation is taken care of in the next two ways. First, the remembering transactions are covered by considering all created C-facts to be stored in the transaction bank of the corresponding transaction kind. Second, the sharing transactions are covered by considering actors to have reading access to the transaction banks in which the facts reside that they need. Derived facts are defined on the basis of these original facts.

The foremost practical importance of the ALPHA theory is in the PIF analysis (PIF is the abbreviation of Performa-Informa-Forma), as discussed in [7]. Applying the PIF analysis to narrative descriptions of organisations or business processes, or to structured descriptions like flow charts or the diagramming techniques of current BPM approaches (cf. Chap. 7), has proven to be a most effective way of revealing the essence of organisations, provided it is combined with the application of the transactor concept from the PSI theory (Chap. 6) and the tree structures of business processes from the OMEGA theory (Chap. 7). The resulting insight and the short time in which an essential model can be produced are unprecedented.

Another practically important contribution of the ALPHA theory is the clarification of the notion of enterprise information system (EIS), and consequently of the way in which EISs should be developed, namely, from the communication-centric view on information systems, as discussed in Chap. 4. The emerging simple and powerful understanding is that developing an EIS is the devising and engineering of a new implementation of a part of the I-, D- and M-organisation (cf. Fig. 8.14), no more and no less. Only when taking this approach can one be confident that all functional requirements are met, even those that are not mentioned by the interviewed employees in the analysis phase, like the tacitly performed C-acts and the 'exceptional' declines, rejections and revocations (cf. Chap. 6).

References

1. Dietz, J. L. G., & Mulder, J. B. F. (2024). *Enterprise ontology—A human-centric approach to understanding the essence of organisation* (Enterprise engineering) (2nd ed.). Springer Nature.
2. Searle, J. R. (1995). *The construction of social reality*. Free Press. xiii, 241 p.
3. De Jong, J. (2013). *A method for enterprise ontology based design of enterprise information systems* (p. 195). MPrise Group.
4. Austin, J. L. (1962). *How to do things with words*. Harvard University Press.
5. Searle, J. R. (1969). *Speech acts: An essay in the philosophy of language*. Cambridge University Press. vii, 203 p.
6. Habermas, J. (1986). *The theory of communicative action*. Polity Press.
7. Dietz, J. L. G. (2006). *Enterprise ontology: Theory and methodology*. Springer. xiii, 243 p.
8. Harari, Y. N. (2017). *Homo deus: A brief history of tomorrow* (First U.S. ed.). Harper, an imprint of HarperCollins Publishers. 449 p.
9. Dennett, D. C. (2017). *From bacteria to Bach and back: The evolution of minds* (1st ed.). W.W. Norton & Company. xviii, 476 p, 2 unnumbered pages of plates.

Chapter 9
The EE Organisational Design Theory

Abstract The EE organisational design theory or BETA theory is a theory about the development of a system, called the object system (OS), which is going to support another system, called the using system (US). The US uses the services that are (going to be) offered by the OS. The development process is conceived as the sequence of function design, construction design and implementation design, where the notion of design corresponds fully with its definition in Chap. 3. Although the BETA theory is generally applicable, we apply it specifically to the development of O-organisations and enterprise information systems (EISs), which comprise parts of an enterprise's I-, D- and M-organisation as defined by the ALPHA theory. Both Enterprise Ontology and Enterprise Architecture are crucial notions in the General System Development Process (GSDP), which is the general development model. Function design starts from the ontological model of the US, and construction design ends up in the ontological model of the OS. The notion of architecture appears to be ambiguous in current theory and practice. In Enterprise Engineering, it is exclusively used in its meaning of guidelines (principles, standards) that are applied in the system development process. These guidelines apply to a class of systems, in contrast to user requirements, which apply to a particular system. Consequently, the applied architecture in a development process is a source of both functional and constructional requirements, in addition to the functional and constructional requirements that are provided by the future users of the OS. In order to manage the, usually large, set of user and architectural requirements, GRAF (General Requirements and Architecture Framework) is presented.

9.1 Introduction

The EE organisational design theory is also labeled B-theory. The Greek capital letter is pronounced as BETA, which is an acronym for Building from Essence with Technology and Architecture. It is a theory about developing artefacts, where

J. L. G. Dietz, H. B. F. Mulder, *Enterprise Design Fundamentals*, The Enterprise Engineering Series, https://doi.org/10.1007/978-3-031-83262-8_9

developing is conceived as designing and implementing the design. The notion of design and the process of designing have been introduced in Chap. 3.

The BETA theory guides one in designing a system, while the ETA theory (cf. Chap. 10) guides one in making it concrete and operating. In Sect. 9.2 (Foundations), the *General System Development Process* (GSDP) is presented. It is a general framework for understanding the development of an *object system* for the benefit of a *using system*. In conformity with the TAO theory (cf. Chap. 5), a distinction is made between the function and the construction of the object system, thereby clarifying that the function of the object system supports the construction of the using system. The design phases in a development process are function design, construction design and implementation design.

Function design starts from the ontological model of the using system (which may have to be produced first, through reverse engineering) and ends with the specification of the object system function. There are two inputs: user requirements (determined by the using system construction) and architectural requirements (determined by the applicable architecture). To assess the functional user requirements, that is, the intended affordances they are in need of, one may like to apply specific approaches, like BMC and SCP (cf. Chap. 3). *Construction design* starts from the object system function and ends with the ontological model of the object system. There are two inputs: user requirements (determined by the using system construction) and architectural requirements (determined by the applicable architecture). *Implementation design* (also called *engineering*) starts from the ontological model of the object system and ends with the fully detailed specification of a possible implementation. The inputs to this phase are both the (constructional) user requirements and the architectural requirements. Implementation design is fully covered by the ETA theory (cf. Chap. 10).

A general problem in system development is the (too) large amount of design freedom that is left when all requirements are satisfied. The notion of *architecture* helps designers use this freedom in a purposeful and systematic way. The notion of architecture and its role in system development is addressed in Sect. 9.2.4. Next, the *General Requirements and Architecture Framework* (GRAF) is introduced. It is a framework for classifying functional and constructional requirements, both the ones provided by the users and the ones provided by the applicable architecture.

In Sect. 9.3 (Elaborations), the GSDP and the GRAF are applied to the development of the O-organisation, the I-organisation and the D-organisation of an enterprise and to the development of an enterprise information system (EIS). We discuss more specifically what it means for the function design and the construction design phases of each of them.

In Sect. 9.4 (Discussions), we reflect on the BETA theory. First, the GSDP is compared to current system development approaches, notably TOGAF/ADM. Second, the GRAF is compared with other architecture frameworks (TOGAF and IAF).

9.2 Foundations

By *system development* we understand the bringing about of a brand-new system or of changes to an existing system. The system development process comprises all activities that have to be performed up to and including the implementation of the system. In this section, we will investigate the nature of the development process, which will lead to the conception of a generic model of this process. In particular, we will study the role of ontology and technology.

There are two actors involved in any development process: the customer and the supplier. The *customer* places the order with the supplier for developing the system. The *supplier* performs the development activities and delivers the system in the end to the customer. By conceiving the customer and the supplier as actors (cf. Chap. 6), their authorities and responsibilities are clarified, as well as the competences they need to have.

9.2.1 Designing

Every development process involves two systems, which we will call the using system and the object system. By the *object system* (OS) is understood the system which is going to be developed. By the *using system* (US) is understood the system that is going to use the services (also called the functionality) of the object system.

As the explanatory example of a US, we use the *sales department* of a company, and for that of an OS, we use a *sales information system*. One of the services that the US takes from the OS is the monthly turnover. One of the monthly products that the OS produces is the result of some calculation. This result is interpreted by the US as the monthly turnover.

The goal of this section is to clarify the two major phases in every system design process, called *function design* and *construction design*. To start with, let us have a closer look at the process of designing a system in a very general way. Figure 9.1 exhibits the basic view that we consider appropriate for understanding the system design process.

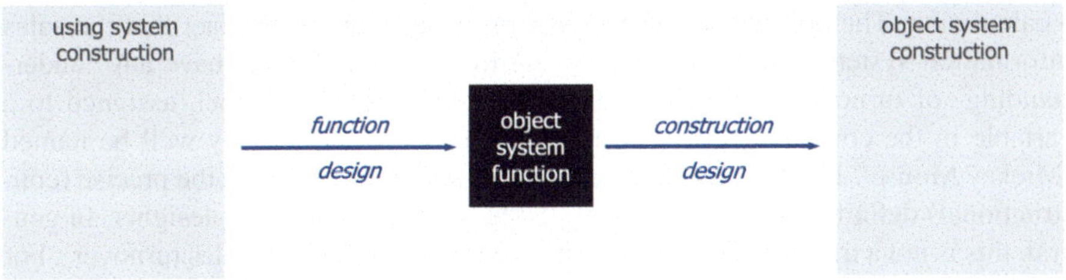

Fig. 9.1 The system design process (1)

The function perspective and the construction perspective on systems, as well as the corresponding black-box model and white-box model (cf. Chap. 5), play a crucial role in understanding the design process. *Function design* starts from the construction of the US and ends with the (specification of the) function of the OS. The function of the OS is considered to be a black-box model. In line with what has been said about black-box models in Chap. 5, it means that the specified function of the OS does not contain any information about the construction of the OS. Instead, it is specified fully and only in terms of the construction of the US.

As said, the function of the OS supports the construction of the US. Put the other way around, the construction of the US uses the functionality offered by the OS. Why does the OS support the construction of the US, and not its function? The answer is that there must always be an alternation of function and construction in the support-use relationship of systems. A function cannot support another function directly, because functions cannot have a need for support; only constructions can. To exemplify this, the sales department as a part of the construction of the enterprise can have a need for the services of a sales information system because the salesmen (the elements in this construction) can be in need of such a support. The sales department as a black box is a functional abstraction that may be useful for some construction above it, but it does not concern the operational activities of selling. Conversely, the function of the OS is always, and necessarily, expressed in terms of the construction of the US. So, for example, the salesmen in (the construction of) the US may have a need to know the monthly turnover of the enterprise. The notion of turnover is an economic notion that takes its rich meaning from the larger economic context in which the enterprise operates. The value of the monthly turnover is something by which people in the sales department can become excited or depressed. In specifying the function of the OS, it is this rich meaning of turnover that the salesmen will share with the function designers of the OS. Needless to say, these function designers must possess sufficient knowledge of the business of the enterprise in order to be well-matched opponents to the salesmen during function design.

The nature of the second design phase, *construction design*, is quite different from the first one. It starts from the specified function of the OS, and it ends with the (specification of the) construction of the OS. Without intending to wrong functional designers, the task of constructional designers is definitely more creative, because they have to bridge the mental gap between function and construction (cf. Chap. 5).

To illustrate this, the notion of turnover must now be 'connected' to the result of a calculation. The constructional designer must be aware of the fact that the sales information system that he or she is going to design will never have any 'understanding' of turnover. The name 'turnover' will at best be a label, assigned to a variable in the computer program, but this variable could equally well be named 'Mickey Mouse'. It is the task of the constructional designer to get the precise (constructional) definition of turnover, with the help of the functional designer. In general, this is not a trivial matter, even not for a simple notion like 'sales turnover'. For example, does a sales order have to be promised in order to be taken into account in calculating the turnover figure (cf. Chap. 6), or is the state requested sufficient?

Does the corresponding payment have to be promised by the customer or not? What about the possible components that may have to be purchased? Must they be taken into account too? All these questions have to be answered before the construction designer can replace the functional or 'business' semantics of turnover by its formal (constructional) semantics. Based on these formal semantics, he/she can then devise an appropriate calculation rule.

The result of the activity function design is a functional model of the OS, which by nature is a black-box model. It contains the *functional specifications* for the OS to be built. In addition to the specifications of the services themselves, they include the specifications for the interface through which the services are provided to the US. The major input for the activity function design are the functional requirements. They are provided by the US, as shown in Fig. 9.2. These requirements need not be equal to the functional specifications, as contained in the functional model of the OS, for several reasons. First, requirements may be unfounded. Fortunately, the ontological model of the US provides an objective yardstick for detecting unfounded requirements, since the ontological model of the US specifies exactly the information that is needed for every actor role (cf. Chap. 6 and [1], Chap. 9). All other information that the actors in the US may want to have is not necessary for executing their roles. Next, determining requirements includes validating them. This can be achieved only in thorough discussions with people 'in the business'. Again, the ontological model of the US offers great help: it is hardly possible to forget essential requirements then.

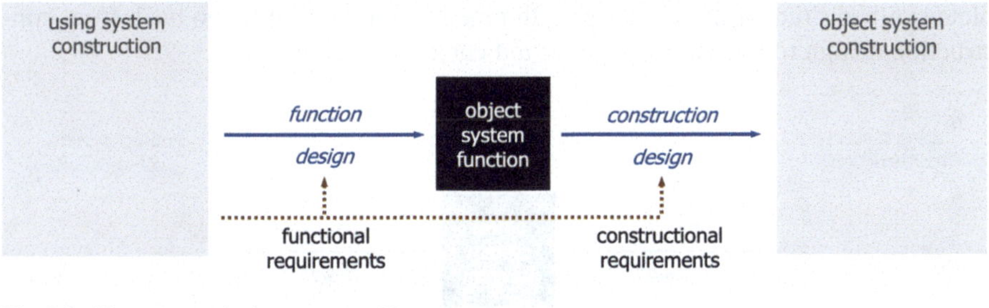

Fig. 9.2 The system design process (2)

The result of the activity construction design is a constructional model of the OS, which by nature is a white-box model. It contains the *constructional specifications* for the OS to be built. These constructional specifications must be feasible, meaning that they can be implemented, given the available technology. This is one aspect of feasibility. Other aspects are that the whole development process can be executed within the agreed-upon time and within the agreed-upon budget. In general, designing includes negotiation, so that the end result is a *balanced compromise* between (reasonable) requirements and (feasible) specifications. This holds both for function design and construction design. The major input for the latter phase are the *constructional requirements*, provided by the US, often also called *non-functional* requirements. Constructional requirements include the performance characteristics with which the OS is going to provide its services. Examples of such characteristics are response time, robustness and security. In practice, the constructional requirements are often made specific by means of service-level agreements (SLAs) regarding each of the performance characteristics.

The negotiation, as mentioned above, is formally conducted by the customer and the supplier but in practice often delegated to, respectively, the future users of the OS and the designers. As said before, the reasonability of the provided functional and constructional requirements can fairly be determined on the basis of the ontological model of the US. The feasibility of the ultimate functional and constructional specifications is something that can only be determined in iteration between function design and construction design, as exhibited in Fig. 9.3.

The figure conforms to the insight of Alexander [2], who understands design as a process of alternate analysis and synthesis steps, as we have discussed in Chap. 3. It elucidates that designing is not a one-way process but that there will be iteration [3]. In other words, the devising of the functional specifications and constructional specifications will usually take place incrementally and alternately. The distinction between analysis and synthesis is a perfect example of the separation of concerns (cf. Chap. 11). During an analysis step, the concerns are the correct understanding of the semantics, the completeness and the consistency of the function of the OS. In a synthesis step, the concerns are the correct replacement of functional semantics by formal semantics, as well as the efficiency of the construction of the OS (although also these two concerns need to be separated). Figure 9.3 shows the ideal path, as discussed in Chap. 3: first the complete analysis (function design) and then the complete synthesis (construction design). In practice, one will often go back from construction design to function design, as indicated in Fig. 9.3.

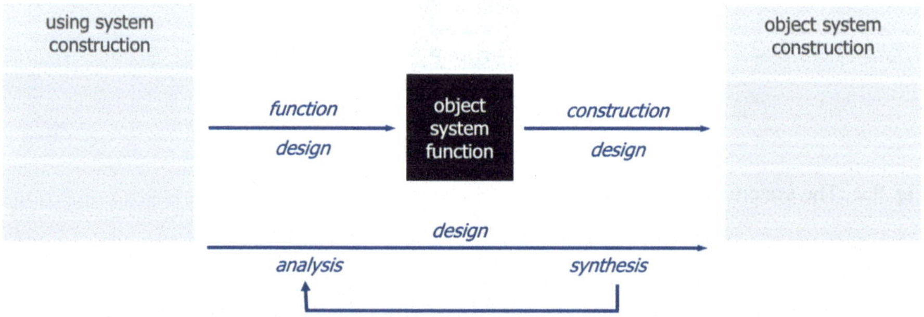

Fig. 9.3 The system design process (3)

9.2.2 The System Development Process

The development phases after designing are engineering and implementing. Next to ontology, another notion plays an important role now, namely, technology. Let us start by focusing on the role of ontology. As we know from Chap. 5, the ontological model of a system is a model of its construction that is completely abstracted from the way in which it is implemented.

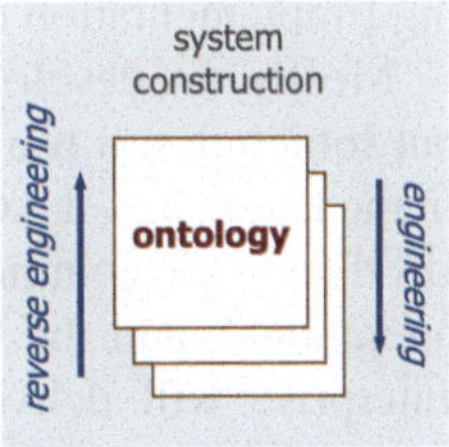

Fig. 9.4 Engineering and reverse engineering

The *engineering* of a system is the activity in which a series of constructional models are produced (cf. Fig. 9.4). Every model is derived from the previous one while taking into account the applicable constructional requirements. We will discuss engineering in Chap. 10.

Often, one or more constructional models are missing, a typical situation being that only the implementation model is available (which is the case for many legacy software systems). The process of reconstructing the higher-level models from the implementation model is known as *reverse engineering* (cf. Fig. 9.4).

Combining Figs. 9.3 and 9.4 results in Fig. 9.5, which we will refer to as the *system development process*. The process starts from the construction of the US, more precisely, from the ontological model (or the ontology) of the US, because only this model provides the appropriate help in guaranteeing that the elicited requirements are *necessary* (all requirements must be deducible from the ontological model of the US), *complete* (the complete ontological model of the US is dealt with) and *sufficient* (redundant or unreasonable requirements are eliminated).

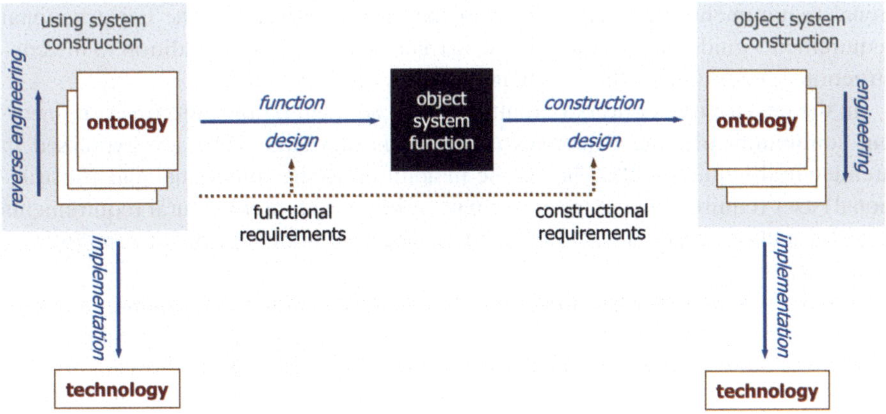

Fig. 9.5 The system development process

If the ontological model of the US is unavailable, it can be produced through reverse engineering (cf. Fig. 9.4). This activity would then be added to the development process. The rest of the process has been discussed in the previous subsections. Note that often construction design is considered to comprise both ontological design (thus producing the ontological model of the OS) and engineering (implementation design).

Mostly, the development regards a minor change in the enterprise's organisation, but sometimes, it is a substantial change. Rarely, a brand-new enterprise is created. In the latter case, the OS is the enterprise to be (re)designed and (re)engineered. The US then is the commercial environment in which the enterprise is or is going to be operational, and the functional model of the OS consists of the services that the enterprise will deliver to the environment. We will elaborate this situation in Sect. 9.3.1.

As said above, the ontological model of the enterprise may be missing. If we take the sales department again as our US, the first step in the development of the supporting sales information system may be producing the ontological model of the sales department through reverse engineering on the basis of lower-level constructional models. Candidates for such models are what is commonly expressed in activity diagrams, EPCs, flow charts, etc. An effective method to 'reveal' the ontological model from such descriptions is the OER method (cf. Chap. 11).

9.2.3 The General System Development Process

Adding the notion of architecture, as defined in Chap. 2, to the system development process in Fig. 9.5 results in Fig. 9.6. The notion of architecture comprises two kinds of architectural requirements: functional and constructional. The functional requirements guide the design of the function of the OS (in addition to the functional requirements that originate from the customers/users). The constructional requirements guide the design of the construction of the OS (in addition to the constructional requirements that originate from the customers/users).

In the prescriptive notion of architecture, as adopted by the enterprise engineering community [4], the objectives of all kinds of stakeholders are expressed in architectural requirements. They come in addition to the (functional and constructional) user requirements in the lower part of Fig. 9.6. If architectural requirements hold for a class of OSs instead of one OS, one commonly speaks of *principles* or *standards*.

An example of a standard in software engineering is the programming language in which the final implementation design is written. Because it makes great practical sense, it is quite common to prescribe the same language for all software components of an enterprise information system or even for all ICT applications in an enterprise. An example of a standard in electricity supply in buildings is the 'standard' outlet in the wall. Unfortunately, there are several standards, like the traffic keeps right in the majority of countries but left in some. Obviously, if there is a choice and no mutual consultation between stakeholders, different 'standards' will arise.

In Fig. 9.6 the field of the BETA theory in the GSDP is marked by the bold-lined and purple-coloured rectangle. Engineering and implementing of the OS are dealt with by the ETA theory, which will be discussed in Chap. 10.

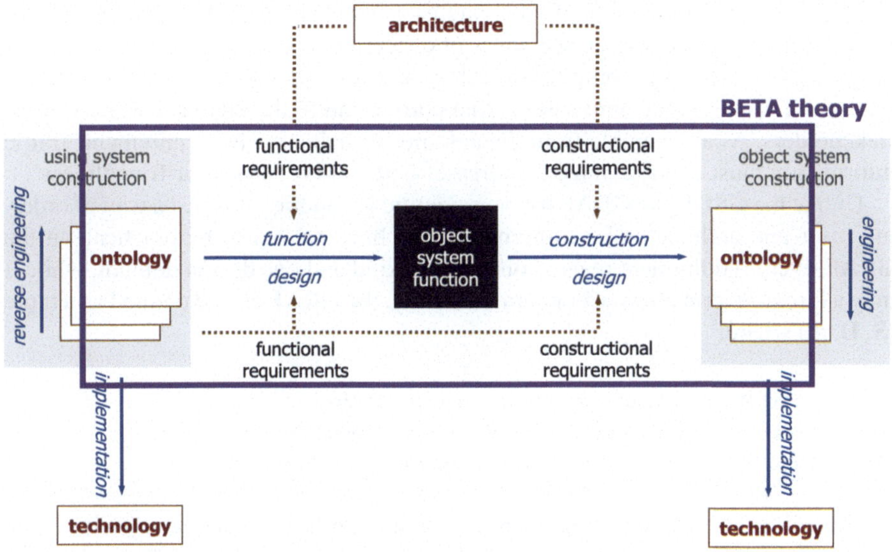

Fig. 9.6 The General System Development Process

9.2.4 The General Requirements and Architecture Framework

In the previous (sub)sections, the GSDP has been presented and discussed, including the role of architecture in the system development process. These discussions have brought insight into the nature of system development, regardless the system category or kind, although our main interest has been in enterprise information systems. But it has left open the question of how the determination of (user and architectural) requirements can be structured and organised in such a way that it is manageable. To address this question, we introduce the General Requirements and Architecture Framework (GRAF). Three dimensions for classifying requirements are distinguished.

The first one is the *system kind* to which a requirement applies. System kind is a specialisation of system category (cf. [1], Chap. 9). In EE, the distinction between system kinds is based on the ALPHA theory (cf. Chap. 7): original, informational, documental and material. Therefore, we distinguish between four system kinds: O-organisations, I-organisations, D-organisations and M-organisations.

The second dimension is the *design domain* to which a requirement belongs. Based on the TAO theory (cf. Chap. 5), we distinguish between two basic domains: function and construction. Systems can be decomposed in each of these domains.

The third dimension is the area of concern that is addressed by a requirement. An *area of concern* is a grouping of focal interests of stakeholders. Usually, this grouping is arbitrary. As a consequence, areas of concern may overlap. Examples of areas of concern are security, compliance, safety and user-friendliness. They divide the total set of requirements into subsets that correspond to the interests of the various stakeholders. As an example from the automotive industry, the requirement 'traffic information must override music' addresses both 'safety' and 'user-friendliness'.

Unlike the GSDP, the GRAF has no scientific grounding. It is just a way of ordering (user and architectural) requirements that have proven to be practical. In the GRAF, every requirement regards one system kind and one design domain, while it may address several areas of concern. Formally, the GRAF can be defined as a tuple (**S**, **D**, **A**) where:

S:	a set of *system* kinds; a system kind is referred to by S.
D:	a set of design *domains*; a design domain is referred to by D.
A:	a set of *areas* of concern; an area of concern is referred to by A.

Guidelines for decomposing a design domain are functional decomposition and constructional decomposition that have been made or can be made. Taking the car again as the example system, we reproduce Figs. 5.7 and 5.6 as, respectively, Figs. 9.7 and 9.8. Consequently, the components can be viewed as (functional or constructional) design domains. The bold grey line around a black box indicates that there is a constructional component through which the function can be operated directly. The constructional component is commonly called the *user interface*.

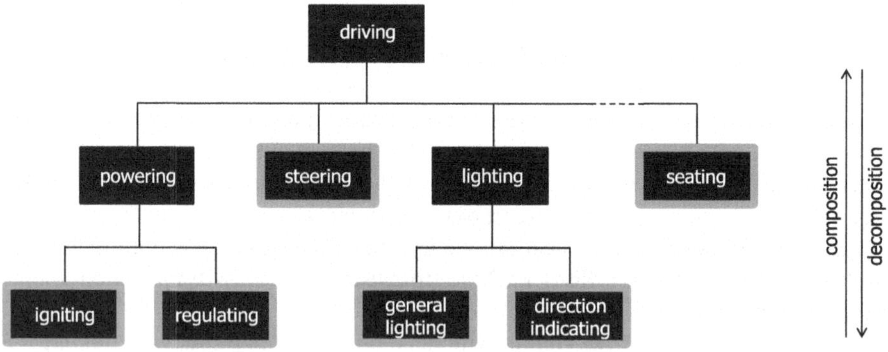

Fig. 9.7 Functional design domains of a car

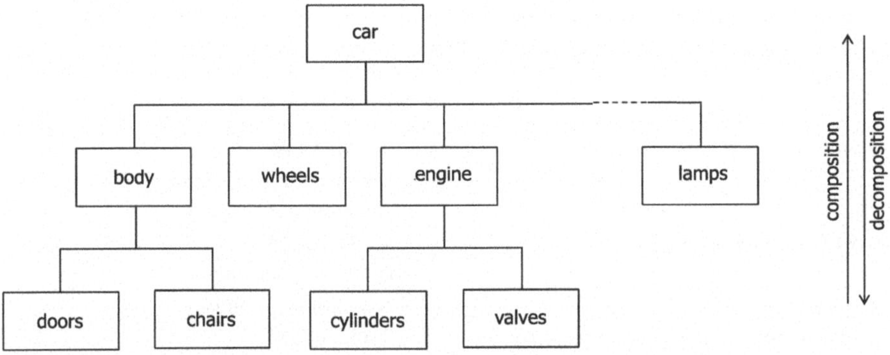

Fig. 9.8 Constructional design domains of a car

Below, we present some possible constructional requirements in the automotive industry, again together with the system kind (S), the design domain (D) and the applicable areas of concern (A).

the total mass must be less than 1500 kg	S = car
	D = car
	A = usage costs
grilles must be made of composite matter	S = car
	D = car/body
	A = durability
all lamps must be LEDs	S = car
	D = car/lamps
	A = sustainability, maintenance

Cars are useful for illustrating the practical applicability of the GRAF, but how to apply it to the design of enterprises? We will show it hereafter, taking MALUM [5] as the example enterprise. In Fig. 9.9, a functional decomposition of the business of the enterprise MALUM is exhibited. The business components are now considered as functional design domains. For each of them, requirements can be formulated.

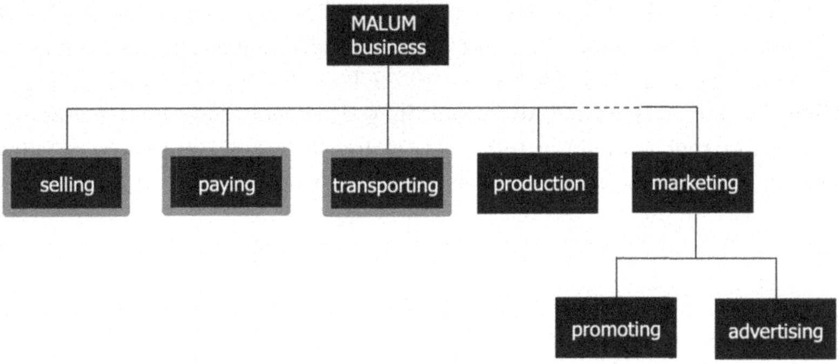

Fig. 9.9 Functional design domains of an enterprise

Below, we provide some examples of functional requirements for MALUM's business, mentioning again system kind (S), design domain (D) and areas of concern (A):

possibility to customise services	S = MALUM
	D = business/production
	A = customer intimacy
easy to use ordering services	S = MALUM
	D = business/selling
	A = customer intimacy
low environmental damaging effect of services	S = MALUM
	D = business/production
	A = environmental awareness

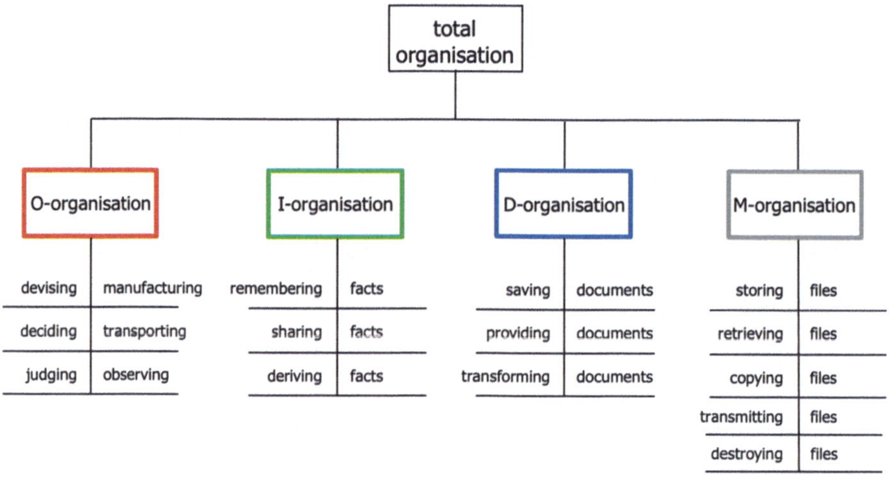

Fig. 9.10 Generic partitioning of an organisation into system kinds

Let us have a look now at the constructional requirements for organisations. Regarding the system kinds (S), we apply the generic partitioning of organisations that is offered by the ALPHA theory (cf. Chap. 6), as exhibited in Fig. 9.10. Regarding the design domains, we apply the generic constructional decomposition of organisations that is made in Fig. 9.11. Below it, we present some examples of constructional requirements for organisations, with indications of the system kind (S), the design domain (D) and the areas of concern (A).

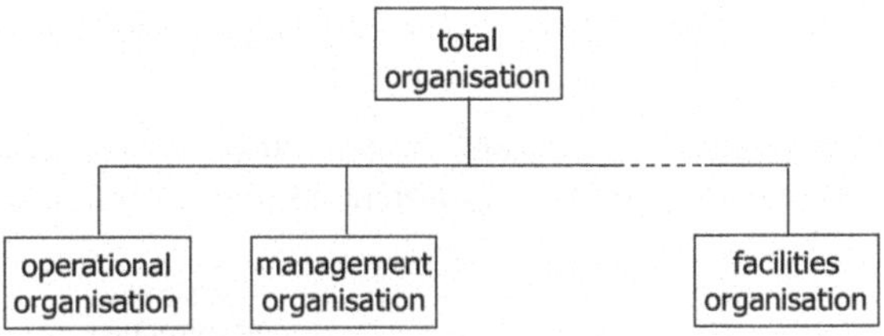

Fig. 9.11 Generic constructional decomposition of an organisation into design domains

real-time workload distribution	S = total organisation
	D = operational organisation
	A = throughput time
Internet-based communication facilities	S = D- and M-organisation
	D = facilities organisation
	A = speed, traceability
percentage of knowledgeable managers ≥ *75*	S = total organisation
	D = management organisation
	A = professionalism

Above we said that the distinction between requirements and design principles or standards is simple and straightforward: a requirement holds for the design of one system, and a principle or standard holds for a class of systems. In this respect, the design of a new car model must be considered as the design of one system, because the manufacturing of the model means creating exact copies. Next, the requirements we discussed above need not be specific for one car model; they may hold for a class of car models and thus be design principles or standards. In particular, the second functional requirement and the third constructional requirement above can very well be taken as standards and thus be architectural requirements.

9.3 Elaborations

The question we will address in this section is how one applies the new notions that we introduced in Sect. 9.2, namely, the GSDP (in Sect. 9.2.3) and the GRAF (in Sect. 9.2.4). To this end, we will discuss the development of the O-organisation of an enterprise, together with the corresponding I-, D- and M-organisation. It will be done, respectively, in Sects. 9.3.1–9.3.3.

9.3.1 Developing the O-Organisation of an Enterprise

Developing the O-organisation of an enterprise, as presented in Fig. 9.12, is nothing less than designing and implementing the core of a new enterprise.

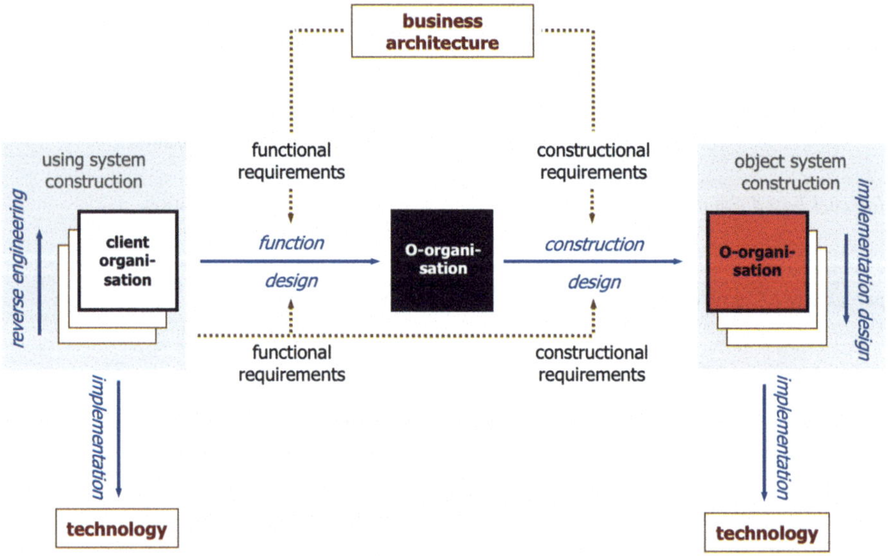

Fig. 9.12 Developing the O-organisation of an enterprise

The black-coloured box in the middle is the functional model of the O-organisation, and the red-coloured box to the right is its ontological model. It is the result of the phase 'construction design', as discussed in Sect. 9.2. Likewise, the functional model of the O-organisation is the result of the phase 'function design', which starts from the ontological model of the using system (on the left side of Fig. 9.12). But what is the using system of an enterprise? A correct but too broad answer is: everything in the environment of the enterprise that uses one or more functions offered by the enterprise. Let us narrow it down to everything that uses the customer or client services that the enterprise offers. Think, for example, of the customer services that a pizzeria offers. Let us next call this narrowed down environment the 'client organisation' of the enterprise, knowing that it is not really an organisation but the collection of clients or customers (though parts of it may be organised).

As we know from the previous section, the function design of the O-organisation is fed by the functional requirements from the using system, thus from the client organisation, as well as by the functional requirements from the applied architecture. Compliant with current terminology, we label the latter 'business architecture'. Likewise, the construction design is fed by the constructional requirements from the using system, as well as by the constructional requirements from the applied architecture.

In applying the GRAF, to keep the (user and architectural) requirements manageable, the next functional requirements could have been classified (cf. Sect. 9.2.3):

possibility to customise services	S = enterprise business
	D = business/production
	A = customer intimacy
easy to use ordering services	S = enterprise business
	D = business/selling
	A = customer intimacy
low environmental damaging effect of services	S = enterprise business
	D = business/production
	A = environmental awareness

The applicable business architecture for designing enterprises 'from scratch' will often consist of standards that are set by government. The third requirement could be an example of such a standard. It will generally be made more specific, for example, by limiting the emission of greenhouse gasses to a specific amount. The other two requirements could very well be the result of a marketing investigation among potential future clients.

As discussed in Chap. 3, the functional user requirements are part of the change mission that the (direction of the) enterprise wants to establish. In order to assess all requirements thoroughly and conveniently, approaches like the ones mentioned in Chap. 3 (BMC and SCP) are needed. In the current chapter, we will not elaborate the application of these approaches. Instead, their application will be demonstrated in the practical cases in Chaps. 12–14. As will become clear there, most changes in practice regard the implementation of the OS, not its essential model.

Regarding the constructional requirements that apply to the development of the O-organisation of an enterprise, we present the following examples (having a take-away and delivery pizzeria in mind as the new enterprise):

kitchen and counter must be adjacent	S = O-organisation
	D = operational organisation
	A = throughput time
sanitary unit close to deliverers room	S = O-organisation
	D = facilities organisation
	A = hygiene, employee well-being
all actors must be human	S = O-organisation
	D = operational organisation
	A = employment, user friendliness

The last requirement actually is a requirement concerning the implementation of the object system. Such requirements, however, do belong to the constructional requirements, since they affect the lowest-level implementation design. Consequently, no robot technology is allowed in the implementation of the pizzeria.

Above, we have discussed the development of the (operational) O-organisation of a brand-new enterprise. It is more common that one wants to re-design a part of the O-organisation of an enterprise. Then this part will be the object system. From the OMEGA theory (cf. Chap. 7), we know that the object system is always a tree or a subtree in the interaction structure of the O-organisation (and that every tree is a business process kind). To illustrate the point, Fig. 10.8 from [1] is copied as Fig. 9.13.

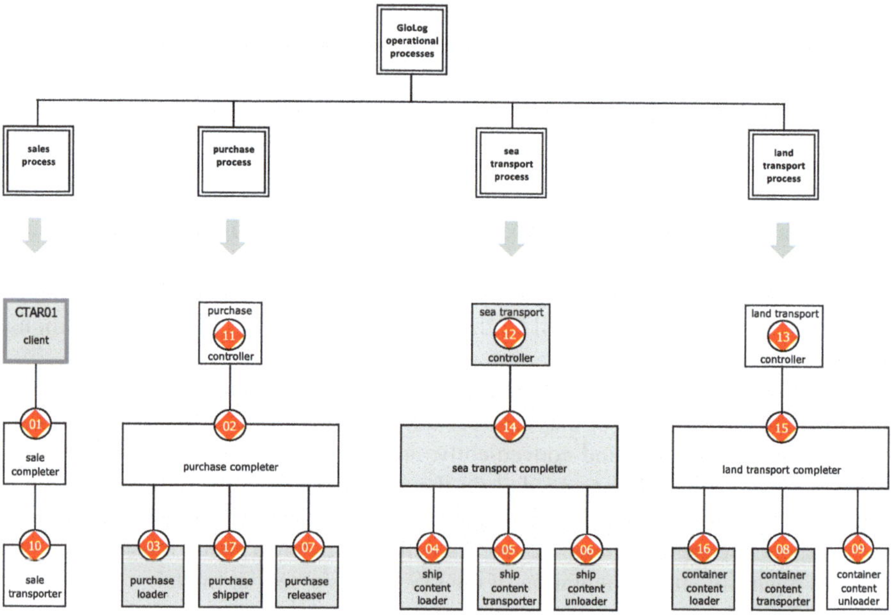

Fig. 9.13 The interaction structure in the GloLog enterprise

The object system to be re-developed could be one of the transactor role trees, thus one of the business process kinds or a subtree of it. An example is the subtree consisting of transactor roles TAR02, TAR03, TAR17 and TAR09. As explained in Chap. 7, all four trees together constitute the Scope of Interest of the case GloLog, whereas the collective white-coloured transactor roles form the focus. They are all executed by actors in the same company, as follows from the case description. From the point of view of this company, the grey-coloured transactor roles may be considered as being outsourced. As explained in the same chapter, in- and outsourcing are changes to an enterprise that concern only its implementation—more precisely, the assignment of actor roles to people.

9.3.2 Developing an Enterprise Information System

Figure 9.14 shows the GSDP for developing an enterprise information system (EIS). As Fig. 8.14 exhibits, an EIS covers a part of the enterprise's I-organisation, D-organisation and M-organisation. In Fig. 9.14, this is expressed by representing the ontological level of the EIS by three boxes on top of each other, one for the part of the I-organisation, one for the part of the D-organisation and one for the part of the M-organisation. As the implementation technology of all three parts, we have chosen ICT, as this is currently the common technology for implementing EISs. The implementation model (coloured yellow and called 'software') comprises the source code of the EIS.

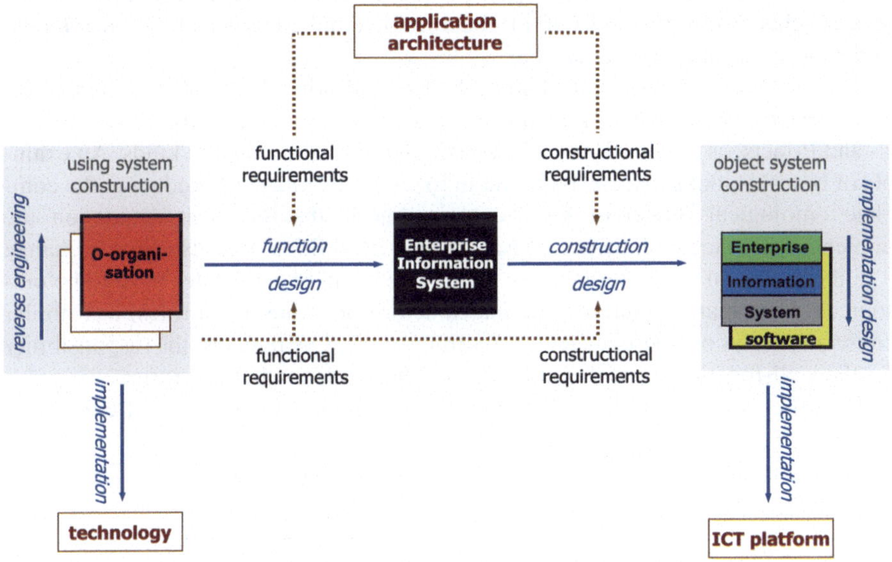

Fig. 9.14 Developing an Enterprise Information System

The black-coloured box in the middle is the functional model of the EIS, and the red-coloured box to the left is the ontological model of the supported O-organisation. The green-blue-grey-coloured box to the right represents the combined ontological models of the concerned parts of the I-, the D- and the M-organisation. It is a result of the phase 'construction design', as discussed in Sect. 9.2. Likewise, the functional model of the EIS is the result of the phase 'function design', which starts from the ontological model of the using system.

As we know from the previous section, the function design of the EIS is fed by the functional requirements from the using system, thus from the sales department, as well as by the functional requirements from the applied architecture. In conformity with current terminology, we label it 'application architecture'. Likewise, the construction design is fed by the constructional requirements from the using system, as well as by the constructional requirements from the applied architecture.

From the ALPHA theory as discussed in Chap. 8, we know that the interface between the O-organisation and the I-organisation consists of two generic transaction kinds, called remembering and sharing. This knowledge simplifies both the function design phase and the construction design phase of the EIS to be developed. It suffices to identify which original C- and P-facts must be remembered and which may need to be shared. They are fully determined by the Action Model of the O-organisation, as discussed in Sect. 6.3. The only remaining design activity is the specification of the derived fact types, of which instances may need to be shared. For example, if the O-organisation is the sales department and if the salespersons need to know the daily turnover, then the fact type 'daily turnover' needs to be specified, such that it can be computed in an internal I-transaction. Note that the access rights of O-actors to C- and P-facts are determined by the ontological model of the O-organisation (cf. Chap. 10).

The ontological model of the part of the I-organisation that is covered by the EIS to be developed consists of remember and share transaction kinds for the distinct C- and P-facts, as well as of the needed computational transaction kinds. An example of how this looks like can be found in [6]. The advantage of producing the complete ontological model of the I-organisation is that one can decide on the implementation technology per transactor role. In addition, it is also easy to change it in the course of time, for example, when one or more actor roles have to be outsourced. Note that outsourcing automated actor roles (thus agent roles) has similar consequences as outsourcing actor roles that are filled by humans: the responsibility for the well-functioning of the software now lies with another enterprise.

Hereafter, we present the following examples of constructional requirements:

all actors are agents	S = I-organisation
	D = operational organisation
	A = efficiency, reliability
development method X must be applied	S = I-organisation
	D = operational organisation
	A = efficiency, maintainability
program code must be in C-sharp	S = I-organisation
	D = operational organisation
	A = efficiency, maintainability

Most likely, all three requirements are architectural requirements, which means that they apply to the development of all ICT applications of the enterprise, not only to the current EIS. The first requirement means that there are no human actors in the I-organisation. In other words, the I-organisation is fully automated. The second and the third requirements are examples of standards in software engineering. They may be enterprise specific, but they mostly have a broader applicability.

Because we actually skipped the function design phase of the GSDP, we also will skip the classification of functional requirements in the GRAF.

9.3.3 Developing the D- and M-Organisation in an EIS

With respect to developing an enterprise's D-organisation and the corresponding M-organisation, one must keep in mind that in EE, a data-processing system, like a database system, is defined on the ontological level, thus abstracted from the implementation technology (cf. Fig. 6.14). As the implementation technology of the D- and M-organisation, we have chosen ICT because it is the common technology nowadays.

From the discussion of the ALPHA theory in Chap. 7, we know that the interface between the I-organisation and the D-organisation consists of two generic transaction kinds, called saving and providing. The things to be saved and provided are documents (including datasets) which contain the O-organisation facts (both original and derived) that the I-actors have decided to save in this way in order to not forget them. The knowledge that we get from Fig. 7.14 about the construction of the I-organisation and the D-organisation simplifies the function design and the construction design of the D-organisation. Moreover, because both the I-organisation and the D-organisation will be fully automated, the construction design of the D-organisation is fully included in the construction design of the EIS: it is determined by the programming language, the database management system, the communication system (including e-mail and networks), etc. We only apply the GRAF to the next constructional requirements that are specific to the D-organisation:

all actors are agents	S = D-organisation
	D = operational organisation
	A = efficiency, reliability
DBMS Y must be used	S = D- and M-organisation
	D = operational organisation
	A = efficiency, maintainability
DMS[1] *Z must be applied*	S = D- and M-organisation
	D = operational organisation
	A = efficiency, maintainability

Most likely, all three requirements are architectural requirements. The first one means that there are no human actors in the D-organisation. In other words, the D-organisation is fully automated. The second and the third requirement are examples of standards in data and document management. They may be enterprise specific, but they mostly have a broader applicability.

[1] DMS stands for Document Management System.

9.4 Discussions

9.4.1 System Development

The BETA theory is a well-founded technological theory in Enterprise Engineering, solidly supported by the ontological theories (cf. Fig. 4.5). Because of this solid grounding, the GSDP offers great practical advantages over other system development approaches. One of them is that the organisation for which one develops a (software) system is considered a system itself that therefore may also (partly) be re-developed. Moreover, this organisation consists of a layer of three (aspect) organisations. Another advantage that the GSDP offers is the distinction between the ontological model of a system and its implementation. The crucial insight that one gets from the underlying ALPHA theory is that an automated (enterprise) information system is just a part of the I-organisation (and the corresponding part of the D- and M-organisation) of the enterprise. It is only implemented by means of ICT instead of 'human technology' and paperwork.

A rather popular approach to developing ICT applications is TOGAF/ADM.[2] Figure 9.15 shows the main picture of it. One may be inclined to equate the three organisational layers (Business, Application, Technology) to the three organisational layers in EE: O-organisation, I-organisation and D-organisation. The most frustrating point in discussing the possible equivalence is that one cannot be sure. The TOGAF layers are too ill-defined to make any sensible decision about it. A similar remark holds for ADM (Application Development Method). Why does it consist of the eight steps that are shown in Fig. 9.15? Why not less or more?

[2] https://www.opengroup.org/togaf

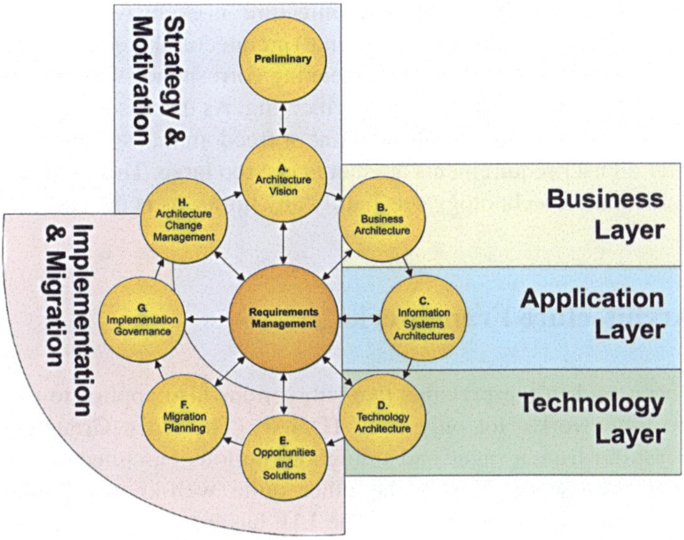

Fig. 9.15 Main picture of TOGAF/ADM

Using the GSDP, user requirements are not elicited by interviewing people in the organisation, like TOGAF does, for example. Instead, they are objectively based on the ontological model of the supported organisation. Eliciting requirements through interviewing, even when supported by studying representations of the business processes, inevitably gives rise to two kinds of errors: (1) crucial requirements are overlooked (people just forget to mention them), and (2) irrelevant requirements are granted (people use their influential power to insist on including them). We discussed this topic already in Sect. 9.2.3 and from a slightly different angle in Chap. 4.

9.4.2 The Notion of Architecture

"When I *use a word," Humpty Dumpty said in rather a scornful tone, "it means just what I choose it to mean—neither more nor less."*

"The question is," said Alice, "whether you can *make words mean so many things."*

"The question is," said Humpty Dumpty, "which is to be master—that's all."
(from *Through the Looking-Glass* by Lewis Caroll)

It is an illusion to think that we would be able to change the current situation where self-declared professionals don't seem to bother about the vagueness and ambiguity that surrounds the notion of architecture, at which we pointed in Sect. 9.2.4. Yet, we stick to our position that no professional progress can be expected until this situation is somehow 'solved'.

The descriptive notion of enterprise architecture, representing the global structure of an enterprise or in some other way describing it, is totally redundant. There is already a notion that does the job and in a very appropriate way: enterprise ontology. That's why in EE, the word 'architecture' is exclusively used for the prescriptive meaning it (also) has: the (additional) architectural requirements that guide the development of a system. Only this meaning corresponds with the origin of the notion at all: the discipline of building engineering. As discussed in Sect. 9.2, there is an urgent need for this notion. The amount of freedom that system developers are left with after all user requirements are met is just too large. This holds in particular if the implementation technology sets hardly any limits, as is the case for ICT.

9.4.3 Architecture Frameworks

What has been said in the previous two subsections also applies to the notion of architecture framework. Not only does TOGAF (The Open Group Architecture Framework) suffer from a vague and ambiguous notion of architecture [7]; it also is not a proper framework. Nor is the other quite well-known framework IAF (Integrated Architecture Framework).[3] The IAF has been extensively discussed in [8]. Both TOGAF and IAF are primarily development methods. A framework, however, should be nothing more (nor less) than a skeleton or frame that serves to organise, classify or categorise things.

The GRAF that we presented and elucidated in Sect. 9.2 is a proper framework. It serves to organise and classify both user and architectural requirements. The distinction between the two kinds of requirements is simple and clear: user requirements hold for a particular system, while architectural requirements hold for a class of systems. Their effect on the development process is similar: they both limit design freedom. Formulated in other words, they guide and constrain the design process.

References

1. Dietz, J. L. G., & Mulder, J. B. F. (2024). *Enterprise ontology—A human-centric approach to understanding the essence of organisation* (Enterprise engineering) (2nd ed.). Springer Nature.
2. Alexander, C. (1964). *Notes on the synthesis of form*. Harvard University Press. 216 p.
3. Dietz, J. L. G., & Albani, A. (2005). Basic notions regarding business processes and supporting information systems. *Requirements Engineering, 10*, 175–183.
4. Dietz, J. L. G., Hoogervorst, J. A. P., et al. (2013). The discipline of enterprise engineering. *International Journal of Organisational Design and Engineering, 3*, 28.
5. Dietz, J. L. G. (2012). *Red garden gnomes don't exist*. Sapio Enterprise Engineering.
6. de Jong, J. (2013). *A method for enterprise ontology based design of enterprise information systems* (p. 195). MPrise Group.
7. Dietz, J. L. G., & Hoogervorst, J. A. P. (2012). A critical investigation of TOGAF. In *Advances in enterprise engineering V* (Spinger-Verlag LNBIP series). Springer.
8. Dietz, J. L. G. (2009). *Architecture: Building strategy into design*. SDU Publishing.

[3] https://en.wikipedia.org/wiki/Integrated_Architecture_Framework

Chapter 10
EE Organisational Implementation Theory

Abstract After the ontological design of an organisation, this design must be made operational. The bridge between the ontological design of an organisation and its being operational consists of four phases. The first one is engineering (or implementation design). It comprises the selection of proper technological means for the elements of the ontological model. The second phase is the actual implementation, that is, the assignment of concrete technological means to the elements of the ontological model. After this phase come installation and operation. Installation is about the specific assignment of technological means, depending on time and space. Operation starts when the 'on button' is pressed. A special section is devoted to (hierarchical) organisational structures as opposed to ontological structures.

10.1 Introduction

The EE organisational implementation theory is also labeled H-theory (cf. Table 4.1). The Greek capital letter H is pronounced as ETA, which is an acronym for Engineering with Technology under Architecture. The word 'engineering' is used here in its narrow sense, thus equal to implementation design (cf. Chap. 9). Figure 10.1 exhibits the place of the ETA theory in the framework of the GSDP. The ETA theory thus covers both engineering and implementation of the resulting implementation design with appropriate technological means. The engineering phase is steered by constructional requirements, both from the applicable architecture and from the using system.

J. L. G. Dietz, H. B. F. Mulder, *Enterprise Design Fundamentals*, The Enterprise Engineering Series, https://doi.org/10.1007/978-3-031-83262-8_10

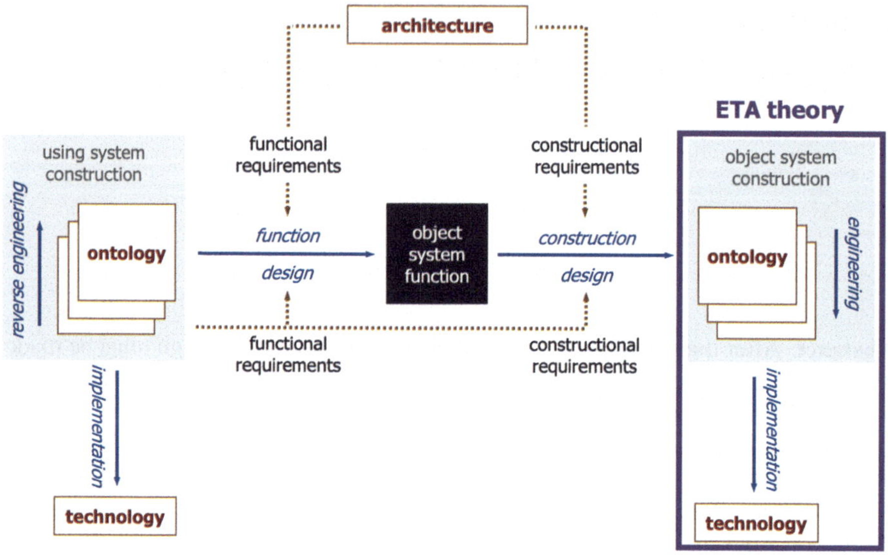

Fig. 10.1 The ETA theory in the GSDP framework

Usually, the number of user requirements will be low, whereas the number of architectural requirements are high. There is a large design freedom that somehow must be narrowed down. The architectural requirements include common standards and common practices.

According to the placement of the ETA theory in the EE framework in Sect. 4.3, it is a technological theory, which means that it is about designing and making things. The validity of a technological theory is justified by its rigour and relevance.

As suggested by the PSI theory (cf. Chap. 6), there are basically three kinds of technology involved in the implementation of an organisation: actor technology, production technology and coordination technology. *Actor technology* concerns the 'active things' that are suited to fill the actor roles in all aspect organisations of an enterprise: the O-, the I-, the D- and the M-organisation (cf. Chap. 8). This topic will be discussed in Sect. 10.2.1. *Production technology* concerns the technologies that actors need in performing production acts. They are addressed in Sect. 10.2.2. *Coordination technology* concerns the technologies that are used in deciding on how to respond to agenda (cf. Chap. 6), in gathering the knowledge needed for this response, as well as in carrying out the communication that is needed to perform the coordination acts. These subjects will be discussed in Sect. 10.2.3.

As explained in [1], in order to let an implemented organisation be operational, it must be installed first. The notions of installation and operation will be discussed in Sect. 10.3. Section 10.4 contains the conclusions of the chapter.

10.2 Foundations

Engineering (or implementation design) is a phase in the GSDP that starts from the ontological model of the OS and ends with its implementation model (cf. Fig. 10.1). Whereas the ontological model of the OS (or of any system) is fully abstracted from all implementation technologies,[1] the implementation model is fully dependent on the technologies that are applied or that are going to be applied.

In [2], Chap. 6, the notion of model is discussed. A conceptual model of a system is defined as the understanding of the system within a specific theory. As Einstein states in the quote above Chap. 4, 'Whether you can observe a thing or not depends on the theory that you use. It is the theory that decides what can be observed'. The ontological model of an organisation is the understanding of the organisation within the ontological EE theories (cf. Fig. 4.5), notably the PSI theory (cf. Chap. 6). In a similar way, the implementation model of an organisation is its understanding within the ETA theory.

There are three implementation technologies that we distinguish: actor technology, production technology and coordination technology. In the subsections hereafter, we will discuss each technology and present how the ETA theory addresses the implementation of the ontological notions of actor role, production act and coordination act. Where the PSI theory speaks of P-acts and C-acts, the ETA theory speaks of P-steps and C-steps.

10.2.1 Actor Technology

By actor technology is understood the technological means or 'active elements' that are eligible to fill the actor roles in an O-, I-, D- or M-organisation. Because we consider the assignment of specific 'things' to actor roles as a matter of installation (cf. Sect. 10.3.2), we will use the notion of organisational function or position, like secretary and administrator, for discussing the implementation design of an organisation. Since the word 'function' has a specific meaning in EE, as discussed in Chap. 5, we will use the term 'organisational position' or just 'position' to denote particular clusters of competence. So, secretary and administrator are labels of specific clusters of competence. As explained in Sect. 6.3.3.4, competences are acquired through talents, education and experience.

Consequently, the implementation design of an organisation includes assigning (organisational) *positions* to the actor roles in the ontological model of the organisation. To present this, a simple Actor role Position Table (APT) suffices, like the one that is shown in Table 10.1 (which is a taken from Table 11.6). An X in a cell means

[1] Although the original meaning of the Greek word for 'technology' is 'knowing how to make', we will use of the term in this chapter as it is mostly used nowadays, namely, as 'technological means', like pencil and paper, digital computers and robots.

that the position (in the row) is assigned to the actor role (in the column). Note that there may be multiple *X*s in a row or in a column. The positions that are listed in the first column are considered to indicate sufficiently the competences (regarding production and coordination) that fillers of the mentioned actor roles need to possess. Ideally, there are educational institutes that offer educational programs leading to diplomas that ensure the correspondent competences.

The example in Table 10.1 regards the O-organisation of the Pizzeria (cf. Chap. 12). Similar tables can be made for the implementation design of the I-, the D- and the M-organisation of an enterprise. As discussed in Chap. 8, we abstain from producing these tables for the reason that nowadays almost always ICT is used as the implementation technology.

As discussed in Chap. 6, there is always a human being responsible for the deeds of the technological artefacts, because it is a human actor who has decided to employ artefacts. Most likely, the choices stem from the applicable architecture: in all pizzerias and comparable enterprises, the actor roles in Table 10.1 are filled by people who possess the competences that are implied by the mentioned organisational positions.

Table 10.1 Actor role position table of the Pizzeria (second phase)

Actor role/position	AR01	AR02	AR03
Desk officer	X		
Baker		X	
Deliverer			X

In current practice, enterprises use organisational charts (also called organigrams or organograms) to exhibit the structure of their organisation. According to Wikipedia,[2] an organisational chart 'is a diagram that shows the structure of the organisation, as well as the relationships and relative ranks of its parts and positions/jobs'. Undoubtedly, by 'the structure of the organisation' is meant a decomposition of the organisation in parts. But then questions arise: is it a functional decomposition, like the one in Fig. 10.6, or a constructional decomposition, like the one in Fig. 9.8? How deep should the decomposition be? How is a part defined? Neither Wikipedia nor the literature in the organisational sciences provides satisfactory answers.

In current practice, there are extremely hierarchical organisational structures next to flat and matrix-shaped ones. To the first category belong 'traditional' enterprises like banks and governmental agencies. To the second category belong 'modern' enterprises, like Semco[3] and Buurtzorg Nederland.[4] Because there is no relationship with the operational construction of the organisation, one cannot derive the organisational structure of an organisation from its ontological model. An

[2] https://en.wikipedia.org/wiki/Organizational_chart

[3] https://en.wikipedia.org/wiki/Ricardo_Semler

[4] https://en.wikipedia.org/wiki/Buurtzorg_Nederland

attempt to address organisational structures scientifically is presented by Mintzberg in [3].

Such structures reflect the perspective of 'people' managers on organisations, thus of 'bosses' of all kinds. These managers are needed to keep human actors in O-, I-, D- and M-organisations 'happy'. The perspective of 'people' manager is perpendicular to the 'process' perspective that is taken in this book.

10.2.2 Production Technology

By production technology is understood the technological means that support actors in performing P-acts, as defined in Chap. 6. We distinguish between tangible and intangible production. Regarding *intangible* production (everything on the left side of Fig. 7.4), actors can basically do without support. However, to speed up production time and/or to increase reliability, modern (automated) decision support systems are often applied. In an implementation model, every intangible production act (P-act) is represented by a single P-step. As an example, the P-act kind TK01/ex in the Pizzeria (cf. Chap. 12) is represented in the implementation model by the P-step kind < decide the completion of [sale] to be a fact >.

Regarding *tangible* production (everything on the right side of Fig. 7.4), actors need machines, tools and other technological means to create their products. In fact, the production time and the product reliability are heavily dependent on the available technological support. As an example of designing the implementation of a tangible P-act kind, we take again the Pizzeria. In the first phase of the Pizzeria, the ontological P-act kind TK02/ex (sale preparing) is represented in the implementation model by the next sequence of P-step kinds: < inspect the pizza kind of [sale] on the pink copy of [sale] > < take a piece of dough that fits the pizza kind of [sale] > < put the ingredients on the dough that belong to the pizza kind of [sale] > < put the dough with the ingredients in the oven > < wait the time needed, as indicated by the pizza kind of [sale] > < retrieve the pizza from the oven > < put the pizza in a fitting box > < shift the box together with the pink copy of [sale] through the hatch to the order taker >.

Note that the instruction < take a piece of dough that fits the pizza kind of [sale] > presumes that there is an inventory of prepared pieces of dough from which the baker can take one. This is normally the case in a pizzeria. Managing this inventory is a separate process that is not dealt with in Chap. 12.

Like we said, when dealing with actor technology in the previous subsection, it is most likely that the choice of the sequences of P-step kinds is steered by the applicable architecture. These sequences have just proven to be the best ways to perform the related ontological production acts.

Notations of sequences of P-step kinds are commonly known as *Work Instruction Specifications* (WIS). Every manufacturing facility uses instructions of this kind. They are the outcome of engineering (in the narrow sense of the word) sales orders.

Shop floors are happy to dispose of detailed step-by-step instructions to do their work.

10.2.3 Coordination Technology

By coordination technology is understood the technological means that support actors in performing C-acts. Performing a C-act is always the outcome of a decision, which on its turn is in principle guided by an action rule (to be discussed in Chap. 11).

So, first of all, actors may need support from decision support systems (DSS) in order to decide on the response to the C-event they are dealing with. A DSS may just be an Enterprise Information System (EIS) that provides the actor with the facts that are needed to execute the action rule. EISs are discussed in Chap. 8. If more support is needed, the actor may use a specific DSS in order to determine the response.

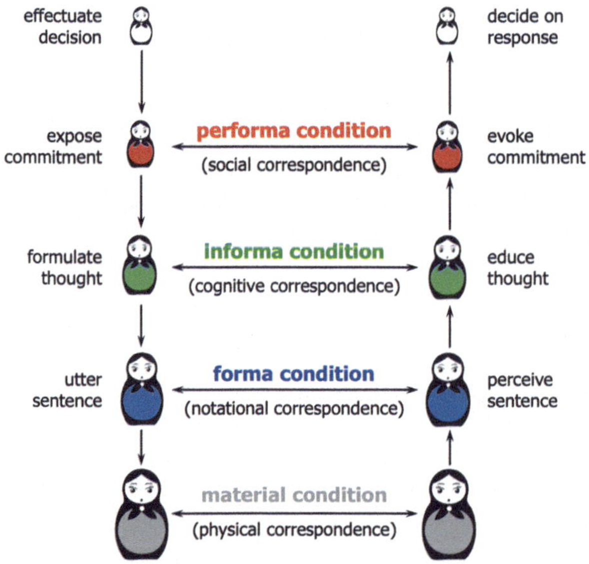

Fig. 10.2 The process of a coordination act

In addition to the decision support, an actor may need help in performing the C-act itself, thus in communicating with the addressee, as exhibited in Fig. 10.2, which is a copy of Fig. 6.5. The minimum level of support consists of transmitting the message from the performer to the addressee, thereby satisfying the material condition as presented in Fig. 10.2.

The support may be extended, however, to include verifying the satisfaction of the forma condition, the informa and the performa condition. This can be done by letting the addressee confirm to the performer of the C-act what he/she has understood, at each level, except of course the highest one (with the 'blank' shapes). At this level, it is the addressee's turn to act.

During engineering, the technological support of performing C-acts has to be decided upon for every step of every transaction kind in the ontological model of the organisation. If the two actors in a transaction communicate face to face, there is no support needed. That's why shopping in a physical shop is so easy. However, when the buyer wants to shop from home, he/she needs equipment to connect to the Internet, find the Web site he/she wants to visit, select the things he/she wants to buy and place the customer order, which is performing the request in the transaction.

The addressee of this C-act is usually not known. Therefore, we stress in Chap. 11 that in the corresponding action rule, the request is directed to some individual who is filling the role of executor in the transaction kind, for example, to 'some sales person'. We think it is crucial that an authorised person is connected to the transaction as the executor of this transaction (actually, this should just be normal practice). Then the customer knows whom to address in case it is needed, for example, when he/she wants to revoke an act. Is this current practice? Unfortunately, not at all. When somebody nowadays orders a drink in a bar or restaurant with a waiter, some other waiter will bring the drink, and yet another one will settle the payment. Most customers will not understand the need for these delegations (or do not want to understand them). Fortunately, most people also don't care, as it seems. But it remains utterly wrong from the point of view of EE.

In addition to the P-steps, which we discussed in the previous subsection, the C-steps that are the outcome of assigning coordination technology are also contained in the *Work Instruction Specifications* (WIS). Likewise, the choice of the sequences of C-step kinds will mostly be steered by the applicable architecture, for the same reasons as the ones that are used when deciding about the implementation of P-acts.

10.3 Elaborations

In this section, we elaborate selected subjects of Sect. 10.2, in order to make sure that the reader has got the right understanding of the subjects. We will also extend the scope of the ETA theory by presenting two phases that come right after the implementation of an organisation (or a system in general): installation and operation.

10.3.1 Implementation

The development phases after designing are engineering and implementing (cf. Fig. 10.5). Next to ontology, another notion plays an important role now, namely, technology. Let us start, however, by focusing on the role of ontology. As we know from Chap. 5, the ontological model of a system is a model of its construction that is completely abstracted from the way in which it is, or will be, implemented.

The *engineering* of a system is the activity in which a series of constructional models are produced (cf. Fig. 10.3). This figure is a copy of Fig. 9.4. Every model is derived from the previous one while taking into account the applicable constructional requirements, both those from the applicable architecture and those from the using system. Contrary to designing, engineering is rather a matter of craftsmanship than of creativity. It starts from the ontological model (or the ontology) and ends with the implementation model. The implementation model is fully dependent on the applied technology. For example, if the applied technology is ICT, the implementation model consists of the program code that is produced by computer programmers.

As we have demonstrated in Sect. 10.2, the implementation model can be produced in most cases directly from the ontological model. In current practice, the ontological model is often missing, while a number of intermediate models are produced, like ArchiMate models, ARIS models, BPM models, UML models, etc.

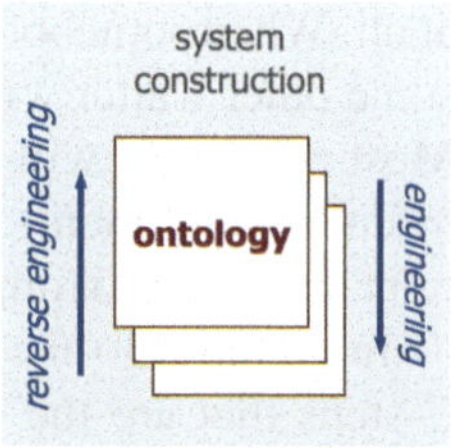

Fig. 10.3 Engineering and reverse engineering

To illustrate that various technologies may be applied to implement organisations, Fig. 10.4 shows two quite different implementations of a withdrawal transaction. To the left, the old-fashioned 'technology' of going to a bank employee in a bank office is shown. To the right, one sees the implementation that is common nowadays, the ATM, with seemingly no responsible human actor (cf. Chap. 6).

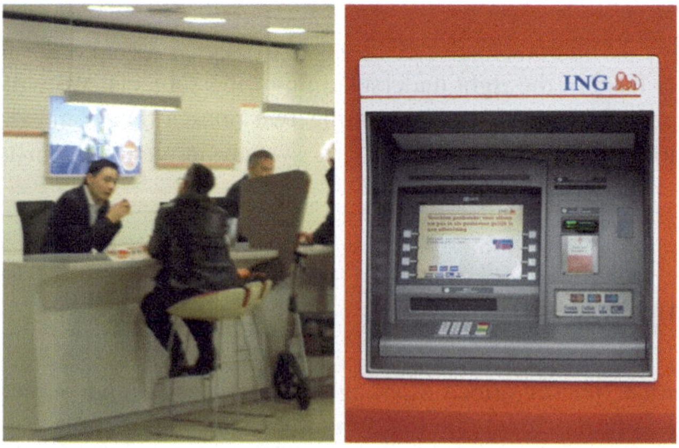

Fig. 10.4 Alternative implementation technologies of a withdrawal transaction

In the previous sections, the implementation of P-acts and C-acts has been sequences of P-steps and C-steps, respectively. In general, such implementations consist of structures of steps, which may contain selections and repetitions, in addition to sequences. These three fundamental ordering principles are described by Dijkstra [4] and Jackson [5] already long ago. As an example of selection, one may think of selecting a particular sequence of P-steps based on the kind of pizza in the pizza-preparing process. As an example of repetition, one may think of a while-do construct in the process of making dough, where the while condition is 'the dough doesn't have the right texture' and the sequence of P-steps after 'do' is < mould the dough for one minute > < check the texture of the dough >, from which the while condition is checked again and so forth.

Fig. 10.5 Implementing a system

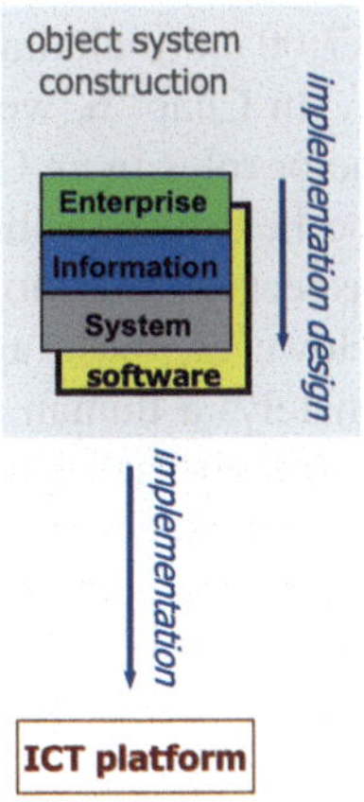

Fig. 10.6 Depiction of software engineering

After having produced the (technology dependent) implementation model, comes *implementing* the system. By this phase is understood the assignment of technological means to the constructional elements in the implementation model. Once implemented properly, the system can be put into operation. The implementation activity is exhibited in Fig. 10.5. As an example, taken from Sect. 9.3.2, Fig. 10.6 shows the implementation of computer software plus the preceding implementation design phase. The yellow-coloured implementation model is a computer program in a programming language that can 'run' on some ICT platform.

Starting from the implementation design of an organisation, the actual *implementation* is quite straightforward. Regarding the actor technology, one has to decide who is going to fill the various positions, as presented in the produced APT (Actor role Position Table), like the one in Table 10.1. A person may fill several positions, and (of course) a position may be filled by several persons. Regarding the production technology and the coordination technology, the sequences of P-step kinds and C-step kinds that are created in the implementation design phase can just be taken over.

10.3.2 Installation

By the installation of an organisation, we understand the assignment of specific technological means or resources to the actor roles, the production and the coordination in the organisation. Usually, these assignments are valid for specific time periods. For example, the installation of the Pizzeria (cf. Chap. 12) comprises, among other things, the assignment of Mario to actor role AR02 for every day of the week except Monday, from 14:00 to 22:00. This assignment is a valid one because Mario has the position of baker and because the Pizzeria is open to customers from 17:00 to 21:00. Mario thus has sufficient time to be ready for baking pizzas from 17:00 on (including doing the needed shopping) and for cleaning up in the evening.

In Chap. 6, we have discussed and explained that only human beings can fill actor roles in an O-organisation, for the simple reason that only human beings can be held responsible and accountable for their deeds. For actor roles in the other aspect organisations, it holds that they can be filled by agents, thus by artefacts. However, these agents have only delegated authority, and there is always (ultimately) a human actor responsible for the acts of the agents, namely, the human actor who has delegated (part of) its authority. Regarding production and coordination, the technological means that are assigned to the distinct P-steps and C-steps in the implementation phase are made ready to use during the installation of the organisation.

10.3.3 Operation

An installed organisation has to be put into operation before it can be called 'life' or operating. Somehow, a 'switch' has to be turned on. For every business process tree, as defined in Chap. 7, it means that the self-activating actor at the top of the tree starts to activate itself. Because the agenda of this actor is initially empty, somehow the first agendum must be created. Fortunately, this is not a big deal in practice.

If a business process starts externally, so if there is an external (composite) transactor that initiates the process, then the organisation is put into operation as soon as the first request in a transaction of the 'top' transaction kind is performed. As an example, the business process in the Pizzeria (cf. Chap. 12) starts as soon as a customer has performed the first request in a transaction of the kind TK01. Then the organisation of the Pizzeria is said to have become operational.

Given the opening hours that were introduced in Sect. 10.3.2, the Pizzeria is put into operation every day when the first customer has performed the first request in a transaction TK01. If this order is fully completed, and there is no other TK01/rq yet, the business process (kind) is said to be idle, but the organisation is still operational.

10.3.4 Organisational Structures

The ontological model of an organisation is a white-box model of the operating core, in terms of Mintzberg [3], we would state cautiously. Why cautiously? Because in [3], it is quite unclear whether the constructional (white-box) perspective on organisations is taken or the functional (black-box) perspective. Since most books on organisations, their structure and their management are written from the functional (black-box) perspective, most people adhere to this perspective (although often unconsciously). Yet the difference between the two perspectives is immense. As immense is the difference between the ontological model of the O-organisation of an enterprise, notably its coordination structures, and the organisational (mostly hierarchical) structures that Mintzberg and other organisational experts are talking about.

In Chaps. 4 and 6, we introduced and discussed the CIAO! Paradigm. It constitutes the basis of Enterprise Ontology by considering communication as the primary notion and information as secondary. Taking the communication-centric view on enterprises and enterprise information systems leads automatically to the 'rich' constructional perspective as discussed in this book as well as in [2].

Still, it appears to be difficult for people who are used to think primarily in terms of hierarchical structures when talking about organisations to get rid of this perspective and to think instead in terms of the coordination structures in the essential model of an enterprise. We can only encourage the reader to try to think along the lines of the CIAO! Paradigm and hope we succeed. As discussed in Sect. 10.2.1, these ontological structures are perpendicular to organisational structures from the perspective of the 'people' managers.

10.4 Conclusions

The EE organisational implementation theory is a technological theory intended to support enterprise engineers during step 3 (implementation design) and step 4 (implementation) of the DAO method (cf. Chap. 11). It also covers the steps after the implementation of an organisation, namely, installation and operation.

The validity of a technological theory is justified by its rigour and relevance. The rigour of the ETA theory appears from its being based on the outcomes of the other EE theories, in particular the BETA theory (cf. Chap. 9) and the PSI theory (cf. Chap. 6). Its relevance appears from the fact that it provides clarity as well as effective support to and insight in the implementation, the installation and the operation of organisations.

Engineering (or implementation design) is steered by the constructional requirements. They come from the using system and from the applicable architecture. We have shown above that they mostly stem from the applicable architecture and that they are mostly the result of long-term experience.

The reader is encouraged to discard for the moment the hierarchical organisational structures that everybody is using and talking about, in favour of adopting the CIAO! Paradigm and consequently of first having a constructional (and ontological) perspective on enterprises.

References

1. Dietz, J. L. G., & Hoogervorst, J. A. P. (2014). *EE theories overview*. Czech Technical University at Prague.
2. Dietz, J. L. G., & Mulder, J. B. F. (2024). *Enterprise ontology—A human-centric approach to understanding the essence of organisation* (Enterprise engineering) (2nd ed.). Springer Nature.
3. Mintzberg, H. (1983). *Structures in fives: Designing effective organisations*. Prentice Hall.
4. Dijkstra, E. W. (1976). *A discipline of programming* (Prentice-Hall series in automatic computation). Prentice Hall. XVII, 217 p.
5. Jackson, M. A. (1975). *Principles of program design. A P I C studies in data processing*. Academic Press. xii, 299 p.

Part III
Applications

I hear and I forget
I see and I remember
I do and I understand
(Confucius)

Part III is about the application of the theories in Part II. Chapter 11 contains an extensive description of the DEMO methodology, specifically of the DAO method, which guides the (re)design of enterprises. In Chaps. 12–14, exercises are presented and discussed on the use of DEMO in the (re)design of enterprises. These exercises in organisational redesign and digital transformation are particularly suited as course material. In Chapter 15, practical applications of DEMO in various industrial areas are reported.

Chapter 11
The DEMO Methodology

Abstract DEMO (Design and Engineering Methodology for Organisations) comprises a Way of Thinking (WoT), a Way of Modelling (WoM) and a Way of Working (WoW). The WoT consists of a number of theories. The WoM consists of an integrated whole of four aspect or sub-models: the Cooperation Model (CM), the Action Model (AM), the Process Model (PM) and the Fact Model (FM). The CM of a Scope of Interest (SoI) is the ontological model of its construction, thus of the identified transactor roles and the coordination structures among them: the interaction structure, the interimpediment structure and the interstriction structure. The AM of an SoI is the ontological model of its operation. For every actor role in the focus (of the SoI), it provides the rules that guide the role fillers in doing their work. The guidelines for responding to coordination events are called action rules; the ones for performing production acts are called work instructions. The PM of an SoI is the ontological model of the state space and the transition space of its coordination world. It contains the existence laws and occurrence laws for all transaction kinds in the SoI. The FM of an SoI is the ontological model of the state space and the transition space of its production world. It contains the existence laws and occurrence laws for all identified entity types, value types, property types, attribute types and event types. The four sub-models are expressed in the DEMO Specification Language (DEMO-SL), which comprises diagrams, tables and formal textual descriptions. For producing essential models of enterprises, the WoW of DEMO offers the OER method (Organisational Essence Revealing). It consists of a number of steps in which the four DEMO models are produced, preferably in a spiral way. For (re)developing organisations as well as for developing Enterprise Information Systems, DEMO offers the DAO method, which is an acronym for Designing under Architecture from Ontology.

J. L. G. Dietz, H. B. F. Mulder, *Enterprise Design Fundamentals*, The Enterprise Engineering Series, https://doi.org/10.1007/978-3-031-83262-8_11

11.1 Introduction

Everyone who understands the EE theories, as discussed in Chaps. 5 through 10 and in [1], Chaps. 5 through 11, disposes of the intellectual ability to analyse organisational problems and to solve them accordingly. Yet most people appear to be uncomfortable with only theories in their toolbox, even if they agree with Kurt Lewin's adage, 'Nothing is more practical than a good theory'. They like to have more concrete bridges to their practical work. With reference to the CIAO tree in Fig. 4.1, they like to have methods that guide them in doing the work.

By a *method* is commonly understood a systematic procedure for accomplishing a task. Examples are teaching methods, learning methods, methods to develop software and methods to make lasagna. Next to 'method', there is the word 'methodology'. By a *methodology* is commonly understood a system of methods, used in a particular area of study or activity, whereas the original meaning is: doctrine or principles of methods, specifically concerning scientific research. We will adopt the first meaning while requiring in addition that a methodology is firmly rooted in theoretical foundations, like the trunk of the CIAO tree in Fig. 4.1 is firmly rooted in the EE theories. In Fig. 11.1, the so-called Five Ways Framework is presented, as an aid to discuss methodologies. It is an adapted version of the one in [2].

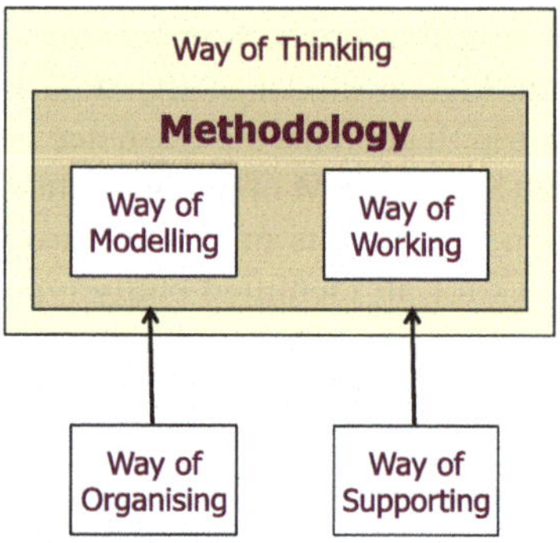

Fig. 11.1 The Five Ways Framework

The core of every methodology is a Way of Modelling (WoM) and a Way of Working (WoW). By a WoM is meant a collection of meta-models (cf. [1], Chap. 6) that guide one in understanding a system. The WoW comprises the methods that are used for producing the models that constitute this understanding, as well as the methods for bringing about devised changes.

The WoM and the WoW must firmly be rooted in a common Way of Thinking (WoT)—thus in a theoretical foundation that is coherent and consistent and that is appropriate for the subject matter. Consequently, a *methodology* is defined as a matching triple WoT, WoM and WoW. It may be supplemented by a Way of Organising (WoO) and a Way of Supporting (WoS). The WoO regards the organising and managing of applying the methodology, and the WoS comprises (software) tools that support both the WoM and the WoW.

In the next sections, DEMO, the principal methodology in Enterprise Engineering, is introduced. In Sect. 11.3, the (meta) models, comprising together the WoM, are summarised. The WoW for revealing the essential model of an enterprise is discussed in Sect. 11.4. This OER method is needed when one has to produce the ontological model of an organisation through reverse engineering (cf. Fig. 9.11). Next, the DAO method is presented. It is the method one needs for (re)developing organisations and for developing EISs. Section 11.5 contains the conclusions of the chapter.

11.2 DEMO: Essence and Simplicity

DEMO (Design and Engineering Methodology for Organisations) is the result of scientific research, constantly fed by practical applications, from 1990 to 1994 at the University of Maastricht and from 1995 to 2009 at Delft University of Technology. Since 2010, its development takes place within the worldwide DEMO community. From the late 1990s on, courses in DEMO are taught under the auspices of the Enterprise Engineering Institute (EEi).[1] Next to commercial courses, the methodology is taught at several member institutes of the CIAO! Network,[2] as well as at universities and polytechnic schools outside the network.

The motto of DEMO is 'essence and simplicity'. The notion of *essence* is specifically discussed in the PSI, DELTA, OMEGA and ALPHA theories (cf. Chap. 4). It refers to the essential model of the organisation that one wants to study, in order to get deep insight into the problems one is facing and subsequently to solve them by means of re-design, re-engineering and re-implementation. In addition to presenting the essence of a problem situation, it is crucial for a methodology to follow Ockham's razor[3] and keep things as simple as possible. This is of paramount importance for intellectually managing the complexity of a problem situation and of enterprises in general. In [1], Sect. 12.4.1, five intellectual techniques are presented that offer help in achieving both essence and simplicity. These techniques for mnemonic reasons, called *sapiences*, are summarised in Fig. 11.2.

Separation of concerns
Use of **a**bstraction
Devising **p**roper concepts
Verification by **i**nstantiation
Validation from **o**ntology

Fig. 11.2 The five sapiences

[1] For more information, visit www.ee-institute.org.

[2] The CIAO! Network is an international group of researchers and practitioners who develop and practise the discipline of Enterprise Engineering. For more information, visit www.ciaonetwork.org.

[3] https://en.wikipedia.org/wiki/Occam%27s_razor

Examples of the first sapience, *separation of concerns*, are making the distinction between function and construction (cf. Chap. 5), distinguishing between production and coordination (cf. Chap. 6) and distinguishing between the O-, I-, D- and M-organisation of an enterprise (cf. Chap. 8). Examples of the second sapience, *use of abstraction*, are abstracting from the implementation of a system and, in doing so, arriving at its ontology, as well as additionally abstracting from the realisation of an enterprise and, in doing so, arriving at its essential model (cf. Chap. 8). Examples of the third sapience, *devising proper concepts*, are the transaction concept as well as concepts like membership, flight, sale and purchase, in formulating uniquely identifiable products (cf. Chap. 6). We owe the three techniques above to Edsger Dijkstra, who provides convincing applications of them in [3]. The fourth sapience, *verification by instantiation*, is an indispensable intellectual technique for making sure that one really understands a conceptual model at the schema (or meta-model) level (cf. [1], Chap. 6). It serves to convince oneself that a produced model is a correct model in the applied methodology. The technique has been articulated by Sjir Nijssen for the field of information systems engineering [4]. The fifth sapience, *validation from ontology*, serves to make sure that a produced ontological model is a faithful conception of the system (organisation, information system, data/document system) that one wants to understand. It does so by systematically checking for every ontological element whether it has a counterpart in reality. It is also a valuable technique for discovering errors in the realisation and implementation of an ontological model.

The development of DEMO was triggered by the dissatisfaction with the state of the art in requirements determination in the 1980s and 1990s, when the information-centric view was dominant. A satisfying solution of this problem had to wait for the communication-centric view being conceived (cf. Chap. 4). Once DEMO was under construction, it became clear that it could provide more benefits than only solving the requirements determination problem. As an illustration, DEMO is (also) considered a coordination-based business process modelling approach [5]. Therefore, the original reading of the acronym (Dynamic Essential MOdelling) was replaced, around the year 2000, by the current one (Design and Engineering Methodology for Organisations).

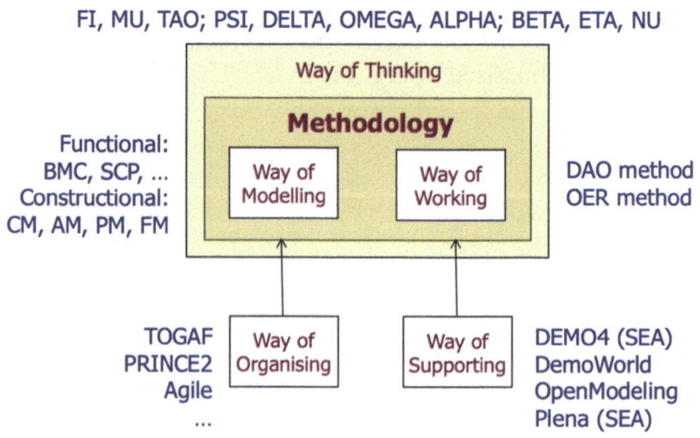

Fig. 11.3 DEMO in the Five Ways Framework

Up to now, DEMO is used almost exclusively as the methodology for producing ontological models of organisations and for improving organisations based on these models [1]. In this book, DEMO is applied to (re)design organisations and (re) implement them. Consequently, the Way of Thinking (WoT), the Way of Modelling (WoM) and the Way of Working (WoW) have to be extended.

Figure 11.3 exhibits the new position of DEMO in the framework of Fig. 11.1 (new compared to its position in [1]). The WoT comprises ten EE theories; the new ones are the BETA theory (Chap. 8), the ETA theory (Chap. 9) and the NU theory. The WoM comprises not only the four constructional models (CM, AM, PM and FM) but also several functional modelling approaches, notably BMC (Business Modelling Canvas) and SCP (Solving Complex Problems). The WoW comprises two methods now: the OER method (cf. [1], Chap. 12) and the DAO method. Together, they offer the support to (re)develop enterprises. The methodology does not include a specific WoO. Therefore, Fig. 11.3 just shows a few candidate project management methods. As for the WoS, several existing tools are listed. The list is not exhaustive since new tools may become available in the course of time. An overview of current tools can be found on www.ee-institute.org.

11.3 Way of Modelling

11.3.1 Functional Modelling

As discussed in Chap. 5, the functions of a system are the affordances that it offers to stakeholders. Regarding enterprises, the stakeholders are in particular its customers or clients. The functional model of the OS of an enterprise is actually not a black-box but a grey-box, since it can only be understood by assuming an internal state. It means that the OS has knowledge of the history of its operation and that this knowledge is applied in determining how the system will respond to inputs. For a discussion of the grey-box model, one is referred to [1], Chap. 9.

Taking the *function* perspective on a thing means that one exclusively considers the affordances that are offered by the thing, given the purposes or needs one has in mind. For example, one could think of sitting on a chair or of using it as a temporary store, one could create a baby's crib by putting two armchairs together, etc. The distinctive characteristic of the function perspective is that we take the position of an observer who has purposes in mind for which the chair could be used. Consequently, two persons, even if they are equipped with the same generic knowledge of chairs, could easily 'see' different affordances of the chair, dependent on the purposes they have in mind. That's why the function perspective is said to be *subjective*, although functions are actually subject-object relationships, as we have seen in Chap. 5.

But who are the observers of an enterprise, and how different can the purposes that they have in mind be? Instead of observers, one commonly discerns the stakeholders of an enterprise. In general, several kinds of stakeholders are distinguished. There are three kinds we consider crucial: the customers or residents (the people that are affected by the activities of the enterprise), the employees (the people that bring about these services) and the shareholders (the people that supply the needed capital).

11.3.2 Constructional Modelling

In modelling the construction of a system, we distinguish between its implementation independent ontology and the implementation dependent construction. The latter is the outcome of the implementation design phase (cf. Chap. 9).

The ontological model of an organisation in DEMO consists of the integrated whole of four aspect models, each taking a specific view on the organisation: the Cooperation Model (CM), the Action Model (AM), the Process Model (PM) and the Fact Model (FM). Models constitute one's understanding of a system or a situation, as discussed in [1], Chap. 12. Here, we will describe the four models only briefly.

The relationships between the four models is presented in Fig. 11.4. As illustrated by the triangular shape and the division of this shape into the four sub-models, the CM and the AM cover both coordination and production, while the PM regards only coordination and the FM only production. The PM connects the CM and the AM as far as the coordination between actors is concerned. In a similar way, the FM connects the CM and AM as far as production is concerned. The AM is the solid foundation on which the other three models are standing. In a sense, they are already 'contained' in the AM; they only need to be 'extracted'. Lastly, there is nothing 'above' the CM.

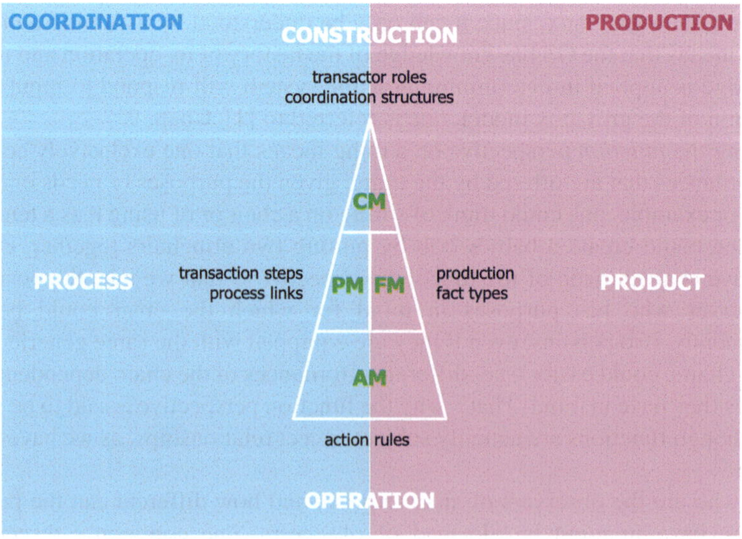

Fig. 11.4 The integrated ontological aspect models

The *Cooperation Model* (CM) of an organisation is a model of its *construction* (cf. [1], Chaps. 9 and 10), thus of the identified transactor roles and the coordination structures between them. A CM is expressed in a Coordination Structure Diagram, supplemented by a Transaction Product Table and a Bank Contents Table.

The *Action Model* (AM) of an organisation is a model of its *operation*, thus the manifestation of the construction in the course of time (cf. [1], Chaps. 8 and 9). An AM is represented by Action Rule Specifications. They guide actors in performing coordination acts.

The *Process Model* (PM) of an organisation is a model of the (business) *processes* that take place as the effect of acts by actors. In systemic terms, it is a specification of the state space and the transition space of the coordination world (cf. [1], Chap. 9). A PM is expressed in a Process Structure Diagram, optionally supplemented by a number of Transaction Process Diagrams and a Create Use Table.

The *Fact Model* (FM) of an organisation is a model of the *products* of the organisation. In systemic terms, it is a specification of the state space and the transition space of the production world (cf. [1], Chap. 9). An FM is expressed in an Object Fact Diagram, supplemented by Derived Fact Specifications, if applicable.

11.4 Way of Working

11.4.1 The OER Method

The method in DEMO that supports the making of essential models is called the OER method (cf. Fig. 11.3). OER is an acronym of Organisational Essence Revealing. The notion of revealing is crucial. One does not devise an essential model or create it in some other way; the operational essence is already present in the organisation under consideration—it only has to be revealed. But how does one proceed to reveal the essence of an organisation effectively and efficiently? We come close to the answer by observing the organisation through the glasses that are constituted by the Way of Thinking as presented above.

Recognising that the essence of an organisation inheres in the actors, the best way of working is to address these people and to reveal the essence together with them. By involving them, they will also feel appreciated, and they will most likely support your proposals to improve the organisation later. You will need them anyhow in the end for validating your models. The second-best option is to rely on written documentation of the operational processes. It is second best for two reasons. First, there is most likely a difference between the descriptions in the documentation and reality. Second, you miss the positive effects of involving the 'shop floor' from the beginning. Yet, the second-best option is by far the most widely spread approach in practice.

Hereafter, we present the OER method as one would use it for producing the ontological model of an organisation through reverse engineering (cf. Fig. 11.11, step 0). As the example organisation, we take the O-organisation of (a part of) the Ford company, as presented in [6]. Our starting point is a narrative description of the case and a picture of the accounts payable process.

11.4.1.1 OER Step 1: Distinguishing Performa-Informa-Forma

The first goal of applying the OER method is to determine the transaction kinds and the actor roles (or the transactor roles for short) in the O-organisation of the enterprise (cf. [1], Chap. 12). A very helpful aid in achieving this goal is to distinguish carefully between the Performa, Informa and Forma shapes. Figure 11.5 resumes these human abilities both for coordination and for production. It is a copy of Fig. 12.19 in [1]. Note that we ignore the medium level or physical world, as presented in Fig. 6.3, for the sake of simplicity.

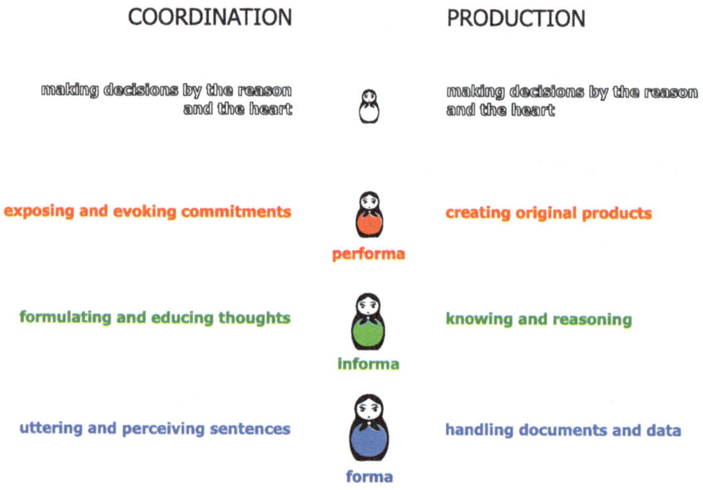

Fig. 11.5 The human abilities in coordination and production

The most inner ability (the 'blank' me) is added to emphasise the humanness of actors. OER step 1, also called the PIF analysis (PIF from Performa-Informa-Forma), consists of traversing the available documentation and marking pieces of text as expressing performa or informa or forma matters. For illustrating the PIF analysis, we take the case Ford, as discussed in the seminal paper by Michael Hammer, titled 'Reengineering Work: Don't Automate, Obliterate' [6]. The paper evoked a variety of endeavours that were all directed to improving the effectiveness of information systems engineering. It was published in 1990, after a decade of fruitless attempts to decrease the costs of automating business processes. People didn't understand business processes nor how automation could improve them.

There was only the feeling that automating existing processes was not enough; there was more to be gained.

In the early 1980s, when the American automotive industry was in a depression, Ford's top management put Accounts Payable under the microscope in search of ways to cut costs. In North America alone, Accounts Payable employed more than 500 people. Management thought that by rationalising processes and installing new computer systems, it could reduce the head count by some 20%. Ford was enthusiastic about its plan to tighten Accounts Payable until it looked at Mazda, where the accounts payable organisation consisted only of five people. Even after adjusting for Mazda's smaller size, Ford figured that its accounts payable organisation was five times the size it should be.

The current way of working in the accounts payable organisation is illustrated in Fig. 11.6. *It is taken from* [6]. *When Ford's purchasing department wrote a purchase order, it sent a copy to Accounts Payable. Later, when Goods Receiving received goods of the purchase, it sent a copy of the receiving document to Accounts Payable. Meanwhile, the vendor sent an invoice to Accounts Payable. It was up to Accounts Payable then to match the purchase order against the receiving document and the invoice. If they matched, payment was issued.*

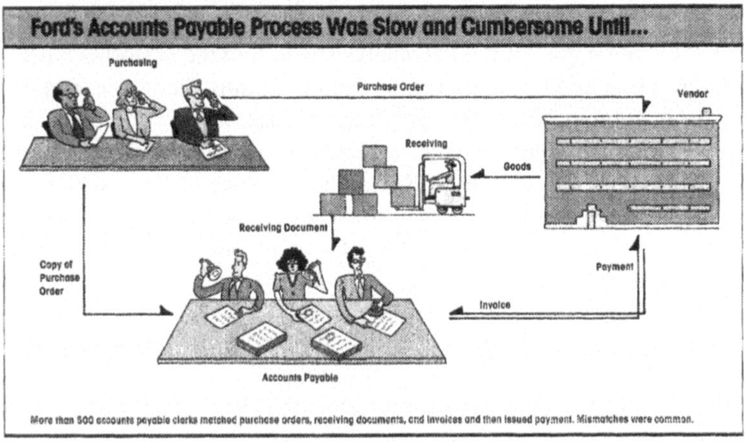

Fig. 11.6 The Accounts Payable work and related information flows

The department Accounts Payable spent most of its time on mismatches, instances where the purchase order, the receiving document and the invoice disagreed. In these cases, an accounts payable clerk would investigate the discrepancy, hold up payment, generate new documents and all in all gum up the works.

In applying OER step 1 to the case Ford, the first thing is to mark those pieces of text that seem to express the performa, informa or forma level in coordination or in production. Doing this yields the result below. The uncoloured pieces are considered to be irrelevant for our purpose. They include specifically the first paragraph, which is meta-text concerning accounts payable.

In the early 1980s, when the American automotive industry was in a depression, Ford's top management put Accounts Payable under the microscope in search of ways to cut costs. In North America alone, Accounts Payable employed more than 500 people. Management thought that by rationalising processes and installing new computer systems, it could reduce the head count by some 20%. Ford was enthusiastic about its plan to tighten Accounts Payable until it looked at Mazda, where the accounts payable organisation consisted only of 5 people. Even after adjusting for Mazda's smaller size, Ford figured that its accounts payable organisation was five times the size it should be.

The current way of working in the accounts payable organisation is illustrated in Fig. 11.6. *It is taken from* [6]. *When Ford's purchasing department wrote a purchase order, it sent a copy to Accounts Payable. Later, when Goods Receiving received goods of the purchase, it sent a copy of the receiving document to Accounts Payable. Meanwhile, the vendor sent an invoice to Accounts Payable. It was up to Accounts Payable, then, to match the purchase order against the receiving document and the invoice. If they matched, payment was issued.*

The department accounts payable spent most of its time on mismatches, instances where the purchase order, the receiving document and the invoice disagreed. In these cases, an accounts payable clerk would investigate the discrepancy, hold up payment, generate new documents and all in all gum up the works.

Although the main goal of the PIF analysis is to find the performa parts, colouring also the informa and forma parts may help in finding them. It is certainly most helpful in the beginning. After one has got experience, it will suffice to use only the red marker. At the same time, one must be cautious. In particular, one must be attentive to avoid the so-called blue trap. Sometimes, a piece of text expresses a forma level P-act but is at the same time the forma level of a C-act. A good example is the piece 'sent an invoice to accounts payable' in the second paragraph. Next to being 'blue' production (right side of Fig. 11.5), it expresses the 'blue' way in which a request is done to get payment (left side of Fig. 11.5). To indicate the additional performa meaning, the text is underlined. From now on, we consider the text thus as being 'red'.

As said, the main goal is to find the performa parts in a description. Nevertheless, being aware of the 'green' and 'blue' parts may help achieve this goal.

11.4.1.2 OER Step 2: Identifying Transaction Kinds and Actor Roles

The second step of the OER method is to find the relevant transaction kinds, the corresponding product kinds and the executing actor roles, based on the 'red' results of the PIF analysis.

Part of the case description is Fig. 11.6, in which the flows are indicated that are related to the work of Accounts Payable. In Fig. 11.7, we have put transactor roles (so transaction kinds and their executor roles) on Fig. 11.6. The parts of the figure that are covered by the actor role boxes are considered to be the filler(s) of the actor roles.

So, we have identified three transaction kinds and consequently three executing actor roles. They are specified in the TPT in Table 11.1. TK03 (purchase shipping) is added to cover the physical transport of goods from the vendor to Ford. The result of a transaction TK03 is the delivery of the goods of a purchase to the receiving department of Ford.

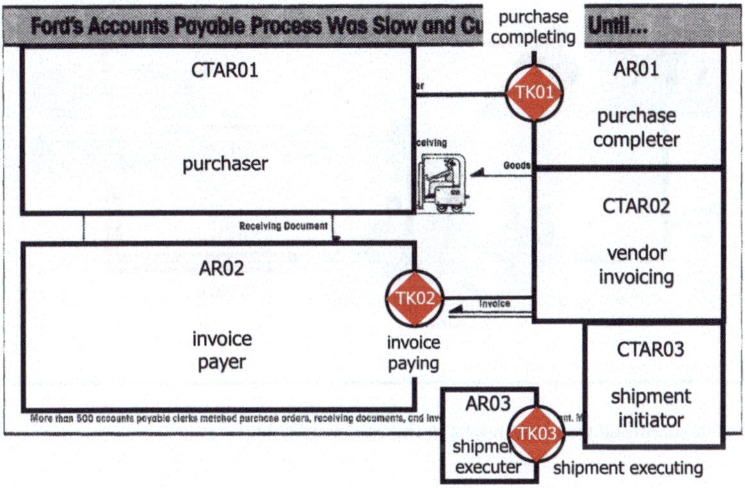

Fig. 11.7 Drawing of the identified transactor roles on Fig. 11.6

Table 11.1 TPT of the case Ford (old)

Transaction kind	Product kind	Executor role
TK01 purchase completing	PK01 [purchase] is completed	AR01 purchase completer
TK02 invoice paying	PK02 [invoice] is paid	AR02 invoice payer
TK03 shipment executing	PK03 [shipment] is executed	AR03 shipment executer

The words 'purchase', 'invoice' and 'shipment' between '[' and ']' represent the variable in the product kind (cf. Chap. 6). It is instantiated by the individual purchases, invoices and shipments. In Fig. 11.8, the transaction acts are indicated that are performed in the 'red' flows in Fig. 11.6. The green lines represent information flows. They regard the contents of the purchase orders and the receiving documents.

The key problem of Ford is perfectly expressed by the TPT in Table 11.1. It is that purchases, shipments and invoices are only loosely connected. Shipments are about some purchase, as invoices are, but they may be only about a part of a purchase. It can easily occur that a vendor responds to a purchase order for 1000 tyres of some brand and model by sending an invoice for 500 tyres, expecting that this quantity can be delivered now and the rest next week. But when loading the truck to ship the tyres, there appear to be only 497 in stock. Consequently, the workers in the Accounts Payable department are quite busy in trying to match the three flows: copies of purchase orders, received shipments and invoices. From Fig. 11.8, it is clear that the workers in the Receiving Goods department accept all shipments, for the simple reason that they don't know the purchase orders. Therefore, they forward all Receiving Documents to Accounts Payable.

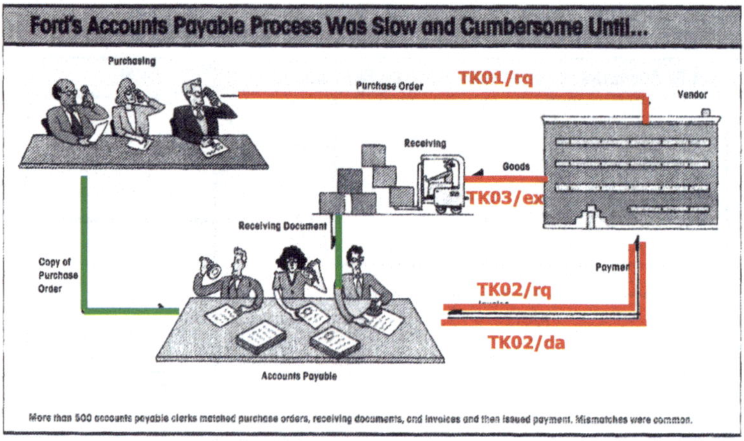

Fig. 11.8 The identified transaction acts in the case Ford (old)

11.4.1.3 OER Step 3: Composing the Ontological Model

After having completed OER step 2, one has basically identified all transaction kinds and their executing actor roles in the organisation. It is now time to build the DEMO model of it. Figure 11.9 summarises the ways in which the four sub-models of an organisation are expressed, in diagrams, tables and (formal) texts (cf. [1], Chap. 12).

After having identified the transaction kinds TK01, TK02 and TK03 and subsequently the product kinds PK01, PK02 and PK03, as well as the executing actor roles AR01, AR02 and AR03, we can produce the CSD (Coordination Structure Diagram). It is presented in Fig. 11.11. Together with the TPT in Table 11.1, it represents the CM of the case Ford in the 'old' situation. Note that the three actor roles on the vendor side (AR01, CTAR02 and CTAR03) are all mapped on the vendor shape.

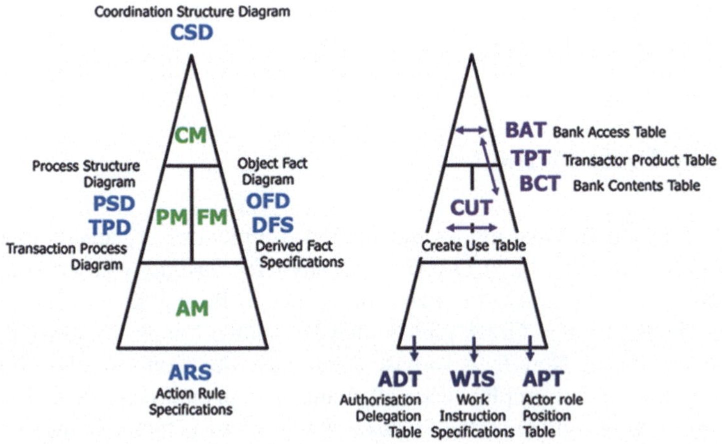

Fig. 11.9 Ways of representing the four sub models

CTAR01 (Ford purchasing) belongs to the Ford organisation, whereas transactor role TAR01 (purchase completer) is part of the vendor. CTAR02 (vendor invoicing) and CTAR03 (vendor shipping) belong to the vendor organisation, whereas TAR02 (invoice payer) is part of Ford. TAR03 can be part of the vendor organisation, but it can also be a third party. The access links from AR02 to TK01 and TK03 represent that actors AR02 get copies of the purchase orders and the receiving documents (Fig. 11.10).

Fig. 11.10 CSD of the case Ford 'old'

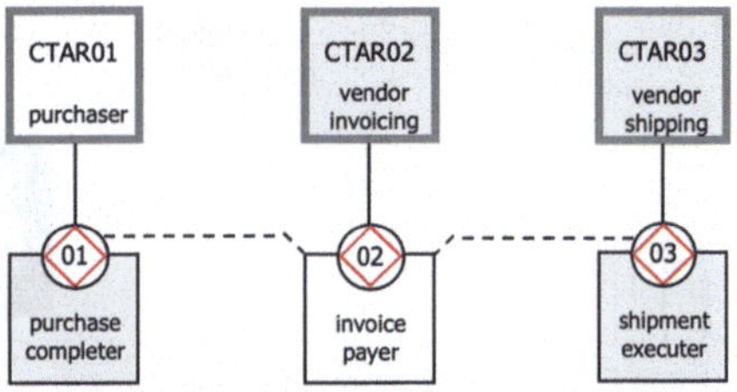

Because the three trees of transactor roles are only 'loosely' coupled, there is little sense in producing also the other aspect models: the AM, the PM and the FM.

11.4.1.4 OER Step 4: Validating the Essential Model

In the previous steps of the OER method, we have applied the first four sapiences (cf. Fig. 11.2): *separation of concerns* (taking exclusively the construction perspective), *use of abstraction* (applying in particular the PSI, OMEGA and ALPHA theories), *devising proper concepts* (notably in Sect. 11.4.1.3) and *verification by instantiation*. It is time now to practice the fifth sapience: *validation from ontology*. Where verification of a model ensures that the model is correct according to the applied methodology, validation ensures that a model offers a faithful understanding of the modelled piece of reality. The reader is referred to [1], Chap. 12 for a discussion of OER step 4.

11.5 The DAO Method

The method in DEMO that guides the (re) development of organisations is called the DAO method (cf. Fig. 11.3). DAO is an acronym for Designing under Architecture from Ontology. DAO is also the name of a river in Portugal.[4] As brought to our knowledge by the ancient Greek philosopher Heraclitus,[5] rivers are never the same. So are organisations. New facts to base a purchase decision on, admitting a new vendor and hiring a new employee are all changes of an enterprise. Not always does a change imply redesign. Only the first example leads to a change in the ontological model of the enterprise's O-organisation. The others are only implementational changes.

Figure 11.11 shows the distinct steps of the DAO method. Step 0 is added for the sake of completeness. It is actually what the OER method brings about. As we did in Chap. 8, 'using system' is abbreviated to 'US' and 'object system' to 'OS'.

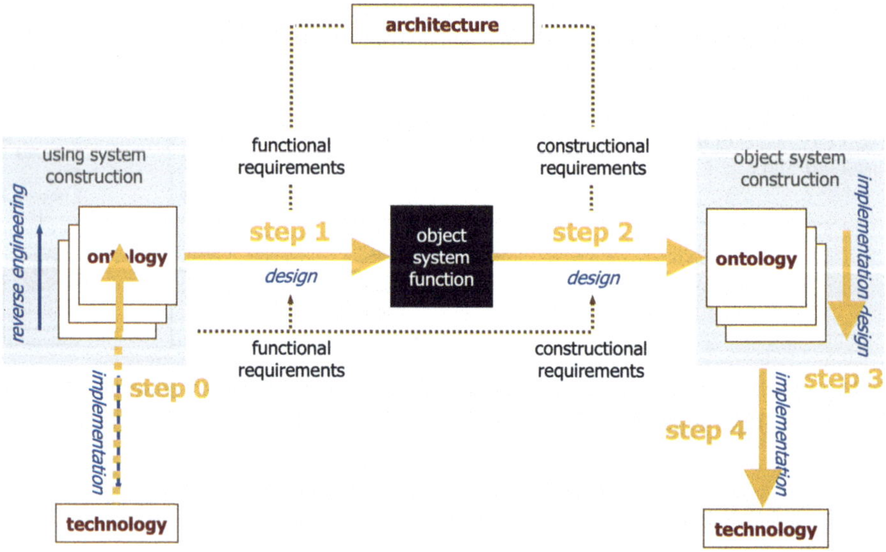

Fig. 11.11 The GSDP with the five DAO steps

[4] By referring to the DAO river, we want to pay tribute to our Portuguese colleagues in the CIAO! Network, who always have been loyal to the cause of Enterprise Engineering and who have contributed immensely to its development and spread.

[5] One of the famous sayings of Heraclitus is *Panta rei*, 'everything flows'.

Both the GSDP (General System Development Process) and the GRAF (General Requirements and Architecture Framework) are crucial intellectual tools of the DAO method. They are presented in Sect. 9.2. Hereafter, we will discuss how the distinct steps in the GSDP are performed and how the GRAF is used in performing a step, if applicable. As hinted at already in Sects. 9.2.3 and 9.2.4, the DAO method is applied to the (re)development of O-organisations and to the development of Enterprise Information Systems (EISs). Application of the DAO method to the development of O-organisations is presented in Sects. 11.5.1 through 11.5.5, with the case Ford for illustration. It is used in real-life cases in Chaps. 11 through 14. The application of the DAO method to the development of an EIS is presented in Sect. 11.5.6. Steps 1 and 2 are steered by the BETA theory (cf. Chap. 9). Steps 3 and 4 are steered by the ETA theory (cf. Chap. 10).

11.5.1 DAO Step 0: Producing the Essential Model of the US

DAO step 0 consists of applying the OER method, as discussed in Sect. 11.3. One starts from an available lower-level constructional model or even from a description of the implementation itself (like the case descriptions in Chaps. 11 through 14) and reveals the ontological model of the US. If the OS is an O-organisation, then the model of the US is mostly an informal description of the future customers of the enterprise, as discussed in Sect. 8.3.1. This step needs only be performed if the ontological model of the US (using system) is needed but missing.

Fortunately, the description of the case Ford in [6] provides us with pictures of the constructional models of the US and the OS. In Sect. 11.4.1, we have discussed the revealing of the ontological model of the US of the case Ford.

11.5.2 DAO Step 1: Defining the Function of the OS

In DAO step 1, the function of the OS is defined. The important distinction between the construction of a system and the functionality it may offer to any other system is discussed in Chap 5 (the TAO theory). This functionality is completely based on the construction of the US. It is also expressed in terms of this construction, as we exemplified for a sales department in Chap. 9.

We distinguish between two sources of input: the functional requirements that are provided by the actors in the US and the functional requirements in the applied architecture (cf. Fig. 11.11). In order to discuss and analyse the needs for change, we dispose of the BMC and the SCP approaches (cf. Chap. 3).

The most important change goal in the case Ford is to reduce costs, specifically through a 75% reduction of the staff working in Accounts Payable. The formulated change mission is what Ford calls 'invoiceless processing'. In [6], this change is articulated by the slogan 'Ford's old rule: we pay when we get the invoice. Ford's new rule: we pay when we get the goods'. It entails more, however: incomplete deliveries would just be sent back. This has enormous impact on the daily operations of Ford.

The last paragraph of the case description reads: *The department Accounts Payable spent most of its time on mismatches, instances where the purchase order, the receiving document and the invoice disagreed. In these cases, an accounts payable clerk would investigate the discrepancy, hold up payment, generate new documents and all in all gum up the works*. Based on this text, we formulate the next QoS (Quality of Service) indicators. The quantities (20, 5 and 5) are chosen quite arbitrarily.

- The time delay between receiving and paying an invoice is less than 20 days.
- The number of refused invoices per month is less than 5.
- The number of refused goods deliveries per month is less than 5.

Because the description of the case Ford in [6] is not very elaborate, we apply only BMC to the case. The result is exhibited in Fig. 11.12. Due to the chosen change goal, a number of fields in the BMC template are called 'not applicable'. We consider them as irrelevant topics for the redesign of the company. We assume that the deciders within Ford, in a group decision session, agree on the formulated change goal and all of the consequences for the implementation of the enterprise.

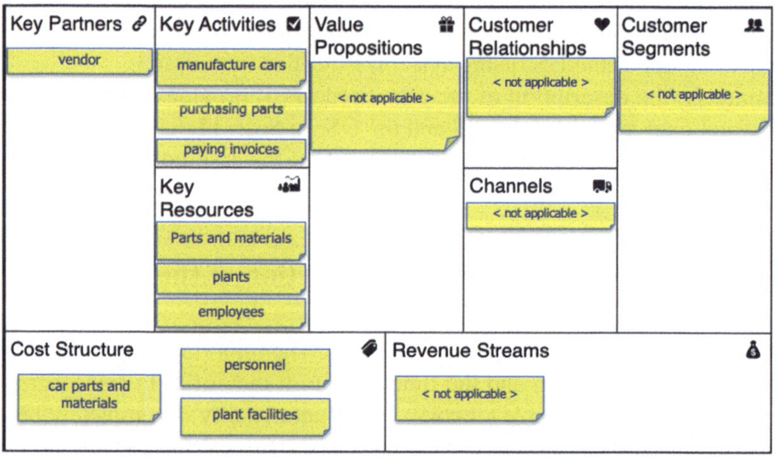

Fig. 11.12 BMC applied to the case Ford

11.5.3 DAO Step 2: Creating the Ontological Model of the OS

The starting point of the *ontological design* step is the object system function, thus the outcome of DAO step 1. Because of the fundamental difference between function and construction, as explained in Chap. 5, this design step is the most creative step: a construction must be conceived in the mind of the designer that, once put into operation, offers the required functionalities to the distinguished stakeholders.

Next to the specification of the object system function, the constructional designer has to satisfy two groups of (constructional) requirements. One is provided by the stakeholders of the US, and the other one is provided by the applicable architecture (cf. Fig. 11.11). Both groups of requirements are discussed in Chap. 9. Conceiving a construction of the OS within the restrictions that are set by the functional model and the constructional requirements is the greatest challenge in designing things of any kind. Fortunately, the designer can rely on proven practices, like design patterns in software engineering [7], in addition to her/his skills. One should at the same time be aware that relying on proven practices may have its drawbacks, as our discussion in Sect. 3.2 of the design of the one-whole kettle in [8] convincingly demonstrates.

Concluding, constructional design is the hardest part of every design effort. The key element is the creativity of the designer, who also has to find a balance between reasonable requirements and feasible specifications [9]. In the case Ford, the design of the new construction of the enterprise's organisation has been done already. The directors of Ford have decided that the main goal, namely, the reduction of the staff of Accounts Payable by 75%, will be achieved by the introduction of what they call 'invoiceless processing'. It means that deliveries of goods that do not fully match an issued purchase order are refused and that the acceptance of matching deliveries will count as having received the corresponding invoice.

The new situation is perfectly expressed in the TPT in Table 11.2. Instead of the three core entity types in Table 11.1, there is only one now, namely, the purchase. The loosely coupled three processes, as shown in Fig. 11.10, are now strongly coupled, as shown in the CSD in Fig. 11.13. We also produce the other aspect models.

Table 11.2 TPT of the case Ford (new)

Transaction kind	Product kind	Executor role
TK01 purchase completing	PK01 [purchase] is completed	AR01 purchase completer
TK02 purchase paying	PK02 [purchase] is paid	AR02 purchase payer
TK03 purchase transporting	PK03 [purchase] is transported	AR03 purchase transporter

On the right side of Fig. 11.13, the corresponding PSD (Process Structure Diagram) is shown. In a PSD, the shape of a transaction kind is stretched out horizontally to a 'sausage'. It shows that a transaction TK02 is initiated from the state promised of a transaction TK01 and that the executing actor AR01 has to wait with performing the production act (represented by the small grey-coloured box) until the TK02 is accepted, which means that it is successfully carried out. A similar reasoning holds for transaction kind TK03. As soon as both the enclosed transaction TK02 and the enclosed transaction TK03 are finished, [TK01/ex] can be performed. Next, the transaction TK01 can be finished by performing the [TK01/da] and [TK01/ac].

In the new situation, delivering the goods of a purchase to Ford also counts as performing the C-act [TK02/rq] (invoiceless processing). In the PSD, this is expressed by the wait link from (TK03/ac) to [TK02/rq]. In other words, requesting for payment has to wait until the state (TK03/ac) is reached (which is the receiving of the goods). Like it holds for the case Pizzeria (cf. Chap. 12), the acceptance of goods deliveries, so the act [TK03/ac] is (implicitly) delegated to the people in Goods Receiving. In a similar way, [TK03/da], thus the delivery of goods, also counts as [TK01/da], which is the completion of the purchase by the vendor. By accepting this, so by performing the act [TK01/ac], Ford agrees with the completion. This act is performed tacitly.

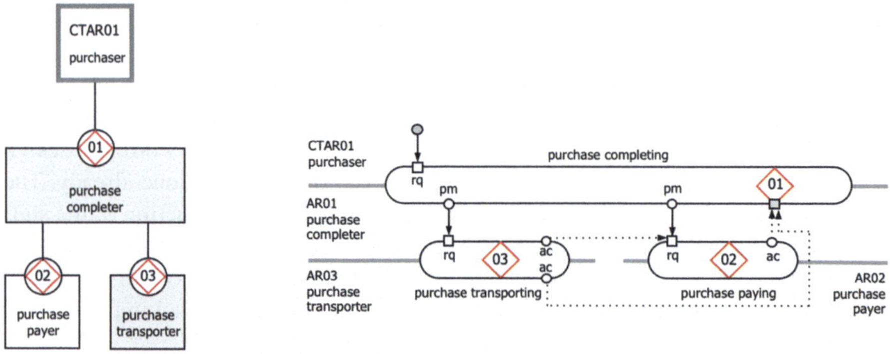

Fig. 11.13 CSD and PSD of the case Ford 'new'

The picture of the new situation in [6] is shown in Fig. 11.14. Mapping the three transaction kinds on Fig. 11.14 yields Fig. 11.15. Note that the difference with Fig. 11.7 is (only) in actor role AR01.

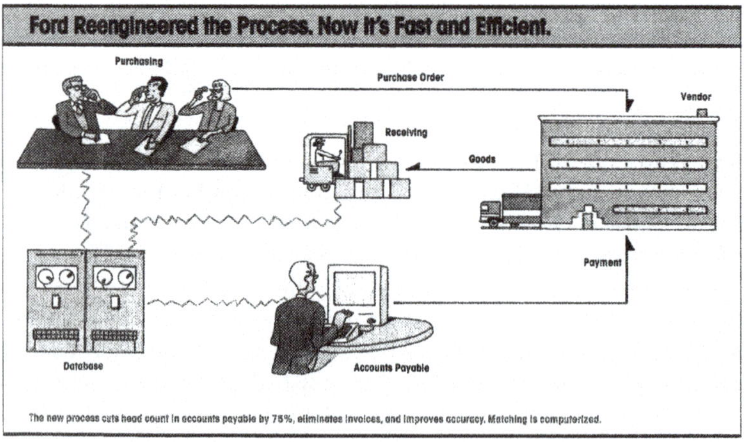

Fig. 11.14 Picture of the new situation

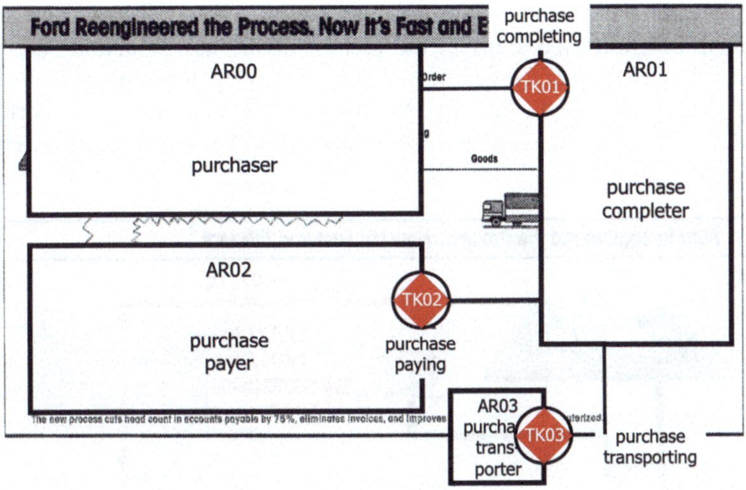

Fig. 11.15 Drawing of the identified transactor roles on Fig. 11.14

Being guided by the transaction pattern, notably the standard transaction pattern as exhibited in Fig. 6.8, we can now produce the action rule specifications that apply to settle the agenda in transactions TK01 and TK02, as far as actors AR02 are concerned. They are presented in Tables 11.3 and 11.4. In these tables, some details are just made up, though they look realistic and appropriate.

Table 11.3 ARS01

when	purchase completing **for** [purchase] is promised		(TK01/pm)
	while purchase transporting **for** [purchase] is accepted		
	given	**the** payer **of** [purchase]	
assess	*rightness:*	**the** performer **of the** promise **is the** purchase completer **of** [purchase]	
		the addressee **of the** promise **is the** purchaser **of** [purchase] ;	
	sincerity:	< no specific condition >	
	truth:	< no specific condition >	
if	*performing the action after **then** is considered justifiable*		
then	request	purchase paying **for** [purchase]	[TK02/rq]
	to	**the** payer **of** [purchase] ;	
	with	**the** requested amount **of** [purchase]	

Table 11.4 ARS02

when	purchase paying **for** [purchase] is declared		(TK02/da)
	given	**the** declared amount **of** [purchase]	
assess	*rightness:*	**the** performer **of the** declare **is the** payer **of** [purchase] ;	
		the addressee **of the** declare **is the** purchase completer **of** [purchase] ;	
	sincerity:	< no specific condition >	
	truth:	**the** declared amount **is equal to the** requested amount **of** [purchase];	
if	*performing the action after **then** is considered justifiable*		
then	accept	purchase paying **for** [purchase]	[TK02/ac]
	to	**the** performer **of the** declare ;	
else	reject	purchase paying **for** [purchase]	[TK02/rj]
	to	**the** performer **of the** declare ;	
	* justification of rejecting *		

Like we did for the situation before re-engineering in Fig. 11.8, we now indicate the main transaction kind steps in the picture of the new situation. This yields Fig. 11.16. Because of the new policy of Ford, receiving goods now counts as performing [TK03/da] and [TK02/rq]. As discussed, it also counts as performing [TK01/da]. There is no separate communication between actors AR01 and actors AR00.

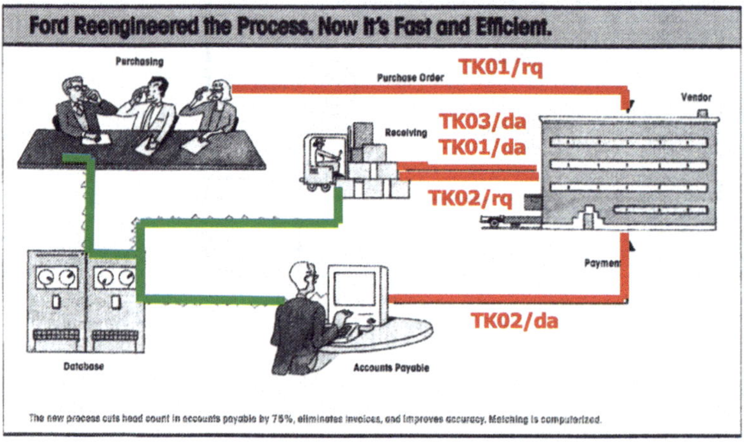

Fig. 11.16 The identified transaction acts in the case Ford (new)

In the foregoing discussion, we have seen several instances of delegation. They can be expressed conveniently in an ADT (Authorisation Delegation Table). Table 11.5 exhibits the delegations, both in the old (left side) and the new situation (right side). They appear to be the same. The delegation of [TK01/ac] from the purchaser to the goods receiver is a classical one: purchasers in a company are generally not accepting the results of their purchasing, although as a consumer in a flower shop, they do. The delegation of [TK03/ac] has purely logistic reasons: one cannot expect the vendor, who anyhow initiated the transaction TK03, to be present at the site of Ford where the goods are delivered and received.

Table 11.5 Delegations in the case Ford

Agendum/position	TK01/da	TK03/da
Purchaser	A	
Goods receiver	D	D
Shipper		A

Agendum/position	TK01/da	TK03/da
Purchaser	A	
Goods receiver	D	D
Shipper		A

In Fig. 11.17, the OFD (Object Fact Diagram) of the case Ford is presented. Recall that the event types '[purchase] **is** completed', '[purchase] **is** paid' and '[purchase] **is** transported]' are identical to, respectively, the product kinds PK01, PK02 and PK03.

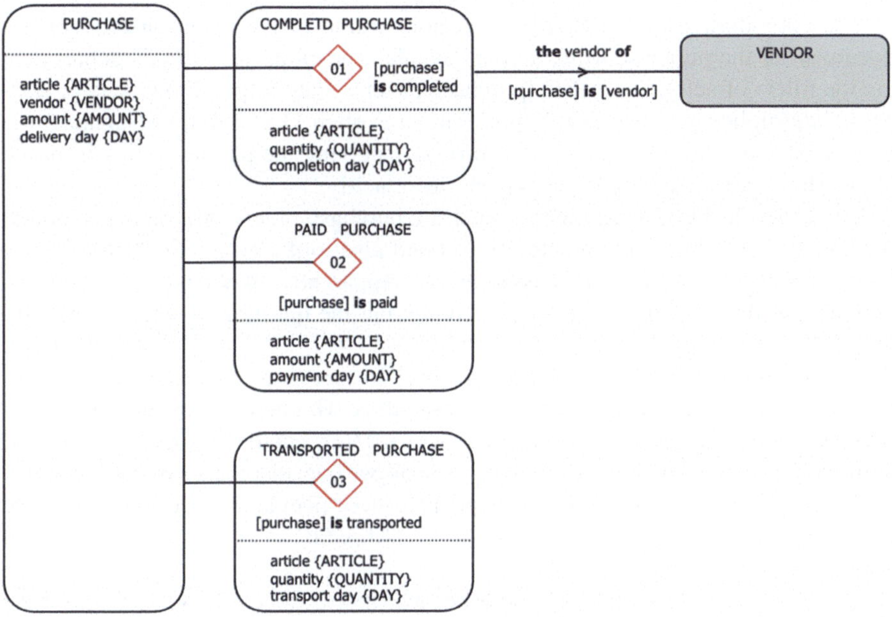

Fig. 11.17 OFD of the case Ford

11.5.4 DAO Step 3: Creating the Implementation Model of the OS

The starting point of the *implementation design* step is the ontological model of the object system (OS). In general, we distinguish between three kinds of technologies in the implementation of an ontological model: actor technology, production technology and communication technology. The process of engineering (implementation design) is clarified by the ETA theory in Chap. 10. Hereafter, we demonstrate DAO step 3, thus the design of the implementation model to the case Ford.

The CM of the case Ford is represented in the CSD in Fig. 11.13, left side, and the TPT in Table 11.2. The corresponding PM is expressed in the PSD in Fig. 11.13, right side. The AM is expressed in the action rules in Tables 11.3 and 11.4, and the FM is expressed in the OFD in Fig. 11.14. These model expressions are sufficient to start designing the implementation of the new situation at Ford.

The employees in Purchasing are the fillers of actor role CTAR00 (purchaser), and the various vendors (presumably the sales persons within the vendor organisations) are the fillers of actor role AR01. C-acts [TK01/rq] are performed through sending purchase orders (on paper by postal mail or digital/electronically). C-acts [TK01/pm] are performed tacitly, which means that there is no evidence of having performed them, as explained in Chap. 6. The delivery of the goods of a purchase is the act [TK03/da]. It counts also as performing the [TK01/da] of the same purchase and of the corresponding [TK02/rq] (cf. Fig. 11.16).

The embodiment of [TK02/rq] is the forwarding of the (electronic) receiving document of the purchase to Accounts Payable. The employees in this department are the fillers of actor role AR02 (purchase payer). They respond to C-acts [TK02/rq] by an implicit promise [TK02/pm] and an explicit [TK02/da]. Presumably, the vendor becomes aware of these acts through receiving the payment slips from the bank. The acceptance [TK02/ac] is performed tacitly.

The actors in Purchasing, who issued the purchase orders (and thus performed the C-acts [TK01/rq], should actually respond also to the events (TK01/da). They won't however, as we have discussed above. Apparently, they have delegated this authority to the workers in Goods Receiving, but the question is whether they are aware of this.

Transactions TK03 (purchase transporting) are necessary, but there are no Ford actors involved in carrying out these transactions. The delivery of the goods of a purchase is the effect of performing the P-act TK03/ex, but the [TK03/da] is directed to the transporter or shipper. For logistic reasons, we consider the act being addressed to the goods receivers in Ford. Consequently, these people are considered to have the delegated authority to respond to acts [TK03/da], as shown in the ADTs in Table 11.5.

Lastly, refusing a shipment of goods because it does not (fully) match a purchase means two things. First, the goods are sent back to the vendor straight away (the people at Ford just refuse to receive them). Second, there is no performing of C-acts, neither of a [TK03/da] nor of a [TK02/rq]. There is also no performance of a [TK01/da], which means that the TK01 is still alive. It can only be ended in the way as described above.

11.5.5 DAO Step 4: Implementing the OS

The implementation of the object system is carried out according to the ETA theory, as discussed in Chap. 10. By implementing is understood the assignment of actor technology, production technology and communication technology to the elements of the implementation model, thus to the outcomes of DAO step 3. To these outcomes belongs also the assignment of actor roles to (organisational) positions, which is presented in an Actor role Position Table (APT). Table 11.6 shows these assignments for the Ford organisation.

Table 11.6 APT for the Ford organisation

Actor role/position	**AR02**
Accounts payable officer	X

Since our focus is Accounts Payable, we only care about transactor role TAR02. The fillers of actor role AR02 are the officers in the Accounts Payable department. The production technology that they use in order to execute transactions TK02 is only their minds: they decide on the payments they do. Regarding the coordination technology that actors AR02 use in carrying out transactions TK02, the implementations of the coordination acts are discussed already in Sect. 11.5.4 (DAO step 3).

11.5.6 Developing an Enterprise Information System

As Fig. 11.14 clarifies, as much communication as possible is automated. It means that an Enterprise Information System (EIS) has been developed that has a user interface with Purchasing, with Goods Receiving and with Accounts Payable. Let us call this EIS APIS (Accounts Payable Information System) because the work of Accounts Payable is at the core of it. The NU theory or EE automation theory (cf. Sect. 4.4.10) guides the development of this EIS.

Hereafter, we will apply the DAO method to the development of APIS, in the way as explained in Chap. 9, notably in Fig. 9.14. Since we have already the ontological model of the using system's O-organisation, we can skip DAO step 0. As discussed in Sect. 8.3.2, we can also skip DAO step 1 and proceed directly to step 2, creating the ontological model of the OS.

In order to do this, we present in Tables 11.7 and 11.8 the relevant action rules in the O-organisation of Ford, including the indications of transactions of the general kinds 'remembering' and 'sharing' that constitute the ontological interface between the O-organisation and the supporting APIS. In Sect. 8.3.8, we have clarified how these transaction kinds are related to the coordination structures in the CM. The facts to be remembered or shared are put between brackets **rem** and **mer** or **sha** and **ahs**, respectively.

Table 11.7 ARS01 of Ford

event part	**when** **sha** completing **for** [purchase] **is** promised **ahs** **given** **sha** **the** payer **of** [purchase]; **ahs**
assess part	* no specific condition *
response part	**if** *performing the action after **then** is considered justifiable* **then** **rem** request purchase paying **for** [purchase] **to** **the** payer **of** [membership] **with** **the** requested amount **of** [purchase] **mer**

Table 11.8 ARS02 of Ford

event part	**when sha** purchase paying **for** [purchase] **is** declared **ahs** **given sha the** declared amount **of** [purchase]; **ahs**	
assess part	**sha the** performer **of the** declare **is the** payer **of** [purchase];	**ahs**
	sha the addressee **of the** declare **is the** purchase completer **of** [purchase];	**ahs**
	sha the declared amount **of** purchase paying **for** [purchase] **is equal to** **the** requested amount **of** purchase paying **for** [purchase]	**ahs**
response part	**if** *performing the action after* ***then*** *is considered justifiable* **then**	
	rem accept purchase paying **for** [purchase] **to the** performer **of the** declare	**mer**
	else	
	rem reject purchase paying **for** [purchase] **to the** performer **of the** declare * justification of rejecting *	**mer**

When the indicated items are shared or remembered, APIS has all the knowledge of the ongoing purchases and payments. From the presented action rules, we deduce that the interface transaction kinds that are listed in Table 11.9 are needed between the O-organisation and APIS (actually, the I-organisation of Ford, but this has become an integral part of APIS now).

Table 11.9 TPT of I-transactions of Ford

Transaction kind	Product kind	Executor role
I-TK04 delivery day sharing	I-PK04 **the** delivery day **of** [purchase] **is** shared	I-AR04 delivery day sharer
I-TK05 payer sharing	I-PK05 **the** payer **of** [purchase] **is** shared	I-AR05 payer sharer
I-TK06 derivation value sharing	I-PK06 [derivation value] **is** shared	I-AR06 derivation value sharer
I-TK07 amount sharing	I-PK07 **the** amount **of** [purchase] **is** shared	I-AR07 amount sharer
I-TK08 transaction step remembering	I-PK08 [transaction step] **is** remembered	I-AR08 transaction step rememberer

NOTE. In order for the product kinds to be unique, the specification of all five product kinds should be '[sharing] **is** done' or the like. But then it would not be possible to be more specific about the distinct kinds of sharing. Therefore, we allow the (non-unique) formulations of the product kinds, as presented in Table 11.9.

The derivation values that are shared with O-actors in transactions I-TK03 are the evaluations of the computational formulas in the assess parts. They are the results of internal I-transactions, which are initiated by actors I-ARS03 and executed by other actors. Note that these 'computational' actors are themselves initiators in various sharing transactions. We will not elaborate them nor do we elaborate the derivations.

As for the remember transactions, we identify transaction kind I-TK08 'transaction step remembering' in Table 11.9. The transaction steps to be remembered are the ones in the response parts of action rules, enclosed between **rem** and **mer**.

What we have presented above is the ontological model of APIS. It is represented by the green layer in the object system construction in Fig. 9.17. The realisation of this (ontological) I-organisation of Ford into the corresponding D- and M-organisation is dependent on the specific implementation technology, thus on the programming language, the DBMS, etc. We will therefore not elaborate the design of the D-organisation (the blue level of the OS in Fig. 9.17) and the M-organisation (the grey level of the OS in Fig. 9.17).

Although we do not want to interfere with a company's decision on implementation technology, we recommend a relational or graphical database and corresponding DBMS (Data Base Management System) for the construction of APIS because they have solid mathematical foundations. The DBMS should anyhow allow for indicating the access rights as determined by the CM of the O-organisation.

11.6 Conclusions

In this chapter, we have presented the DEMO methodology: the Way of Thinking, the Way of Modelling and the Way of Working. We have demonstrated how the essential model of an enterprise can be produced by applying the OER method to the implementation of an organisation, like the narrative description of the case Ford. Next, we have demonstrated how a new organisation can be designed by applying the DAO method, using the case Ford again for illustration. In addition, we have shown how an EIS (Enterprise Information System) can be developed by applying the DAO method.

As discussed in [6], the organisation of Ford has been re-engineered, and the results are astonishing: a reduction of the staffing of Accounts Payable with 75% is achieved! From the discussion in [6], it has also become evident that the re-engineering approach of Michael Hammer lacks a theoretical basis. Therefore, it is hard to reproduce the outcome or to transfer the approach to other organisations. Based on their experiences, Michael Hammer c.s. formulated several 'principles of reengineering', which are included in the cited paper. These principles were revolutionary at the time when most companies were organised according to the divisional ideas of Frederic Taylor [10]. As discussed in [11], Taylor actually ignored the human nature of workers. One could even say that Taylor invented the assembly line, where the workers are actually robots instead of human beings who have autonomy in decision-making.

In particular through the tree-thinking approach (cf. Chap. 7), DEMO clarifies the distinct responsibilities in the Ford organisation. They have been discussed in the preceding sections.

Let us conclude this chapter by emphasising four crucial properties of the DEMO methodology. First, DEMO is at the same time a process modelling approach, a data modelling approach, a business rules modelling approach and a business product modelling approach. Moreover, these approaches are fully and properly integrated. In addition, DEMO offers the overarching Cooperation Model, something that none of the current approaches to enterprise modelling incorporates.

Second, producing DEMO models is to a large extent a straightforward undertaking. The essential model of an organisation is not the outcome of a creative action nor something that one can have differences of opinion about. The essence of every organisation is 'hidden' in its implementation—it only has to be revealed. By applying the OER method properly, one gets it, irrespective of the person(s) who produce(s) it. If two knowledgeable professionals would get the task of producing the essential model of the same SoI, they will deliver the same model. If not, one of them (or both) has made one or more mistakes. Modelling approaches without such a solid and proper theoretical foundation allow for subjectivity and consequent boundless discussions about the correctness and rightness of a model.

Third, next to offering full confidence regarding the correctness (through verification) and rightness (through validation) of a model, applying the OER method assures one of the most valuable approval and support by the actors in the organisation, the people 'on the shop floor'.

Fourth, because of its firm rooting in the BETA theory (cf. Chap. 9), notably the GSDP, DEMO's way of working that is called DAO method can be applied quite straightforwardly. It supports both the (re)design of organisations and the development of (automated) EISs. The latter has become a guaranteed successful endeavour because of its firm rooting in the ALPHA theory (cf. Chap. 8).

References

1. Dietz, J. L. G., & Mulder, J. B. F. (2024). *Enterprise ontology—A human-centric approach to understanding the essence of organisation* (Enterprise engineering) (2nd ed.). Springer Nature.
2. Seligmann, P. S., Weijers, G. M., & Sol, H. G. (1989). Analyzing the structure of IS methodologies—An alternative approach. In *First Dutch Conference on Information Systems, Amersfoort, The Netherlands*.
3. Dijkstra, E. W. (1976). *A discipline of programming* (Prentice-Hall series in automatic computation). Prentice Hall. XVII, 217 p.
4. Nijssen, G. M. (1976). *Modelling in data base management systems: Proceedings of the IFIP Working Conference on Modelling in Data Base Management Systems* (p. 418). North-Holland Pub. Co.
5. Keen, P. G. W. (1997). *The process edge: Creating value where it counts*. Harvard Business School Press. xvii, 185 p.

6. Hammer, M. (1990, July–August). Reengineering work: Don't automate, obliterate. *Harvard Business Review*.
7. Marciniak, J. J. E. (2002). *Encyclopedia of software engineering*. Wiley.
8. Alexander, C. (1964). *Notes on the synthesis of form*. Harvard University Press. 216 p.
9. Dietz, J. L. G. (2009). *Architecture: Building strategy into design*. SDU Publishing.
10. Taylor, F. W. (1911). *The principles of scientific management*. Harper & Brothers.
11. Dietz, J. L. G., Hoogervorst, J. A. P., et al. (2013). The discipline of enterprise engineering. *International Journal of Organisational Design and Engineering, 3*, 28.

Chapter 12
Exercise: Pizzeria

An Exercise in Organisational Redesign and Digital Transformation

Abstract The Pizzeria is an exercise in understanding and applying the GSDP to two organisational transitions that a pizzeria experiences in the course of time. The transition from the first to the second phase consists of adding the home delivery service. It implies a change in the essential model. This change appears to have interesting consequences for the allocation of authority: the performing of several C-act kinds has to be delegated, just for logistic reasons. Despite the huge differences between the second and the third phase in terms of implementation, their ontological models do not differ.

12.1 Introduction

The case Pizzeria is presented in [1] as an exercise in understanding and applying the abstraction from realisation and implementation, and thus modelling the O-organisation of an enterprise, as proposed by the ALPHA theory (cf. Chap. 8). In terms of the categorisation of enterprises by the OMEGA theory (cf. Chap. 7), the business of the pizzeria is the creation and the transfer of ownership of tangible things (preparing and selling pizzas), as well as the transfer of ownership of intangible things (paying).

In this chapter, we discuss the re-development of the Pizzeria, when transiting from the first to the second phase, as well as from the second to the third phase. We will apply the BETA theory (cf. Chap. 9) while re-using the ontological models that are produced already in [1], Chap. 14. The ETA theory (cf. Chap. 10) is not applied. Instead, an informal way is followed to discuss the changes in the implementation design and the implementation itself. We abstain fully from discussing the automation of the I-, D- and M-organisation.

Section 12.2 contains the narrative description of the operational activities in the three phases of the Pizzeria. The transition from the first to the second phase is

J. L. G. Dietz, H. B. F. Mulder, *Enterprise Design Fundamentals*, The Enterprise Engineering Series, https://doi.org/10.1007/978-3-031-83262-8_12

discussed in Sect. 12.3 and the transition from the second to the third phase in Sect. 12.4. The last section (Sect. 12.5) contains the conclusions from the exercise.

In Fig. 12.1, The GSDP is presented with the distinct DAO steps as introduced in Chap. 11. We will use it from Sect. 12.3 on to indicate the design steps we are dealing with. In addition, we will apply the GRAF (cf. Chap. 9) to the design of the object system (OS), in particular to the implementation design of the OS.

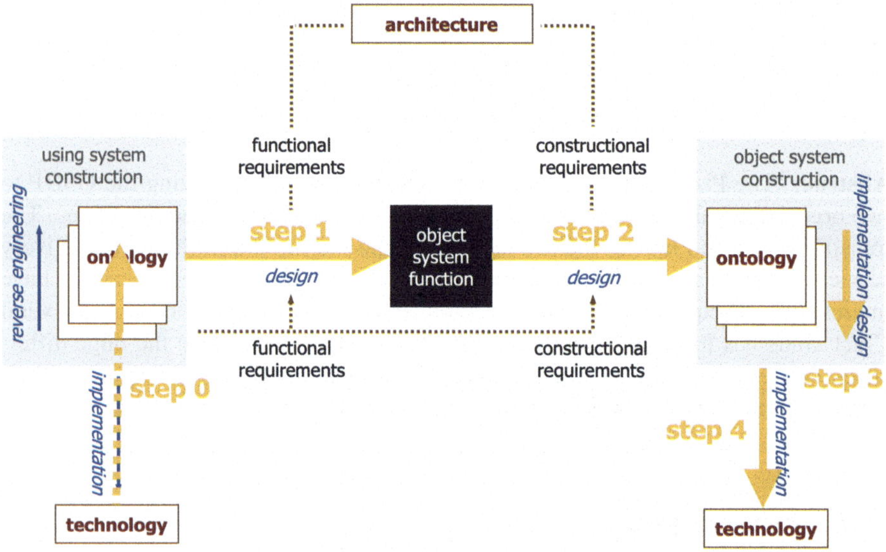

Fig. 12.1 The GSDP with the DAO steps

12.2 Narrative Description

The Pizzeria Mama Mia was established in 1970 by the owner at the time, Mia, and her son, Mario. In the first phase of its existence, there was only a take-away service. Customers could just walk in and place their orders at the counter, or they could order by telephone. In both cases, they had to take away the pizzas themselves. In 1980, an important new service was introduced: home delivery. To realise this service, Mia hired students, who deliver the pizzas on their mopeds. This appeared to be a good decision: within a year, less than 20% of the orders were taken away by the customers themselves. Let us call the situation from 1980 on the second phase of Mama Mia.

The year 1990 marks the start of the third phase, a time about which Mia still does not know whether she should be glad or sad. The pizzeria was bought by a global chain of pizzerias, called Domina. Mia and Mario have returned home to Italy, with the proceeds from the sale. Rumour goes that they still do not really enjoy the *dolce far niente*. For each of the three phases, the operational activities are described in detail below.

The First Phase

Customers present themselves at the counter of the pizzeria or make a telephone call. In both cases, Mia writes on an order form the name of the customer, the ordered pizzas and the total price. On the counter lies a menu of the available pizzas and their prices. Usually, she produces this list every year during the holiday. In case of a telephonic order, she also notes the telephone number. Moreover, she repeats the ordered items and informs the customer about the price and the expected time that the order will be ready. If needed, she also informs the customer about the available assortment of pizzas.

The order forms have a serial number and are produced in duplicate: a white and a pink copy. Mia slides the pink copy through a hatch in the wall to the kitchen, where Mario takes care of preparing the pizzas. She keeps the white copy at the counter. As soon as Mario has finished an order, he slides the pizzas in boxes through the same hatch to Mia, including the pink order copy. Mia then seeks the matching white copy, hands it together with the boxes over to the customer and waits for payment.

It can happen that Mario is not able to fulfil an order completely because of missing ingredients. In such a case, he puts his head through the hatch and notifies Mia of the problem. He then also returns the pink copy. If the customer is present in the shop, Mia confers with her/him on what to do about it and modifies the order. If the customer is not present, which is of course the case for orders by telephone, she modifies the order often at her own discretion. This leads sometimes to vigorous debates in the pizzeria when the customer comes to take away the pizzas. Thanks to Mia's temperament, she always comes to an agreement that is not disadvantageous for her.

The Second Phase

The operations in this phase are basically similar to the operations in the first phase; only the deliveries have been added. However, the big success of the new service has made it necessary that a second baker be employed. His name is Giovanni.

An extra duplicate is added to the order forms; next to the white and the pink copies, there is a blue one. If an order has to be delivered home, Mia writes down the delivery address on the order form and slides both the white and the blue copies through a hatch to the room where the students are waiting.

The deliverer whose turn it is fills in her or his name on the blue copy and puts it in a tray. He/she then waits for Mario or Giovanni to slide the pizzas, together with the pink copy, through a hatch to the transporters' room. Then, the deliverer leaves with the pizzas and the pink and white copies of the order form. At the customer's address, he/she hands over the pizzas and the white copy and waits for payment. After the customer has paid and has signed the pink copy, the deliverer goes back to the pizzeria and hands the money and the pink copy over to Mia. The students use their own mopeds; Mia did not want the trouble of having the pizzeria own the mopeds.

The Third Phase

The takeover of Mama Mia by the Domina chain has brought a lot of changes to the pizzeria. Mia and Mario have left, and Giovanni has become branch manager. Both the inside and the outside of the building are modified so drastically that one cannot find anything that reminds of the old days of the pizzeria; it has just become one of the many Domina pizzerias. The assortment as well as the prices are determined by the central office. There is a choice out of 12 kinds of pizza in three sizes: 25 cm Classic Medium, 25 cm Pan Pizza Medium and 35 cm Classic Large. The selection is printed on colourful flyers, which are given to customers and dropped at locations where one expects gatherings of young people. Giovanni manages about ten youngsters on a part-time basis. Their function is either baker or deliverer. Baking is not much of a job anymore; the pizzas are produced in automatic ovens. There is also no more a separate kitchen and transporters' room. The inside of the pizzeria is one big open space, except for a small office for Giovanni. Everything carries the Domina logo, including the mopeds, which are owned by the company now.

Both the bakers and the deliverers take orders from customers, of which over 95% are placed through the Web shop, with payment in advance. There is a fully automated order entry system that is integrated with other administrative functions. After entering an order, stickers are automatically printed, which are put on empty boxes. On the stickers are printed the kind of pizza, the order number, the total price, the name of the customer and the delivery address.

As soon as a pizza is discharged by the baking machine, one of the bakers puts it in the right box, which he/she takes from a rack. The baker then enters a record of the pizza being baked in the automatic order system. The boxes of the same order are kept together on a table with infrared lamps. If an order is complete, a deliverer takes the boxes to the customer address. In case of a take-away order, the deliverer hands the boxes over to the customer, after he/she has paid in cash or by bank transfer.

12.3 The Transition from the First to the Second Phase

In this section, we will present and discuss the re-development of the Pizzeria, which is needed to make the transition from the first to the second phase. Our OS is of course the organisation of the Pizzeria. The US consists primarily of the collective customers. Secondarily, one may think of other stakeholders, but we will ignore them.

In [1], Chap. 14, the essential model of the Pizzeria in the first phase is already produced. It is the ontological model of the OS (object system) in the GSDP that we start from. As the effect of the redesign of the OS (DAO step 2), the ontological model is extended, to accommodate the addition of the home delivery option.

In order to understand fully what it means to add the optional service of home delivery, we start with presenting the ontological model of the OS in the first phase.

12.3.1 The CM of the Pizzeria in the First Phase

The CM (Cooperation Model) of the Pizzeria in the first phase is expressed in the TPT in Table 12.1 and the CSD in Fig. 12.2. As said before, the CM (as well as the other aspect models) is taken from [1], Chap. 14.

Table 12.1 TPT of the Pizzeria organisation (first phase)

Transaction kind	Product kind	Executor role
TK01 sale completing	PK01 [sale] is completed	AR01 sale completer
TK02 sale preparing	PK02 [sale] is prepared	AR02 sale preparer
TK03 sale paying	PK03 [sale] is paid	AR03 sale payer

Actors in actor roles customer (CTAR01), sale completer (AR01) and sale preparer (AR02) have access to the contents of the multiple (external) transaction bank MTK01, which contains facts like the assortment of pizzas. Only actors AR01 have access to facts about customers, like their phone numbers.

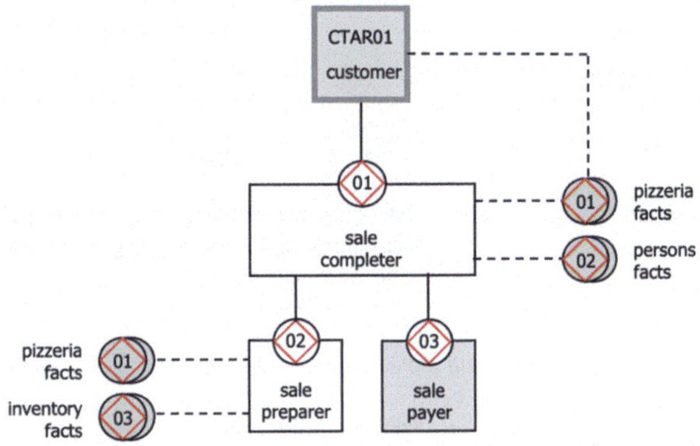

Fig. 12.2 CSD of the Pizzeria organisation (first phase)

12.3.2 The AM of the Pizzeria in the First Phase

In this section, we present the action rules in the first phase of the existence of the Pizzeria. They are applied by the actors within the chosen focus (the internal actors) of the coordination acts in the basic transaction pattern (cf. Chap. 6). As usual, the other coordination acts in the complete transaction pattern are not considered because they commonly lack explicit action rules.

ARS01

when sale completing **for** [sale] **is** requested (TK01/rq)
given **the** delivery time **of** [sale];
for each [sale item] **in** [sale]:
the pizza kind **of** [sale item];
the number **of** [sale item];

assess *rightness:* **the** performer **of the** request **is the** customer **of** [sale]
the addressee **of the** request **is some** sale completer;
sincerity: < no specific condition >
truth: **for each** [sale item] **in** [sale]:
the pizza kind **of** [sale item] **is** deliverable **and**
the number **of** [sale item] **is** deliverable;
the delivery time **of** [sale] **is equal to or greater than**
now plus min prep time **in the** year **of** [sale];

if *performing the action after **then** is considered justifiable*
then promise sale completing **for** [sale] [TK01/pm]
to the performer **of the** request
else decline sale completing **for** [sale] [TK01/dc]
to the performer **of the** request
* justification of declining *

ARS02

when sale completing **for** [sale] **is** promised (TK01/pm)

assess *rightness:* **the** performer **of the** promise **is the** sale completer **of** [sale];
the addressee **of the** promise **is the** customer **of** [sale];
sincerity: < no specific condition >
truth: < no specific condition >

if *performing the action after **then** is considered justifiable*
then
request sale paying **for** [sale] [TK02/rq]
to the sale payer **of** [sale]
with the amount **of** [sale] **is equal to the** total price **of** [sale]

ARS03

when sale completing **for** [sale] **is** promised (TK01/pm)
while sale paying **for** [sale] **is** promised (TK02/pm)

assess *rightness:* **the** performer **of the** promise **is the** sale completer **of** [sale];
the addressee **of the** promise **is the** customer **of** [sale];
sincerity: < no specific condition >
truth: < no specific condition >

if *performing the action after **then** is considered justifiable*
then
request sale preparing **for** [sale] [TK03/rq]
to a sale preparer

ARS04

when sale paying **for** [sale] is declared (TK03/da)

assess *rightness:* **the** performer **of the** statement **is the** sale payer **of** [sale];
the addressee **of the** statement **is the** sale completer **of** [sale];
sincerity: < no specific condition >
truth: **the** declared amount **is equal to**
    the promised amount;
the declared ot **of** sale paying **for** [sale] **is equal to**
    the promised ot **of** sale paying **for** [sale]

if *performing the action after* ***then*** *is considered justifiable*
then
accept sale paying **for** [sale] [TK03/ac]
to the performer **of the** declaration
else reject sale paying **for** [sale] [TK03/rj]
to the performer **of the** declaration
* justification of reject *

ARS05

when sale preparing **for** [sale] is declared (TK02/da)

assess *rightness:* **the** performer **of the** statement **is the** sale preparer **of** [sale];
the addressee **of the** statement **is the** sale completer **of** [sale];
sincerity: < no specific condition >
truth: **the** declared contents **of** [sale] **is equal to**
    the promised contents **of** [sale];
the declared ot **of** sale preparing **for** [sale] **is equal to**
    the promised ot **of** sale preparing **for** [sale]

if *performing the action after* ***then*** *is considered justifiable*
then
accept sale preparing **for** [sale] [TK02/ac]
to the performer **of the** declaration
else reject sale preparing **for** [sale] [TK02/rj]
to the performer **of the** declaration
* justification of reject *

ARS06

when sale completing **for** [sale] **is** promised (TK01/pm)
while sale paying **for** [sale] **is** accepted **and** (TK03/ac)
sale preparing **for** [sale] **is** accepted (TK02/ac)

assess *rightness:* **the** performer **of the** promise **is the** sale completer **of** [sale];
the addressee **of the** promise **is the** customer **of** [sale];
sincerity: < no specific condition >
truth: < no specific condition >

if *complying with promise is considered justifiable*
then execute sale completing **for** [sale] [TK01/ex]
declare sale completing **for** [sale] [TK01/da]
to the customer **of** [sale]

12.3.3 The PM of the Pizzeria in the First Phase

In this section, we present and discuss the PM (Process Model) of the pizzeria in the first phase of its existence. The exhibited PSD in Fig. 12.3 is fully based on the AM, as expressed in the action rules AR01 through AR06 and the CSD in Fig. 12.2.

As one may expect, the PSD shows the transaction kind TK01 (sale completing), which encloses two other transaction kinds: TK02 (sale preparing) and TK03 (sale paying). Because there are no indications that the initiation of transactions of the enclosed kinds is performed otherwise, we assume that the 'normal way' holds, thus that they are initiated from the state promised (pm) of the enclosing transactions TK01. In other words, as soon as the order taker has promised the customer to fulfil her/his wishes, the transactions TK02 and TK03 are started (cf. ARS02 and ARS03).

The transactions TK02 and TK03 must have been carried out before the enclosing transaction (TK01) can be completed. This condition is represented by the wait links from (TK02/ac) and (TK03/ac) to [TK01/ex]. It is an obvious condition since the products of the enclosed transactions, so the PK02 and PK03, are components of the product PK01. In other words, a completed sale presupposes that the sale is prepared and paid.

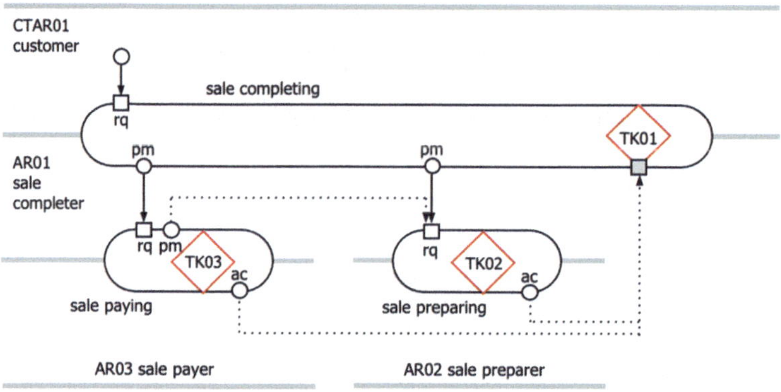

Fig. 12.3 PSD of the Pizzeria organisation (first phase)

Basically, and ideally, enclosed transactions are carried out in parallel, but this is not always possible. The wait link from (TK03/pm) to [TK02/rq] expresses that the order taker will only ask for preparing the pizzas of a sale if the customer has promised to pay. This is a common condition in sale situations. It is also common that the seller deduces the condition from the having accepted of the claim to sincerity in ARS01, which means that the customer complies with the general sale conditions.

12.3.4 The FM of the Pizzeria in the First Phase

In Fig. 12.4, the OFD of the Pizzeria organisation in the first phase is presented. It is based on the AM in Sect. 12.3.2. A sale is defined as a set of sale items. Every sale item is unique, but two sale items may have the same attribute values. So if a customer orders two pizza pepperoni and one pizza marguerita, the corresponding sale consists of three sale items of which two have the same attribute values.

The derived facts are specified in Table 12.2. Note that the specifications in this table are informal. It is clear however what they express. The first and the second item occur in ARS01, the third one occurs in ARS02.

Table 12.2 DFSs of the Pizzeria organisation (first phase)

the pizza kind **of** [sale item] **is** deliverable ≡ * the pizza kind is included in the list of available pizza kinds *;
the number **of** [sale item] **is** deliverable ≡ * the stock of ingredients is sufficient *;
the total price **of** [sale] ≡ * the sum of the prices of all sale items in the sale minus the discounts, possibly plus the delivery costs, plus the taxes *;

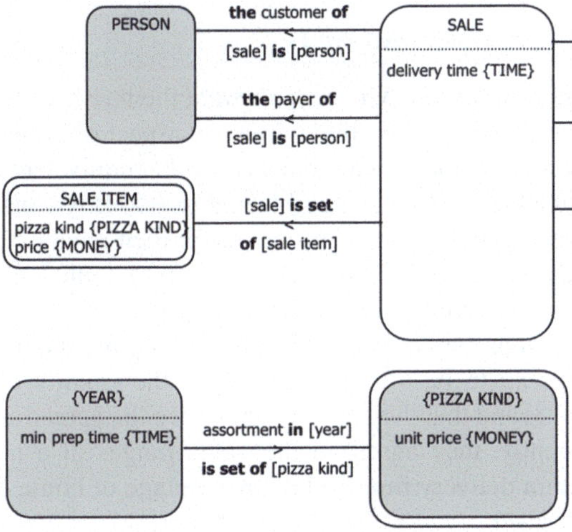

Fig. 12.4 OFD of the Pizzeria organisation (first phase)

12.3.5 The Function Design of the OS in the Second Phase

The next step in re-developing the Pizzeria is performing DAO step 1, thus the function design step. The new function that is going to be offered by the Pizzeria to its customers (collectively constituting the US) is the home delivery of pizzas. We consider this as a functional requirement from the using system (cf. Fig. 12.1). For the sake of simplicity, we assume that there are no other user requirements nor any architectural requirements. Mia decides to have a group decision session with Mario and a few future deliverers to discuss the impact of home delivery. As the basis for the discussion, she has produced the BMC template that is presented in Fig. 12.5.

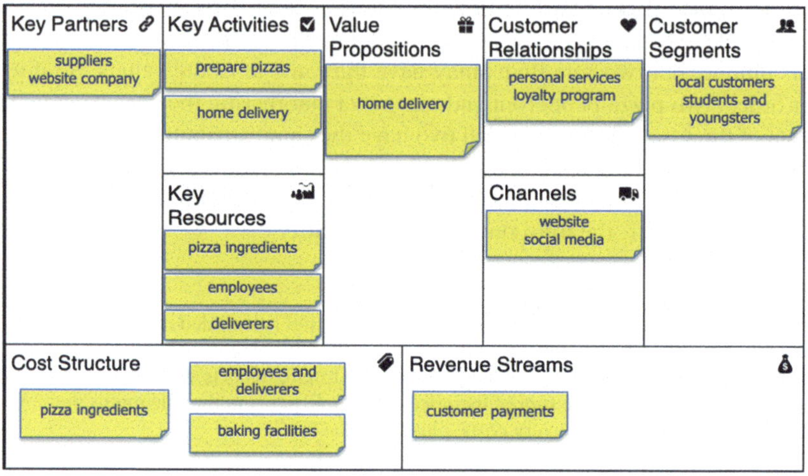

Fig. 12.5 The BMC template for performing DAO step 1

As mentioned in the case description, Mia doesn't want the hassle of having her own mopeds. Therefore, the decision about this important aspect of home delivery is clear: the deliverers must acquire their own mopeds (or other equivalent means of transportation). Because students seem to be flexible and trustworthy workers, they start acquiring deliverers among student associations. As for their payment, Mia and Mario think of some amount per travelled kilometre, on top of some base amount per working hour. The future deliverers agree with the proposal.

Mia and Mario are aware that they also need to think about the quality level at which the new service is going to be offered, thus about the Quality of Service (QoS) as discussed in Chap. 3, and that they have to announce the agreed-upon QoS to the customers. Consequently, they agree on the value ranges of a number of parameters, like the maximum delivery time and the percentage of home deliveries that has to meet this quality level.

They also agree, on a suggestion by Mario, that they need to assess the actual performance of the home delivery service after a month. When needed, they will adapt the various parameter values of the new service. In the worst-case scenario, they may have to withdraw the whole idea of home delivery. However, they both think, as do the future deliverers, that this will not happen, given the increasing indolence of consumers in all branches, which they read about in the newspapers and on their social media.

In Sects. 12.3.6, the ontological model of the Pizzeria in the second phase is presented. As one may expect, the difference with the first phase is mainly the addition of a transactor role that is responsible for the home delivery.

In Sect. 12.3.8, we discuss the implementation of the new ontological model, in particular the addition of the fourth transactor role.

12.3.6 The Construction Design of the OS in the Second Phase

12.3.6.1 The CM of the Pizzeria (Second Phase)

In order to make the function of home delivery happen, we extend the ontological model of the O-organisation with transactor role TAR04, as expressed in the TPT in Table 12.3 and the CSD in Fig. 12.6. They are the results of performing DAO step 2, the design of the ontological model of the OS.

Table 12.3 TPT of the Pizzeria (second phase)

Transaction kind	Product kind	Executor role
TK01 sale completing	PK01 [sale] is completed	AR01 sale completer
TK02 sale preparing	PK02 [sale] is prepared	AR02 sale preparer
TK03 sale paying	PK03 [sale] is paid	AR03 sale payer
TK04 sale delivering	PK04 [sale] is delivered	AR04 sale deliverer

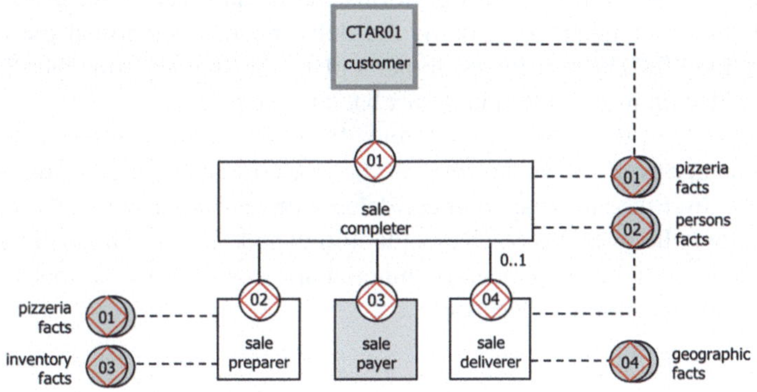

Fig. 12.6 CSD of the Pizzeria organisation (second phase)

For completeness sake, we have added a multiple transaction bank (MTK04) to give the deliverers access to geographic facts, for example, by means of digital maps on their smartphones.

Table 12.4 ADT of the Pizzeria (second phase)

Agendum/position	TK01/pm	TK02/da	TK03/da	TK04/da
Customer				D
Order taker	A	A	A	A
Baker				
Deliverer	D	D	D	

As discussed in [1], Chap. 14, the new implementation of transactions TK01, TK02, TK03 and TK04 asks for delegation of some authorities in case of home delivery. They are displayed in the ADT (Authorisation Delegation Table) in Table 12.4. The table tells us that the organisational position order taker (filled by Mia in the first and the second phase) is authorised to respond to the declare act in transactions TK02 (sale preparing), TK03 (sale paying) and TK04 (sale delivering). These authorisations are marked by an 'A'. For take-away orders, there is no problem: the order taker can accept the preparing and the paying and subsequently declare the transaction TK01 to be completed. However, in case of home delivery, the delegations are needed that are marked by a 'D'. In transactions TK02 (sale preparing), it is not the order taker but the deliverer who accepts the pizzas from the kitchen (or rejects them). In transactions TK03 (sale paying), it is the deliverer who accepts or rejects the payment from the customer, instead of the order taker. In transactions TK04 (sale delivering), it is the customer who accepts or rejects the delivery, instead of the order taker. This is less strange than it may look, because it is also the customer who performs the accept act in the enclosing TK01. Needless to say that this act is performed tacitly, the customer will mostly be unaware of it. Next, it is now the deliverer who performs the declare act in these transactions instead of the order taker. As soon as the deliverer has performed the delegated [TK04/da] and [TK03/ac] at the customer's place, he/she performs the [TK01/da], most likely also unaware of it, and drives back to the pizzeria.

The necessity of these delegations stems from the inability of the order taker to be in two locations at the same time (in the pizzeria and at the customer's home address). As discussed in Chap. 6, these delegations presuppose that the authorised performer, thus the order taker, shares the norms and values that he/she applies in the delegated acts with the delegated functionaries or persons, so that everything runs as smooth as without delegations.

12.3.6.2 The AM of the Pizzeria (Second Phase)

In this section, we present the action rules in the second phase of the existence of the Pizzeria. They are applied by the actors within the chosen focus (the internal actors) of the coordination acts in the basic transaction pattern (cf. Chap. 6). As usual, the other coordination acts in the complete transaction pattern are not considered because they commonly lack explicit action rules.

ARS01

```
when      sale completing for [sale] is requested                               (TK01/rq)
          given      the delivery time of [sale];
                     the delivery mode of [sale];
                     for each [sale item] in [sale]:
                                the pizza kind of [sale item];
                                the number of [sale item];
assess    rightness: the performer of the request is the customer of [sale]
                     the addressee of the request is some sale completer;
          sincerity: < no specific condition >
          truth:     for each [sale item] in [sale]:
                          the pizza kind of [sale item] is deliverable and
                          the number of [sale item] is deliverable;

if        performing the action after then is considered justifiable
then
          sel the delivery mode of [sale] is 'take away':
          promise    sale completing for [sale]                                 [TK01/pm]
                     to the performer of the request
                     with the delivery time of [sale] is equal to now plus min prep time
                          in the year of [sale];
             the delivery mode of [sale] is 'home delivery':
          promise    sale completing for [sale]                                 [TK01/pm]
                     to the performer of the request
                     with the delivery time of [sale] is equal to now plus min prep time
                          in the year of [sale] plus estimated transport time of [sale];
          les
else      decline    sale completing for [sale]                                 [TK01/dc]
                     to the performer of the request
                     * justification of declining *
```

ARS02

```
when      sale completing for [sale] is promised                                (TK01/pm)

assess    rightness: the performer of the promise is the sale completer of [sale];
                     the addressee of the promise is the customer of [sale];
          sincerity: < no specific condition >
          truth:     < no specific condition >

if        performing the action after then is considered justifiable
then
          request    sale paying for [sale]                                     [TK02/rq]
                     to the sale payer of [sale]
                     with the amount is equal to the total price of [sale]
          sel the delivery mode of [sale] is 'home delivery':
                     request    order delivery for [sale]                       [TK04/rq]
                     to a sale deliverer
                     with the delivery address is the home address of [sale]
          les
```

ARS03

when sale completing **for** [sale] **is** promised (TK01/pm)
while sale paying **for** [sale] **is** promised (TK02/pm)

assess *rightness:* **the** performer **of the** promise **is the** sale completer **of** [sale];
the addressee **of the** promise **is the** customer **of** [sale];
sincerity: < no specific condition >
truth: < no specific condition >

if *performing the action after **then** is considered justifiable*
then
request sale preparing **for** [sale] [TK03/rq]
to a sale preparer

ARS04

when sale paying **for** [sale] is declared (TK03/da)

assess *rightness:* **the** performer **of the** statement **is the** sale payer **of** [sale];
the addressee **of the** statement **is the** sale completer **of** [sale];
sincerity: < no specific condition >
truth: **the** declared amount **is equal to**
the promised amount;
the declared ot **of** sale paying **for** [sale] **is equal to**
the promised ot **of** sale paying **for** [sale]

if *performing the action after **then** is considered justifiable*
then
accept sale paying **for** [sale] [TK03/ac]
to the performer **of the** declaration
else reject sale paying **for** [sale] [TK03/rj]
to the performer **of the** declaration
* justification of reject *

ARS05

when sale preparing **for** [sale] is declared (TK02/da)

assess *rightness:* **the** performer **of the** statement **is the** sale preparer **of** [sale];
the addressee **of the** statement **is the** sale completer **of** [sale];
sincerity: < no specific condition >
truth: **the** declared contents **of** [sale] **is equal to**
the promised contents **of** [sale];
the declared ot **of** sale preparing **for** [sale] **is equal to**
the promised ot **of** sale preparing **for** [sale]

if *performing the action after **then** is considered justifiable*
then
accept sale preparing **for** [sale] [TK02/ac]
to the performer **of the** declaration
else reject sale preparing **for** [sale] [TK02/rj]
to the performer **of the** declaration
* justification of reject *

ARS06

when	sale completing **for** [sale] **is** promised		(TK01/pm)
	while	sale paying **for** [sale] **is** accepted **and**	(TK03/ac)
		sale preparing **for** [sale] **is** accepted **and**	(TK02/ac)
		if the delivery mode **of** [sale] **is** 'home delivery':	
		order delivery **for** [sale] is accepted	(TK04/ac)
assess	*rightness:*	**the** performer **of the** promise **is the** sale completer **of** [sale];	
		the addressee **of the** promise **is the** customer **of** [sale];	
	sincerity:	< no specific condition >	
	truth:	< no specific condition >	
if	*complying with promise is considered justifiable*		
then	execute	sale completing **for** [sale]	[TK01/ex]
	declare	sale completing **for** [sale] **to the** customer **of** [sale]	[TK01/da]

12.3.6.3 The PM of the Pizzeria (Second Phase)

In this section, we present and discuss the PM of the pizzeria in the second phase of its existence. The exhibited PSD in Fig. 12.7 is fully based on the CM in Sect. 12.3.6.1 and the action rule specifications in Sect. 12.3.6.2.

As one may expect, the PSD shows the transaction kind TK01 (sale completing), which encloses three other transaction kinds: TK02 (sale preparing), TK03 (sale paying) and TK04 (sale delivering). Because there are no indications that the initiation of transactions of the enclosed kinds is performed otherwise, we assume that the 'normal way' holds (cf. Chap 11), thus that they are initiated from the state promised (pm) of the corresponding transaction TK01. In other words, as soon as the order taker has promised the customer to fulfil her/his wishes, the enclosed transactions can be started. Transaction kind TK04 has a cardinality range 0…1 next to the response link from (TK01/pm) to [TK04/rq], as well as to the wait link from (TK04/ac) to [TK01/ex]. It expresses that this transaction is optional: not every sale is delivered home.

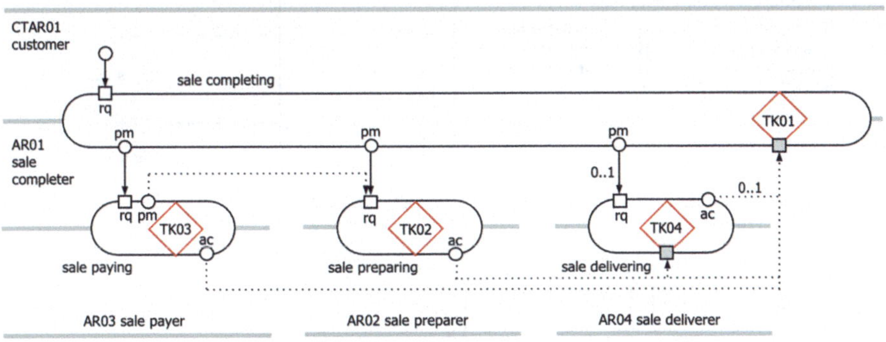

Fig. 12.7 PSD of the Pizzeria organisation (second phase)

All enclosed transactions (so TK02, TK03 and optionally TK04) must have been carried out before the enclosing transaction (so TK01) can be completed. This condition is represented by the wait links from (TK02/ac), (TK03/ac) and (TK04/ac) to [TK01/ex]. It is an obvious condition since the products of the enclosed transactions, so the PK02, PK03 and PK04 are components of the PK01.

Basically, and ideally, enclosed transactions are carried out in parallel, thus simultaneously, but this is not always possible. In the case Pizzeria, there are two conditions that prevent the (ideal) full parallel carrying out of the transactions TK02, TK03 and (optionally) TK04. The first one is represented by the wait link from (TK03/pm) to [TK02/rq]. It is a matter of policy of the pizzeria, which we discussed earlier.

The other additional wait condition is the one from (TK02/ac) to [TK04/ex]. The reason for the presence of this condition is purely a matter of logistics: one cannot transport pizzas that are not yet prepared, given the used implementation technology. It is important to understand though that ontological models are only abstracted from implementation; they are not independent from it (cf. Chap. 6). One could, for example, imagine vans that have an oven inside. With this implementation technology, one could carry out transactions TK02 and TK04 in parallel. Then the wait condition from (TK02/ac) to [TK04/ex] would disappear.

12.3.6.4 The FM of the Pizzeria in the Second Phase

In Fig. 12.8, The OFD of the Pizzeria organisation in the second phase is presented. It is based on the AM in Sect. 12.3.6.2. Compared to the FM in the first phase, there is only a small extension of the OFD, namely, the product kind PK04.

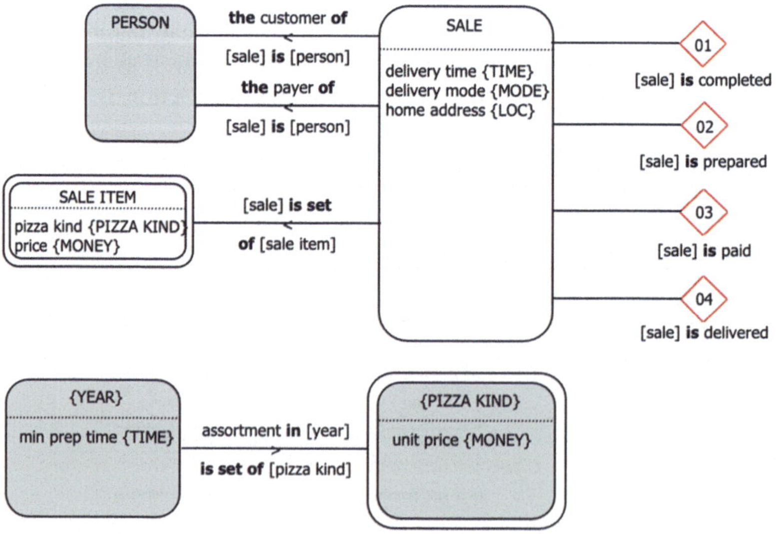

Fig. 12.8 OFD of the Pizzeria organisation (second phase)

12.3.7 Application of the GRAF

In Chap. 9 the GRAF (General Requirements and Architecture Framework) was introduced for ordering user and architectural requirements. We will apply the GRAF in the exercise Pizzeria to the requirements that hold for the design of the implementation of the second phase.

Full outsourcing home delivery	S = total organisation
	D = operational organisation
	A = delivery costs
Home deliverers must be students	S = total organisation
	D = operational organisation
	A = delivery reliability, delivery costs

What these two architectural requirements specify is first that the Pizzeria doesn't want to acquire mopeds (or other means of transportation) in order to reduce delivery costs. It is a formal expression of Mia's firm statement, made in Sect. 12.3.5, that she doesn't want the hassle of having her own mopeds.

The second architectural requirement states that the persons who deliver pizzas to the customers must be students. This is a formal expression of another statement in Sect. 12.3.5, namely, that students seem to be flexible and trustworthy workers. Students thus raise the reliability of the delivery service and reduce the incurred costs, because their payments can be lower than regular deliverers.

12.3.8 The Implementation of the Second Phase

The next steps in the re-development of the Pizzeria are DAO step 3 (engineering or implementation design) and DAO step 4 (implementation). As discussed above, the engineering implies mainly the hiring of students (with their own mopeds) and letting them deliver ordered pizzas at the customer's home address. Next to these changes, the blue copy of the order form has to be produced.

The implementation itself comprises the choice of a particular deliverer for a particular home delivery and the addition of the blue copy of the order form to the baked (pizzas of a) sale. Mia and Mario have decided to start addressing this implementation choice in a simple way: the student among the deliverers (on a particular day) who has waited longest will be assigned the next home delivery order. If there are more students with the same (longest) waiting time, an arbitrary choice is made. By lack of a better rule, the students agree.

12.4 The Transition from the Second to the Third Phase

In this section, we will present and discuss the re-development of the Pizzeria that is needed to make the transition from the second to the third phase. According to the description in Sect. 12.2, the third phase is very different from the second. This is unquestionably the case. At the same time, the changes regard specifically the ownership and the financial position of the Pizzeria (now being a branch of a big company) and the implementation of the organisation.

The ontological model of the Pizzeria in the third phase, however, is the same as the one in the second phase. It means that there are the same four actor roles and transaction kinds. Except for actor role AR03 (sale payer), these actor roles are filled by the 'youngsters'. Although the ordering and paying process is automated, the 'youngsters' are the authorised and responsible fillers of actor roles AR01, AR02 and AR04. So in case of a breakdown of the automatic ordering and paying system or of the automatic ovens, they have to take appropriate actions. The question is whether the manager of the new Domina branch is aware of these crucial consequences of automation. Probably not. It stresses the importance that both the branch manager and the employed 'youngsters' deeply understand the PSI theory (cf. Chap. 6).

Also the delegations as exhibited in Table 12.4 are still in place. It doesn't matter whether the same 'youngster' or different 'youngsters' fill the distinct actor roles for a particular sale; the delegations remain valid.

The question is whether we need to reconsider the function of the Pizzeria in the third phase, put more concretely: whether we need to give attention to the function design (DAO step 1). Actually we should, but wc will not do it because the results of the next steps (step 2, step 3 and step 4) are already fully determined as follows from the narrative description in Sect. 12.2. Moreover, Mia and Mario are gone; it is all up to Domina to solve occurring problems.

12.5 Conclusions

We have demonstrated in this chapter the application of the DAO method to the Pizzeria. Because the functional changes are either clear and straightforward, or the resulting consequences for the construction were already determined, the functional analysis approaches, as discussed in Chap. 3, were not applied, except the use of the BMC template in Fig. 12.5. In particular, we didn't need to apply the ETA theory (cf. Chap. 10) for the simple reason that the implementation decisions were already taken.

The huge transformation from a small local pizzeria to a branch of a large pizzeria chain, with huge consequences for the way in which it is 'organised', hardly appears to have consequences for the essential model of the Pizzeria. This is probably the most important insight that the case Pizzeria offers. It shows the strength of the ontological model. At the same time, one must be attentive: abstracting from implementation seems to make it less important, but this may be misleading. In the end, it is its implementation and installation as dealt with by the ETA theory in Chap. 10 that makes a system real, ready to become operational.

Another insight may be the consequences of the apparently 'simple' extension of the business with home delivery for the allocation of authority (and the necessary delegations). As illustrated by Table 12.4, these consequences are not trivial.

The case Pizzeria also demonstrates the importance of the transaction pattern in determining and discussing authorisation and delegation (cf. Chap. 6). Only on the basis of deep knowledge of the transaction pattern can one understand the necessity of some delegations. They are consequences of the way in which the ontological model is implemented.

Reference

1. Dietz, J. L. G., & Mulder, J. B. F. (2024). *Enterprise ontology—A human-centric approach to understanding the essence of organisation* (Enterprise engineering) (2nd ed.). Springer Nature.

Chapter 13
Exercise: Library

An Exercise in Organisational Redesign and Digital Transformation

Abstract The Library is an exercise in understanding and applying the GSDP to an organisational transition that a library goes through. The essential model appears to be a stable beacon when discussing the impacts of alternative ways of implementing the organisational changes. Far-reaching changes in the operational activities appear to have no or little impact on the essential model because they mainly regard the implementation of these activities. Special attention is given to showing how revocations can be indicated in the process structure diagram.

13.1 Introduction

The case Library is an exercise in re-designing an enterprise. In [1], Chap. 16, the essential model of the enterprise is developed. In terms of the categories that are distinguished in Chap. 7, the library offers both the obtaining of usufruct of tangible things (borrowing books) and the creating of intangible things (starting and ending memberships).

Section 13.2 contains the description of the operational activities of the Library. It is the basis for applying the OER method (cf. Chap. 11) in order to produce the essential model. This is discussed in Sect. 13.3, along with presenting (parts of the) essential model in diagrams, tables and formal text. The analysis of the second phase, and the application of the DAO method, is presented in Sect. 13.4, with its consequences for the initial essential model. In Sect. 13.5, the application of the ETA theory is presented, while Sect. 13.6 contains the conclusions from this exercise.

J. L. G. Dietz, H. B. F. Mulder, *Enterprise Design Fundamentals*, The Enterprise Engineering Series, https://doi.org/10.1007/978-3-031-83262-8_13

13.2 Narrative Description

Description of the First Phase

The Library described hereafter is a small public library. In the building in which it is located is a desk for lending books, called the out-desk, and a desk for returning books, called the in-desk. At a third desk, called the information desk, one can get information about the opening hours, the library regulations and the membership fees. At the information desk is a desktop computer where members can browse through the library catalogue to find the books they want to borrow.

In order to become member of the library, one has to present oneself at the information desk and provide the next data to the staff member: surname, first name, middle initials, city of residence, street name, house number, postal code, date of birth, place of birth and the starting day of the membership (which must be the first day of a month in the Gregorian calendar). The provided data are entered into the Library Information System (LIS). LIS automatically prints a membership card (with a bar code) and an invoice for the fee of the first year. The amount to pay is proportional to the remaining part of the year. From then on, membership fees are invoiced annually.

New members also get a letter of welcome, informing them about the library regulations that they are supposed to know. It is handed over to the new member after payment of the first membership fee, in cash or by bank transfer (in which case one has to provide a debit card). The minimal age for new members is 8 years. Moreover, if a new member is under 18, an adult must be entered as the payer of the fee and one as the payer of possible fines.

Memberships are automatically extended every calendar year, until they are explicitly ended by the member. The termination of a membership is always per the 1st of January. In addition, the librarian decides every month about ending memberships by the Library. Reasons for ending a membership in this way are, for example, repeatedly late returns of books and/or refusals to pay the fee or the incurred fines. If a membership is ended by the Library, the member may claim the refund of the fee that has been paid for the remaining part of the current year. Refunds are made in cash or by bank transfer.

Members are entitled to borrow books from the library. Books are put on shelves, sorted by category and title. Normally, there are several copies of the same title. Every book copy is uniquely identified by a bar code. It consists of the ISBN (International Standard Book Number) and a serial number of the book copy. If someone wants to borrow books, he/she has to take the books from the shelves to the out-desk. There, one of the staff members scans the bar codes on the membership card and on the books. These data are automatically entered into LIS, where a loan contract for every borrowed book is created. After this process is finished, the member can take the books along.

There is a maximum number of books that one can have in loan simultaneously, and there is also a maximum loan period. Borrowed books must be returned within this period. When a member returns one or more books, he/she goes to the in-desk and hands the books to a staff member, who then scans the book codes and the membership number, which are automatically entered into LIS. On the screen of the computer, the staff member sees whether the loan period of a book is exceeded. If it is, the fine to be paid is also shown. Fines have to be paid by the member right away (in cash or by bank transfer).

Description of the Second Phase
After about 10 flourishing years, the librarian decides to improve the services of the library substantially by two major changes. The first one is that people don't need to visit the library in order to become a member. It can now be done from home via a Web extension of LIS. It implies, however, that payments can only be made by periodic direct debits. Instead of a membership card, members can identify themselves in LIS by means of a membership number and a password. Every member has a personal section in LIS, called MyLIS.

The second major change regards the way in which books are issued and returned. There are no more shelves with books in the library building. Instead, there is a central repository in the cellar, where book copies are automatically stored and retrieved by a warehouse system.

Either from home or from desktop computers in the library, one can browse through the catalogue and select the books one wants to borrow. Like it was in the first phase, a loan is created for every book copy. After finishing such a borrow session, the borrowed books are automatically retrieved from the central repository and put in a locker. The member has access to this locker, by keying the membership number and the password at the locker wall, during five workdays. If the books are not taken out within this period, they are put back in the repository.

Returning books is made as easy as picking up. In the hall of the library building is a conveyer belt on which one can put the returned books, one after the other. The handling of the books, as well as the processing of the corresponding loan, is done automatically. If a fine is incurred, the amount is automatically charged to one's bank account (also through direct debit).

13.3 Analysis of the First Phase

Because it is not possible to involve the employees of the Library directly, we have to apply the second best way of working, as discussed in Chap. 11. It is to study the case description and to find clues for the presence of original (thus O-organisation) transaction kinds and corresponding actor roles. We will do this below, paragraph after paragraph. The pieces of text that are taken from the case description are written in italics. We apply the OER method to the case description in a spiral way (cf. Chap.11). All transaction kinds and involved actor roles are identified and discussed, and most corresponding parts of the aspect models are presented. The described operational processes determine the Scope of Interest (SoI) we take. The actor roles that are filled by employees of the Library are internal; all other ones are external.

The Library described hereafter is a small public library. In the building in which it is located are a desk for lending books, called the out-desk, and a desk for returning books, called the in-desk. At a third desk, called the information desk, one can get information such as the opening hours, the library regulations and the membership fees. At the information desk is a desktop computer where members can browse through the library catalogue to find the books they want to borrow.

Although this piece of text does contain indications of essential transaction kinds, we consider it primarily as introductory text.

In order to become member of the library, one has to present oneself at the information desk and provide the next data to the staff member: surname, first name, middle initials, city of residence, street name, house number, postal code, date of birth, place of birth and the starting day of the membership (which must be the first day of a month in the Gregorian calendar). The provided data are entered into the Library Information System (LIS). LIS automatically prints a membership card (with a bar code) and an invoice for the fee of the first year. The amount to pay is proportional to the remaining part of the year. From then on, membership fees are invoiced annually.

In the first sentence, we find, in red, evidence of one of the services that the library offers: becoming member of the library. Let us identify this transaction kind as TK01 and give it the name 'membership starting', in accordance with the discussion of how to model 'becoming member' in the case Volley (cf. [1], Chap. 12). In the subsequent sentences, one learns how a request to do so (thus a TK01/rq) must be performed and what data one has to provide. Let us identify the corresponding product kind as PK01 and formulate it as '[membership] **is** started' in DEMO-SL [2]. So, every PK01 is an instance of becoming member of the library by some person. We identify the executor role as AR01 and call it 'membership starter'. The initiator role in transactions TK01 is filled by the aspirant members. Because this role is clearly an environmental one (outside the focus of the chosen Scope of Interest), we consider it to be contained in the composite transactor role CTAR01.

Becoming member of the library belongs to the category of creating intangible things in the distinctions made in Chap. 7 (cf. Table 7.2). Consequently, we can take the CSD in Fig. 7.6 as the reference model, although the tree we come up with is quite small: there is only one transaction kind enclosed in TK01, which we will call TK02. The presence of this transaction kind can be deduced from the piece of text *invoice for the fee of the first year*. Let us identify the corresponding product kind as PK02 and formulate it as '**the** fee **for** [membership] **in** [year] **is** paid'. Adding '[year]' as the second entity variable is a convenient way to deal with the time aspect in memberships. The alternative way is to formulate PK02, for example, as '[fee payment] **is** done'. But then, one needs to introduce a new entity type, with the inherent property (or attribute) types 'membership of fee payment' and 'year of fee payment'. Although this formulation is also fully correct, it is recommended to adhere to the principle of minimality, often referred to as Ockham's Razor.[1]

[1] https://en.wikipedia.org/wiki/Occam%27s_razor

To accommodate the annual occurrence of transactions TK02, we deduce from the same piece of text (being in addition confirmed by the fourth paragraph, to be discussed later) the presence of a third transaction kind. Let us identify it as TK03, name it 'fee payment controlling' and formulate the product kind PK03 as 'fee payment controlling **for** [year] **is** done'. The executing actor role, AR03, can properly be named 'fee payment controller'. As it holds for all repeating or periodic activities, actors AR03 are not only the executors TK03 but also their initiators (cf. Chap. 7). Every time that a TK03 is carried out, a number of transactions TK02 are carried out. The number is of course the number of current memberships.

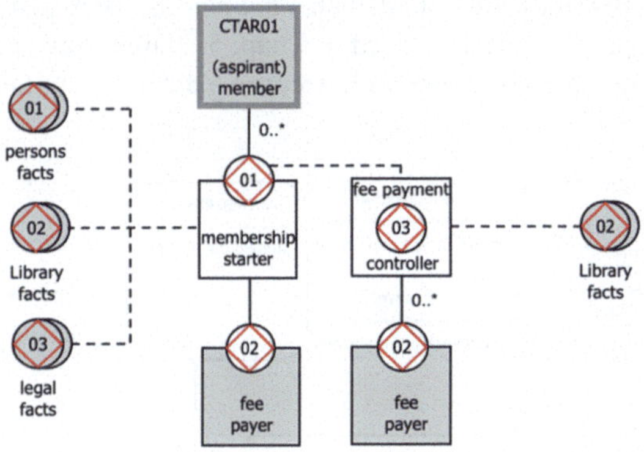

transaction kind	product kind	executor role
TK01 membership starting TK02 fee paying TK03 fee payment controlling	PK01 [membership] **is** started PK02 **the** fee **for** [membership] **in** [year] **is** paid PK03 fee payment controlling **for** [year] **is** done	AR01 membership starter AR02 fee payer AR03 fee payment controller

Fig. 13.1 CSD and TPT of the Library organisation (first part)

Based on the analysis so far, we produce the first part of the CSD and the first part of the TPT in Fig. 13.1. The access links can be deduced from the AM, of which one rule is discussed later. The external facts are contained in the multiple transaction kinds MTK01 through MTK03. In addition, we present the part of the FM that can be deduced from our findings up to now in the OFD in Fig. 13.2. It shows the presence of the core entity type membership (actually its extension, thus the object class MEMBERSHIP, as discussed in [1], Chap. 5), as well as the external entity type person and the value type year, which is by definition external.

The property type '**the** member **of** [membership] **is** [person]' determines who is the member of a membership. Note that every membership has exactly one associated person as the member but that, conversely, a person may be member in a number of memberships. Although this is not explicitly stated by the case description (and thus has to be validated), it makes perfect sense: by having several memberships simultaneously, one can have more books in loan simultaneously. We assume that the legal age (contained in MTK03) does not change more than once in a year, like the facts that are determined by the Library and contained in MTK02 (like membership fee and minimal age). The annual fee payment is an aggregation type of MEMBERSHIP and YEAR (cf. [1], Chap. 6).

The P-event kind PK01 (which is identical to the product kind PK01 in the TPT) concerns the entity type membership, and the P-event kind PK03 concerns the value type year. The entity type that the P-event kind PK02 concerns is the aggregation of membership and year: every instance of PK02 regards one membership and one year.

The attribute types that are listed in Fig. 13.2 can directly be deduced from the part of the case description that we have analysed. Note that the entity type person doesn't have the attributes surname, first name and middle initials, for the simple but crucial reason that they are not attributes but names. They just and only serve to refer to particular persons, as discussed in Chap. 5. Names have no ontological relevance, but they may of course very well occur in a database containing the data that are used by LIS.

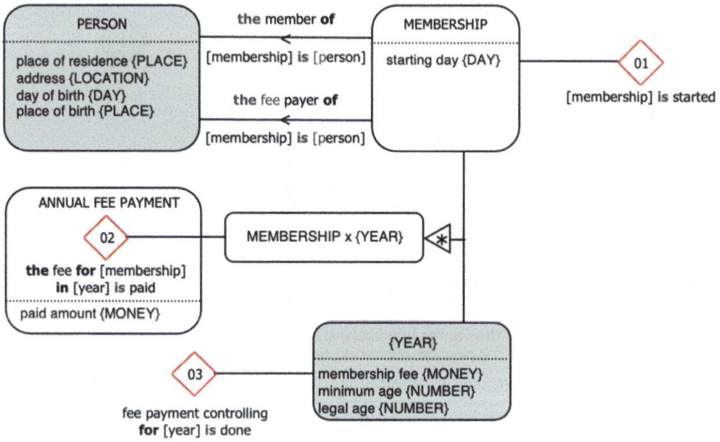

Fig. 13.2 OFD of the Library organisation (first part)

Next, the fact type 'paid amount' is an attribute type of the entity type 'fee payment', which is a specialisation of the aggregate entity type 'membership × year' (cf. [1], Chap. 6). This specialisation can conveniently be defined graphically, as is done in the OFD in Fig. 13.2.

As an example of an action rule specification, we provide below the one for dealing with requests for memberships. It is assumed that a new instance of membership is created as soon as the first request for it is performed. From then on, the membership is referred to as the entity variable [membership].

when membership starting **for** [membership] **is** requested (TK01/rq)
  given **the** member **of** [membership];
    the fee payer **of** [membership];
    the starting day **of** [membership]

assess *rightness:* **the** performer **of the** request **is the** member **of** [membership]
  the addressee **of the** request **is a** membership starter
  sincerity: * no specific condition *
  truth: **the** starting day **of** [membership] **is the** first day **of some** month;
  the age **of the** member **of** [membership] **on the** starting day **of** [membership] **is equal to or greater than the** minimum age **in the** year **of the** starting day **of** [membership];
  the age **of the** fee payer **of** [membership] **on the** starting day **of** [membership] **is equal to or greater than the** legal age **in the** year **of the** starting day **of** [membership];

*if performing the action after **then** is considered justifiable*
  then promise membership starting **for** [membership] [TK01/pm]
    to the performer **of the** request
  else decline membership starting **for** [membership] [TK01/dc]
    to the performer **of the** request

The first condition in the rightness division is not a trivial one (cf. Chap. 11). If it is omitted, anyone could perform the request. After execution of the action rule, a particular employee is allocated to the membership as its membership starter.

New members also get a letter of welcome, informing them about the library regulations that they are supposed to know. It is handed over to the new member after payment of the first membership fee, in cash or by bank transfer (in which case one has to provide a debit card). The minimal age for new members is 8 years. Moreover, if a new member is under 18, an adult must be entered as the payer of the fee and one as the payer of possible fines.

The only ontologically interesting piece of text in this paragraph (marked in red) does not lead to an extension of the essential model because transaction kind TK02 (fee paying) has been identified already. The other parts of the text refer to informational (… *informing them about the library rules* … and … *an adult must be entered as the payer* …) or documental/material (… *in cash or by bank transfer* …) matters.

Memberships are automatically extended every calendar year, until they are explicitly ended by the member. The termination of a membership is always per the 1st of January. In addition, the librarian decides every month about ending memberships by the Library. Reasons for ending a membership in this way are, for example, repeatedly late returns of books and/or refusals to pay the fee or the incurred fines. If a membership is ended by the Library, the member may claim the refund of the fee that has been paid for the remaining part of the current year. Refunds are made in cash or by bank transfer.

The red-marked text in the first line indicates the presence of a fourth transaction kind, which we will identify as TK04 and name ‘membership ending’. Let us formulate the product kind PK04 as '[membership] is ended' and name the executing actor role (AR04) 'membership ender'. A possible initiator of transactions TK04 is the member of the membership, thus an actor role within the composite transactor role CTAR01. The other possible ender of memberships is the librarian. According to the second part of text in red, he/she makes such decisions once per month. Clearly, we need another self-activating actor role (like AR03) to model this properly. Let us identify this actor role as AR05, name it 'membership controller', name the corresponding transaction kind (TK05) 'membership controlling' and formulate the product kind (PK05) as 'membership controlling **for** [month] **is** done'.

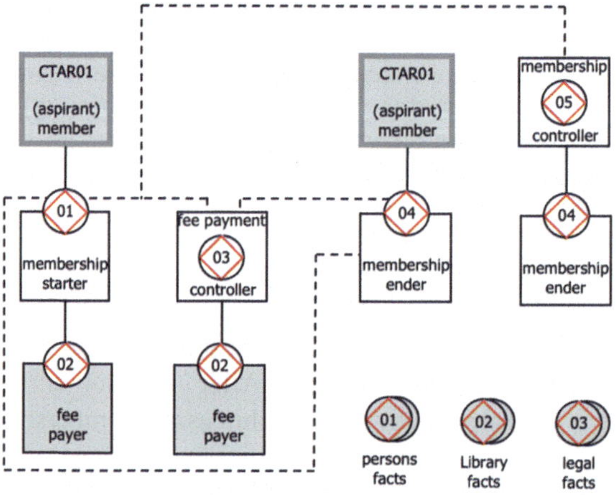

transaction kind	product kind	executor role
TK01 membership starting TK02 fee paying TK03 fee payment controlling TK04 membership ending TK05 membership controlling	PK01 [membership] **is** started PK02 **the fee for** [membership] **in** [year] **is** paid PK03 fee payment controlling **for** [year] **is** done PK04 [membership] **is** ended PK05 membership controlling **for** [month] **is** done	AR01 membership starter AR02 fee payer AR03 fee payment controller AR04 membership ender AR05 membership controller

Fig. 13.3 CSD and TPT of the Library organisation (plus second part)

The analysis up to now leads to the extension of the CM as presented in Fig. 13.3. The access links to the external banks are omitted, in order to keep the diagram readable. In order to specify access rights completely, we will introduce the Bank Access Table later on.

Refunding the membership fee that has been paid for the remaining part of a membership year means ontologically that the payer, so the actor AR02, revokes her/his promise in the corresponding transaction TK02, followed by a new transaction TK02 for the remaining amount to be paid, in much the same way as the agreed reduction of the price to pay for the repair in the case Fixit is handled (cf. [1], Chap. 13). It is presented in Fig. 13.4. Path 1 (coloured green) represents the successful payment of the fee for the current membership year, and path 2 (coloured tangerine) represents the revoke by the payer of her/his promise to pay. He/she does so in response to the declaration by the librarian that the membership has been ended, thus to the C-event (TK04/da). The revoke may be allowed by the librarian, but it may as well be refused, for a valid reason, like a behind on payment.

If it is refused, the main process of the transaction TK02 remains in the state (ac). If it is allowed, this process will be rolled back to the state (rq), from which the payer can decline the (original) request. In the discussion state (dc), the parties agree on the (reduced) amount that the payer has to pay, after which the librarian performs a renewed request for the agreed-upon amount. This is represented by the tangerine-coloured path 3. Finally, the payer pays this amount, represented by path 4 (in blue).

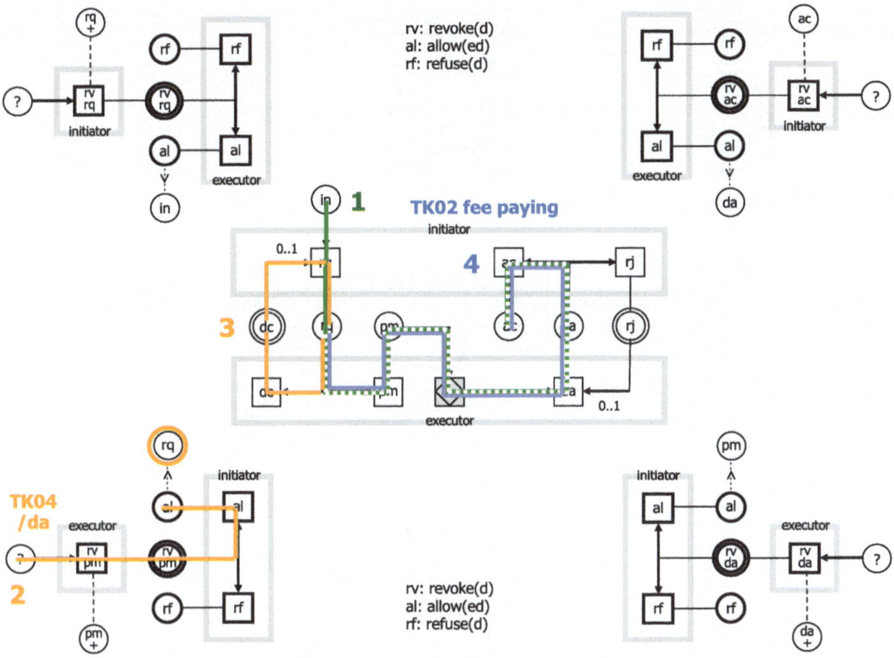

Fig. 13.4 Claiming the refund of the paid membership fee

Rolling back the transaction process up to the state (rq), indicated by the dashed green line, logically implies 'undoing' the production act. Undoing the performed fee payment would mean giving back the paid amount to the payer. The second pass of the same transaction process regards paying the reduced amount. The practical solution is of course to subtract the first amount from the second one and to ask for paying the difference. Because the result of the subtraction is negative, the librarian 'pays' the difference to the payer.

The PM of the case Library, based on the analysis up to now, is represented by the PSDs in Fig. 13.5. It shows how transactions TK02 are enclosed in transactions TK01 and TK03 and how memberships are ended by the librarian (bottom part). In blue, the response link is added, which represents the [rv-pm] act by the fee payer in the (last carried out) TK02, in order to get a refund, after the membership has been ended by the librarian (as stated earlier, endings of memberships by members are always per the 1st of January). Although this revoke can be performed in any state of the main process, it is most likely performed from the state (T04/ac), so when the membership is ended. As shown, this link must also be drawn to the [rv-pm] act in the shape of TK02 in the upper part of Fig. 13.5, because it can already happen in the first year.

Because the ending of memberships by the members themselves doesn't have enclosed transactions, the (trivial) corresponding PSD is not presented.

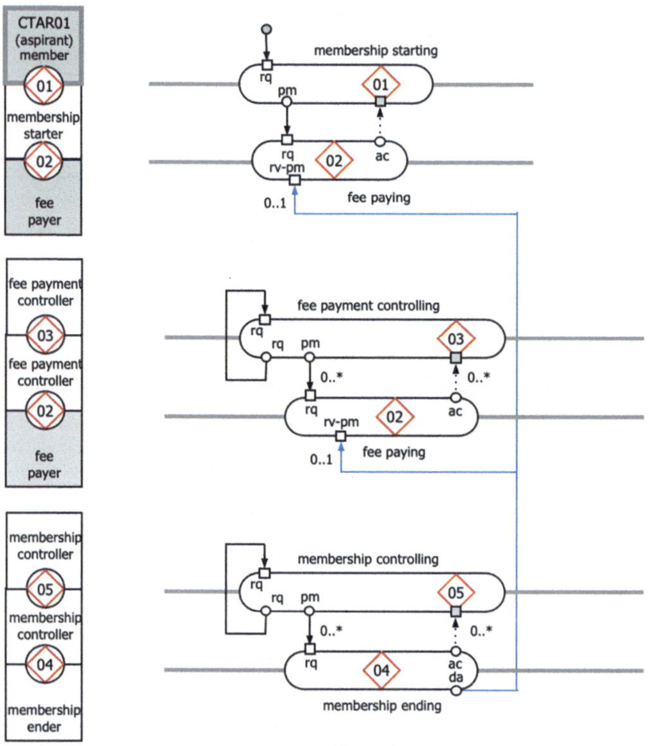

Fig. 13.5 PSD of the Library organisation (first part)

Members are entitled to borrow books from the library. Books are put on shelves and sorted by category and title. Normally, there are several copies of the same title. Every book copy is uniquely identified by a bar code. It consists of the ISBN (International Standard Book Number) and a serial number of the book copy. If someone wants to borrow books, he/she has to take the books from the shelves to the out-desk. There, one of the staff members scans the bar codes on the membership card and on the books. These data are automatically entered into LIS, where a loan contract for every borrowed book is created. After this process is finished, the member can take the books along.

This part of the case description regards the borrowing of books, which is a specialisation of the general category of obtaining the usufruct of tangible things,[2] according to the division in Chap. 7 (cf. Table 7.2). Therefore, we start from the general reference model in Fig. 7.19 and its tailored variant in Fig. 7.21.

From the red-coloured parts in this piece of text, we deduce indeed the presence of two transaction kinds in the reference model. The first one is about concluding a loan contract. Let us identify it as TK06 and name it 'loan completing'. Next, let us name the executor role (AR06) 'loan completer' and formulate the product kind (PK06) as '[loan] **is** completed'. Transactions TK06 enclose a transaction regarding the taking along of borrowed books, as expressed by the third piece of text in red. Let us identify it as TK07 and name it 'book taking'. Next, let us name the executor role (AR07) 'book taker' and formulate the product kind (PK07) as '**the** book **of** [loan] **is** taken'.

Note that a loan concerns one book (copy), as also expressed in the second piece of text above in red. As a general rule, and again as an application of Ockham's Razor, it is recommended to have one book per loan, one car per rental, one order entry per order, etc. One may open, however, several loans, rentals, order entries, etc. simultaneously. The advantage is that one or more of the concurrent loans may be completed (after having returned the related book), while the others still go on. So if a member borrows a number of books at the same time, an equal number of loans are created.

Note also that a formulation of PK07 like '[book] **is** taken', which one may be inclined to choose as a first attempt, is incorrect. It would imply that every book (copy) can only be taken once in its lifetime. This is obviously not what one wants. The unsuitability of the formulation can easily be discovered by applying the sapience 'verification by instantiation', which we applied before in verifying other fact type formulations (cf. Chap. 12).

Based on the analysis above, we arrive at the extension of the CM of the Library, as expressed in the CSD and the TPT in Fig. 13.6. It contains also the two transaction kinds (and involved actor roles) that can be deduced from the part of the case description above.

There is a maximum number of books that one can have in loan simultaneously, and there is also a maximum loan period. Borrowed books must be returned within this period. When a member returns one or more books, he/she goes to the in-desk and hands the books to a staff member, who then scans the book codes and the membership number, which are automatically entered into LIS. On the screen of the computer, the staff member sees whether the loan period of a book is exceeded. If it is, the fine to be paid is shown also. Fines have to be paid by the member right away (in cash or by bank transfer).

[2] One might disagree with the tangibility of books since it is commonly not the physical representation of the contents that one is interested in, but the contents itself. That is why a digital (electronic) representation (eBook or PDF) is often a good alternative. Nevertheless, we stick to the case description, which is clearly about physical books. An additional argument to do this is that the borrower of a book may have other affordances in mind than reading (cf. Chap. 7).

The first and the second red-coloured piece of text in this paragraph indicate the existence of another transaction kind. Let us identify it as TK08 and name it 'book returning'. Next, let us give the name 'book returner' to the executor role (AR08) and formulate the product kind (PK08) as '**the** book **of** [loan] **is** returned'. The third piece of text in red gives rise to identifying transaction kind TK09, which we name 'penalty paying', with product kind PK09, formulated as '**the** penalty **of** [loan] **is** paid'. The executing actor role is AR09, named 'penalty payer'. Figure 13.6 exhibits the consequent extension of the (final) CSD and TPT, following the reference model in Fig. 10.21.

The figure also contains the (external) multiple transaction kinds MTK01 through MTK03. They are the conceptual stores of facts that are created outside the chosen SoI but needed by the internal actors. MTK01 contains facts about persons, like place of residence and day of birth, and MTK02 contains facts that are created by actors within the Library as a whole, but outside the chosen SoI. Examples are the minimum age of members and the maximum loan period. Their values are typically decided upon (annually) by the librarian. MTK03 contains the current legal age.

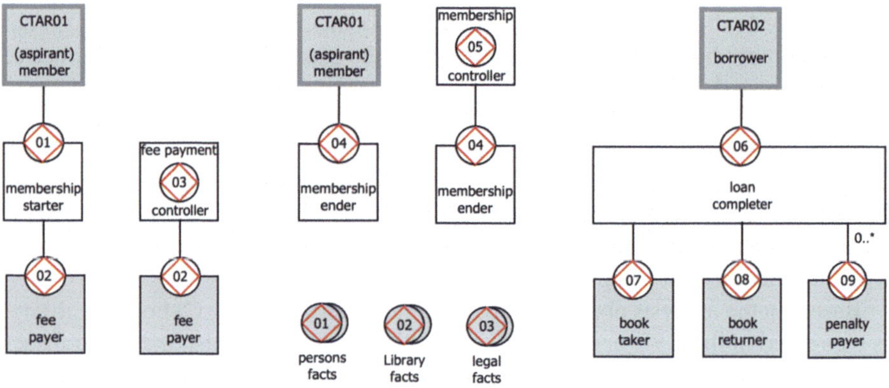

transaction kind	product kind	executor role
TK01 membership starting	PK01 [membership] **is** started	AR01 membership starter
TK02 fee paying	PK02 **the** fee **for** [membership] **in** [year] **is** paid	AR02 fee payer
TK03 fee payment controlling	PK03 fee payment controlling **for** [year] **is** done	AR03 fee payment controller
TK04 membership ending	PK04 [membership] **is** ended	AR04 membership ender
TK05 membership controlling	PK05 membership controlling **for** [month] **is** done	AR05 membership controller
TK06 loan completing	PK06 [loan] **is** completed	AR06 loan completer
TK07 book taking	PK07 **the** book **of** [loan] **is** taken	AR07 book taker
TK08 book returning	PK08 **the** book **of** [loan] **is** returned	AR08 book returner
TK09 penalty paying	PK09 **the** penalty **of** [loan] **is** paid	AR09 penalty payer

Fig. 13.6 Final CSD and TPT of the Library organisation

Table 13.1 BAT of the Library organisation

Bank Actor	TK01	TK02	TK03	TK04	TK05	TK06	TK07	TK08	TK09	MTK01	MTK02	MTK03
AR01	Ex	In								U	U	U
AR02		Ex									U	
AR03	U	In	Ex	U						U	U	
AR04	U			Ex				U	U	U	U	
AR05	U			In	Ex					U	U	
AR06	U			U		Ex	In	In	In	U	U	U
AR07							Ex				U	
AR08								Ex			U	
AR09									Ex		U	
CTAR01	In			In							U	
CTAR02						In					U	

Figure 13.6 only shows the interaction structure, thus the set of initiator links between the transactor roles. There are five trees, thus five business processes: TK01 with enclosed TK02, TK03 with enclosed TK02, TK04, TK04 with enclosed TK05, and TK06 with enclosed TK07, TK08 and TK09. There appear to be no impediments between these processes, so there are no process dependencies. There are, however, quite some state dependencies, represented by the interstriction structure, which is exhibited in Fig. 13.7. What is still missing in the figure are the access links from the various actor roles to the external multiple transaction kinds MTK01, MTK02 and MTK03. Adding these access links would make the CSD a mess of dashed lines, however. Fortunately, there is an alternative way to indicate access links. It is the Bank Access Table (BAT), as explained in [2]. Table 13.1 exhibits the BAT for the Library. Next to showing which actor role has reading access to which transaction bank, indicated by a 'U' (for Use) at the crossing of the corresponding row and column, 'Ex' indicates the executor actor role and 'In' an initiator role of a transaction kind. Full insight into which actor roles use (the instances of) which fact types is gained when also the Bank Contents Table (BCT) and the complete FM are available.

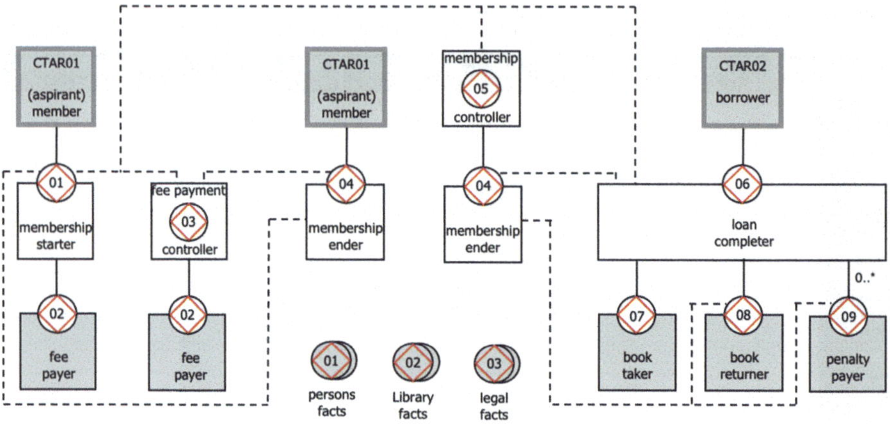

Fig. 13.7 Final CSD plus interstriction structure

Figure 13.8 exhibits the PSD of the loan completion process (the right part of Fig. 13.6). The main structure of this PSD is what one may expect: the transaction kind TK06 (loan completing) has three enclosed transaction kinds: TK07 (book taking), TK08 (book returning) and the optional TK09 (penalty paying). As discussed in Chap. 10, transactions TK07 and TK08 are initiated from the state requested in the enclosing transaction TK06. The transaction TK06 can be promised when the enclosed TK07 and TK08 are promised. Transactions TK09 are initiated from the state (TK01/pm), which is the usual case. Next, book returning cannot be executed before book taking is finished, represented by the wait link from (TK07/ac) to [TK08/ex], and penalty paying cannot be initiated before book returning is finished, represented by the wait link from (TK08/ac) to [TK09/rq]. As said, the final and complete OFD is presented in Fig. 13.9. The left part was already discussed above (cf. Fig. 13.2), except for the event type PK04 ([membership] **is** ended) and the value class MONTH with the event type PK05 (membership controlling **for** [month] **is** done). The two additions are considered to be self-explanatory.

For the right part of Fig. 13.9, we provide the next explanation. The core entity type is 'loan'. The connection with the core entity type in the left part is constituted by the property type '**the** membership **of** [loan] **is** [membership]' of which the domain is the object class LOAN and the range the object class MEMBERSHIP. There are four event types that concern loans: PK06 ([loan] **is** completed), PK07 (**the** book **of** [loan] **is** taken), PK08 (**the** book **of** [loan] **is** returned) and PK09 (**the** penalty **of** [loan] **is** paid). Note that the latter is optional, as follows from the PSD in Fig. 13.8. Based on these event types, three specialisations of the entity type 'loan' are defined graphically: 'taken loan', 'returned loan' and 'penalty paid loan'. They serve to define precisely two property types and one attribute type.

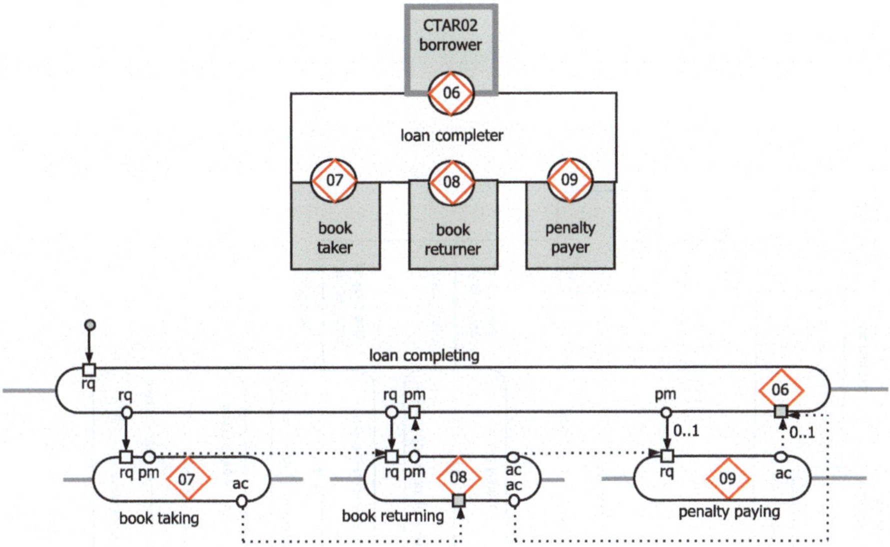

Fig. 13.8 PSD of the Library organisation (second part)

The attribute type is 'paid amount', whose range is the value class MONEY. The class may be refined to, e.g. EURO (cf. Chap. 6), if needed. The two property types are '**the** book **of** [taken loan] **is** [book]' and '**the** book **of** [returned loan] **is** [book]'. The range of both is the external object class BOOK. Note that, consequently, the returned book of a loan may be different from the taken book. This can be determined when the book of a loan is returned. Most likely, one of the (declarative) business rules of the Library is that the two books must be the same.

Next, there is an external object class BOOK TITLE and a value class BOOK CATEGORY. Every book (copy) is a book of some book title. Because one starts a borrowing process by looking for a book of a specific book title, every loan has a particular book title as one of its properties. Which book copy one takes home is actually irrelevant. Finally, to every book title, one or more book categories are assigned, like novel, thriller, etc., and youth, adult, etc., as an aid in finding the book titles one may want to read. Usually, the book categories are created by the publisher, but the Library may refine them or add categories.

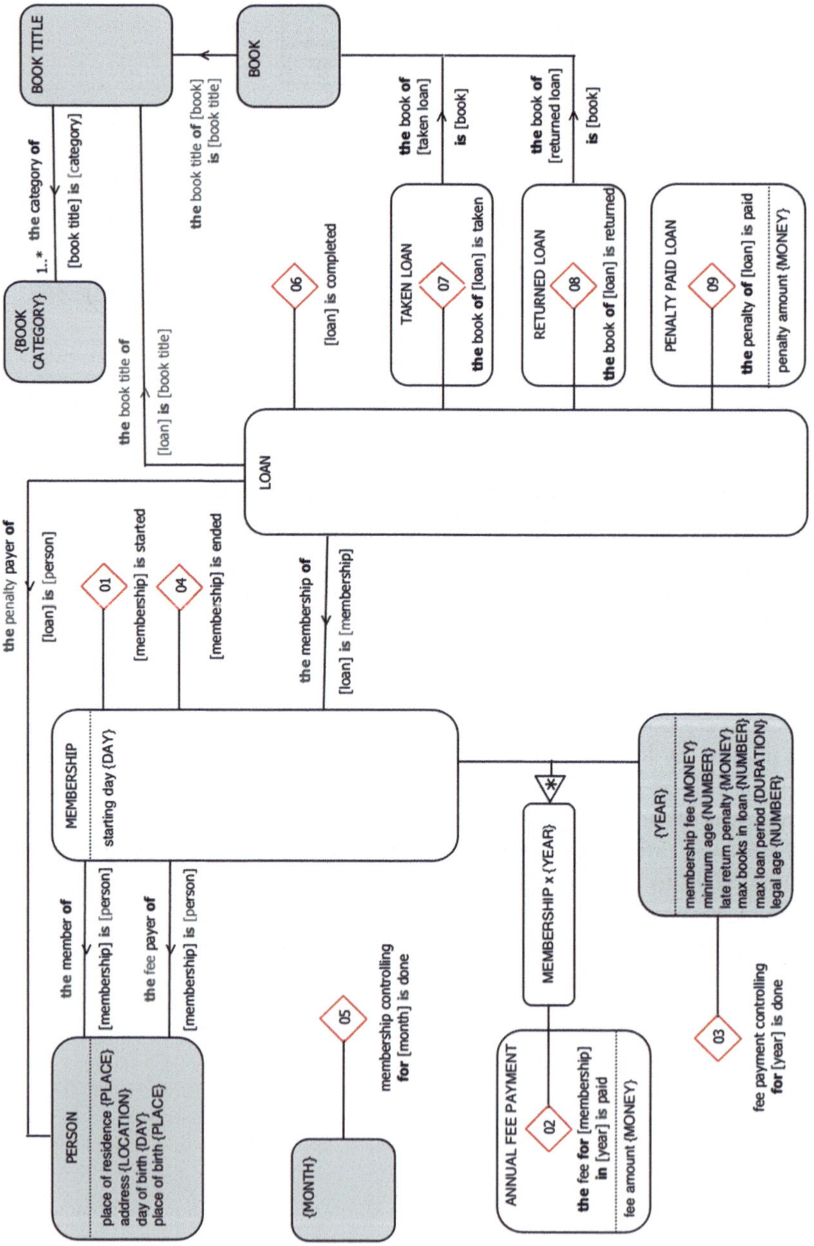

Fig. 13.9 Complete OFD of the Library organisation

13.4 Analysis of the Second Phase

Like it holds for the third phase of the case Pizzeria (cf. Chap. 12), the changes in the second phase of the Library compared to the first phase seem to be substantial. Yet the implications for the essential model that we have produced for the first phase are not dramatic. Nevertheless, we will follow the steps of the DAO method, as presented in Fig. 13.10. The using system (US) consists of the members of the library. Like we did in Chap. 12, we will not formally produce the ontological model of the US (DAO step 0), nor do we formally produce the object system function (DAO step 1), because the Library has already decided to change the construction of the object system (OS) as described in Sect. 13.2 and as repeated below. Let us investigate the changes by analysing the description of the second phase and producing the ontological model of the Library in the second phase (DAO step 2) first and then discuss the implications for the implementation (DAO steps 3 and 4).

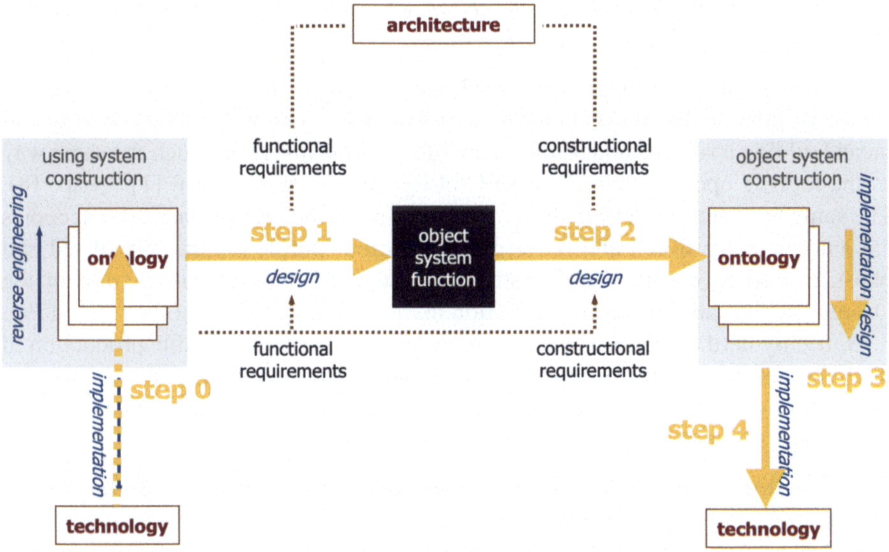

Fig. 13.10 The GSDP with the DAO steps

After about 10 flourishing years, the librarian decides to improve the services of the library substantially by two major changes. The first is that one doesn't need to visit the library in order to become a member. It can now be done from home via a Web extension of LIS. It implies, however, that payments can only be made by periodic direct debits. Instead of a membership card, members can identify themselves in LIS by means of a membership number and a password. Every member has a personal section in LIS, called MyLIS.

Using a Web application to become a member, instead of presenting oneself at the desk in the library, is only a change in the way that the steps in transactions

TK01 are performed. So it is only about the lower-two levels in Fig. 6.5, thus about implementation. Automating transaction steps doesn't affect the responsibilities of the involved actors (cf. Chap. 11). Therefore, as an example, the popping up of a message on the screen, saying that you have successfully become a member of the library, is the declare act in a TK01. The only difference with the way of doing this in the first phase is that the aspirant member and the addressed desk officer communicate via the Web application. Note that the decision that you are a member is not made by the Web application but by the desk officer! That you commonly don't know her/him doesn't matter. A similar reasoning holds for the new way of paying (by periodic direct debits) and for using a password instead of a card for identifying oneself.

The creation of a personal section MyLis for members is primarily also a change at the documental/material level of communication.

The second major change regards the way in which books are issued and returned. There are no more shelves with books in the library building. Instead, there is a central repository in the cellar, where book copies are automatically stored and retrieved by a warehouse system.

In the first phase, one had to take the books to borrow from the shelves. Note that we didn't include this action in the essential model. If one wants to add it, it would mean building a subtree under transactor AR07 (book taker), in much the same way as the logistic operations in the case GloLog can be extended (cf. [1], Chap. 18). The same holds for modelling the way of working in the second phase (book copies are automatically stored and retrieved). The colour purple (as the mix of red and blue) is used to clarify that we are at the edge of 'tangible production in the O-organisation' and 'material production in the M-organisation' of the 'pie' in Fig. 8.13. If only hard copies are considered, we are dealing with tangible production in the O-organisation, but if electronic copies, like eBooks or PDFs, are at stake, we are dealing with material production in the M-organisation (cf. Chap. 8). Electronic copies of documents are easily produced and transported.

Either from home or from desktop computers in the library, one can browse through the catalogue and select the books one wants to borrow. Like it was in the first phase, a loan is created for every book copy. After finishing such a borrow session, the borrowed books are automatically retrieved from the central repository and put into lockers (one book copy per locker).

The piece of text in red is about the logistic operations that we discussed already above. Because we only deal with hard copies, red is used instead of purple.

Returning books is made as easy as picking up. In the hall of the library building is a conveyer belt on which one can put the returned books, one after the other. The handling of the books, as well as the processing of the corresponding loan, is done automatically. If a fine is incurred, the amount is automatically charged to one's bank account (also through direct debit).

Although the case description in Sect. 2.2 doesn't reveal this, it is not hard to imagine what thoughts the librarian must have had before he/she decided to jump into the huge change that the transition to the second phase is. A BMC template like the one in Fig. 13.11 may have helped get sight on the most important issues that are at stake.

Allowing people to become members from their armchair is a service that every organisation with members offers. Lending books from the same armchair is a logical extension, of course. And for sure, both are important value propositions! Extending the services that are offered by LIS means some work for the company that has developed the system and maintains it since then, but this is not the main brain-racking concern. The real big decision concerns of course the investment in the equipment needed to implement the arrangements in the second phase. They lead to a complete rebuilding of the Library.

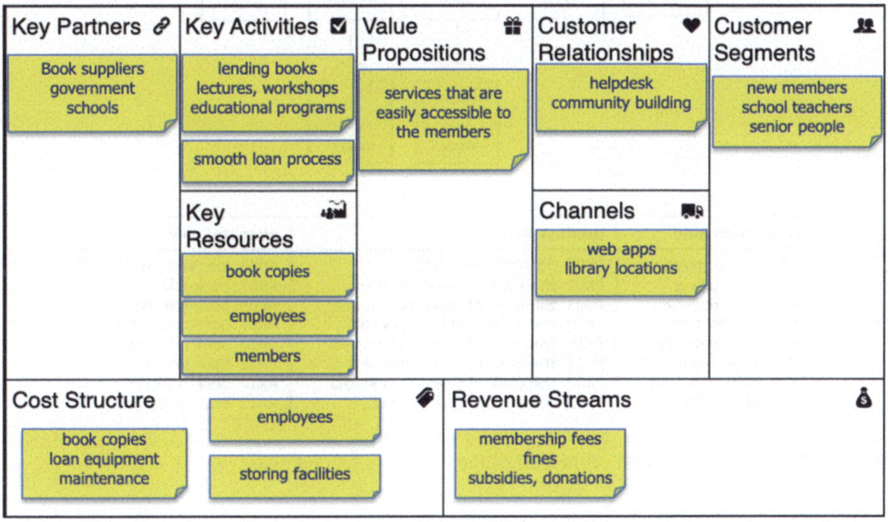

Fig. 13.11 BMC template for the Library—second phase

In Fig. 13.12, a CSD and the corresponding TPT show the possible consequences of the rebuilding for the organisation of the Library. We present it specifically to demonstrate that new transactor roles 'pop up' as subtrees under transactor roles TAR07 and TAR08 and that the new actor roles basically have to filled by human beings. The production acts of transactions TK10 through TK13 are as follows: PK10 (**the** book **of** [loan] **is** retrieved) means that the book copy of a specific loan is taken from the repository, PK11 (**the** book **of** [loan] **is** locked **in** [locker]) means that the book copy is put in a specific locker (where the member has access to), PK12 (**the** book **of** [loan] **is** unlocked **from** [locker]) means that the member of the loan has taken the book copy out of the locker and PK13 (**the** book **of** [loan] **is** put) means that the member has put the book copy on the conveyor belt. Actor roles AR10 and AR11 are filled by somebody in the Library, while actor roles AR12 and AR13 are filled by members.

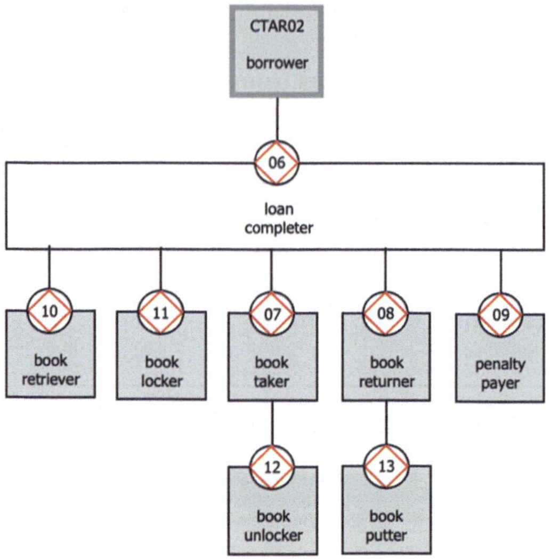

transaction kind	product kind	executor role
TK06 loan completing	PK06 [loan] **is** completed	AR06 loan completer
TK07 book taking	PK07 **the** book **of** [loan] **is** taken	AR07 book taker
TK08 book returning	PK08 **the** book **of** [loan] **is** returned	AR08 book returner
TK09 penalty paying	PK09 **the** penalty **of** [loan] **is** paid	AR09 penalty payer
TK10 book retrieving	PK10 **the** book **of** [loan] **is** retrieved	AR10 book retriever
TK11 book locking	PK11 **the** book **of** [loan] **is** locked	AR11 book locker
TK12 book unlocking	PK12 **the** book **of** [loan] **is** unlocked	AR12 book unlocker
TK13 book putting	PK13 **the** book **of** [loan] **is** put	AR13 book putter

Fig. 13.12 Possible extension of the CM of the Library—second phase

Of course, production acts PK10 and PK11 are performed by the equipment that is bought by the librarian and installed by the supplier, but the responsible person is in first instance not the supplier but somebody in the Library.

13.5 Applying the ETA Theory

In this section, we will elaborate the application of the EE implementation theory, or ETA theory, to the implementation of the second phase of the Library, thus to DAO steps 3 and 4. As discussed in Chap. 10, we have to address three implementation technologies: actor technology, production technology and coordination technology.

Regarding the actor technology, the first change is the filling of AR01 (membership starter) and AR04 (membership ender) by artefacts, namely, parts of LIS. As we have discussed extensively in Chap. 6, this arrangement is fine, as long as there are no problems, but the member must be able to address a human membership starter and a human membership ender if necessary. Because nothing is said about these humans in the description of the second phase in Sect. 11.2, we assume that the librarian is the human filler of AR01 and AR04. A similar reasoning holds for the second change, namely, the 'automation' of actor role AR06 (loan completer). Also here, there must ultimately be a human role filler. Most likely, it is also the librarian (cf. Table 13.2). The same holds for actor roles AR10 and AR11. As long as everything (in particular LIS and the new equipment) runs smoothly, the librarian doesn't need to act. But as soon as people need a human executor of these transactions, the assignment as exhibited by the APT (Actor role Position Table) in Table 13.2 applies. The self-activating actor roles AR03 and AR05 are added for completeness sake.

Table 13.2 APT of the Library (second phase)

Actor role/position	AR01	AR03	AR04	AR05	AR10	AR11
Librarian	X	X	X	X	X	X

Regarding the production technology, the major changes concern the tangible production kinds PK10 and PK11, which are enclosed in PK06 (cf. Fig. 13.12). Special equipment is needed to bring about products PK10 and PK11: books must be retrieved from the repository (PK10) and stored in lockers (PK11).

Regarding the coordination technology, most of the C-acts are performed digitally now and included in the new (extended) design of LIS. This is fully okay of course, provided that the complete transaction pattern (cf. Fig. 6.9) is followed. At this point, current practice is unfortunately rather stubborn. Rarely is the full CTP implemented. The common defence of this attitude is that exceptions never occur (!?).

According to the ETA theory, the implementation, which we discussed above, is followed by installation and operation. Installation of the library in the second phase means basically two things. One is the assignment of specific persons to actor roles, and the other is the installation of the software (LIS) and of the equipment to handle books. Even if there is only one person allowed to have the position of librarian, it is necessary to make this explicit and to fix operating hours.

The operation of the Library starts as soon as somebody wants to start or to end a membership or the librarian performs a request in a TK03 or a TK05 or a member starts a transaction TK06 (borrowing a book).

13.6 Conclusions

There are two clusters of business processes in the case Library, one about starting and ending memberships and one about borrowing books. The product category of the first is creating and changing (cf. Table 10.2), and the product category of the second is obtaining usufruct. So the reference model of libraries is a combination of the one for clubs or associations in general, like the case Volley (cf. Chap. 12), and the one for renting resources, like the case Rent-A-Car (cf. Chap. 15).

Applying Ockham's Razor leads to conceiving only two core entity types: membership and loan, as well as tailored subtypes, as shown in the OFD in Fig. 13.9. It is the perfect starting point for designing a database as part of the Library Information Systems (LIS), both in the first and in the second phase.

There are two issues that deserve special attention. One is the refund of membership fees in case of the ending of a membership by the librarian. As elucidated in Sect. 13.3, and more specifically in Fig. 13.4, refunding can elegantly be accommodated if one conceives it (quite properly) as revoking the initial promise to pay the last annual fee by the member. This illustrates once more the power of ontological thinking in addressing practical problems.

The other issue is the particular way in which the transactions TK07 (book taking) and TK08 (book returning) are enclosed in a transaction TK06, as shown in Fig. 13.8. It is a specialisation of the general case of seizing and releasing a (scarce) resource, as discussed in Chap. 10. Requiring that both the seizing and the releasing of a resource (in the case Library a book) are promised before the usufruct case (in the case Library a loan) can be promised emphasises that actions like checking in and checking out are not non-committal. In this way, no shows are discouraged effectively. Both the step TK07/pm and the step TK08/pm are 'serious' commitments. If necessary, they also offer sufficient ground for legal follow-ups.

Lastly, although the changes in the second phase of the Library are substantial improvements of the services that the Library provides to its (aspirant) members, the essential model of the Library organisation has not changed, obviously, since the essential model is independent of the applied implementation technologies. Still, this condition is a helpful anchor in changing an organisation.

References

1. Dietz, J. L. G., & Mulder, J. B. F. (2024). *Enterprise ontology—A human-centric approach to understanding the essence of organisation* (Enterprise engineering) (2nd ed.). Springer Nature.
2. Dietz, J. L. G. (2024). *DEMO-4 specification language*. Enterprise Engineering Institute.

Chapter 14
Exercise: Regional Police

An Exercise in Organisational Redesign and Digital Transformation

Abstract Regional Police Force is an exercise in understanding and applying the GSDP to a major change in the organisation of the Dutch Police. In the old situation, there was one state police organisation (in Dutch, *Rijkspolitie*) and a huge number of municipal police corpses. In the new situation, there are 25 autonomous regions, each divided into a number of districts. One of the largest regions is the region Rotterdam-Rijnmond. The initiative that the board of this region took was to align the many and various automated systems that were in use. To achieve this, the organisational unit ROSS was established.

14.1 Introduction

This chapter is based on the doctoral thesis of Hans Mulder[1] [1]. ROSS (Regional Operational Support Services) is an organisational unit in the region Rotterdam-Rijnmond, whose task was to guide the transition to a regional police force. It was decided by the board of ROSS that DEMO would be applied to the redesign of the operational organisation. The pragmatic approach that the police force took lead to a slightly adapted application of the DAO method in the GSDP, which we reproduce in Fig. 14.1. The adaptation concerns steps 1 and 2. The board of ROSS wanted to keep close contact with the current organisational structure, as shown in Fig. 14.2. Consequently, the design of the function model of the OS (DAO step 1) and the design of the ontological model of the OS (DAO step 2) were taken together. This

[1] Hans B.F. Mulder is co-author of the current book. He got his doctorate degree in 2006, after defending the doctoral thesis titled 'Rapid Enterprise Design' (written in Dutch).

J. L. G. Dietz, H. B. F. Mulder, *Enterprise Design Fundamentals*, The Enterprise Engineering Series, https://doi.org/10.1007/978-3-031-83262-8_14

was possible, thanks to the support of the design decisions by a Group Decision System (GDS).

Section 14.2 contains the description of the case. In Sect. 14.3, the approach taken is discussed, and in Sect. 14.4, the ontological model of the OS is presented. In Sect. 14.5, the redesign of the organisation is discussed. Section 14.6 contains the conclusions.

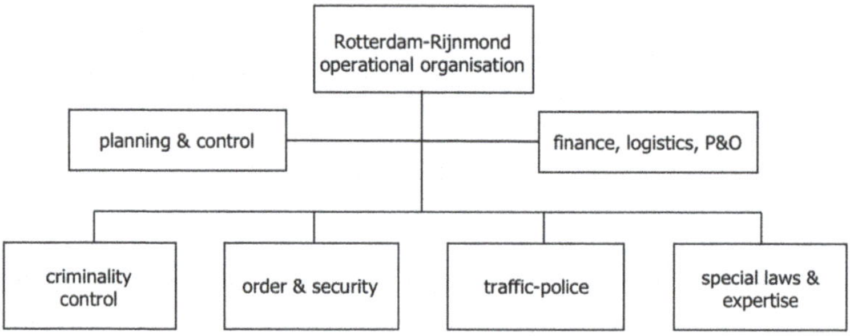

Fig. 14.1 The GSDP with the DAO steps

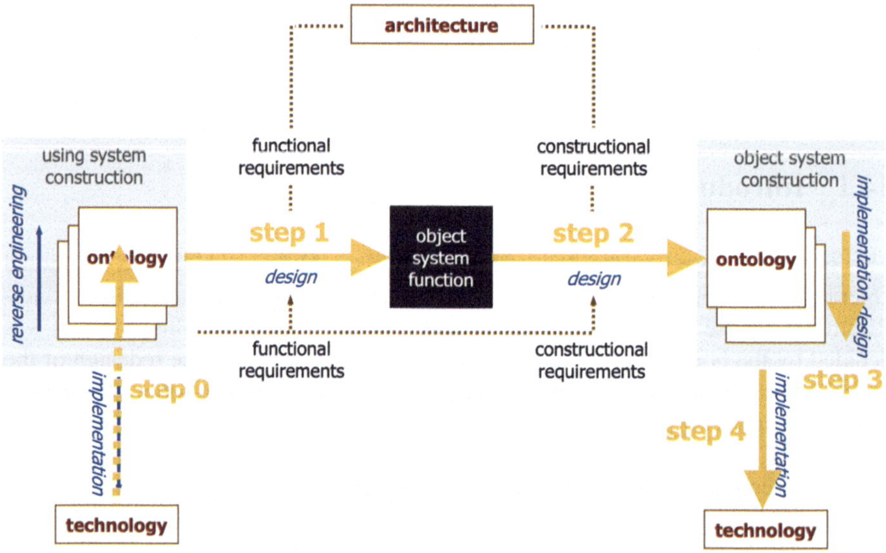

Fig. 14.2 The organisational structure of Ross

In 1993, the Dutch Police Force underwent a major reorganisation, which can be summarised as follows:
National Level
The national police force is led by the ***chief of police****. It is divided into 25 autonomous regions.*
Regional Level
The head of a region is the ***corps administrator****, normally the mayor of the largest municipality within a region. The corps administrator, the regional chief public prosecutor and all mayors of the municipalities within a region constitute together the regional police board.*
District Level
Each region is further divided into districts. Every district is headed by a ***district chief****, who manages the police operations at the district level.*
In a short time, the police officers understood that once you know the ***essential model*** *of your organisation, you are prepared for every change that comes on your path. Because the essential model is independent of region or district or any organisational structure…*

14.2 Description of the Case

In 1994, a major reorganisation took place within the Dutch Police Force. The existing national and municipal police departments were abolished. The nation became divided into 25 autonomous regions, each with its own police corps chief. Every region was divided into a number of districts, headed by a district chief. One mayor from a region (mostly the mayor of the largest municipality) is the corps administrator. He or she is responsible for the functioning of the regional police force. The operational management of a corps (region) lies in the hands of the regional chief, usually a chief commissioner.

Decisions on the main lines of policy are made by the regional board, consisting of the mayors of all municipalities in the region and the (regional) chief public prosecutor. The police force in this case study is one of the largest police regions in the country. In the mid-1990s, there were more than 5000 police officers for over 1.2 million people who live, work and engage in leisure activities in the area. The force is divided into nine districts and four regional services.

The information provision of police forces is a complex matter. The formerly autonomous ICT departments and information systems of the municipal and state police forces in the region were merged. The complexity of this operation was increased as municipal police systems processed data differently, using their own definitions. For example, in the case of 'car theft', most forces distinguish between motorcycles and cars, but six forces combine them under the term 'motor vehicles'.

In the police force of Rotterdam-Rijnmond, the regional responsibility for information provision was placed in the organisational unit Regional Operational Support

Services, abbreviated to ROSS. This reorganisation at the regional level made the consequences of different systems and data definitions clearly visible: duplicate and inconsistent data, discussions about responsibility for tasks, data and systems. As an example, a police manager would sometimes get ten different answers to the question of how many murders had occurred in the region.

Because of all these differences, the board of ROSS thought that the constitution of a well-functioning region Rotterdam-Rijnmond was mainly a matter of getting the municipal information systems aligned. To this end, a regional information manager was appointed. Accordingly, several information planning projects were carried out, among which are the application of James Martin's Information Engineering and Porter's Value Chain. Despite the long time (over a year) that these endeavours took, their results did not help the board of ROSS.

In 1996, the information manager read a paper by Hans Mulder in the national magazine *Automatisering Gids*. He seeks contact with the author of the paper. After several meetings of Hans Mulder and the information manager, the board of the corps Rotterdam-Rijnmond decided to adopt DEMO for the reorganisation of the region, including the redesign and alignment of the supporting information systems, which mostly originated from the municipalities.

14.3 The Approach Taken

The initial assignment was to develop an information plan for the unit Fingerprint Service within the Department of Criminality Control. This would be a pilot in order to investigate the suitability of DEMO for the problems at hand. The plan would outline the information needs and systems required to support the unit's operations. The project began with an inventory of the current situation, including existing information systems and processes. This was followed by a proposal for improvements, focusing on aligning the unit's information systems with the overall strategic objectives of the police force. The inventory and analysis of the business processes and information systems within the fingerprint service were investigated by a team of three researchers of the TU Delft: Jan Dietz, Hans Mulder and Victor van Reijswoud.[2] The first and the third member of the team had limited time to participate in the doctoral project of Hans Mulder, of course. Thanks to the applied methodology (DEMO), the job was completed within the agreed-upon 3 days (!) and presented to the ROSS board on 15 October 1996.

Based on the positive outcome of the first phase, a second study was conducted in which new strategic goals were formulated and in which the understanding of the organisation as well as its redesign would be done by applying the DEMO methodology. Based on the pilot at the Recognition Service, the board of ROSS was able to

[2]Victor E. van Reijswoud was an assistant professor at the time in the department of Information Systems Design (chaired by Jan Dietz). He was the supervisor of Hans Mulder's thesis.

make statements about the organisation, business processes and information processes. As a result of the pilot, the board of ROSS decided to commission the information planning for the entire region. The project started on 21 November 1996, with the task of delivering the results before 1 January 1997 so that the new information policy could be finalised in January. Thanks again to the methodology and the competence of the three researchers, the job was done in time.

During the information planning project, it became clear that the current structure and tasks of ROSS were no longer adequate. The management of ROSS therefore decided to redesign the organisation. The objective of the redesign was to create an organisation that was better able to support the districts in their operational work while also ensuring that the regional responsibilities were adequately fulfilled.

The first step in the redesign process was to redefine the tasks of ROSS. This was done in close consultation with the districts and the regional board. The main task of ROSS was redefined as 'providing operational support to the districts'. This involved tasks such as financial administration, personnel affairs, logistics and information processes. However, it was also decided that ROSS would no longer be responsible for certain tasks. These tasks would be transferred to the districts.

The next step was to redesign the organisation of ROSS. The aim was to create a more flexible and less bureaucratic organisation that was better able to respond to the needs of the districts. The new organisation was based on a matrix structure (cf. Sect. 14.6), with a distinction between functional areas (such as finance, personnel, logistics and information processes) and geographical areas (the districts). Each functional area was led by a manager who was responsible for the support provided to the districts in that area. The managers of the functional areas formed the board of ROSS.

The redesign of the organisation was accompanied by an extensive decision-making process. The management of ROSS involved all relevant stakeholders, including the districts, the regional board and the staff of ROSS. Several workshops were organised to discuss the redesign and to gather input from the stakeholders.

To support the decision-making process, a Group Decision Room (GDR) was set up at the TU Delft. This room houses an electronic Group Decision System (GDS) that allows participants to discuss issues and make decisions in a structured and efficient manner. The GDR was used to discuss the various design options for ROSS and to reach consensus on the final design.

The GDS sessions were attended by the board of ROSS, representatives of the districts, external consultants and the three researchers. The following redesign questions were put forward for decision-making:

1. Which current transaction kinds belong to the organisation?
2. Which new transaction kinds should be added to the organisation?
3. Which organisational units should be responsible for these transaction kinds?
4. How should the regional information systems be managed?

The discussion and analysis of these questions and the decision-making process are discussed in the next section.

14.4 Building the Ontological Models

As said, the board of ROSS wanted to maintain the current high-level organisational structure, which is exhibited in Fig. 14.2. Consequently, the four departments are indicated in the DEMO diagrams in Figs. 14.3, 14.4, 14.5, 14.6 and 14.7, represented by dashed-lined rectangles. First, the product kinds that constitute the relationships of the regional corps with its environment were identified. They are expressed in the CSD (Coordination Structure Diagram) in Fig. 14.3 and the TPT (Transactor Product Table) in Table 14.1. It took some abstraction effort from the commissioners to agree on this set of basic services that the regional police force offers to the environment (citizens, legal entities, corporate organisations, etc., as well as internally). It was also the first time that they had to express their thoughts in the concepts of actors and transactions. Therefore, it was also a learning process, which they enjoyed. For the guiding project team, it was amazing to watch how quickly the ontological concepts were adopted. It reinforced the conviction that these concepts are very natural.

As the initiators of the identified six transaction kinds, we simply have used six composite (environmental) actor roles, all of them called 'customer'. In the DEMO-4 notation (cf. Chap. 11), words between '[' and ']' are entity variables, whose instances are individual entities. So, for example, a concrete product PK2 is a specific advice, produced by a specific advice offerer. The actor who produced it is a person to whom the actor role AR2 (advice offerer) has been assigned based.

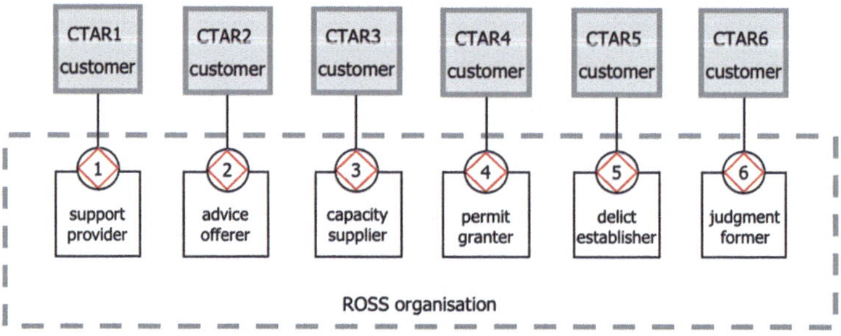

Fig. 14.3 CSD of the total operational organisation

Table 14.1 TPT of the total operational organisation

Transaction kind	Product kind	Executor role
TK1 support providing	PK1 [support] is provided	AR1 support provider
TK2 advice offering	PK2 [advice] is offered	AR2 advice offerer
TK3 capacity supplying	PK3 [capacity supply] is done	AR3 capacity supplier
TK4 permit granting	PK4 [permit] is granted	AR4 permit granter
TK5 delict establishing	PK5 [delict] is established	AR5 delict establisher
TK6 judgment forming	PK6 [judgment] is formed	AR6 judgment former

The six executor roles were of course new to the commissioners, but they could quickly relate them to existing employees and/or organisational units. They also soon liked the strong connection between authority and responsibility and their relationship with required competences.

Note that PK4 is specified as '[capacity supply] is done' instead of '[capacity] is supplied'. The reason is that the instances, so the individual products, must be clearly distinguishable.

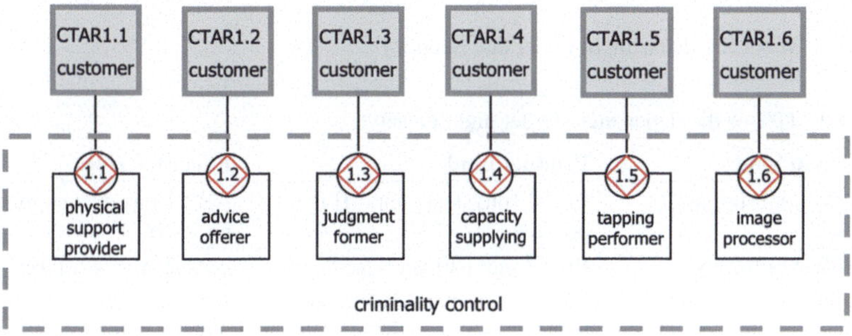

Fig. 14.4 CSD of the department Criminality Control

Table 14.2 TPT of the department Criminality Control

Transaction kind	Product kind	Executor role
TK1.1 physical support providing	PK1.1 [physical support] is provided	AR1.1 physical support provider
TK1.2 advice offering	PK1.2 [advice] is offered	AR1.2 advice offerer
TK1.3 judgment forming	PK1.3 [judgment] is formed	AR1.3 judgment former
TK1.4 capacity supplying	PK1.4 [capacity supply] is done	AR1.4 capacity supplier
TK1.5 tapping performing	PK1.5 [tapping] is performed	AR1.5 tapping performer
TK1.6 image processing	PK1.6 [image] is processed	AR1.6 image processor

The researchers were quite surprised by the quick adaptation of one of the fundaments of DEMO: the abstraction from individual employees and the focus on (elementary) actor roles as the units of authority and responsibility. This was not only encouraging, it demonstrated that the 'communication-centric' view of DEMO is just natural; the widespread 'information-centric' view is the villain (cf. Chap. 4).

The same exercise is done for the four departments that are exhibited in Fig. 14.2. The results are presented in Figs. 14.4, 14.5, 14.6 and 14.7 and in Tables 14.2, 14.3, 14.4 and 14.5.

The transaction kinds TK1.1 through TK1.4 are specialisations of TK1 through TK4. Transactions of these kinds are initiated by customers who are actors within CTAR1 through CTAR4.

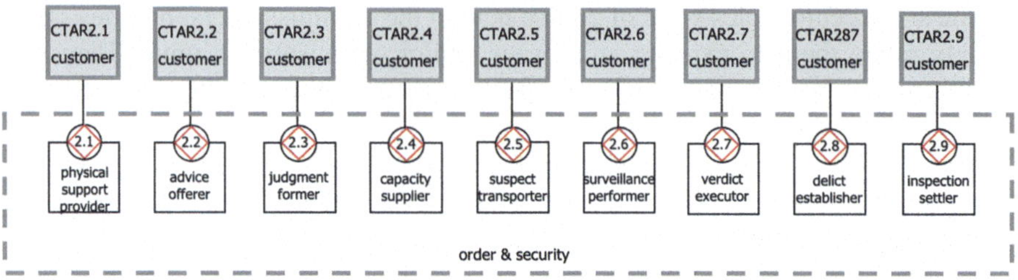

Fig. 14.5 CSD of the department Order and Security

Table 14.3 TPT of the department Order and Security

Transaction kind	Product kind	Executor role
TK2.1 physical support providing	PK2.1 [physical support] is provided	AR2.1 physical support provider
TK2.2 advice offering	PK2.2 [advice] is offered	AR2.2 advice offerer
TK2.3 judgment forming	PK2.3 [judgment] is formed	AR2.3 judgment former
TK2.4 capacity supplying	PK2.4 [capacity supply] is done	AR2.4 suspect transporter
TK2.5 suspect transporting	PK2.5 [suspect transport] is done	AR2.5 capacity supplier
TK2.6 surveillance performing	PK2.6 [surveillance] is performed	AR2.6 surveillance performer
TK2.7 verdict executing	PK2.7 [verdict] is executed	AR2.7 verdict executor
TK2.8 delict establishing	PK2.8 [delict] is established	AR2.8 delict establisher
TK2.9 inspection settling	PK2.9 [inspection] is settled	AR2.9 inspection settler

Likewise, the transaction kinds TK2.1, TK2.2, TK2.3 and TK2.4 are specialisations of, respectively, TK1, TK2, TK3 and TK4. Transactions of these kinds are initiated by customers who are actors within CTAR1, CTAR2, CTAR3 and CTAR4.

Similar remarks hold for the Cooperation Models that are expressed in the CSDs in Figs. 14.6 and 14.7 and in the TPTs in Tables 14.4 and 14.5.

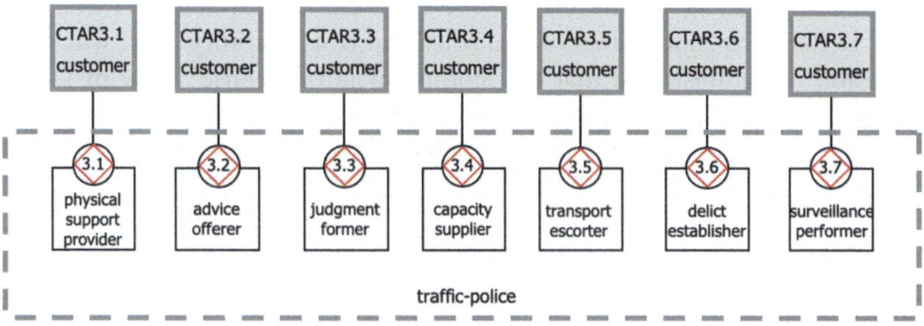

Fig. 14.6 CSD of the department Traffic Police

Table 14.4 TPT of the department Traffic Police

Transaction kind	Product kind	Executor role
TK3.1 physical support providing	PK3.1 [physical support] is provided	AR3.1 physical support provider
TK3.2 advice offering	PK3.2 [advice] is offered	AR3.2 advice offerer
TK3.3 judgment forming	PK3.3 [judgment] is formed	AR3.3 judgment former
TK3.4 capacity supplying	PK3.4 [capacity supply] is done	AR3.4 capacity supplier
TK3.5 transport escorting	PK3.5 [transport escort] is done	AR3.5 transport escorter
TK3.6 delict establishing	PK3.6 [delict] is established	AR3.6 delict establisher
TK3.7 surveillance performing	PK3.7 [surveillance] is performed	AR3.7 surveillance performer

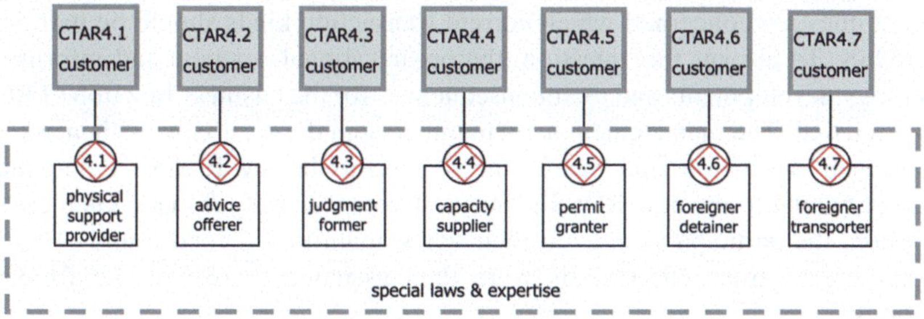

Fig. 14.7 CSD of the department Special Laws and Expertise

Table 14.5 TPT of the department Special Laws and Expertise

Transaction kind	Product kind	Executor role
TK4.1 physical support providing	PK4.1 [physical support] is provided	AR4.1 physical support provider
TK4.2 advice offering	PK4.2 [advice] is offered	AR4.2 advice offerer
TK4.3 judgment forming	PK4.3 [judgment] is formed	AR4.3 judgment former
TK4.4 capacity supplying	PK4.4 [permit] is granted	AR4.4 capacity supplier
TK4.5 permit granting	PK4.5 [permit] is granted	AR4.5 permit granter
TK4.6 foreigner detaining	PK4.6 [detain] is done	AR4.6 foreigner detainer
TK4.7 foreigner transporting	PK4.7 [transport] is performed	AR4.7 foreigner transporter

14.5 The Redesign of the Organisation

During the project, it became clear that the current structure and tasks of ROSS were no longer adequate. The management of ROSS therefore decided to redefine the tasks of ROSS and to redesign the organisation. The objective of the redesign was to create an organisation that was better able to support the districts in their operational work while also ensuring that the regional responsibilities were adequately fulfilled.

The first step in the redesign process was to redefine the tasks of ROSS. This was done in close consultation with the districts and the regional board. The main task of ROSS was redefined as 'providing operational support to the districts'. This involved tasks such as financial administration, personnel affairs, logistics and information processes. However, it was also decided that ROSS would no longer be responsible for certain tasks, such as the coordination of regional operations and the management of regional information systems. These tasks would be transferred to the districts. The following questions were put forward for the decision-making:

1. Which current transaction kinds belong to the new ROSS, and which do not?
2. Which new transaction kinds should be added to the new ROSS?
3. Which organisational units should be responsible for these transaction kinds?
4. How should the regional information systems be managed?

First Question

The first question concerned which current transaction kinds should be part of the new ROSS. To answer this question, the organisational, societal and information technology developments and their consequences for the business function of ROSS were discussed. The management team members and the experts were then asked to vote on each transaction kind: yes meant 'belongs to the new ROSS', and no meant 'does not belong to the new ROSS'. This first vote was not yet made visible. After discussion, the participants entered their votes again in a second round of voting. The considered transaction kinds were then assigned to one of the following categories:

- Retain (more than four 'yes' votes)—these transaction kinds are eligible to be included in the new ROSS.
- Discussion (three or four 'yes' votes)—these transaction kinds will be discussed and then voted on again.
- Eliminate (less than three 'yes' votes)—these transaction kinds do not belong to the new ROSS.

In the matrices in Fig. 14.8 (which are copied from [1]), the framework (left) and the plotting of the decisions on the framework (right) are shown. The top-left square and the bottom-right one are labeled 'further investigation'. The top-right square is labeled 'belongs to the business function', and the bottom-left one is labeled 'does not belong to the business function'. The square in the middle is labeled 'items for discussion'. The numbers at the right side of Fig. 14.8 are the same as the numbers in Tables 14.2, 14.3, 14.4 and 14.5. Numbers that do not occur in these tables are discussed later.

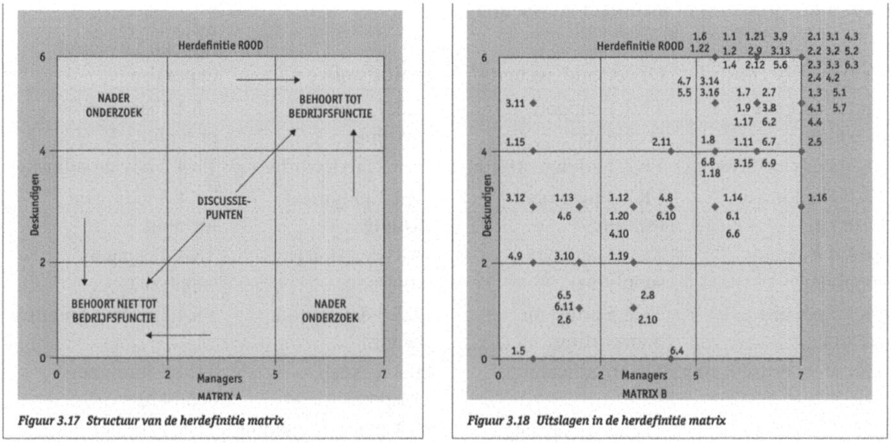

Fig. 14.8 The plotting of the transaction kinds on the business functions

Eliminating a transaction kind does not mean that the transaction kind is redundant, but rather that it should be assigned elsewhere within or perhaps outside the police force. For all transaction kinds in the 'discussion' category (middle square), the managers and experts were asked to reason and discuss them and then take possibly a new position (double-loop learning).

The Other Questions

The second, third and fourth questions were also dealt with by the board of ROSS, but we skip the decision-making about them, as these decisions had less impact than those regarding the first question.

14.6 The Redesign of the Operational Organisation

The next step was to redesign the organisation of ROSS. The aim was to create a more flexible and less bureaucratic organisation that was better able to respond to the needs of the districts. The new organisation is primarily based on the communication (through executing transactions) between the organisational units and the environment, since the police participants were convinced that this would lead to an optimal structure. Meanwhile, new transaction kinds were identified. The final list is presented in Table 14.6.

Table 14.6 Final list of identified transaction kinds

Criminality control	Order and security	Traffic police	Special laws and expertise
TK1.1 support providing	TK2.1 support providing	TK3.1 support providing	TK4.1 support providing
TK1.2 advice offering	TK2.2 advice offering	TK3.2 advice offering	TK4.2 advice offering
TK1.3 judgment forming	TK2.3 judgment forming	TK3.3 judgment forming	TK4.3 judgment forming
TK1.4 capacity supplying	TK2.4 capacity supplying	TK3.4 capacity supplying	TK4.4 capacity supplying
TK1.5 reward granting	TK2.5 arrestant transporting	TK3.5 deposition placing	TK4.5 permit granting
TK1.6 expertise hiring	TK2.6 educating	TK3.6 excep. transporting	TK4.6 foreigner detaining
TK1.13 tapping performing	TK2.7 surveilling	TK3.7 penalty issuing	TK4.7 foreigner transporting
TK1.15 destroying	TK2.8 verdict executing	TK3.8 surveilling	TK4.9 educating
TK1.18 image processing	TK2.9 penalty issuing	TK3.9 object investigating	
TK1.19 equipment hiring	TK2.10 examining		
	TK2.11 securing on smell		

Next to the transaction kinds in Table 14.6, there were another nine ones identified between the four departments. Because of these cross-departmental relationships, the organisational structure of ROSS could not be purely hierarchical (division structure). After several discussions in the board, one agreed on a matrix structure, one of the types that are identified and discussed by Mintzberg in [2]. The managers of the functional areas, as depicted in Fig. 14.2, form the management team of ROSS.

The matrix organisation is often characterised as an evolution of the machine bureaucracy, in which projects play a dominant role. Working in projects is a response to the inability of the machine bureaucracy to handle special tasks that require a quick response. In a project organisation, temporary groups of specialists work under the leadership of a specially appointed project manager on a clearly defined task. The project groups function to some extent as mini-organisations within the larger organisation while utilising the specialists from the functional departments of the overall organisation. Specialists in the projects have a dual responsibility: they report to the project manager regarding the project and have a hierarchical responsibility for general functioning. The strength of the matrix organisation is that it enables large organisations to function in a moderately dynamic environment where complex tasks must be performed.

The main disadvantage of the matrix organisation is that it is often perceived by employees and middle management as a confusing organisational form. In contrast to all other configurations where a clear hierarchical responsible structure is defined, this is not the case in the matrix configuration.

In the discussion of the research results with the management of ROSS, during the concluding phase of the case study, the characteristics of this organisational structure were addressed. The researcher concluded that this configuration was perceived by management as appropriate for the dynamics of the environment, the nature of the business processes, the applied technology as well as the skills and competencies of the employees.

Regarding the redesign of the organisational structure, Hans Mulder drew on existing theories and methods. Specifically, the work of Mintzberg [2] was applied in analysing and designing the organisational structure. Organisational configurations are not stable over the years. As organisations age, adopt new technology and/or grow in workforce size, their structures change. Organisations with a simple configuration need to change as they grow. Depending on the environment in which they operate and the products or services they provide, the simple configuration is transformed into a professional or machine bureaucracy. Bureaucracies are converted into divisional structures or matrix organisations to respond to the rapidly changing demands of the market. Simple structures can also develop into adhocracies or virtual organisations.

Modern Internet technologies, in particular, make this direction of organisational development feasible. Greiner [3] characterises organisational growth in several stages, where evolution and revolution alternate. In designing the new organisational structure, the focus was particularly on desired characteristics. Figure 3.23 in [1] summarises the properties of the organisational configurations discussed, based on four characteristics: specialisation, formalisation, centralisation and the environment and nature of the organisation.

The redesign process was evaluated by comparing the results against the initial expectations. The evaluation showed that the DEMO methodology, with its focus on transactions and business functions, was effective in analysing and redesigning the organisation. The use of the Group Decision Room also proved to be a valuable tool in the decision-making process, enabling a high level of participation and consensus among the stakeholders.

The new structure was implemented within a short period, with the entire redesign process, including decision-making, being completed in just a few weeks. This rapid and participatory approach to organisational design can be characterised as 'Rapid Enterprise Design' (RED) [1].

14.7 Conclusions

The redesign of the region Rotterdam-Rijnmond and of ROSS was carried out with the active participation of both the staff and the management. Thanks to the GDR, where many meetings of the ROSS board have been held, the decision-making was a transparent matter. Looking back at these meetings, we think that using a GDS throughout a change project simplifies the formal design process as expressed in the GSDP in Fig. 14.1. It allows for a combined execution of steps 1 and 2, as we have experienced in this project. It also supports strongly consensus building among the stakeholders. Although the board members were inclined to 'fall back' to the organisational structures they were familiar with, they were at the same time able to appreciate and assess the ontological model of the new organisation (the OS in the GSDP in Fig. 14.1). Based on this ontological model, they were able to devise a new organisational structure for the regional police force.

Given the environmental characteristics of ROSS, which are considered complex and volatile, the current divisional structure of ROSS was deemed unsuitable. A choice for the simple structure of Mintzberg, as well as the machine and professional bureaucracy, was also ruled out. A choice for a virtual network organisation was not considered, leaving the adhocracy and the matrix organisation as the remaining options. The board decided on a matrix organisation because the formalisation within the structure and the functional specialisation of the matrix organisation were well aligned with the nature of the business processes, the applied technology and the skills and competencies of the employees.

The RED method, with its emphasis on participation and rapid decision-making, proved to be effective in addressing the challenges of organisational redesign. The experience gained in the ROSS project provides valuable insights for the further development and application of the RED method.

References

1. Mulder, J. B. F. (2006). Rapid enterprise design. In *Faculteit Elektrotechniek, Wiskunde en Informatica* (p. 160). Delft University of Technology.
2. Mintzberg, H. (1983). *Structures in fives: Designing effective organisations*. Prentice Hall.
3. Greiner, L. (1972). Evolution and revolution as organisations grow. *Harvard Business Review*.

Chapter 15
Real-Life Applications of DEMO

Abstract A number of real-life applications of Enterprise Design are presented, varying in size and impact and in their industrial area of concern. The selected applications are Direct Childcare Financing (Sect. 15.2), Redesigning an Organisation (Sect. 15.3), Redesigning Asset Management (Sect. 15.4), Business Information Security (Sect. 15.5), BPMN Patterns for Process Design (Sect. 15.6), DEMO in Airline Alliances (Sect. 15.7), Designing the My Number System (Sect. 15.8), Developing Process Ownership (Sect. 15.9) and The Sangikyo Case (Sect. 15.10). All applications are reported in the STARR framework.

15.1 Overview

In the next sections, nine appealing real-life applications of DEMO are presented and discussed, selected from a larger collection of interesting practical studies. The next studies are reported in this chapter:

Section 15.2: Direct Childcare Financing
Section 15.3: Redesigning an Organisation
Section 15.4: Redesigning Asset Management
Section 15.5: Business Information Security
Section 15.6: BPMN Patterns for Process Design
Section 15.7: DEMO in Airline Alliances
Section 15.8: Designing the My Number System
Section 15.9: Developing Process Ownership
Section 15.10: The Sangikyo Case

All applications are reported in the STARR framework (Situation, Task, Approach, Results, Reflection):

The **Situation** in which the case is positioned. It includes, but is not limited to, the context of the case organisation (e.g. market, competition), the characteristics of

J. L. G. Dietz, H. B. F. Mulder, *Enterprise Design Fundamentals*, The Enterprise Engineering Series, https://doi.org/10.1007/978-3-031-83262-8_15

the case organisation (facts and figures), its challenges and opportunities, important stakeholders, the reason why the project was initiated, a history of earlier attempts, etc.

The **Task** that has been conducted. It includes, but is not limited to, the goals and objectives of the project, its budget and timelines, special requirements, the roles of the various stakeholders, etc.

The **Approach** taken to conduct the task. It includes, but is not limited to, the method used, the various steps in this method, the paradigm or underlying philosophy of the approach/method, the products and deliverables, the way in which the project was planned and managed, the risk management approach and the tools used, etc.

The **Results** of the project. It includes, but is not limited to, the actual benefits for the case organisation and the stakeholders, a cost/benefit analysis, the extent to which the case organisation was actually transformed, etc.

A **Reflection** on the case. It includes, but is not limited to, a discussion about the faced challenges; the way in which the existing methods, frameworks, etc. aided in dealing with these challenges; omissions and limitations found; thoughts on how to 'fix' such omissions and limitations, etc.

Right after the section head, the name(s) and the email address(es) of the contributor(s) is/are mentioned, so that one can directly make contact if one desires to do so. All references to publications are put together at the end of the chapter.

All sections are illustrations of what Enterprise Design entails, where design is … *devising courses of action aimed at changing existing situations into preferred ones* … as articulated by Herbert Simon [1]. Notably Sects. 15.3, 15.7 and 15.10 report on making the employees in an organisation aware that they are having social interaction and that this is the core of their business processes. Changing only the mindset of the people involved is rightly called a matter of redesigning the organisation.

15.2 Direct Childcare Financing

Ingrid Theuwissen, theuwissen@live.nl

Situation

From 2014, the Dutch governmental agency DUO has been working on a system called 'Direct Childcare Financing' (Dutch abbreviation, DFK), which replaces the existing Childcare Benefit. With DFK, the chain was reversed: The childcare organisation requests the entitlement to reimbursement and sends the invoice to DUO every month. The parents pay their contribution to DUO, and then DUO pays the entire amount to the childcare organisation. The purpose of this change was to offer parents earlier certainty about their right to childcare reimbursement, reduce repayments, simplify the system and minimise errors.

Implementing DFK had become a complex process. Challenges came from various stakeholders, including the childcare organisations (which had varying automation levels), both digitally skilled and unskilled parents, software suppliers (from sole proprietors to professional companies) and associations representing parents and childcare organisations.

Task

DUO was appointed by the Ministry of SZW (Social Affairs and Employment) to implement DFK, the work taking place from 2015 to 2018. The program at DUO can be broadly divided into two phases: the preparatory phase and the realisation phase. In the preparatory phase, the project organisation was set up, and DUO was deeply involved in the legislative process. The realisation phase consisted of implementing the new system and continued involvement in the legislative process.

Approach

During the preparatory phase, so-called E-labs were set up. In these labs, DUO, in conjunction with the Ministry of SZW, gave parents, childcare organisations and industry associations insight into what the new direct funding system was about.

A working prototype was created to demonstrate the new system. This prototype was used to demonstrate through 'storytelling' how the new system would operate. Scenarios were enacted based on fictitious characters: the parents Harry and Christien and their children Barry and Femke. Events included Harry finding a new job, Femke attending childcare for the first time and a failed automatic payment of their personal contribution because Harry impulsively purchased an overly expensive car. This hasty purchase caused so many problems that Harry and Christien ended up getting divorced.

To incorporate a scenario into a prototype, there needs to be an understanding of the sequence in which the steps in the process occur, something that wasn't necessary in the preparatory phase of a program. Fortunately, it was possible to draft an initial version of the Cooperation Model (CM) of DFK based on the draft legislative texts.

It was also possible to find in these legislative texts the essential product kinds and the corresponding transactor roles. The entire Scope of Interest (SoI) is depicted in the CSD in Fig. 15.1. The primary transactor roles (of which the boxes are coloured white) are the focus; these are the roles for which DUO is responsible.

Results

Displaying the scenarios in a working prototype and discussing them in workshops helped identify potential implementation issues early in the legislative process. It also helped build support.

There are numerous questions in the preparatory phase of a system change, but not all can be answered immediately. First, the primary ambiguities must be clarified, such as defining the product kind and understanding responsibilities in the chain. The uncertainties that emerge while setting up the CM are usually the first and most critical questions to be addressed. A CM is expressed in a TPT (Transactor Product Table) and a CSD (Coordination Structure Diagram).

In Table 15.1, the TPT of DFK is presented. It is a list of identified transaction kinds, each with a specification of the corresponding product kind and the corresponding executing actor role. A transaction kind and its executing actor role constitute a transactor role. Transactor roles are represented in a CSD by the transaction shape, which is a diamond in a disk, half 'sunken' in the box of an actor role.

Table 15.1 Transactor product table DFK

Transaction kind	Product kind	Executing actor role
TK01 concluding childcare agreement	PK01 [childcare agreement] **is** concluded	AR01 childcare agreement concluder
TK10 establishing right to compensation	PK10 right to compensation **for** [childcare agreement] **is** given	AR10 right to compensation establisher
TK11 agreeing to provide compensation	PK11 agreement to provide compensation **for** [childcare agreement] **is** given	AR11 compensation agreement giver
TK20 determining right of reduced income scheme	PK20 right of reduced income scheme **for** [childcare agreement] in [year] **is** determined	AR20 right of reduced income scheme determiner
TK30 managing compensation	PK30 [compensation management] **for** [month] **is** done	AR30 compensation manager
TK31 paying compensation	PK31 compensation **for** [childcare agreement] **in** [month] **is** paid	AR31 compensation payer
TK32 determining cost distribution	PK32 cost distribution **for** [childcare agreement] in [month] **is** determined	AR32 cost distribution determiner
TK33 paying parent contribution	PK33 parent contribution **for** [childcare agreement] **in** [month] **is** paid	AR33 parent contribution payer

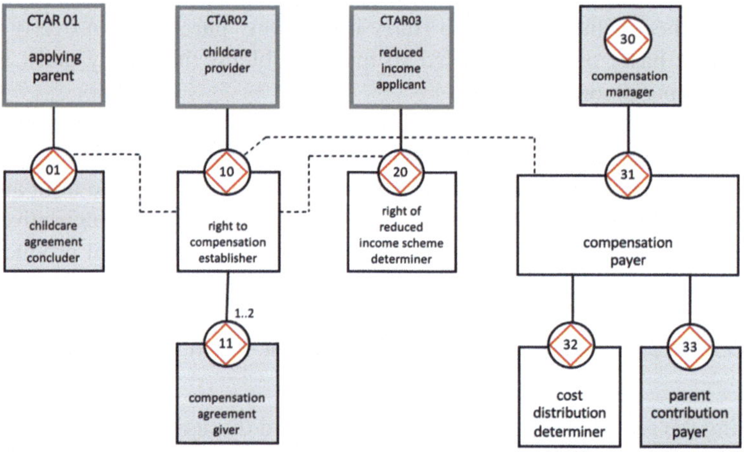

Fig. 15.1 Coordination structure diagram of DFK

In Fig. 15.1, the CSD of DFK is shown. The parents (CTAR01) enter into an agreement (TK01) with a childcare organisation for the care of their child. For DUO, TK01 is outside the focus but is part of the Scope of Interest (SoI).

The childcare organisation offering the care (CTAR02) applies to DUO for the right to compensation (TK10) based on the TK01 agreement. Being eligible for a compensation means that the government contributes to childcare costs. To qualify, the parent, any potential partner, the intended childcare organisation and the concluded agreement must meet the requirements set in the law. One such requirement is that the parent and any potential partner must agree to the provision of the compensation (TK11). Along with this right, the amount of government contribution per hour and the maximum number of childcare hours per year that the government will contribute are determined.

The amount of government contribution depends on the combined income of the parent and their partner from 2 years prior. In cases of a significant drop in income afterwards, this can be adjusted to consider the current year's income. The parent or their partner (CTAR03) can apply to DUO for permission to use the reduced income scheme (TK20).

Each month, the childcare organisation (AR30) will send an invoice to DUO, requesting compensation for the child's childcare costs (TK31). The cost distribution for that month is then determined (TK32): determining which portion the parent pays and which portion the government covers. DUO asks the parent to pay their monthly contribution (TK33), after which DUO pays the total invoice amount to the childcare organisation (TK31).

The Quality of Service is determined for each transaction kind, and there are clear differences. For instance, for TK10 (establishing right to compensation), accuracy and diligence are vital, whereas speed is crucial for TK31 (paying compensation). Moreover, TK10 (establishing right to compensation) is infrequent and depends on many production facts produced outside of DUO. In contrast, for TK31 (compensation paying), childcare organisations send large volumes of cost summaries to DUO at the end of the month. Following that, direct debits for parental contributions and payments to childcare organisations must occur quickly.

Reflection

DEMO makes complexity manageable. Applying DEMO allowed me, as a business analyst, to be effective in a large governmental project where the laws and regulations were still in development. A program like DFK is an environment where there are many uncertainties that were resolved over time.

Looking back, the changes in policy that took place during the course of the program rarely led to changes in the Cooperation Model of DEMO. When they did, they were mostly expansions. With DEMO, it was possible to maintain an overview in such an environment. Having and maintaining this overview allowed me, as a business analyst, to be effective.

15.3 Redesigning an Organisation

Joop de Jong, jdjong@mprise.nl

Introduction

This section is based on an interview that the authors had with Joop de Jong, the founder of Mprise, an enterprise that provides ERP services to small and medium-sized companies (SMEs). In this interview, De Jong reflects on his extensive experience in organisational development and his efforts to translate theoretical knowledge into practical applications, with a particular focus on small and medium-sized enterprises.

Joop de Jong has also been professor in information management at Hogeschool Utrecht. He holds a doctoral degree at Delft University of Technology. His doctoral thesis is about implementing the essential model of DEMO [2].

Situation

Mprise operates in a competitive market where the demand for effective and efficient business processes is continuously increasing. In this environment, it was necessary to develop a culture of 'ownership', where employees are not only accountable for their tasks but also engaged in the overall success of the company. This was complicated because of the diversity of employees at Mprise, ranging from highly educated consultants to people with more practical backgrounds.

Consequently, the situation in which De Jong found himself was complex. His work at Hogeschool Utrecht and his involvement with Mprise exposed him to various challenges inherent to the academic world and the business sector. At Mprise, he had a key position in defining actor roles and the corresponding responsibilities.

Task

The task De Jong undertook was to drive a transformation within the organisation by applying the theoretical concepts of DEMO in a way that was understandable and useful for all employees. This required not only a revision of existing processes and structures but also a fundamental shift in how employees perceived their roles and responsibilities. He had to develop a framework in which theoretical knowledge could be transformed into practical tools and strategies for day-to-day work.

To achieve this, De Jong needed to develop clear role definitions that went beyond traditional job descriptions. He introduced a system where actor roles were defined based on their added value to the organisation. This meant that each role needed a clearly defined output that contributed to the company's overall objectives.

Approach

The approach taken involved several strategic steps. First, De Jong organised workshops to engage employees in the process of defining actor roles. These workshops were aimed at providing employees with a deep understanding of their roles within the broader context of the organisation and on how filling these roles would contribute to the success of Mprise.

Second, during the workshops, there was a focus on the concept of ownership. Employees were encouraged to reflect on their responsibilities and on how they could contribute to achieving the enterprise's goals. This was supported by Mprise's cultural values, such as 'People First' and 'Sharp Minds', which emphasise that every employee is valued from day one on and that expertise and continuous learning are key to the Mprise culture.

Additionally, the ‘lifeworld’ versus ‘system world’ model was introduced, a concept that helps bridging the gap between employees’ daily experiences and the formal structures of the organisation (Ownership). By showing employees how their work is meaningful both informally (lifeworld) and formally (system world), De Jong was able to foster a deeper level of engagement and understanding.

Results

The workshops and the new way of working (from clearly defined actor roles) resulted in greater employee engagement and better communication regarding roles and responsibilities within the organisation. The concept of ownership became deeply embedded in the organisational culture, leading to higher satisfaction among both employees and customers.

Clarifying roles and responsibilities not only helped Mprise operate more efficiently but also increased overall productivity and customer satisfaction. Employees felt more responsible for their work and were better able to proactively solve problems and make improvements. This led to a culture where learning and improvement were central, as emphasised already in the competency models of Mprise.

Furthermore, De Jong observed that by defining clear actor roles and the corresponding responsibilities, it was possible to establish a system of continuous competence development, which is crucial for the organisation’s further growth and professionalisation.

Reflection

De Jong reflects on the challenges he encountered during this process, including resistance to change and the need to make complex theoretical concepts understandable for a diverse workforce. He acknowledges that while the process of change was difficult, the results justify the efforts. He emphasises that it is important to consider both the lifeworld and the system world when implementing organisational changes and that the notion of ownership is crucial.

A key lesson De Jong learned from this experience is that change cannot be imposed from the top down to the work floor. It requires a collective effort and clear communication about why change is necessary and how it benefits both employees and the organisation as a whole. He highlights the importance of a connective leadership style, where leaders act as facilitators who create the conditions for success and growth.

Joop de Jong’s work at Mprise illustrates the power of a structured and people-centric approach to organisational development. By creating a culture of ownership and responsibility, and by translating theoretical knowledge into practical tools, he has demonstrated how companies can grow and adapt in an ever-changing market. His experiences offer valuable insights for other leaders and organisations striving for sustainable improvements and employee engagement.

15.4 Redesigning Asset Management

Peter Kuipers, peter@eaxpertise.nl
Marien Krouwel, marien.krouwel@make-it-right.nl

Situation

Within Rijkswaterstaat (The Dutch Department of Waterways and Public Works, part of the Ministry of Infrastructure and Water Management[1]), asset management concerns the construction, maintenance and operation of physical infrastructure objects, such as bridges, locks and tunnels, that keep the Netherlands dry and safe. The responsibility of asset management is further subdivided into separate organisational units (cf. Fig. 15.2): Major Projects and Maintenance (MPM) and Programmes, Projects and Maintenance (PPM) are responsible for the construction and maintenance of assets, while Traffic and Water Management (TWM) is responsible for its operations, such as taking measures to (locally) improve traffic flow. All three organisational units are subdivided into domains: *Water Management*, *Road Management* and *Shipping Traffic Management*. In practice however, there is much overlap in the asset management processes as well as in the required support from ICT and other supporting services. It has been shown that a lot of coordination is needed between the three operational domains as well as between the different organisational units, and questions arise whether the current organisational structures facilitate efficient operations and support.

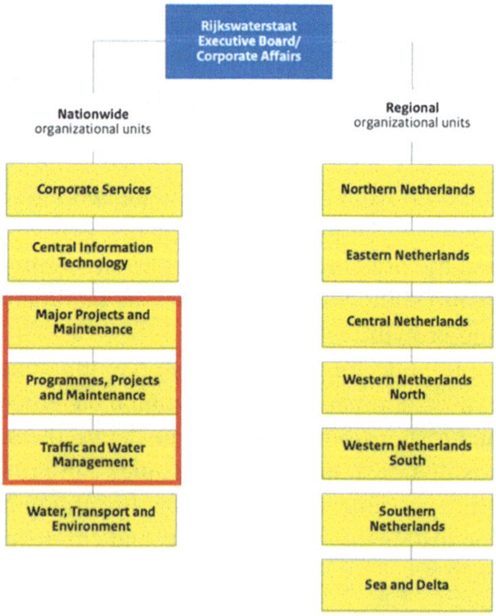

Fig. 15.2 Rijkswaterstaat high level organisational structure

[1] https://www.rijkswaterstaat.nl/en

The focus of this project is TWM (asset operations) and MPM and PPM (asset construction and maintenance), as indicated by the red-coloured border.

Task

The program called 'Asset management 2.0' is aimed at improving asset management, encompassing both the construction, maintenance and operations of assets and its supporting ICT landscape. The main task was thus to design an efficient organisational structure and effective ICT systems to support the asset management processes. In order to do this, it was necessary to get a good but global understanding of the asset management processes within MPM, PPM and TWM, as well as to design a target organisational structure that has the potential to be more efficient than the current one, along with its implications for ICT.

Approach

As the function of Rijkswaterstaat, and of the organisational units in scope specifically, does not change, the function model was not created. Instead, a DEMO ontological model of the different asset management processes was created for the three domains (Water Management, Road Management and Shipping Traffic Management). Based on these models, overlapping processes were identified and abstracted, resulting in a CSD (cf. Fig. 15.3) and the corresponding TPT (cf. Table 15.2). The models show that asset management, after carefully considering both the static constructional and dynamic operational asset facts, consists of building (including renewing and remediating) assets and deploying operational measures. The latter is modelled as the starting and stopping of a measure kind, such as operating a bridge or lock and closing (and opening) a road or waterway, where different priorities may be influencing the actual completion of those measures.

Additionally, an analysis was made for crisis situations, which unfortunately happen sometimes. Examples include the malfunctioning of a dike, bridge or lock, but also resolving after a vessel has crashed into a bridge, taking measures for (expected) flooding or dealing with water pollution.

Table 15.2 TPT of asset management within Rijkswaterstaat

Transaction kind	Product kind	Executing actor role
TK05 asset managing	PK05 asset managing for [period] **is** done	AR05 asset manager
TK06 asset building	PK06 [asset] **is** built	AR06 asset builder
TK13 measure kind starting	PK13 [measure kind] **is** started	AR13 measure kind starter
TK15 measure kind stopping	PK15 [measure kind] **is** stopped	AR15 measure kind stopper
TK16 measure completing	PK16 [measure] **is** completed	AR16 measure completer
TK21 measure priority determining	PK21 priority **of** [measurement] **is** determined	AR21 measure priority determiner

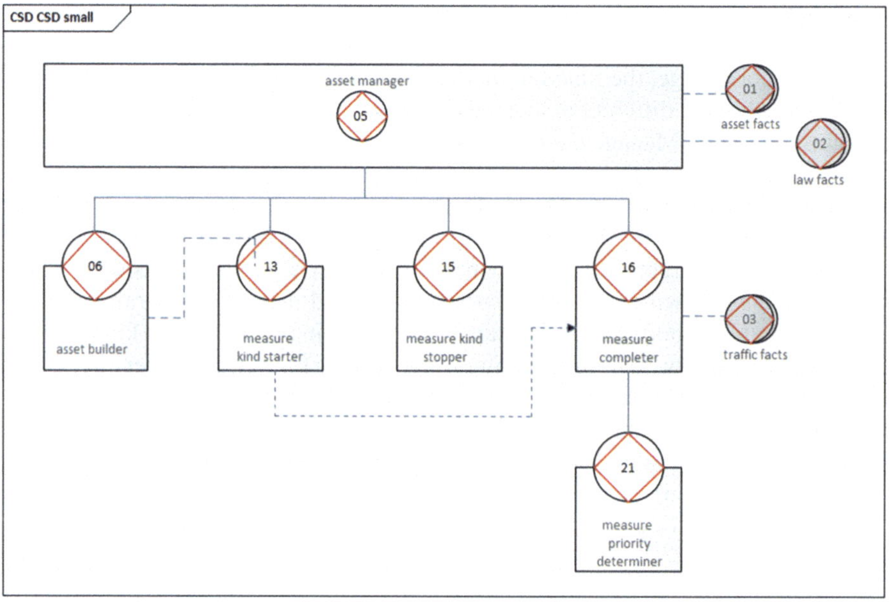

Fig. 15.3 DEMO CSD of asset management within Rijkswaterstaat

Results

In analysing the different ontological models for the three domains, it turned out that most of the asset management processes could be abstracted, with minor differences between the three domains. It was also shown that both the construction, maintenance and operations of assets within the three domains has exactly the same ontological model and that, for example, the concepts of road inspector and operator hold for both roads and waterways.

It was also shown that in case of an emergency, the ontological model does not change but that some responsibilities may be shifted to other functionaries or even to other organisations. Also, the response time (time between request and execution of a transaction) may differ in such situations.

This analysis has laid the foundation for a renewed organisation structure for asset management as well as a design of the ICT landscape, in which the separation between the three domains is less dominant than currently. It is expected that this will improve efficiency and effectiveness of both the organisation and ICT, in both operational asset management and crisis solving processes.

Reflection

The DEMO ontological model helped in showing that the differences between the three domains were not as big as initially expected. It also helped in identifying critical differences, as well as the current allocation of responsibilities. From there, with the help of (parts of) Enterprise Design, and implementation details specifically, it was possible to design a future organisation structure and supporting ICT systems, in which the current domains (Water Management, Road Management and Shipping Traffic Management) play a less dominant role. This has the potential to improve collaboration and learn from each other over the different domains. It is also expected that it can decrease ICT costs, as similar processes can now be supported with a single software product.

Moreover, it shows the dependencies between constructional and operational activities within asset management, where operations may put additional requirements when designing and building an asset. This dependency stresses the need to involve operations (TWM) early in the design process of an asset (MPM and PPM).

The DEMO ontological model also helped in showing that the processes and responsibilities do not really change in case of a crisis, only the allocation of the responsibilities and the Quality of Service change. Although in such situations it is often desirable to have clarity on who is responsible, separated from the operational organisation, the DEMO ontological model showed that it is not needed to build a separate ICT landscape to deal with crises. The Enterprise Design approach did help in identifying the needs to be flexible in authorisation with regard to the ICT landscape, to allow different users and parties to deal with a crisis effectively.

15.5 Business Information Security

Yuri Bobbert, yuri.bobbert@uantwerpen.be
Hans Mulder, hans.mulder@viagroep.nl

Situation

The research by Bobbert and Mulder [3] reported on in this section addresses the complexities and challenges in implementing and maintaining Business Information Security (BIS) within enterprises. Historically, organisations rely on IT security controls and spreadsheets to manage and report on information security, which proved insufficient due to their limited scope, subjective nature and siloed implementation. This fragmented approach challenges ensuring visibility, control and assurance for business information security [4]. The need for a more integrated and objective approach led to developing a new artefact, the SecuriMeter, to improve visibility, control and assurance in BIS through an integrated dashboard and reporting tool.

Task

The primary task addressed in this research is developing and validating a new artefact to enhance BIS management. The goal is to move away from silo-based spreadsheet management to a more integrated and effective solution providing comprehensive visibility, control and assurance for BIS.

The three main tasks involved in this research are:

Literature Review and Expert Consultation. A comprehensive review is conducted of existing BIS frameworks. In addition, experts are consulted to identify key parameters and requirements for the new artefact.

Development of the SecuriMeter. Design and engineer an artefact that integrates various BIS functionalities, including the ability to capture, measure and report on BIS maturity across multiple enterprise levels (strategic, tactical and operational).

Validation and Comparison. Validate the artefact through case studies and compare its effectiveness against existing tools, such as the ISF Accelerator, using predefined criteria, under the supervision of the University.[2]

Approach

The approach taken during this research consists of the next elements:

1. Using the Design and Engineering Methodology for Organisations (DEMO) to develop an ontological model for BIS and to engineer the SecuriMeter artefact. The Design Science Research (DSR) Approach was used over a span of 10 years; the authors engaged in DSR to create and refine the SecuriMeter. This process involved iterative cycles of designing, testing and improving the tool based on real-world applications and feedback.
2. Case Studies: The development and effectiveness of the SecuriMeter were illustrated through three detailed case studies: a government entity, a financial firm and a utility company. These case studies demonstrated how the tool was used in different organisational contexts to improve BIS practices and to assess its practical contributions and effectiveness in real-world scenarios.

[2]Videos with Artefact Demonstrations. Based on criteria, two video demonstrations are recorded and delivered: SecuriMeter video, accessible via: https://youtu.be/wBNg2oyK4c4. Recorded on 1 August 2017 in Ede. ISF Accelerator video, accessible via: https://youtu.be/EXLyGUFDwu0. Recorded on 18 July 2017 in Nieuwegein.

3. Comparison Study and Group Support System (GSS): First, an in-depth comparison was conducted to assess the SecuriMeter against existing BIS frameworks and methods. This comparison aimed to validate the SecuriMeter's comprehensiveness and effectiveness in meeting core BIS requirements. Second, a GSS Session with experts was conducted to prioritise BIS criteria, evaluate the artefact and gather feedback for further refinement [4].

Results
The research concluded with these significant findings:

Enhanced BIS Management. The SecuriMeter effectively emancipated boards from the limitations of spreadsheet-based management. It provided a more integrated and user-friendly platform for BIS management.
High Compliance with BIS Requirements. The comparison study revealed that the SecuriMeter met 90% of the core BIS requirements, indicating its completeness, validity, robustness and applicability across various BIS contexts.
Improved Visibility and Control. Users of the SecuriMeter reported better visibility and control over their BIS processes, which contributed to more informed decision-making and enhanced security posture. The SecuriMeter artefact significantly improved BIS management by integrating subjective, intersubjective and objective data into a cohesive dashboard. This integration allowed for better decision-making, enhanced visibility and improved control over security measures across different organisational layers.

Reflection
The research highlighted the limitations of traditional BIS approaches that rely heavily on spreadsheets and subjective assessments—by developing and validating the SecuriMeter, Bobbert and Mulder showcased the potential of using enterprise engineering principles to enhance BIS. The artefact addressed current BIS challenges and provided a scalable and adaptable solution for future needs. However, the study also noted the importance of continuous validation and refinement of the artefact to keep pace with evolving security threats and organisational requirements. Hence, the SecuriMeter found its successor in the LockChain initiative [4] as well as the AnoveAI technology launched in 2023, marking a 10-year research journey for the authors.[3]

In conclusion, Bobbert and Mulder's study significantly contributes to the field of BIS by introducing a comprehensive method that bridges the gap between IT security and business objectives, ensuring a more holistic and effective approach to

---

[3] www.anove.ai

information security management. For further reading, go to https://doi.org/10.17026/dans-zbu-hfdc

15.6 BPMN Patterns for Process Design

Sérgio Guerreiro, sergio.guerreiro@tecnico.ulisboa.pt

Situation

The organisation under consideration is a higher education institution (HEI) encompassing approximately 600 known business processes, organised into 16 departments, spanning across 3 campuses. The HEI's strategic principles are to offer excellence in the areas of education and research.

Two major sets of business processes help realise these principles: the first involving academic processes and the second involving administrative processes. Academic processes are those supporting the execution of education before, during and after classes. Examples include course, class, enrolment, internationalisation and certificate management. Administrative processes support the organisation in fulfilling the educational and research missions, such as human resources, building and financial management and student grant support.

Initially, there was only a partial catalog of known business processes, produced manually and managed via spreadsheets. Moreover, the business process catalog was constructed from user forms made available through various HEI Web sites. Each HEI service had its own separate system. Users were required to print forms, fill them out, sign them, scan them and then send them by email to the corresponding HEI service.

The limitation of this approach was that user forms only represented the starting point of each business process, without consideration of the entire sequence or the back-office business processes that were not accessible through these forms. Examples of such processes are auditing and grade certification. Additionally, some existing business processes in the catalog were just disjointed parts of an end-to-end business process. For example, some processes were sequences of activities conducted by one organisational unit, requiring handover to another unit for completion. A full representation of these business processes was lacking.

Compounding this situation was the absence of a governance process for deploying new business processes, which hindered the organisation's efforts to implement digital transformation.

Task

The task involved documenting a sample of the most important business processes of the HEI. To start with, a subset of the estimated 600 business processes was selected. The specified timeframe for completing the task was 2 months, with the expectation of reaching a consensus among stakeholders on the representation of the business processes. The next steps were taken.

First, the existing documentation was used to create BPMN 2.0[4] skeletons using a tool based on DEMO[5] [5]. Eliciting the network of DEMO business transaction kinds consists of describing its name and description, the involved actor roles, the returned outcome of each business transaction kind and the dependencies between them (options are a Request after Promise pattern or a Request after Execution pattern or a Request after Declare pattern). This step helped minimise variability in BPMN representations.

Second, a direct meeting approach was followed. Initial assessments were conducted through interviews with the actors involved in the business processes. When necessary, additional actors were invited to join the discussions. The purpose of these interviews was to gather descriptions regarding the execution of tasks. A total of 43 meetings, spanning approximately 90 h, were held to discuss process details and correct any inaccuracies within the business processes.

Third, the BPMN elements were extracted and normalised to a database to address inconsistencies in naming. The produced BPMN representations were validated by a second group of stakeholders to reduce any potential biases from the discussions.

Approach

The meta-model used to bootstrap the process design in the HEI is depicted in Fig. 15.4. The simplicity of this meta-model aims to facilitate communication among stakeholders regarding the HEI's enterprise architecture. We believe that if stakeholders can communicate using the same set of concepts and relationships, fewer misunderstandings and inconsistencies will arise [6].

The meta-model is explained as follows: each business actor is assigned to business roles, representing the roles they can fulfil. This relationship is directly observable in the daily routines of the HEI. Each business role is then assigned to one or more business processes. Each business process realises a business capability, which, in turn, is associated to a strategic principle. To emphasise that the implementation of business processes requires applications, the application component concept is represented with the relation of serving the business processes. It means that each business process will require application components. Finally, the data accessed by an application component realises a business object, which represents a more abstract concept when compared to a data object. A business process accesses the concept of a business object to perform its tasks. Later, this meta-model will be expanded to include, at a minimum, the concepts of service, interface, value and product.

[4] Specification available at https://www.omg.org/spec/BPMN

[5] Source code publicly available at https://github.com/SemantifyingBPMN

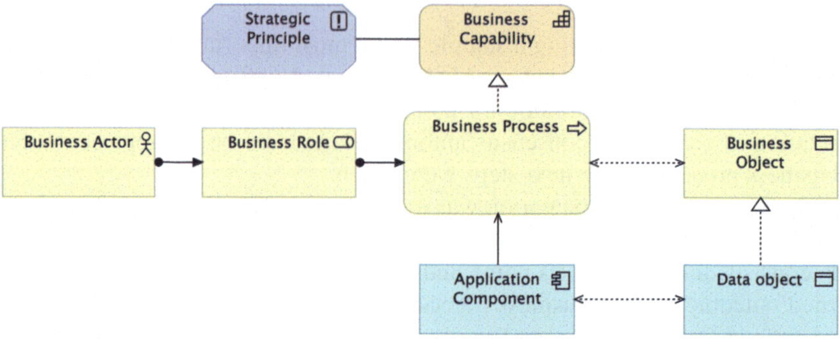

Fig. 15.4 HEI essential meta-model, using ArchiMate 3.2 (https://pubs.opengroup.org/architecture/archimate3-doc/) notation

Since the business process is the central concept in the meta-model, it has been employed to reflect the realities of academic and administrative units. Each DEMO business transaction kind is captured by the information detailed in Table 15.3. Following this, a corresponding BPMN diagram, illustrating the basic DEMO transaction pattern, is generated as shown in Fig. 15.5. An advanced pattern integrating the standard DEMO transaction pattern is presented in [7].

Table 15.3 Example of a DEMO business transaction kind

Transaction kind	Product kind	Executing actor role
TK01 budget changing	PK01 [budget change] **is** done	AR01 budget changer

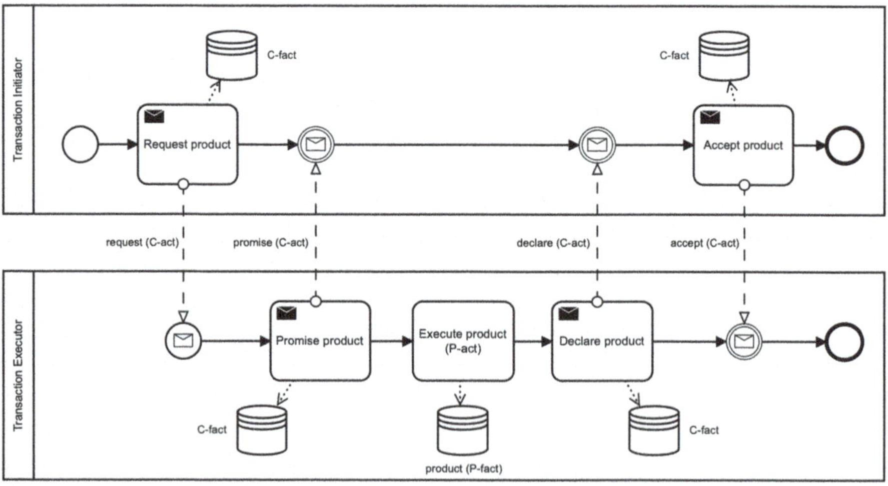

Fig. 15.5 BPMN diagram of the basic DEMO transaction pattern

Results

Through direct contact methods, including meetings and focus groups, approximately 100 DEMO business transaction kinds were identified, corresponding to the automatic generation of 65 BPMN processes involving 22 distinct participants. An analysis of the elements in these BPMN processes reveals the distribution shown in Fig. 15.6.

The significant number of elements involved in the BPMN processes, with a strong emphasis on the process control flow, highlights the complexity and detail required by the BPMN modelling technique. This complexity, however, was mitigated using a forward engineering approach, which facilitated the generation of the BPMN patterns from DEMO business transactions. Despite this, the lack of reverse engineering from BPMN to DEMO limited the ability to propagate BPMN changes across different versions.

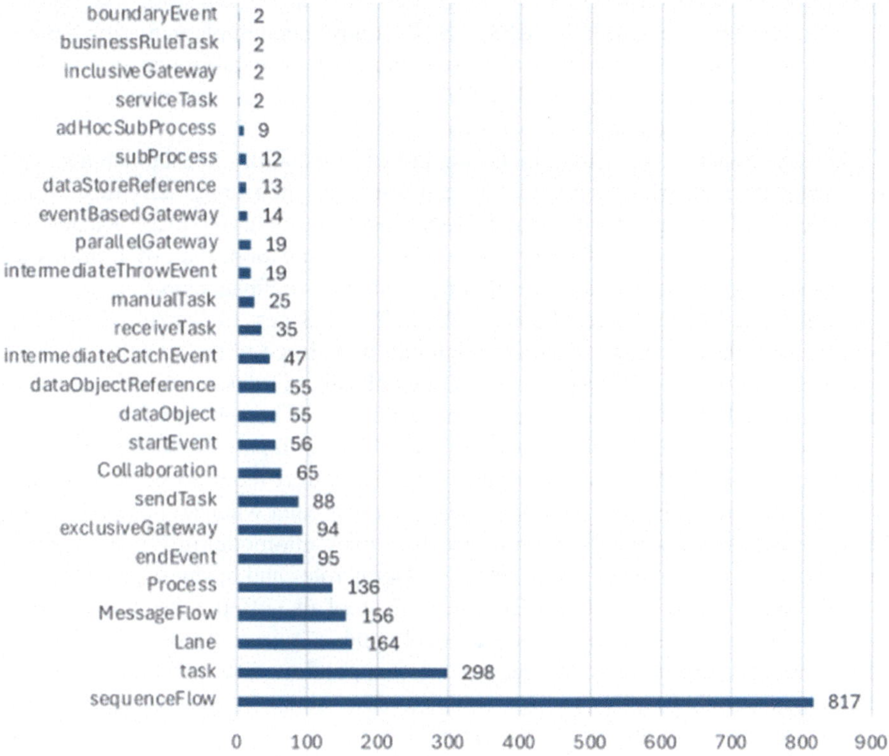

Fig. 15.6 Number of BPMN elements instantiated across the 65 elicited BPMN processes

Another key observation from analysing the generated BPMNs was the bias introduced during meetings and focus groups. The knowledge captured was largely constrained to the perspectives of the participating stakeholders, who were primarily business oriented. As a result, the technical integration between different application components and the data architecture aspects was underrepresented. The next phase of this project will involve a new round of elicitation to address these implementation issues and align with the details of the existing workflow engine, as previously studied in [8].

Reflection

Despite the importance of DEMO for capturing the essence of an organisation, it is well-known that BPMN is the lingua franca for designing and implementing business processes in the industry. Therefore, a reasonable approach is to maximise the production of DEMO artefacts and generate abstract BPMN models from them. It is understood that even abstract BPMN models are still far from meeting the requirements imposed by executable BPMNs, which require much implementation details, to be deployed in a process engine. Establishing clear traceability between DEMO business transactions and executable BPMN models seems like an ambitious objective that could be beneficial for most organisations.

The importance of utilising a meta-model lies in its ability to establish a shared framework through which stakeholders can articulate their daily activities, which are subsequently designed within the BPMN models. By adhering to a consistent set of concepts, the meta-model ensures focused communication, thereby minimising the introduction of extraneous ideas that fall outside its defined scope.

Creating the BPMN process based on the DEMO business transaction definitions facilitates the development of patterns that can be tailored to the specific needs of each organisation. The full context of a DEMO business transaction is inherited to streamline the BPMN design process. This efficiency is corroborated by the small number of elicited DEMO business transaction kinds compared to the significantly larger number of BPMN elements generated. The effort required to design these processes directly in BPMN would be substantially greater when compared to using DEMO business transactions. As referenced in the meta-model in Fig. 15.4, these elements are classified as business actors, business roles and business processes.

In the specific context of this HEI project, the tool also offered the ability to suggest exception flow scenarios, such as declinations, rejections or cancellations, which could be incorporated into the primary (happy) flow. These recommendations encouraged stakeholders to engage in discussions about integrating daily workarounds into new business process designs.

Additionally, an important outcome was the creation of the information architecture, initially derived from the DEMO Fact Model, which represent the outcomes of each business transaction kind. As the BPMN models were refined, more specialised fact types were identified, corresponding to the business objects as described in the meta-model in Fig. 15.4.

Future research will focus on automating this approach, whereby only DEMO business transaction kinds are defined and the BPMN processes are generated automatically.

15.7 DEMO in Airline Alliances

Dirk Gemke, dirk.vincent.gemke@gmail.com
Rob Mocking, rob.mocking@klm.com

Situation

The airline business is one of the most internationally oriented businesses in the world. Paradoxically, this is the result of the value national governments attach to their national airline and the associated limitations to mergers and acquisitions that would result in global companies and brands like Apple, Google, Microsoft, Amazon, Booking, Philips, Shell, etc.

To nevertheless create continental and global network reach for customers without having to operate flights themselves, airlines started to cooperate in 1947 based on so-called interline agreements. This was still the age of handwritten, paper tickets. The next and deeper level of cooperation started during the migration to electronic tickets and emergence of Global Distribution Systems; the pioneers of so-called code sharing were Qantas and American Airlines in 1987.

Unsurprisingly, airlines with a smaller home market, like KLM, SAS, Sabena and Swissair, were pioneering the most, based on new air-political agreements, and by creating as many interline and code-share agreements as possible to anchor their vulnerable market position. Around 2000 further clustering of cooperating airlines took place to create alliances: STAR, Oneworld and SkyTeam were born.

SkyTeam is an alliance of airlines (a co-operative of members, incorporated in The Netherlands) founded by Aeromexico, Air France, Delta Air Lines and Korean Air in New York City on June 22, 2000. In 2005, KLM Royal Dutch Airlines joined the alliance, which grew to its current 19 members, including SAS that switched this year from STAR to SkyTeam. Two airlines joined but also left SkyTeam: China Southern Airlines and Czech Airlines.

Some members only cooperate to the level of code sharing, while others further deepened their cooperation to the level of Joint Ventures with Anti-Trust Immunity to coordinate networks and schedules, prices and share revenues. Membership involves implementing a series of membership requirements that enable day-to-day inter-operability between members to ensure SkyTeam members fulfil their agreed mission:

> SkyTeam is dedicated to powering the most seamless customer journey of any global alliance. Our members work together to connect millions of passengers across an extensive global network. SkyTeam offers the most comprehensive priority services of any alliance, easy and efficient transfers and the opportunity to earn and redeem miles across all member airlines.

The common goal of all these efforts, whether with one partner or in an alliance-context with many, is reaching seamlessness for the customer, followed by flexibility and scalability for future changes, at the lowest possible cost and shortest time. Seamlessness means that customers search for, select, order, pay, claim loyalty awards and check in with the airline of their choice and receive tickets, seats, flight statuses and awards for their entire journey even if this involves other airlines.

Task
Until around 2008, the projects dealing with creating partnerships followed IATA- and GDS-standards as much as possible but were mostly undertaken as one-offs, every time again. And since each airline is organised differently with different silos leading the same effort, this resulted in tightly coupled solutions with low flexibility and scalability. Some elements of the desired seamlessness were achieved, for example, ticket issuance, while mobile check-in for the full journey remained impossible and loyalty credits could not always be awarded. So while outcomes for customers were the same (a ticket plus ancillary services, a seat number with a boarding pass, a checked bag and awarded loyalty credits), different IT implementations resulted in seams and increasing complexity and cost to close them.

After being actively involved in the post-merger projects to connect Air France and KLM, enterprise architects also became involved in new partnership and alliance projects, to help steer towards more flexible and scalable solutions. In 2008, KLM's CIO Office team of enterprise architects and the alliance liaison to the business side of Air France and KLM discovered DEMO, became DEMO professionals and never looked back. The team were encouraged to experiment with DEMO in actual projects.

Approach
The first application of DEMO was Air France and KLM Cargo Post Merger Decision-Making (discussed in [9], Chap. 19). The next was the so-called Lounge access (IT) service for verifying eligibility of customers for the comforts of various SkyTeam member lounges across the world. Learning from such explicit as well as more covert use of DEMO resulted in the creation of a so-called praatplaat (reference diagram) of the Construction Model[6] (CM) for (network) airlines. This praatplaat enabled focusing on different perspectives of airlines: the need to find and work with actor roles instead of hierarchical departments, separation of concerns and working with source (transaction) data instead of creating yet another copy of data.

The CM reconciles all different actor roles and transaction kinds independent of hierarchical organisational structures in a consistent, coherent and complete way. As a result, the airline construction model is also an airline alliance construction model. The praatplaat was shared and discussed with the Enterprise Architects of all 19 SkyTeam members in the biannual Architects meeting of 2015 in Nairobi, Kenya.

Results
The only full IT implementation following enterprise engineering and service-oriented thinking is the lounge access service of SkyTeam. Traditionally, the eligibility checks required lounge agents to apply the rules of the customer's airline or loyalty program and, on behalf of them, to allow the customer in, or not. Changes to

[6]At the time, the standard was DEMO-2, in which the term Construction Model was used. It has evolved into Cooperation Model in DEMO-4.

the rules involved distributing new rules booklets to all lounges in the world. And settlement of the cost required lounges sending an excel with all the lounge visits to the relevant airlines and loyalty programs and await the settlement, often involving controllers with questions.

Using DEMO changed the entire process and service to having the customer's boarding pass or loyalty card scanned, after which a real-time request is made to the loyalty program and airline to let the customer in, or not. And, if yes, to send an invoice number to the lounge for settlement of the cost. The result was a dramatic reduction of complexity of changes to the eligibility rules, and the process of settlement became beyond dispute. The service pattern can be applied infinitely for any type of eligibility check, including the boarding on a flight.

Elsewhere, the CM served as reference to nudge traditional approaches, and each airline's own implementation, in the direction of the reference. However, often new off-reference implementations were preferred to save project time and cost: short-term cost over long-term value. Nudging was applied for the review of SkyTeam Membership requirements, Air France-KLM application rationalisation and two major business transformation programs.

More recently, IATA's Modern Airline Retailing program was subjected to DEMO and the airline CM. In essence (pun intended), this program aims to modernise and replace (a.k.a. renovate and innovate) the business actor roles and standards and IT standards from the very beginning of digitisation of the airlines in the 1960s: marketing and operating carrier, tickets, passenger name records, electronic miscellaneous documents, boarding passes and all inter-operability needed to produce them within and across airlines. On its turn will this enable airlines to broaden the scope of their products and services beyond the capabilities of tickets, PNRs and EMDs and hence create more value. Unsurprisingly, IATA also had to resort to actor roles instead of traditional hierarchical departments that are different in name and scope across airlines and to outcomes for these actor roles instead of detailed legacy processes and system names.

We found that our airline CM can also be the model for IATA's Modern Airline Retailing vision and in support of airlines subscribing to the IATA program but also for (blockchain-enabled) travel consortia like Chain4Travel that have a much broader scope than IATA. Key actors for IATA and our CM are Customer, Retailer and Supplier. The key ambiguity created and needing resolution by IATA is the cross- and duplicate use of organisations and actor roles. The resulting key discussion is if the split between the Retailer and the Supplier role should not only apply between airlines but also within airlines. Test questions for any proposal not based on the construction model: does it also work when the Retailer is not an actor in an airline, and does it work when the Supplier is not an airline? Also, who recovers disrupted orders, with all legal consequences, the retailer or the supplier?

Reflection

Johan Cruijff's saying, 'You'll only see it when you understand it', applies to DEMO and using it to maximum effect with uninitiated colleagues. So helping them take the perspective of an engineer is key but may not always be achieved: hierarchical perspectives are extremely difficult to eradicate.

Sometimes, explaining the difference between the Black-box and White-Box perspective helped (cf. Chap. 5). What also may help is Hans Mulder's storytelling[7] on page 95 in 'Blockchain in de Lage Landen'.

Irrespective of the use of DEMO, having a champion in a company's leadership team is all important for success: one who can think out of the usual boxes and silos can helicopter up and down between actors and who deeply understands a need for true transformation.

In the case of each airline's internal implementation of IATA's Modern Airline Retailing, the biggest risk is that without a strong reference architecture team, reporting to overall (business) steering group, the new concepts and standards will be implemented in old organisations: the value destruction will be unsurpassed, and the potential reduction of complexity and cost will not be captured. DEMO can help prevent this.

15.8 Designing the My Number System

Junichi Iijima, junichi.iijima@gmail.com

Situation

After a long and winding road, Japan finally introduced a common number system to identify each citizen, comparable to the UK's National Insurance Number and the Netherlands' BSN. This common number is called the My Number, and this case is a DEMO application example that was used as a reference document for the e-government task force meetings that were held prior to the introduction of the My Number system for public services. The reason for using DEMO was to visualise the changes in the design of public services due to the introduction of the My Number system.

Task

Once information sharing is realised, individuals will no longer need to submit certificates that can be arranged through information provision network systems, etc.

---

[7] Start thinking about an organisation with which you are familiar. Now consider its business process, so that you can visualise the activities, workflows, people performing actions, the equipment they use and the machines they operate. Now, set aside all organisational structures, such as grouping employees into departments and business units, or whatever these groups may be called in the organisation you've thought of. When you do this, you will only see people, the equipment they use and the machines they operate. Next, remove all green and blue resources for communication, information storage and information processing, such as computers and networks, pencils, paper and filing cabinets. Afterward, you'll see a group of people interacting with each other and doing things with or without machines. The image of the organisation that you have now created is called its 'OER-form'.

The benefits of the number system include (1) the possibility of simplifying operations in line with the abolition of certificates, (2) the ability to provide one-to-one services tailored to each individual citizen and (3) the ability to keep track of one's own life record in chronological order, and (4) the number of transactions that citizens request from the government will decrease, while those that the government requests from citizens will increase.

In order to make these things possible, the entire range of government services, including those provided by the private sector, should be extensively linked together. If some services cannot be linked together, this will hold back the whole system, and in the end, the system will not be used, which will be a waste of taxpayers' money.

Approach

To demonstrate the advantages of the My Number system, we will take up the 'vaccinations for infants (routine)' and model the current state of the business process as As-Is, and the business process that is expected to be introduced after the introduction of the My Number as TO-BE, using DEMO to explicitly capture the changes in the design. The business process for vaccinations for infants (routine) is as follows:

- Parents with infants and young children who are eligible for vaccinations look at information on vaccinations from their local government in public relations papers, etc. and make an appointment for vaccinations at a medical institution.
- They then receive a preliminary medical examination form from the local government and fill in the necessary information.
- They take their health insurance card, maternal and child health handbook, etc. to the medical institution to have the vaccinations administered.
- After the vaccination, they pay the fee and receive a receipt.
- They submit the receipt to the municipal office along with the necessary documents, such as a bank book, seal and the maternal and child health handbook.
- The municipal office will transfer the subsidy to the relevant account.

Problems with this procedure include the need to pay the fee in advance, so if you lose the receipt, the application process for the subsidy is complicated.

Results

Figure 15.7 shows the Cooperation Structure Diagram (CSD) of the current business process for vaccination procedures for infants and young children. In this diagram, all actor roles are represented as composite actor roles in order to express the general relationship between the people involved, and the system boundary is not shown in particular. Table 15.4 contains the corresponding Transactor Product Table (TPT).

The parents of infants and young children who are to receive vaccinations obtain a preliminary medical examination form from their local government office and take the form and the necessary documents to the medical institution to receive the vaccinations, and after paying the medical institution, they request their local government office to pay the subsidy. Therefore, the four transaction kinds 'preliminary medical examination form issuance', 'vaccination implementing', 'paying of fees for vaccination' and 'paying of subsidy' have been extracted as original transactions.

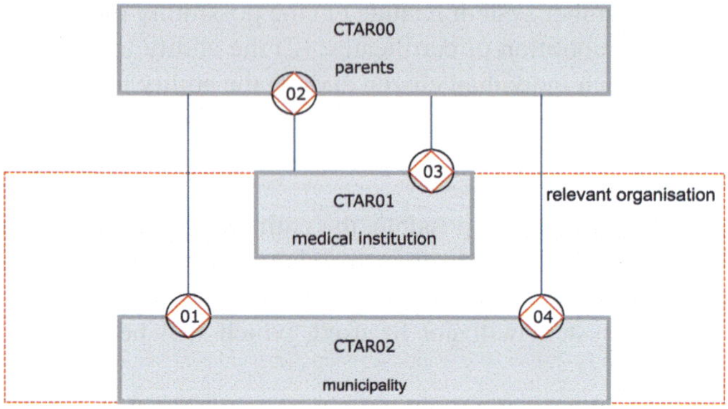

Fig. 15.7 CSD of the AS-IS model of infant vaccination procedure

Table 15.4 TPT of infant vaccination procedure

Transaction kind	Product kind	Executing actor role
TK01 pre-medical check-up form issuing	PK01 [pre-medical check-up form issuing] **is** done	CTAR02 check-up form issuer
TK02 infant vaccination paying	PK06 [infant vaccination] **is** paid	CTAR00 infant vaccination payer
TK03 vaccination implementing	PK13 [infant vaccination] **is** implemented	CTAR01 vaccination implementer
TK04 vaccination subsidy paying	PK15 subsidy for [infant vaccination] **is** paid	CTAR02 vaccination subsidy payer

Figure 15.8 shows the Cooperation Structure Diagram (CSD) of the TO-BE model that is expected to be implemented after the introduction of the My Number system. Table 15.4 contains the corresponding Transactor Product Table (TPT). The change is in the initiator role of transaction kind TK04. Therefore, the TPT for the TO-BE situation is the same as the one for the AS-IS situation.

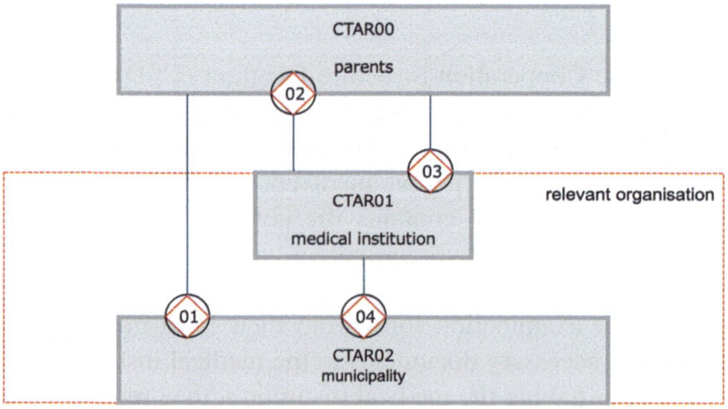

Fig. 15.8 CSD of the TO-BE model for infant vaccination procedure

Reflection

When comparing the two models, it is immediately apparent that the method of payment of subsidy will change from parents making a claim to the municipality to medical institutions making a claim to the municipality. This is thought to resolve various problems caused by advance payments. What we need to be careful of here is that, because the initiators are not specified in the TPT, both the AS-IS and TO-BE situation have the same TPT, but the difference can be seen in the CSDs.

Also, before the introduction of the My Number system, parents would come to pick up the pre-medical check-up form after seeing the notice of vaccination. However, after the introduction of the My Number system, the municipality will send a pinpointed guide to the parents. Since this is a change in implementation, it is not visible in the CSD.

After the introduction of the My Number system, parents will be able to check which vaccinations their children have received using a system called the 'My Portal Maternal and Child Health Handbook', and they will be able to refer to information about vaccinations at any time. Furthermore, health check information will also be recorded for the whole of their lives. The My Number system is reported about in [10].

15.9 Developing Process Ownership

Maryka Erasmus, mkuyler@mweb.co.za
Marné De Vries, marne.devries@up.ac.za

Situation

Co. INS is a short-term insurance company in South Africa that identified an opportunity to improve process performance by developing a new function at the enterprise, namely, a process ownership function. A current-reality tree (CRT), used to model a complex system by relating multiple undesirable effects of the core problem [11], highlighted a number of root causes for poor process performance, namely, (1) limited system development budget, (2) lack of a holistic approach, (3) lack of customer focus and (4) not focusing on process measurement. The root causes indicated that Co. INS searched for quick wins via system development or drove people harder for better performance, rather than having a good understanding of the underlying process. People and/or systems are frequently prioritised for improvement initiatives at the expense of detailed process optimisation.

The result of this misalignment between different design domains demanded a new approach for sustainable process excellence. A detailed literature study suggested that a solution to the problem at Co. INS was to deploy *process ownership* (PO), based on the foundational belief that process is a strategic asset. In accordance with [12], deployment of PO as a new function at the enterprise had to acknowledge that the enterprise is an intentionally created entity, that is, highly complex, as well as highly organised, where multiple enterprise design domains need to be (re-) designed [13].

Task

The task was to develop an approach artefact that any enterprise designer could use, namely, the *Enablers that Support effective Process Ownership* (ESPO), to develop a new PO function at an enterprise. The enterprise designer must distinguish between three different artefacts:

1. The *enterprise* as an artefact, consisting of multiple design domains
2. The *PO function* that requires some essential tasks to govern and improve the development of enterprise operations
3. The *ESPO* as an artefact to guide the enterprise designer in deploying the PO function

The deployment of ESPO within Co. INS was approved with the condition that no additional resources were allowed. The PO function had to fit into an existing enterprise where employees already performed certain tasks, which might overlap with that of a new PO function.

Solving the problems at Co. INS required more focus on the (re-)design of the organisation design domain, where the organisation of an enterprise can be partitioned into four partial organisations, the O-organisation (O from original), the I-organisation (I from informational), the D-organisation (D from documental) and the M-organisation (M from material), presented in Chap. 8. A PO function at Co. INS therefore required a deep understanding of underlying processes where human beings play a central role in organisational operations, as defined by several Enterprise Engineering (EE) theories to design a human-centric enterprise [9].

Approach

In developing ESPO as an artefact, the ESPO developer extracted existing knowledge from literature about PO. Since ESPO was also used to (re-)design some parts of the enterprise, enterprise design knowledge, especially the *general system development process* (GSDP, cf. Chap. 9), was used to guide the development of enterprise constructs that relate to the new PO function, as indicated in Fig. 15.9.

First, we provide an interpretation of the GSDP when the entire *enterprise* as an artefact is developed, using the three purple comments to interpret the GSDP constructs. The enterprise designer starts with the *environment as the using system* to design *multiple enterprise functions as object system functions*, ending with *enterprise constructs as object system constructs*.

Next, we provide an interpretation of the GSDP when *process ownership constructs* are developed within the context of an existing enterprise, using three yellow comments to interpret the GSDP constructs. The enterprise designer starts with the *environment as the using system* to design the *process ownership function as the object system function*, ending with *process ownership constructs as object system constructs*.

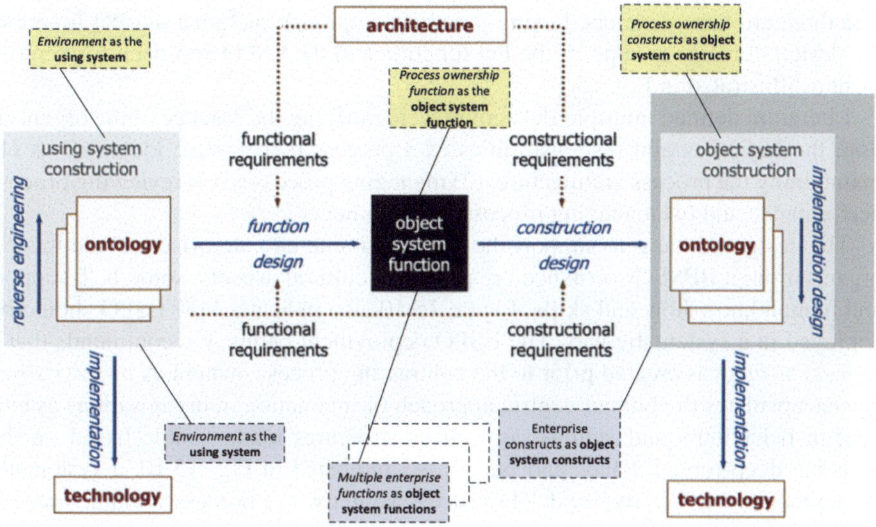

Fig. 15.9 ESPO's design scope using the GSDP from

ESPO could now be developed, drawing knowledge from existing PO literature to extract generic functional requirements and constructional requirements that would guide the design of PO constructs.

Apart from the literature study to inform the requirements for the PO constructs, ESPO also draws on the different EE theories to ensure intentional design, alignment and governance between the different domains of the enterprise. Different design domains include amongst others the organisation domain where human actors perform essential tasks, the ICT domain to support the organisation with software applications and hardware and the aspects of culture and human skills and know-how [14].

Next DEMO's Way of Thinking was used to identify the essential organisation by making a distinction between the production and coordination activities identified in literature for a new PO function. Given the required PO function was compiled from literature, white-box models of the object system were specified. The white-box models represent only the essence of operation for a PO function, using aspect models. Aspect models apply the ALPHA theory (cf. Chap. 7) to only specify one abstraction of the organisation domain of an enterprise, namely, the original organisation.

Since we had to ensure that ESPO was useful to the enterprise designer when developing PO as a new function, we also applied approach design principles [15] to package ESPO as a coherent approach. ESPO had to answer three questions: (1) Why is process ownership required (i.e. defining the paradigm of using ESPO)? (2) What are the main constructs of ESPO? (3) How should ESPO be deployed?

Results

The three artefacts developed using the above approach included the PO function, the design domains to support the PO function and the ESPO approach for deployment as illustrated in Fig. 15.10.

Literature defined multiple PO activities. Identifying the essence of the organisation, the key roles and responsibilities of a process owner were identified as (1) maintaining the process architecture, (2) managing processes, (3) reviewing process performance and (4) managing process improvements.

The design domains to support the PO function at an enterprise include the PO organisation, a BPM Governance organisation, cultural aspects, some ICT support and human know-how and skills. Figure 15.10 also indicates how ESPO should be deployed in a systematic way. The ESPO deployment pathway recommends that a *process strategy* is created prior to the contracting process owners. A *process strategy* encapsulates the human-centric approach of interaction in organisations as evident in behaviours and actions, as well as structures made visible based on the invisible deep-rooted values and beliefs. As indicated in Fig. 15.10, a systematic deployment of PO is required: (1) process strategy, (2) process architecture, (3) process ownership, (4) process measurement and (5) process improvement.

Culture emerged as a critical design aspect, as a prerequisite for an effective deployment of process ownership. Creating a culture where a lean mindset is fostered needs servant leadership, process performance metrics and rigorous visual management. Several structures, for example, budget for process improvement initiatives and process performance, were identified as most important contributions to the cultural aspect.

During the first phase of deploying ESPO at Co. INS, the team performed a readiness assessment, especially regarding the cultural readiness that forms part of the first deployment phase of ESPO, called *process strategy*, as indicated in Fig. 15.10. The cultural readiness assessment indicated that one of the two candidate teams scored higher on cultural readiness and was therefore chosen for further deployment of PO.

During the second phase indicated in Fig. 15.10, called *process architecture*, Co. INS needs to identify a scope of interest that should be modelled, using aspect models to represent the essence of some existing enterprise operations. Co. INS already adopted concepts that are not aligned with EE theory. For instance, where the BETA theory (cf. Chap. 9) interprets *architecture* as design principles or generic requirements that constrain solution development, Co. INS uses *architecture* as a composite term to describe the essence of enterprise operations but also describe the implementation details, i.e. adding technology, process measurements/metrics and identifying real-world actors as process owners.

The guidance provided in Sect. 7.3 will be useful to indicate how an elementary actor role owns a particular process in which a single product kind is brought about. In addition, the elementary actor role may also be responsible for multiple initiations of other transactors. When composite actors defined at Co. INS, such as a business analyst, product owner or first line manager, need to be allocated to multiple processes as composite process owners, the trees of responsibility graphically indicated by a cooperation structure diagram, indicating multiple elementary process owners, will be useful.

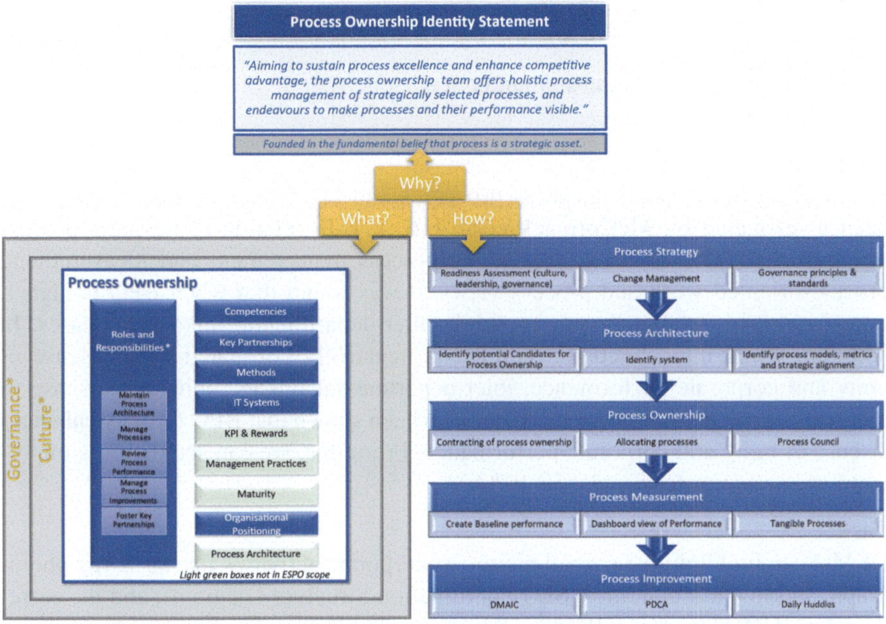

Fig. 15.10 ESPO's constructs and guidance for the deployment of a PO function

Reflection

Developing and implementing PO as a new function at Co. INS required a systematic approach. Although the existing literature on PO highlighted several mechanisms to develop PO at an enterprise, a holistic and complete approach for deployment was not available. The GSDP (cf. Chap. 9), the EE theories and the design principles were instrumental in consolidating existing PO knowledge within a coherent ESPO.

The EE theories, especially the ALPHA theory, have been instrumental to communicate the essence of organisation by reducing complexity from multiple tasks allocated to a process owner by the different publications extracted from literature, i.e. representing the O-organisation of the PO function via multiple aspect models. It is apparent that the ALPHA theory can be used on multiple levels and throughout the design of the enterprise. In ESPO, it is used for two different scopes: (1) Defining the essence of PO activities to construct PO as a new function at an enterprise and (2) defining the essence of the new/adapted enterprise activities as part of the *process architecture*, indicated in Fig. 15.10.

Process ownership creates a narrative which embodies an intentional culture of commitment towards process as a strategic asset. Although *culture* is indicated as a design aspect for enterprise design [14], the necessity of the lean mindset' culture that is fundamental to the success of process ownership required additional design guidance, as demonstrated in the ESPO approach. The necessity of understanding and selecting the appropriate cultural environment for deployment of ESPO acknowledges the sociological nature of a human-centric enterprise design.

15.10 The Sangikyo Case

Junichi Iijima, junichi.iijima@gmail.com

Situation

The relationship between business processes and IT investment effectiveness has been investigated by McCormack et al. [16, 17]. In relation to business process orientation (BPO), which is defined by process management and measurement, process-oriented work and process views, it was found that when BPO is higher, inter-functional conflict decreases, while inter-departmental linkage increases. In addition, while inter-functional conflict is negatively correlated with a sense of unity and corporate performance, inter-departmental linkage enhances a sense of unity and corporate performance. It has also been shown that BPO directly enhances a sense of unity and corporate performance. From this, we can see that it is important for companies to increase its BPO.

Task

DEMO can highlight the overall picture of corporate activities like an X-ray photograph, and in particular, the CSD (Coordination Structure Diagram), and the corresponding TPT (Transactor Product Table), is suitable for taking a bird's-eye view of the overall activities of the company in question. Therefore, it can be expected that if each employee understands the relationship between the transactions in the CSD, their own actor role and the actor roles of other people, it will have the effect of increasing BPO in the organisation in question. The goal in this project is to investigate the relationship between understanding CSDs and process-oriented thinking, self-efficacy, etc.

This project was carried at Sangikyo Co. Ltd., a medium-sized company with a corporate philosophy of 'continuing to create value through optimisation thinking' that is involved in businesses such as mobile communications, wireless broadband and in-house information and communications. The company has just under 1000 employees. The project is reported about in [18].

Approach

We produced the CSD and the corresponding TPT of the business processes for the construction and on-site adjustment work, dispatch work and on-site contracting work that make up the majority of Sangikyo's operations. Based on this, we created a sheet called 'Sangikyo's Work' that is made up of the following three parts:

1. Employee number and name
2. How to read the 'Sangikyo no Shigoto': Explanation of how to read the DEMO cooperation model (CM)
3. The DEMO cooperation model (cf. Fig. 15.11 and Table 15.5), with the actor roles handled by the relevant employee coloured in

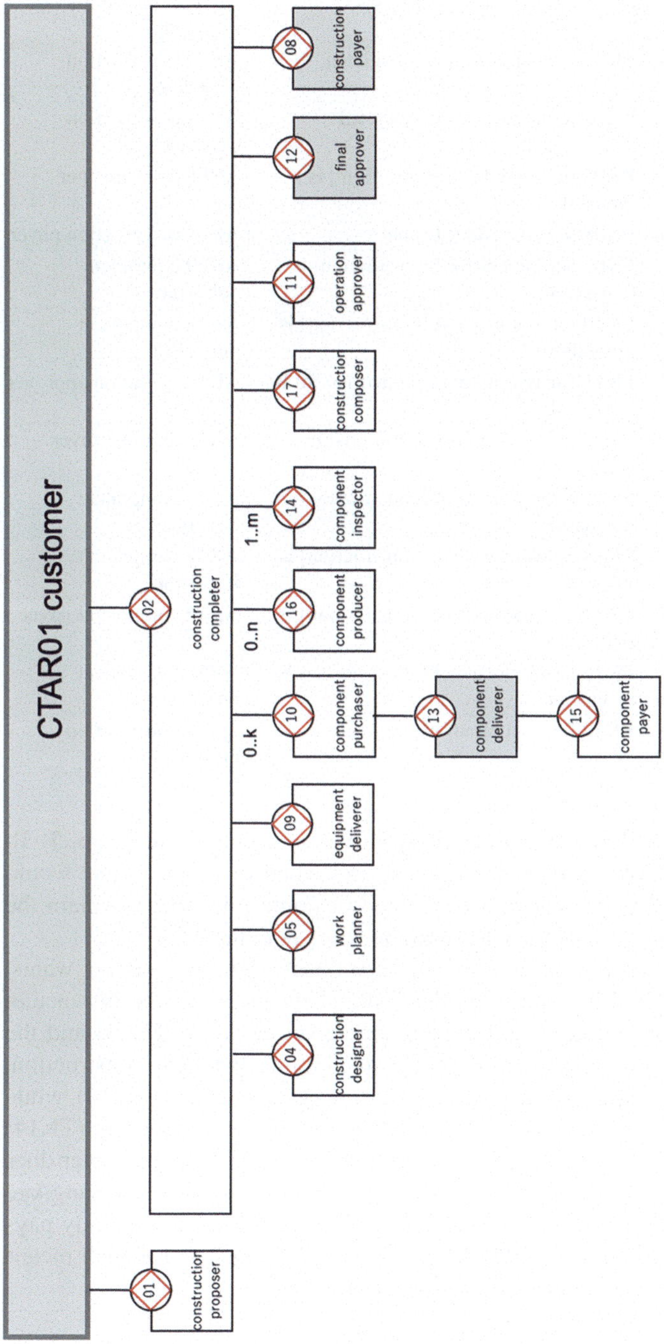

Fig. 15.11 CSD of the case Sangikyo

Table 15.5 TPT of the case Sangikyo

Transaction kind	Product kind	Executing actor role
TK01 construction proposing	PK01 [construction] **is** proposed	AR01 construction proposer
TK02 construction completing	PK02 [construction] **is** completed	AR02 construction completer
TK04 construction designing	PK04 [construction] **is** designed	AR04 construction designer
TK05 work planning	PK05 the work for [construction] **is** planned	AR05 work planner
TK08 construction paying	PK08 [construction] **is** paid	AR08 construction payer
TK09 equipment delivering	PK09 equipment for [construction] **is** delivered	AR09 equipment deliverer
TK10 component purchasing	PK10 [component] **of** [construction] **is** purchased	AR10 component purchaser
TK11 operation approver	PK11 **the** operation **of** [construction] **is** approved	AR11 operation approver
TK12 final approving	PK12 the final approval **of** [construction] **is** done	AR12 final approver
TK13 component delivering	PK13 [component] **of** [construction] **is** delivered	AR13 component deliverer
TK14 component inspecting	PK14 [component] **of** [construction] **is** inspected	AR14 component inspector
TK15 component paying	PK15 [component] **of** [construction] **is** paid	AR15 component payer
TK16 component producing	PK16 [component] **of** [construction] **is** produced	AR16 component producer
TK17 construction producing	PK17 [construction] **is** produced	AR17 construction producer

The presented CSD shows the 'tree' perspective, as explained in Chap. 7. To fully understand the 'flow' perspective, as also explained in Chap. 7, one would need to produce the PSD (cf. Chap. 10). Instead of doing this, let us explain the business process on the basis of the CSD and the corresponding TPT.

First, a construction proposal is made (TK01). If this is what the customer wants, the construction is ordered by requesting the TK02. This results in first instance in the design of the construction (TK04), the planning of the work (TK05) and the delivery of the needed equipment (TK09) for assembling the final construction. Some, possibly zero, components are purchased from subcontractors (TK10), while the others are produced by Sangikyo (TK16). All components are inspected (TK14) before they are assembled into the construction (TK17). Before the customer does the final approval (TK12), the operation of the construction is tested by Sangikyo (TK11). Next, the customer does the final approval (TK12) and subsequently pays for the produced construction (TK08). Then TK02 can be finalised, which means that the customer accepts the delivered construction.

The 'Sangikyo's Work' sheet was distributed to the employees, and they were asked to keep it in a place where they could see it and to refer to it several times a day. Three months after the sheets were distributed, a survey was conducted using a questionnaire. The questionnaire covered self-assessment of understanding of the business process expressed in the CSD and TPT, external communication, internal communication, process-oriented thinking and self-efficacy.

Results

Based on the results of the survey, we divided the participants into two groups, a group of 21 participants with low understanding of business processes and a group of 50 participants with high understanding of business processes, based on their subjective evaluation of their understanding of business processes. We then tested for differences between the two groups in the values of these four variables: external communication, internal communication, process-oriented thinking and self-efficacy.

The result was that the group with a high level of understanding of the business process scored higher than the group with a low level of understanding for all variables. With the exception of internal communication, these differences were all statistically significant.

Reflection

It was found that the deeper the understanding of the business process of the company in question, the more it would activate communication with the outside world and give an image of what procedures should be taken to obtain the desired results.

It was also found that the deeper the understanding of the business process, the more confident employees became in their ability to carry out their work, and the clearer their image of the procedures that should be followed to achieve the desired results in business.

The reason why there was no significant difference in the scores for internal communication is thought to be that the work carried out at Sangikyo is relatively strictly defined by rules, culture and information systems, so there was no difference in the scores according to the level of understanding of the business process.

Because the adjustment structure diagram can concisely express the overall picture of the business in question, it is hoped that it will improve employees' understanding of the business process. However, on the other hand, the fact that there were a certain number of employees with a low level of understanding shows that it is necessary to take the time to explain the CM in a way that will help them understand it, rather than simply distributing it.

References

1. Simon, H. A. (1981). *The sciences of the artificial* (2nd ed.). MIT Press, xiii, 247 p.
2. de Jong, J. (2013). *A method for enterprise ontology based design of enterprise information systems* (p. 195). Mprise Group.

3. Bobbert, Y., & Mulder, J. (2022). *25 years of Group Support Systems, from Fata Morgana to Silver Bullet.*
4. Bobbert, Y., & Opzkanli, N. (2020). LockChain technology as one source of truth for cyber, information security and privacy. In *SAI 2020.* AISC.
5. Guerreiro, S., & Sousa, P. (2020). *A framework to semantify BPMN models using DEMO business transaction pattern.* eprint=2012.09557, archivePrefix=arXiv, primaryClass=cs.SE.
6. Guerreiro, S. (2021). Conceptualizing on dynamically stable business processes operation: A literature review on existing concepts. *Business Process Management Journal, 27*(1), 24.
7. Guerreiro, S., & Dietz, J. L. G. (2024). *DEMO enhanced BPMN.*
8. Lopes, T., & Guerreiro, S. (2023). Assessing business process models: A literature review on techniques for BNPMN testing and formal verification. *Business Process Management Journal, 29*(8), 133.
9. Dietz, J. L. G., & Mulder, J. B. F. (2024). *Enterprise ontology—A human-centric approach to understanding the essence of organisation* (Enterprise engineering) (2nd ed.). Springer Nature.
10. Iijima, J. (2014). *DEMO—A modelling methodology for visualising the framework of corporate activities (in Japanese).* NTT Publishing.
11. Doggett, A. M. (2005). Root cause analysis: A framework for tool selection. *The Quality Management Journal, 12*(4), 34–45.
12. Dietz, J. L. G., et al. (2013). The discipline of enterprise engineering. *International Journal of Organisational Design and Engineering, 3*(1), 86–114.
13. Hoogervorst, J. A. P. (2018). *Practicing enterprise governance and enterprise engineering—Applying the employee-centric theory of organization.* Springer.
14. De Vries, M. (2017). Towards consistent demarcation of enterprise design domains. In S. De Cesare & U. Frank (Eds.), *Advances in conceptual modeling* (pp. 91–100). Springer.
15. De Vries, M. (2016). Guiding the development of enterprise design approaches. *The South African Journal of Industrial Engineering, 27*(3), 12–22.
16. McCormack, K. P., & Johnson, W. C. (2001). *Business process orientation: Gaining the E-business competitive advantage.* CRC Press.
17. McCormack, K. P. (2007). *Business process maturity: Theory and application.* BookSurge Publisher.
18. Ishiwata, S., Geok, P. L., & Iijima, J. (2012). Enhancing business process understanding to support employee's work. In *Spring national research conference, H1-7, JASMIN.*

Glossary[1]

Access link A link between an *actor role* and a *transaction kind*, indicating that fillers of the actor role have (reading) access to the *facts* in the corresponding *transaction bank*. An access link represents the existence of one or more *sharing transaction kinds* between the *O-organisation* and the *I-organisation* of an *enterprise* (Chap. 7).

Act The atomic unit of action in *systems*. Two kinds of acts are distinguished: *coordination acts* and *production acts*. Acts are performed by *actors* (Chap. 6).

Actagenic conversation A *business conversation* in which the participants strive to reach consensus about a *product* that one of them is going to bring about at the other's request (Chap. 6).

Action rule [Synonym of *business rule*] a guideline for *actors* to settle *agenda*. An action rule consists of three consecutive parts: the *event part*, the *assess part* and the *response part*. Action rules are the imperative equivalent of *business laws* (Chaps. 6 and 11).

Actor A *subject* in her/his filling an *actor role*. An actor is referred to by a tuple <actor role, subject>, commonly noted down as <actor role>/<subject> (Chap. 6).

Actor role The term 'actor role' has two interpretations. The constructional interpretation is that it represents the *authority* to perform the *coordination acts* and the *production act*, within the *responsibility area* of the *executor*, in *transactions* of the *transaction kind* to which the actor role is linked by an *executor link*. The operational interpretation is that it represents the guidelines, ranging from culture (norms and values) to specific *action rules* and *work instructions*, that *actors* filling the actor role apply when they carry out transactions (Chap. 6).

Addressee [*Property* of *coordination act*] the *actor* to whom the *coordination act* is addressed (Chap. 6).

Agenda Plural of *agendum*. At every *point in time*, every *actor* disposes of her/his agenda, also called to-do list (Chap. 6).

[1] Hereafter, the definitions of the key terms in Enterprise Design, as used in this book, are summarised, in alphabetical order. At the end of every entry, the chapter(s) where the term is defined is/are indicated between '(' and ')'.

J. L. G. Dietz, H. B. F. Mulder, *Enterprise Design Fundamentals*, The Enterprise Engineering Series, https://doi.org/10.1007/978-3-031-83262-8

Agendum A *coordination event* to which the *addressee* of the corresponding *coordination act* has to respond (Chap. 6).

Agent An ICT-artefact, used by an *actor* as its digital proxy. Unlike actors, agents cannot be held responsible for their deeds; they only support actors (Chap. 8).

Architecture In Enterprise Engineering, architecture is defined in the next way. Theoretically, architecture is the normative use of design freedom. Practically, it is a consistent and coherent set of requirements, both *functional requirements* and *constructional requirements*. Architectural requirements hold for a class of *systems* (or *system kinds*), whereas user requirements hold for one *system* (or one *system kind*) (Chap. 3).

Aspect model Partial *ontological model* of an *organisational layer*. Unlike a *submodel*, an aspect model takes a specific view on the organisational layer and is therefore in itself not a complete ontological model (Chap. 8).

Assess part The part of an *action rule* containing the propositions regarding the *state* of the *coordination world* and the *production world* to be evaluated (Chap. 11).

Attribute Instance of an *attribute type* (Chap. 11).

Attribute type A binary *type*. The *extension* of an attribute type is a mapping from a concrete (object) class or an abstract (object) class, called the domain of the attribute type, to an abstract (object) class, called its range, so that every object in the domain is mapped to exactly one object in the range and that every object in the range is mapped to zero, one or more objects in the domain (Chap. 11).

Authorisation One of the two ways in which *authority* can be assigned to *subjects*. The other way is *delegation*. Through authorisation, a subject gets the authority to fill a complete *actor role* (Chap. 6).

Authority The right to perform one or more specific *coordination acts* in *transactions* of some *transaction kind*. Authority can be assigned to a *subject* through *authorisation* or *delegation* (Chap. 6) [see also responsibility and competence].

Basic transaction pattern [See *transaction pattern*].

Business Term to refer to the *function perspective* on an *enterprise*, in particular the function as perceived by its customers (the consumers of its *services*) (Chap. 5) [see also organisation].

Business conversation A conversation that takes place in an institutional setting and of which the participants aim at achieving a common goal. Four kinds of business conversations are distinguished: *actagenic* conversations, *factagenic* conversations, *reversiogenic* conversations and *cogitatiogenic* conversations (Chap. 6).

Business event [Synonym of *coordination event* in the *O-organisation* of an *enterprise*].

Business fact *Fact* in the *production world* of the *O-organisation* of an *enterprise*.

Business law A (first-order) logical formula determining the lawfulness of *states* and *transitions* in the *coordination world* or the *production world* of an *organisation* (Chap. 6) [see also business rule].

Business process A sequence of *process steps* in *transactions* of some *business process kind* in the *O-organisation* of an *enterprise* (Chap. 7).

Business process kind A set of *transactor roles* (possibly only one) and the *interaction structure* between them, together constituting a tree structure. Every transactor role in the tree is enclosed in a transactor role on the next higher level (except the 'highest' one) and encloses one or more transactor roles on the next lower level (except the 'lowest' ones) (Chap. 7).

Business rule [Synonym of *action rule*].

Causal link Link between a *coordination act* and its resulting *coordination fact*, indicating that the fact is the immediate result of performing the act (Chap. 6).

Claim to rightness One of the three *validity claims* in a *coordination act*. The claim to rightness regards the *authority* of the *performer* to perform the act (Chap. 6).

Claim to sincerity One of the three *validity claims* in a *coordination act*. The claim to sincerity regards the sincerity of the *performer* in performing the act (Chap. 6).

Claim to truth One of the three *validity claims* in a *coordination act*. The claim to truth regards the (potential) existence of the concerned *product* (Chap. 6).

Cogitatiogenic conversation A *business conversation* in which the participants strive to reach consensus about an idea or plan for future action (Chap. 6).

Cognitive correspondence The mutual understanding of actors concerning a *coordination act* at the *informa level* of *communication*. Cognitive correspondence is reached if the *addressee* thinks he/she has understood the semantic content of the communicated *coordination fact* correctly. Success or failure is conveyed by a *confirmation* or a *disconfirmation* (Chap. 6).

Commitment The being bound by the *performer* of a *coordination act* to its *intention*. A commitment implies that the performer has the moral obligation to let her/his future actions be in agreement with the intention (Chap. 6).

Communication The sharing of thoughts between *subjects*. It is brought about by exchanging *information* (Chap. 6).

Competence The collective capabilities of a *subject* that makes her/him eligible to perform specific *acts*, in particular to be assigned one or more *actor roles* (Chap. 6) [see also authority and responsibility].

Complete transaction pattern [See transaction pattern].

Composite transactor role A collection of *transactor roles*, connected by *initiator links*, possibly also by *access links* and *wait links* (Chap. 7).

Conceptual schema A coherent collection of *types*. A conceptual schema works as a mental lens through which one perceives concrete complexes and subsequently creates corresponding *conceptual complexes* in the mind. If the concrete complex is the *world* of a *system*, the conceptual schema determines the *state* space and the *transition* space of the world (Chap. 11).

Confirmation The statement by the *addressee* of a *coordination act* towards the *performer* that he/she thinks they have reached (*notational* or *cognitive* or *social*) *correspondence* (Chap. 6) [see also disconfirmation].

Construction There are two fundamentally different perspectives on any system: the construction perspective and the *function* perspective. In the construction perspective, one considers the composition, the environment and the structure of the system, regardless of the function(s) it may offer (Chap. 5).

Construction design The phase in the GSDP that starts from the *function* of the *object system* and ends with the *construction* of the *object system* (Chap. 9). It is fed by *constructional requirements* from the *using system* and from the applied *architecture*. The construction design of a system is split into two consecutive phases: *ontological design* and *implementation design* [see also function design].

Constructional requirements *Requirements* that apply to the *construction design* of a *system*. They originate from the *using system* (user requirements) and from the applied *architecture* (architectural requirements) (Chap. 9) [see also functional requirements].

Coordination act The atomic act in *business conversations*. It has four components or properties: *performer*, *intention*, *addressee* and *product*. The result of a successfully performed coordination act is the immediate creation of the corresponding *coordination fact* (Chap. 6) [see also process step].

Coordination event An *event* in the *coordination world*. The occurrence of a coordination event is identical to the becoming existent of a *coordination fact* (Chap. 6).

Coordination fact *State* element in the *coordination world*. It has four components: *performer*, *intention*, *addressee* and *product*. A coordination fact is the immediate result of a performed *coordination act*. More precisely: the immediate result of a coordination act is a state of affairs that gives rise to a *conceptual fact* representing the state of affairs (Chap. 6) [see also process step].

Coordination world One of the two *worlds* in which the elements in a *system* cause *transitions* (Chap. 6) [see also production world].

Creation time [*Attribute* of *fact*] the *point in time* at which a *fact* is created. It may be equal to its *event time*, but it may also precede the event time (Chap. 6).

Data set A structured collection of signs. Examples of datasets are customer data, article data and sales data (Chap. 8).

Delegation An *authorisation* may include the right of the authorised person to delegate a part of the assigned *authority* to other subjects. Delegation regards the responding to one or more *coordination events* (Chap. 6).

Dependent production fact A production *fact* that starts to exist dependent on, and together with, an *independent production fact* (Chap. 6).

Design Devising courses of action aimed at changing existing situations into preferred ones (Chap. 3).

Design process (1) In software engineering, the design process is conceived as a path from a point R (Requirements) to a point C (program Code) in a two-dimensional space. One dimension is formality (ranging from fully informal to fully formal), and the other one is concreteness (ranging from fully concrete to fully abstract). The point R is (fully) informal and abstract; the point C is (fully) formal and concrete (Chap. 3).

Design process (2) In constructional engineering, the design process is conceived as a stepwise path from a point P (Problem) to a point S (Solution) in a two-dimensional space. One dimension is analysis; the other one is synthesis. A path from P to S is a sequence of alternative analysis and synthesis steps. The process stops when the result of a synthesis step is considered satisfactory (Chap. 3).

Disconfirmation The statement by the *addressee* of a *coordination act* towards the *performer* that he/she thinks they have not reached (*notational* or *cognitive* or *social*) *correspondence* (Chap. 6) [see also confirmation].

Discussion state *Transaction state* in which the *initiator* and the *executor* have to 'sit together' and discuss the cause of having ended up in this state and how to proceed. The *standard transaction pattern* has two discussion states: 'declined' and 'rejected'. Each of the four *revocation patterns* has one discussion state: 'revoked' (Chap. 6).

Document An un- or ill-structured collection of signs. Examples of documents are reports, books and letters (Chap. 8).

Documental production In every enterprise, four sorts of *production* can be distinguished: *original*, *informational*, documental and *material*. Documental production consists of saving, transforming and providing *documents* or *datasets* (Chap. 8).

D-actor (role) [Shorthand for *actor* (*role*) in the *D-organisation* of an *enterprise*].

D-organisation (D from documental) the *organisational layer* of the *organisation* of an *enterprise* in which *documental* production takes place. The ontological model of a D-organisation comprises a number of *D-transactor roles* and the *coordination structures* between them. The D-organisation supports the *I-organisation* by providing *documental services* (Chap. 8).

D-transaction (kind) [Shorthand for *transaction* (*kind*) in the *D-organisation* of an *enterprise*].

D-transactor (role) [Shorthand for *transactor* (*role*) in the *D-organisation* of an *enterprise*].

Enterprise The general term to refer to any kind of collaborative activity by human beings. An enterprise commonly is, but need not necessarily be, an economic and/or legal body. Examples of enterprises are companies, governmental agencies, healthcare institutions, sports clubs and building projects. Every enterprise has a *business* and an *organisation* (Chap. 6).

Essential model The essential model of an *SoI* is defined as the *ontological model* of its *O-organisation* (Chap. 8).

Event The becoming existent of a *fact*. Events occur instantly, meaning that their duration falls within one *time unit*. Events that occur in the same time unit are said to occur simultaneously (Chap. 6).

Event part The part of an *action rule* containing the *agendum* to be settled when executing the action rule (Chap. 11).

Event time [*Attribute* of *fact*] the *point in time* at which a *fact* starts to exist. It may be equal to its *creation time* or later (Chap. 6).

Execution phase The *transaction* phase in which the *executor* performs the *production act*. It starts when the *transaction state* 'promised' is reached, and it ends when the production act is performed (Chap. 6).

Executor One of the two roles that *actors* have in a *transaction*; the other role is *initiator*. The executor in a transaction is *authorised* and *responsible* for performing the *coordination acts* in the executor's *responsibility area* of the *complete transaction pattern* (Chap. 6).

Executor link A link between an *actor role* and a *transaction kind*, indicating that *actors* in the actor role play the role of *executor* in *transactions* of the transaction kind (Chap. 6).

Fact Something that is taken to be the case. A distinction is made between *conceptual facts* and *concrete facts*, as well as between *coordination facts* and *production facts* (Chap. 6).

Factagenic conversation A *business conversation* in which the participants strive to reach consensus about the *production fact* that one of them has brought about on the other's request (Chap. 6).

File A physical embodiment of a *document* or *dataset*. Examples of files are collections of ink marks on paper and optical marks on disk or tape. A document or dataset may be inscribed in many files, called its copies (Chap. 8).

Focus When applying DEMO to an enterprise, one always chooses a *Scope of Interest* (*SoI*). Within this SoI, one chooses a focus. In the CSD, the focus is indicated by the white colour of the shapes. The shapes of the elements outside the focus but within the SoI are coloured light grey. The AM is only made for the actor roles within the focus (Chap. 11).

Forma Term to refer to the general *competence* of a *subject* to perform *coordination acts* at the *forma level* of communication, as well as *documental production* acts (Chaps. 6 and 8) [see also informa and performa].

Forma condition The collective prerequisites for reaching *notational correspondence* in performing a *coordination act* (Chap. 6).

Forma level The level of *communication* in performing a *coordination act* at which the *performer* and the *addressee* strive for *notational correspondence* (Chap. 6).

Function There are two fundamentally different perspectives on any system: the *construction* perspective and the function perspective. In the function perspective on an *enterprise*, one considers the functions of the enterprise as perceived by its various stakeholders (Chap. 5) [see also business and service].

Function design The phase in the GSDP that starts from the *ontological model* of the *using system* and ends with the (specification of the) *function* of the *object system* (Chap. 9) [see also construction design].

Functional requirements *Requirements* that apply to the *function design* of a *system*. They originate from the *using system* (user requirements) and from the applied *architecture* (architectural requirements) (Chap. 9) [see also constructional requirements].

Impediment The influencing between actors through *wait links* (Chap. 8).

Implementation The phase in the GSDP that starts from the *implementation model* of the *object system* and ends with the implemented *object system* (Chap. 10).

Implementation design [Sub phase of object system design]. Implementation design starts from the *ontological model* of the *object system* and ends with the *implementation model* of the *object system* (Chap. 10).

Implementation model A conceptual model (cf. [1], Chap. 6) of the *object system* within the ETA theory. Where the *ontological model* of the *object system* is fully abstracted from implementation technology, its implementation model is fully dependent on the applied actor technology, production technology and coordination technology (Chap. 10).

Independent production fact The core of the *product* that is brought about in a *transaction*. It starts to exist as the direct effect of the accept act by the *initiator*. It is represented by a unary fact (like 'sale 1618 is delivered') or a binary fact (like 'the fee for membership 387 in year 2019 is paid') (Chap. 6) [see also dependent production fact].

Informa Term to refer to the general *competence* of a *subject* to perform *coordination acts* at the *informa level* of communication, as well as *informational production acts* (Chap. 6) [see also forma and performa].

Informa condition The collective prerequisites for reaching *cognitive correspondence* in performing a *coordination act* (Chap. 6).

Informa level The level of *communication* in performing a *coordination act* at which the *performer* and the *addressee* strive for *cognitive correspondence* (Chap. 6).

Informational production In every enterprise, four sorts of *production* can be distinguished: *original*, informational, *documental* and *material*. Informational production comprises remembering, recalling and computing *facts* (Chap. 8).

Initiator One of the two roles that *actors* can have in a *transaction*; the other role is *executor*. The initiator in a transaction is *authorised* and *responsible* for performing the *coordination acts* in the initiator's *responsibility area* of the *complete transaction pattern* (Chap. 6).

Initiator link A link between an *actor role* and a *transaction kind*, indicating that *actors* in the actor role play the role of *initiator* in *transactions* of the transaction kind (Chap. 6).

Installation The assignment of specific technological means or resources to the *actor roles*, the *production* and the *coordination* in an *organisation* (Chap. 10).

Intangible Concrete things are *tangible* or intangible. A thing is intangible if it cannot be physically grasped. Examples of intangible things are observations, decisions and judgements (Chap. 8).

Intellectual manageability One of the three general goals of EE. Intellectual manageability means that one has insight into and overview over the *organisation* of an *enterprise*. It is achieved through appropriate and well-controlled reduction of complexity, notably the one that is offered by the *essential model* of an enterprise (Chap. 1).

Intention [*Property* of *coordination act*] the social disposition of the *performer* of a *coordination act* towards the *addressee*, with respect to a *product*. Examples of intentions are 'request', 'promise', 'decline', 'declare', 'accept' and 'reject' (Chap. 6) [see also commitment].

Interaction The mutual influencing of *actors* in an *organisational layer* that consists of performing *coordination acts* (Chap. 6).

Interaction structure One of the three coordination structures in an *organisation*. It consists of a number of *interaction trees* (Chap. 8).

Interaction tree Building block of the *interaction structure* in an *organisation*. It consists of a collection of *transactor roles* that are connected to each other by *initiator links* (Chap. 8).

Interimpediment structure One of the three coordination structures in an *organisation*. It consists of *wait links* between *transactor roles* in different interaction trees (Chap. 8).

Interstriction The mutual influencing of *actors* in an *organisational layer* that consists of taking into account the current state of the *coordination world* and/or the *production world* when being active, i.e. when settling *agenda* (Chap. 8).

Interstriction structure One of the three coordination structures in an *organisation*. It consists of *access links* between *transactor roles* (Chap. 8).

I-actor (role) [Shorthand for *actor* (*role*) in the *I-organisation* of an *enterprise*].

I-organisation (I from informational) the *organisational layer* of the *organisation* of an *enterprise* in which *informational* production takes place. The ontological model of an I-organisation comprises a number of *I-transactor roles* and the *coordination structures* between them. The I-organisation supports the *O-organisation* by providing *informational services* (Chap. 8).

I-transaction (kind) [Shorthand for *transaction* (*kind*) in the *I-organisation* of an *enterprise*].

I-transactor (role) [Shorthand for *transactor* (*role*) in the *I-organisation* of an *enterprise*].

Material production In every enterprise, four sorts of *production* can be distinguished: *original*, *informational*, *documental* and material. Material production comprises storing, retrieving, copying, transmitting and destroying *files* (Chap. 8).

Medium level The level of communication in performing a *coordination act* at which the *performer* transmits the file to the *addressee* that carries the *document* or *dataset* (possibly containing only one sentence) that must be made perceivable to the addressee (Chap. 6).

Multiple transaction kinds A collection of *transaction kinds*. Multiple transaction kinds may be useful if one does not (need to) know exactly the constituent transaction kinds (e.g. because they are outside the *Scope of Interest*) (Chap. 6).

Notational correspondence The degree of mutual understanding of a *coordination act* at the *forma level* of *communication*. Notational correspondence is reached if the *addressee* thinks he/she has understood the form of the message correctly. An example of a form is a sentence in English. Success or failure is conveyed by a *confirmation* or a *disconfirmation* (Chap. 6).

Object system (OS) The *system* in the GSDP (General System Development Process) that is going to be developed (Chap. 9).

Ontological design [Sub-phase of object system design] ontological design starts from the (specified) *function* of the *object system* and ends with the *ontological model* of the *object system* (Chap. 9).

Operating principle [*Property* of *system*] the mechanism that makes a system 'tick'. If the system is an *organisation*, it is the ability and readiness of the *actors* in the organisation to enter into and comply with *commitments* regarding the bringing about of *products* (Chap. 6).

Operation The state of a *system* in which it is operating or life. The operation of an *organisation* starts when the first *coordination event* is dealt with (Chap. 10).

Operative time [*Attribute* of *product*] the time period[2] during which the product of a *transaction* is operative or valid (Chap. 6).

Order phase The *transaction* phase in which the *initiator* and the *executor* strive to reach consensus about the *product* that the executor is going to bring about. It starts by performing the 'request' act and ends in the state 'promised'. Ending up in the state 'declined' means that the transaction is in a deadlock (Chap. 6).

Organisation Term to refer to the *construction* perspective on an *enterprise* (Chap. 6) [see also business].

Organisational concinnity One of the three general goals of *EE*. Organisational concinnity means that the organisation of an enterprise is a harmoniously integrated whole. This can be achieved through coherent and consistent *enterprise design* (Chap. 1).

Organisational layer The *organisation* of an *enterprise* consists of three organisational layers: the *O-organisation*, the *I-organisation* and the *D-organisation*. The D-organisation supports the I-organisation by *documental services*. The I-organisation supports the O-organisation by *informational services* (Chap. 8).

Original In every enterprise, four sorts of *production* can be distinguished: original, *informational*, *documental* and *material*. Original production comprises manufacturing, transporting, observing, deciding and judging. They all result in the creation of (new, original) *facts* (Chap. 8).

O-actor (role) [Shorthand for *actor* (*role*) in the *O-organisation* of an *enterprise*].

O-organisation (O from original) the *organisational layer* of the *organisation* of an *enterprise* in which *original* production takes place. The ontological model of an O-organisation comprises a number of *O-transactor roles* and the *coordination structures* between them (Chap. 8).

O-transaction (kind) [Shorthand for *transaction* (*kind*) in the *O-organisation* of an *enterprise*].

Performa Term to refer to the general *competence* of a subject to perform *coordination acts* at the *performa level* of communication, as well as *original production acts* (Chap. 6) [see also forma and informa].

Performa condition The collective prerequisites for reaching *social correspondence* in performing a *coordination act* (Chap. 6).

Performa level The level of communication in performing a *coordination act* at which the *performer* and the *addressee* strive for *social correspondence* (Chap. 6).

Performer [*Property of coordination act*] the performing *actor* of a *coordination act* (Chap. 6).

---

[2]As discussed in the DELTA theory (Chap. 9), every point in time is actually a time period, but possibly very small. This holds always for the attribute event time. The operative time, however, may be so large (minutes, hours, days) that one preferably speaks of a time period.

Point in time A particular value on a *time scale*, expressed in the corresponding *time unit*. Examples: week 36 (week), today (day), tomorrow at 11:25 h (min) (Chap. 11).

Process A sequence of *events* in a *world*, as well as the sequence of the causing *acts* in the corresponding (discrete event) *system*. In other words, a process is a sequence of performed process steps (Chap. 6).

Process step The atomic building block of a *transaction process*. It consists of a *coordination act* and its resulting *coordination fact*. Every process step has a specific *process step kind* (Chap. 6).

Process step kind [*Property* of *process step*] a process step kind is defined by two *properties:* a *transaction kind* and an *intention*. If 'TK01' denotes a particular transaction kind and 'rq' denotes the intention 'request', then 'TK01/rq' denotes a process step kind (Chap. 6).

Product [*Property* of *coordination act*] the product of a coordination act consists of an *independent production fact* and its *dependent production facts* (Chap. 6).

Product kind [*Property* of *product*] *products* of the same product kind are brought about in *transactions* of the same *transaction kind*. Examples of product kinds are '[membership] is started', '[rental] is completed' and 'the fee for [membership] in [year] is paid'. The variables in the formulation of a product kind are placeholders for *entities* (Chap. 6).

Production act The *act* in a *transaction* by which the *executor* brings about the *product* of the transaction (Chap. 6) [see also transaction pattern].

Production fact *State* element in a *production world*. A production fact is the result of performing a *production act*. More precisely: the result of a production act is a state of affairs in the production world that gives rise to a number of *conceptual facts* representing the state of affairs (Chap. 6) [see also product].

Production world One of the two *worlds* in which the elements in a *system* cause *transitions* (Chap. 6).

Property Instance of a *property type* (Chap. 11).

Property type A binary *fact type*. The extension of a property type is a mapping from a concrete (object) class, called the domain of the property type, to a concrete class, called the range of the property type, in such a way that every object in the domain is mapped to exactly one object in the range and that every object in the range is mapped to zero, one or more objects in the domain (Chap. 11).

Response link A link between a *coordination fact* and a *coordination act*, indicating that the *coordination act* is performed in response to the *coordination event* through which the coordination fact has started to exist (Chap. 6).

Response part The part of an *action rule* containing the *act(s)* to be performed in response to settling the *agendum* in the *event part* (Chap. 11).

Responsibility Disposition of a *subject* to be committed to the *coordination acts* he/she has performed, as well as the *agenda* he/she has to respond to. *Authority* and responsibility are like the two sides of a coin (Chap. 6) [see also authority and competence].

Responsibility area The set of process steps in the (complete) *transaction pattern* for whose performing either the *initiator* or the *executor* is responsible.

Consequently, a distinction is made between the responsibility area of the initiator and the responsibility area of the executor (Chap. 6).

Result Term to refer to the *product* of a *transaction* during the *result phase* (Chap. 6).

Result phase The *transaction* phase in which the *initiator* and the *executor* strive to reach consensus about the *product* that the executor has brought about. It starts by performing the 'declare' act and ends in the state 'accepted' (Chap. 6).

Reverse engineering The phase in the GSDP that starts from the implemented *using system* and ends with the *ontological model* of the *using system* (Chap. 9).

Reversiogenic conversation A *business conversation* in which the participants strive to agree on reverting (turning back) the current state in an actagenic and/or a factagenic conversation, in which they (also) participate (Chap. 6).

Revocation Every step in the *basic transaction pattern* (so 'request', promise', 'declare' or 'accept') can be revoked, at any time and from any state in the main *transaction process*. The effect of a successful revocation is that the state of the main process is 'rolled-back' to the previous basic state (accepted → declared, declared → promised, promised → requested, requested → initial state) (Chap. 6) [see also reversiogenic conversation].

Revocation pattern A pattern of *process steps* through which one can revoke one of the steps in the *basic transaction pattern* (Chap. 6) [see also revocation].

Scope of Interest (SoI) The delineation of the (part of the) *enterprise* or the collection of enterprises that one has chosen to model with DEMO (Chap. 11).

Self-activating actor role An *actor role* is called self-activating if its fillers are *initiator* as well as *executor* of the same *transaction* (Chap. 11).

Sentence The syntactic form in which thoughts, especially *facts*, are expressed (Chap. 6).

Service The functional appearance of a *product* to its consumers (Chap. 6).

Settlement time [*Attribute* of *coordination fact*] the *point in time* at which the *performer* of the corresponding *coordination act* wants the addressee to settle the created *coordination event* (Chap. 6).

Social correspondence The degree of mutual understanding of a *coordination act* at the *performa level* of *communication*. Social correspondence is reached if the *addressee* thinks he/she has understood the *intention* of the message correctly. Success or failure is conveyed by a *confirmation* or a *disconfirmation* (Chap. 6).

Social devotion One of the three general goals of *EE*. *Enterprises* should be designed in such a way that its employees get all the opportunities and facilities they need to develop and exert their *competences*. Social devotion implies that the employees are empowered with proper *authorities* (Chap. 1).

Standard transaction pattern [See *transaction pattern*].

Subject A human being in her/his quality of social individual—in particular her/his ability to enter into and comply with *commitments* (Chap. 6).

System A complex of *concrete things* that is able to act, i.e. to bring about changes in the corresponding *world*. Formally, a (homogeneous) system can be defined as a triple (C, E, S), where C is a set of concrete things of the same category, called the composition of the system; E is a set of concrete things of the same category as the elements in C, called the environment of the system; S is a set of influencing bonds among the elements in C and between them and the elements in E, called the structure of the system. Most interesting systems, like enterprises, are heterogeneous systems: layered nestings of homogeneous systems ([1], Chap. 9).

System design See *design*.

System development The bringing about of a brand-new *system* or of changes to an existing *system* (Chap. 9).

System kind A specialisation of system category (cf. [1], Chap. 9). In EE, the distinction between system kinds is based on the ALPHA theory: *O-organisations*, *I-organisations*, *D-organisations* and *M-organisations* (Chap. 9).

Tangible Concrete things are tangible or *intangible*. A thing is tangible if it can be physically grasped. Examples of tangible things are goods (of all kinds) but also electrons and magnetic fields (Chap. 8).

Time scale A division of a (discrete and linear) time dimension in consecutive pieces of equal length (duration), called *time units* (Chap. 11).

Time unit The unit for indicating or measuring amounts of *time* on a *time scale*. The length of a time unit depends on the needed precision. Examples: day, hour, minute, second (Chap. 11) [see also point in time].

Transaction The unit of *production* in an *organisation*. The result of a successfully carried-out transaction is the becoming existent of a *product* (Chap. 6).

Transaction bank The conceptual store associated with a *transaction kind* in which all *coordination facts* and all *production facts* are stored, in all of its carried-out *transactions* (Chap. 7).

Transaction kind [*Property* of *transaction*] there are two interpretations of the term *transaction kind*: the constructional interpretation and the operational interpretation. In the constructional interpretation, it represents the *complete transaction pattern*. Every *transaction* of the transaction kind is some path, possibly including iterations, through the complete transaction pattern. *Transactions* of the same transaction kind regard *products* of the same *product kind*. Examples of transaction kinds: membership_starting, rental_completing. In the operational interpretation, the transaction kind represents the conceptual store of all coordination and production facts in transactions of the kind that are created in the course of time. The transaction kind is now conceived as a *transaction bank* (Chap. 7).

Transaction pattern A pattern of *process steps* alternately taken by actors in two roles: one is the *initiator* and the other the *executor* of the transaction. The *basic transaction pattern* consists of the process steps 'request', 'promise', 'declare' and 'accept'. (Note: in between the promise and the declare act, the *production act* is performed; it precedes immediately and unconditionally the declare act, but it is not considered a process step itself.) The *standard transaction pattern* contains in addition the process steps 'decline' and 'reject'. The *complete transaction pattern* consists of the standard pattern and four *revocation patterns* (Chap. 6).

Transaction Phase A *transaction process* consists of three consecutive phases: the *order phase*, the *execution phase* and the *result phase*. They may partly or wholly be 'repeated' as the effect of *revocations* (Chap. 6).

Transaction process A sequence of *process steps* within the *complete transaction* pattern. Process steps of the same kind may occur multiple times, as the effect of *revocations* (Chap. 6).

Transaction state The state of a *transaction process* is defined as the most recently performed *process step* in the *complete transaction pattern* (Chap. 6).

Transactor role Since every *actor role* is connected by an *executor link* with exactly one *transaction* kind (and vice versa), the combination of the two constitutes a transactor role (Chap. 6).

Using system (US) The *system* in the GSDP (General System Development Process) that is using the *services* from the *object system* (Chap. 9).

Validity claim In performing a *coordination act*, three validity claims are raised by the *performer* and validated by the *addressee*: the *claim to rightness*, the *claim to sincerity* and the *claim to truth*. The response to a *coordination event* will depend on the degree in which the three *validity claims* are accepted by the addressee (Chap. 6) [see also action rule].

Value (1) A *typed abstract thing*. Values are commonly ordered in *value scales*. Examples of values are days, meters and Boolean values (Chap. 11).

Value (2) The intensity of the experience that is evoked in a *subject*'s mind by the recognition of an affordance. This notion of value is commonly expressed in economic or monetary terms (Chap. 5).

Value scale An ordered class *value* (according to definition 1). A value scale has a dimension (like time, length, mass, temperature or money) and a scale unit (like minute, meter, gram, degree Celsius or euro) (Chap. 11).

Wait link A link between a *coordination fact* to a *coordination act*, indicating that performing the *coordination act* must wait until the *coordination fact* does exist (i.e. the corresponding event has occurred) (Chaps. 8 and 11).

Work instruction Guideline for performing (the implementation of) a *production act* (Chap. 11).

World With every (discrete event) system, a world is associated in which the effects of the *acts* by (the elements in) the system take place. More specifically, the effect of an act is the creation of a *fact* in the system's world (Chap. 6).

Reference

Dietz, J. L. G., & Mulder, J. B. F. (2024). *Enterprise ontology—A human-centric approach to understanding the essence of organisation* **(Enterprise engineering) (2nd ed.). Springer Nature.**

The manufacturer's authorised representative in the EU is Springer Nature Customer Service Centre GmbH, Europaplatz 3, 69115 Heidelberg, Germany. If you have any concerns regarding our products, please contact ProductSafety@springernature.com

Printed and bound by CPI Group (UK) Ltd, Croydon, CR0 4YY
30/09/2026
02225591-0014